W9-BCC-135

A Guide to

POLITICAL PLATFORMS

A Guide to

Political Platforms

BY

EDWARD W. CHESTER

Archon Books
1977

© Edward W. Chester 1977
First published 1977 as an Archon Book,
an imprint of The Shoe String Press Inc
Hamden, Connecticut 06514

Library of Congress Cataloging in Publication Data

Chester, Edward W
   A guide to political platforms.

   Bibliography: p.
   Includes index.
   1. Political parties—United States—History. I. Title.
JK2261.C48   1977   329'.023'73   77-169
ISBN 0-208-01609-0

Printed in the United States of America

Contents

Foreword

In this issue-oriented history of presidential nominations and elections, Professor Edward W. Chester provides a guide to the party platforms since 1840. It will fill a notable gap in the literature of American politics. Party platforms have always had importance as a register of the issues on which political men divided. Throughout the nineteenth century they provided a roll call of the leading issues of the times—the annexation of Texas, extension of slavery into the territories, abolition of slavery, secession, preservation of the Union, Reconstruction, populism, the tariff, free coinage of silver, and financial and monetary policy generally. More recently, platform drafting has evolved into a major enterprise in which dozens of advisers are mobilized on the whole range of public policy, committees work long hours, and the final result is a major event at each national party convention.

Yet the platforms still involve a remarkable paradox of perception. For generations editorial writers and some leading politicians, usually those who distinguish themselves as dissidents from major trends in their own parties, have made it their business to denigrate the platforms as campaign trivia—ephemera to be forgotten as soon as the campaign is over. But it is not possible to watch the amount of struggle that goes into any major party platform without concluding that the platforms must be highly important to some people for some purposes. In recent times every major party platform has involved literally thousands of man-hours of toil, sweat, and strain from people who value their time highly. Moreover, the amount of this effort is increasing with the wider range and complexity of all public policy. In an article written some years ago, it was my conclusion that the amount of effort going into each major party platform had probably increased by something like an order of magnitude between 1952 and

7

1968—that is, by ten times. Each major party platform now deals with several hundred different issues in such fields as foreign policy, defense policy, economic programs, labor, agriculture, industry, resources, welfare, and civil rights. And the results are the material for debate as each campaign progresses.

As Professor Chester has documented, party platforms have generally been taken most seriously by the presidents who ran on them. President Eisenhower, for example, although less political than most of our recent presidents, frequently surprised his associates by the extent to which he demonstrated commitment to the Republican platform of 1952. During his first year in office, it provided the principal guidelines for his staff in the clearance of proposed legislation, pending the development of more specific legislative proposals.

Recent academic research, most notably that done by Professor Gerald M. Pomper of Rutgers University, has demonstrated that in recent years, platform pledges have generally been carried out. Bipartisan pledges, those found in the platforms of both major parties in the same year, have had an 85 percent rate of fulfillment. Pledges by the party winning the election for president have been fulfilled about 79 percent of the time; those by the losing party, 53 percent. The record, moreover, has been an improving one. It was better during the Eisenhower, Kennedy, and Johnson administrations than it had been during the Truman administration, although probably there was some relapse during the Nixon administration, for which the statistical record is less adequate.

Platforms have long been the subject of preparatory work before the conventions at which they are adopted, but that work has become much more extensive and intensive in recent times. The prospective chairman of the platform committee of each major party national convention is usually designated some months in advance. He in turn mobilizes an initial staff, which begins the collection and drafting of platform proposals. (For the party in power, this may involve a heavy input from the White House staff under guidance of the president.) Beginning in 1960, it became customary for the platform committees of both major parties to come into session at the beginning of the preconvention week, first to hold public hearings and then to complete committee work on the final text of the platform. From 1960 on, the objective was to have the platform ready when the full convention met, although this objective was not always achieved. At Miami Beach in 1968, for example, the Republican platform committee was in session for some thirty-three hours between Thursday and 3:16 A.M. on Sunday morning, when it completed the platform for release that afternoon—the day before the convention convened. The Democrats at Chicago in that same year of political troubles did not complete their platform in committee until the early hours of Tuesday of the convention week, for adoption Wednesday afternoon after the impressive debate and divided vote on the Vietnam plank.

Between 1968 and 1972 the Democrats adopted two major changes in their rules for platform preparation. One change consisted of changing the size and composition of their platform committee to make it more representative. Previously it had consisted of two members from each state and outlying territory. As revised, each state was represented in proportion to the size of its convention delegation on a committee of around 150 members, with 1—10 members per state. The second change consisted of requiring the committee to meet and complete its work in time to mail the draft of the proposed platform to each convention delegate ten days in advance of the convention. This was done and greatly facilitated the consideration of the platform at the 1972 convention. Similar rules were in effect for 1976.

The Republican party has also considered rules changes for platform preparation, but has not so far emulated the Democratic changes. Each state, regardless of size, continues to have the same representation on the Republican platform committee and the work is not brought to final completion until the week before the convention. In 1972, however, a temporary platform committee was established early in the year, and the preliminary preparatory work was more extensive than ever before. Something similar was done in 1976.

Congressional input as well as presidential has been important for platform preparation for many years. Members of Congress have been prominent as the platform committee chairmen of both major political parties, and state delegations have elected their congressional members to represent them on the platform committees with increasing frequency. On the Democratic side in 1975, Speaker Carl Albert called upon the various committee chairmen in the House of Representatives to begin preparatory work for the

Democratic platform of 1976. Party platforms have become too important for neglect by the elected officials who may be called upon to carry them out.

For all of this recent activity, the historical precedents are numerous, ancient, and long-continued. Even under primitive conditions of travel and communication, the delegates at early national conventions strove mightily to achieve platforms conducive to party victory and representative of the views of their constituencies. Professor Chester's narrative has traced these efforts from their earliest beginnings, and is a worthy addition to our knowledge of the history of political issues. It can be heartily recommended to all students in this field.

PAUL T. DAVID

Woodrow Wilson Department
Government and Foreign Affairs
University of Virginia

Preface

In the age of television politics has become more and more involved with images, yet issues remain the backbone of the political process. The Bible of ideology is the collected platforms of the major and minor parties. Unfortunately, the degree of significance of these documents has been matched only by the extent of neglect and contempt lavished upon them by journalistic critics, the politicians themselves, and the general public.

Many new insights into the political process are to be gained by an examination of political platforms. These include:

> What domestic and foreign policy issues have appeared the most frequently in major party platforms?
>
> Which domestic and foreign leaders are mentioned the most often in political platforms?
>
> On what issues have the major parties disagreed most vehemently over the years?
>
> Which major party platforms have represented the greatest break with past traditions?
>
> How have the platforms of certain groups of minor parties represented a continuum of reform?
>
> Why has the originality of such documents as the 1856 Republican, 1892 Populist, and 1912 Progressive Party platforms been overrated?
>
> To what extent have reforms originated in major and minor party platforms?
>
> Which major and minor party platforms have contained planks that are bigoted in nature?
>
> What issues have the major parties evaded or ignored in their platforms?
>
> On which issues have there been floor fights at major party conventions?

11

When has the Presidential candidate of a major party
repudiated planks in his party's platform?

How faithfully has the victorious party executed platform
pledges?

In the process of answering these questions and others the
present volume examines every presidential election since 1832.
Both major and minor party platforms are set in the context of the
preceding presidential administration, the rivalries for the major
party presidential nominations, and the campaign and election;
there is an emphasis on both traditional and innovative planks
relative to a party's ideology. In the lengthy introduction we shall
undertake some extended comparative analysis, as well as go
briefly into the matter of implementation.

The main materials used in the construction of the narrative are
the actual platforms themselves, the platform debates at the major
party conventions, contemporary journalistic reactions, and retrospective scholarly assessments. A great deal of this information has
never been assembled in one place before. As for the popular vote
totals, we have cited these at the appropriate places throughout,
but owing to occasional episodes of "vote buying" and "ballot
burning" throughout American history, they do not always reflect
the popular mandate in a completely accurate manner.

While the audience for any work can depend on forces beyond
the control of the author or the publisher, this volume is addressed
to serious students of American political history, who may use it
either as a reference work or read it as a scholarly monograph. It,
however, is *not* addressed to the quantitatively-oriented political
scientist. If the touch at times is a bit light, and the narrative
intermittently turns from the platforms themselves to related
matters, this is done to break the hypnotic effect of reciting page
after page of planks. To be comprehensive without being tedious
has been our goal.

Department of History   EDWARD W. CHESTER
University of Texas at Arlington

Acknowledgments

Three chronological units of the manuscript have been presented as papers at annual meetings of the Missouri Valley History Conference, the Southwestern Social Science Association, and the Northern Great Plains History Conference. The author has taken note of the discussions and comments engendered there. While the final version of this book is strictly his responsibility, he wishes to thank a number of prominent scholars who have read and criticized portions of it. These include David Burner, James MacGregor Burns, Chester M. Destler, Arthur M. Ekirch, Jr., William H. Harbaugh, Jerome M. Mileur, Horace Samuel Merrill, James Patterson and Joel H. Silbey. Representative John J. Rhodes of Arizona also has been kind in providing data on his role as chairman of the Resolutions Committee at the 1972 Republican national convention, while Senator Charles H. Percy of Illinois has been equally helpful relative to his role in 1960. Henry Cabot Lodge, Chester Bowles, and Richard Neustadt likewise have made valuable bibliographical suggestions. Finally, Executive Secretary Earl F. Dodge of the Prohibition National Committee furnished several historical pamphlets containing information used in the text.

A Guide to

POLITICAL PLATFORMS

Political Platforms in Perspective

Some evaluations by friends . . . and foes

Towards the end of the nineteenth century, Lord James Bryce, who stands with Alexis de Tocqueville at the forefront of foreign commentators on the United States, observed that political platforms are "a mixture of denunciation, declamation, and conciliation" whose "tendency is neither to define nor to convince, but rather to attract and confuse."[1] Even more vitriolic in his denunciations is M. I. Ostrogorski, author of *Democracy and the Organization of Political Parties*, who opined early in the twentieth century that the platform was "the biggest farce of all the acts of this great parliament of the party."[2] Many domestic commentators over the years, too, have been equally grudging in praise of these quadrennial documents. Thus in recent times Republican Senator Barry Goldwater of Arizona has observed that "At best political platforms are a packet of misinformation and lies,"[3] and thus made an attempt (which proved to be unsuccessful) to persuade the Republican Party to adopt a brief statement of principles when it nominated him for President in 1964.

Professional journalists have likewise vented their contempt for political platforms on numerous occasions, although *The Nation* did characterize them a quarter century ago as "an intangible but at times a very real force."[4] William S. White, who long covered Washington for *The New York Times*, has commented: "Not often, in fact, have so many men worked with so many words that are read and long remembered by a few."[5] Similar sentiments have been expressed in liberal quarters as well as conservative ones. Thus Theodore White, author of the volumes on *The Making of the President*, complains that "in actual fact, all platforms are meaningless."[6] Columnists writing in national magazines, too,

17

often look upon these documents with disfavor. To cite two
Newsweek columnists, Henry Hazlitt laments that "Platforms are
seldom anything but an embarrassment anyway, particularly
when they get specific,"[7] while Raymond Moley assesses the
collected platforms as "a monumental example of insecurity,
double-talk, irrelevance, and promises impossible of fulfillment."[8] Even the *Catholic World* has abandoned Christian charity
to proclaim, "The purpose of a platform is not to say anything but
to say nothing while seeming to say something."[9]

It is only when we turn to the world of scholarship that we find a
widespread realization that political platforms may be more than
an unmitigated evil. Gerald Pomper, for example, finds that
"Party platforms can contribute to rational action by voters and
parties";[10] Edward Cook maintains that "Probably no other aspect
of our national political process is depreciated on the basis of so
little analysis or such scant evidence."[11] One might suggest, too,
that it is possible that these documents may today be superior to
their earlier counterparts. In this connection Paul David observes
that "the party platforms are indeed becoming more important,"
as "the process has intermittently moved in the direction of greater
professionalism."[12]

The question next arises as to what should go into a political
platform. Here one might quote the 1950 statement by the
Committee on Political Parties of the American Political Science
Association, which declared that the function of this document is
"to indicate how a party stands on issues, to offer a coherent
program, and to provide the voters with a proper choice between
the alternative policies and programs advanced by the two
parties."[13] To scholar-turned-politician Woodrow Wilson, "the
platform is meant to show what the nation is thinking about, what
it is most concerned about, what it wishes corrected, and what it
desires to see attained that is new and constructive and intended for
its long future."[14] Not every candidate for office or officeholder,
though, has conceived of political platforms in such lofty terms.
Mike Sutton, a practicing lawyer in Dodge City Kansas during the
frontier days, ran for mayor on a platform that had only one plank:
"Like Caesar's wife, I will be all things to all men."[15]

Key problems in platform analysis

It would be most convenient for purposes of analysis if one were able to reduce every aspect of platform evaluation to quantitative terms, but this is not easily done, despite the impressive attempts of Gerald Pomper and other scholars. In fact, for some of these documents it is only with great foreboding that one ventures even tentative judgments. For example, any rating of the platforms in terms of literary excellence, or as "good" or "bad" is largely conjectural, as is any attempt to place a platform at some approximate position on a conservative-liberal continuum, or a traditional-innovative spectrum. One also would like more data on those platforms which were more or less drawn up in advance of the convention by politically influential persons independent of the Resolutions Committee—more data on the impact the wishes of an incumbent president have on a platform—more data on the actual debates in the Resolutions Committee which led to the adding, rewriting, or deleting of various planks. Most of this information unfortunately remains hidden. Finally, it would be edifying to learn in detail which groups voted for or against which parties in which elections on the basis of which platform planks, as well as to find out which groups pressured the inclusion, modification, or omission of certain platform planks at the party conventions.

But it is possible to ask even more cosmological questions. In the words of one scholar who critically read a portion of this manuscript, "Do platforms frequently contain 'conspiratorial' views of history a la Hofstadter or Davis?" Equally important, to what extent do they mirror the ebb and flow of political moods? As to whether these documents do indeed furnish ammunition in support of this or the rival consensus interpretation, the most correct answer probably is that they may be used to prove either hypothesis, depending upon the platforms and planks cited. Like William James' pluralistic universe, conflicting currents are present in these documents; if at times they resemble an ideological supermarket, it is because they must appeal to a galaxy of voter and interest group tastes. In addition, political platforms also reflect the alternation between conservatism and liberalism in American political life, which as Arthur Schlesinger, Sr. has pointed out, takes place at the approximate rate of one complete cycle per generation. Yet, in the broader sense, certainly since the collapse of the Federalists, all three of the major parties—and indeed most of the minor ones, with such obvious exceptions as the Communists on the left and the Christian Nationalists on the right—have adhered to the ideas one finds in the writings of the seventeenth-century English political theoretician John Locke. Thus, to cite Louis Hartz, there has been no Liberal party as such at the national level in the United States because, in the words of Alexis de Tocqueville, America was "born free."

Enduring confrontations in American history

Although the course of American history has been freer from the outbreak of violence and revolution than the histories of many other countries, a number of great antagonisms have been present over the years. Perhaps the earliest of these was the geographical rivalry between the Tidewater and the Piedmont during the colonial era; in 1861 tension between the North and the South erupted into open conflict between the two sections. One, too, might point to various confrontations along other lines: capital versus labor, business versus government, free trade versus high tariff, "cheap" money versus "sound" money, free land versus land companies, and territorial expansion versus "little America."

There have been occasions when these antagonistic elements have reached temporary understandings, but as a rule these conflicts have persisted, sometimes in modified form. The gold standard, for example, is no longer the pivotal issue it once was, but the Federal Reserve Board advocates "sound" money; while land sales have declined since the closing of the frontier in 1890, there remains the confrontation between the exploiters and the environmentalists. As for the controversy surrounding the American presence in Vietnam and Cambodia, it is, of course, an updated version of the turn-of-the-century struggle over the acquisition of colonies by the United States.

Ideological divisions in political platforms

Despite the fact that political parties frequently have taken opposing positions relative to these great antagonisms, or at least assumed stances manifesting some degree of ideological differentation, party members have not always followed the "line" set forth in political platforms. Thus, with respect to the "cheap" money versus "sound" money dispute of the Gilded Age, one might say with complete justification that every shade of opinion could be found in both parties, even though these variations were rarely expressed in the more simplistic platform planks.

Nevertheless, any attempt to trace the shadings of opinion on any given issue within a party over a period of time, especially prior to the inception of the public opinion polls four decades ago, would doubtless require computerized studies of Congressional roll calls, which are beyond the scope of the present volume.

In comparison with the voluminous encyclopedias that most modern political platforms have become, the typical pre-Civil War political platform seems a brief, concise statement of principles. While the Whig party was largely an outgrowth of the reaction against certain practices of the Jackson administration, as well as the personality of "Old Hickory" himself, most Whig platforms tended to be vapid, ambiguous evasions rather than point-by-point rebuttals of their far more specific Democratic counterparts. Rather than change their stance from election to election, the Democrats held firm for two decades to the key planks that they first adopted in 1840, thus establishing a precedent for ideological consistency. Among these were planks advocating economy in government and a strict interpretation of the Constitution, but opposing federally financed internal improvements, the Second Bank of the United States, and the protective tariff. On the slavery issue the Democrats took a laissez faire position. Despite the fact that the Whigs often avoided ideology in their quest for the White House, it was the Democrats who survived as a party after splitting in 1860, while the Whig Party disintegrated following the election of 1856.

Following the Civil War, the recently founded Republican party dominated American politics to the end of Reconstruction; thereafter, it alternated in the White House with the Democrats for two decades. Nevertheless, its conservative, big business orientation faithfully mirrored the mainstream of American public opinion throughout the Gilded Age. Likewise, among the Democrats, the conservative, pro-gold Cleveland faction was more pro-business than the reformist, pro-silver Bryan one. With respect to this period as a whole, neither major party adopted a core statement of principles that compared with those to be found in the Democratic platforms between 1840 and 1860, but significant ideological differences did emerge between the Republicans and the Democrats. Although their positions on this issue did vary somewhat from campaign to campaign, the Republicans generally favored a protective tariff, the Democrats opposed it; it was here that the only Democratic President of the latter nineteenth century, Grover Cleveland, who was in many respects a conservative Republican, placed himself firmly in the Democratic camp.

Republican platforms over these years also tended to be pro-Reconstruction, anti-Southern, and anti-states' rights; their Democratic counterparts anti-Reconstruction, pro-Southern, and pro-states' rights. Upon the return of the former Confederacy to the Union there ensued two decades of sharp competition between the two major parties for the presidency; using the new Solid South as a base of operations in capturing the Electoral College, the Democrats were always a threat. But despite the importance of domestic issues, before the 1890s foreign policy played a decidedly minor role in both major party platforms, and the Republicans and Democrats even found common ground in their pro-Irish and anti-Chinese stances. The great debate over imperialism, however, placed them in opposite camps, with the GOP generally for overseas territorial acquisitions, the Democrats against.

It was, of course, the currency question that was to play the divisive role in American politics that slavery had before the Civil War. The Republicans generally took a stand against cheap money without always openly embracing gold, while the Democrats successively pledged their allegiance to the "Ohio Idea" of Pendleton, the gold standard of Cleveland, and the silver heresy of Bryan. By 1896 the currency issue had become so explosive that not only did it precipitate a walkout of silverite delegates (led by Henry Teller) from the Republican convention, it also caused the Democratic "gold bugs" to field a separate ticket after the convention had embraced Bryan and free silver. While the Republicans recovered to become the majority party for a generation, the Democrats were able to capture the White House again only with Woodrow Wilson—and this was after the Republicans had temporarily split in 1912.

The first third of the twentieth century witnessed two decades of reform, the Progressive Era, followed by a dozen years of status quo. During the Progressive Era the Republicans and the Democrats adopted a number of antithetical stands on a variety of issues, but in many respects they merely continued policies they had endorsed by 1900. The Democrats tended towards anti-imperialism, a pro-League of Nations stance, and a low tariff, while the Republicans favored imperialism, an anti-League position, and a high tariff. As for the money question, the Republicans continued to favor gold, while the Democrats, after losing with Bryan, evaded the currency issue in both 1904 and 1908. During the 1920s the Republicans managed to avoid the touchy Klan issue (they were weak politically in the South), while by 1928 they had reached a modus vivendi on the prohibition question, endorsing the eighteenth Amendment but rejecting the Volstead Act. On the other hand, the Democrats nearly split over the Ku Klux Klan in 1924, when an anti-Klan minority plank was rejected by the delegates in the closest vote in the history of American political conventions; then four years later they promised to enforce the eighteenth Amendment, only to have their "wet" Presidential candidate call for its eventual repeal. Torn between their southern and western rural wing and their northern big city wing, the Democrats seemed unable to agree on a platform and a candidate, let alone become the majority party in American politics again.

One year after Alfred Smith's defeat, though, the nation suffered the greatest economic collapse in its history, and for the first time the man on the street lost faith in the big business leadership that had dominated American life since the Civil War. The Democrats were also most fortunate to have in their midst a gifted political leader, Franklin Roosevelt, who was able to forge a new majority coalition out of the South, organized labor, the big city masses, and such minority groups as the Jews and Negroes. Long identified with big business, the Republican party suffered politically as a result.

Although Franklin Roosevelt served as President of the United States for an unprecedented period of twelve years, from 1933 to 1945, the entire corpus of New Deal domestic legislation dates from the five-year span between 1933 and 1938. To both contemporary and present-day critics, much of this program represented an abandonment of traditional Democratic principles as set forth in the party platform of 1932. Finally, in 1952 the Republicans recaptured the White House after a twenty-year lapse. But the Democratic party nevertheless remains the majority party in

America to this day, as its control of Congress since 1954 attests; an examination of the "something for everyone" domestic programs of the New Deal and Fair Deal helps explain this phenomenon.

On the other hand, the Republicans took a generally conservative stance in their platforms during the 1930s and 1940s. They by no means totally rejected reform, however; in 1936, for example, the Republicans mentioned favorably the Securities Exchange Act and the Public Utility Holding Company Act. The Republicans also were somewhat more liberal on the Negro question than were the Democrats, despite the fact that after 1932 the black vote shifted away from the Republicans, and in 1948 a group of hard-core Southerners bolted the Democratic party after liberals had forced the inclusion of a strong civil-rights plank. With respect to foreign affairs, both parties were generally isolationist during the 1930s, with both shifting to a rather ambiguous isolationist/internationalist stance in 1940. The Democrats perhaps placed a greater emphasis on Latin America. After World War II Democrats and Republicans alike embraced American global leadership, the United Nations, and the independent state of Israel. In 1948, though, the Republicans did fail to mention specifically either the Marshall Plan or the Truman Doctrine in their platform, attributing recent diplomatic successes to the eightieth Congress rather than to HST.

Domestically, the Republicans remained basically anti-New Deal and pro-business in orientation following 1932, as the Democrats embraced the New Deal and FDR attacked the economic royalists. While the Republicans endorsed a gold standard and a protective tariff, Roosevelt took America off the gold standard and inaugurated a reciprocal trade agreements program. In 1940 the Democrats favored a third term for Roosevelt, the Republicans opposed. Following World War II the Republicans praised the work of the eightieth Congress and the Taft-Hartley Act, but the Democrats blasted both that body and its most famous creation. Perhaps even more significant was the fact that after 1932 the Republicans were the party of states' rights, while the Democrats embraced nationalism; although this ideological volte face was not always spelled out in the major party platforms, it was openly affirmed in both 1936 documents.

During the last two decades political platforms have tended to become longer and more complex, especially those of the major parties, and an examination of recent Republican and Democratic platforms reveals a number of antithetical stands, both in the areas of domestic affairs and foreign relations. At home the Republicans continued to defend the record of the eightieth Congress and the Taft-Hartley Act; the Democrats attacked both. In 1952 and 1956 the Republicans advocated the return of the tidelands oil to the states; the Democrats opposed this. During the last two decades the Republicans have tended to support flexible farm supports; the Democrats, rigid ones. Long accused by the Democrats of being the party of big business, the Republicans have been more sympathetic towards private enterprise, assuming a partnership with the government relative to public power and health care, while in recent years the Democrats have embraced the various projects of the New Frontier and the Great Society, including the war on poverty and federally financed welfare programs. Since 1960, too, the Democrats certainly have been more liberal on civil rights than have the Republicans.

Globally speaking, the Democrats have perhaps shown a greater concern for Israel than the Republicans, the latter more enthusiasm for the liberation of the Communist-dominated countries of Eastern Europe. In 1960, pointing to the underdeveloped nations of Asia, Africa, and Latin America, the Democrats charged that the Republicans had concerned themselves too much with the military aspects of the Communist threat. Four years later, with Barry Goldwater the Republican Presidential nominee, the two major parties took opposing stands on nuclear weapons. But for all the talk of a bipartisan foreign policy since the end of World War II, the fact remains that the party out of power has regularly blasted the party in power for its alleged shortcomings in the diplomatic area: Truman vis-a-vis Korea, China, and Eastern Europe; Eisenhower vis-a-vis Suez, Hungary, and the U-2 espionage flights; Kennedy vis-a-vis Cuba; and Johnson vis-a-vis Vietnam. Despite the numerous domestic issues confronting America, our political platforms in recent years have come to revolve around foreign policy to an increasingly greater extent. To paraphrase John Donne, no nation is an island unto itself.

Turning next to the question of which major party platforms have represented the sharpest break with past traditions, an examination of both the Republican and Democratic platforms reveals that the Democrats on at least two occasions have embraced a revolution in principles, while the Republicans have adhered more to a pattern of continuity. In 1896 control of the Democratic party passed from the conservative, pro-gold Cleveland faction to the pro-silver Bryan one, while in 1936 the Democrats rejected their traditional Jeffersonian states' rights philosophy for the centralized nationalism of the New Deal. But in the case of the McGovern candidacy in 1972, one must reserve judgment as to whether the platform adopted by the Democrats was merely a temporary aberration, or whether it indeed marked the end of the reform period beginning with Franklin Roosevelt's New Deal and culminating in Lyndon Johnson's Great Society. Eight years previously, in 1964, the Republicans had departed from tradition somewhat with the Goldwater candidacy, but in 1968 they returned again to the mainstream of party ideology.

The growing proliferation of planks and pledges

As one might expect, political platforms have become longer over the years, but this is far more true of the major party documents than the minor party ones, especially during the last two decades, when both major parties have increasingly offered a "Santa Claus" approach to potential voters. Thus the combined Republican and Democratic platforms in 1968 were four times as long as their 1948 counterparts; since 1960, too, Democratic platforms have been much longer than the Republican ones, this being the era of the New Frontier and the Great Society. Not surprisingly, as Paul David has pointed out, "Each Presidential year since 1948, except 1964, has seen a new high in the total number of platform pledges [made] by each major party, and a corresponding increase in the total number of pledges by the two parties taken together."[16] Aside from 1944 and 1964, when there were more Republican pledges than Democratic ones, the Democrats have outpledged the Republicans.

Prior to 1952 the longest Democratic platform was that of 1920, the longest Republican one that of 1932; the respective party conventions ratified these documents in years when their Presidential candidate went down to a decisive defeat at the polls. The greatest disparity in the length of major party platforms also occurred in 1932, when the Republicans were five times as verbose as the Democrats, yet the latter produced one of the most highly regarded documents in the history of political platforms. Even with the expansion of Federal government activities under the New Deal, each of the three Democratic platforms adopted in 1920, 1924, and 1928 was longer than any ratified in 1932, 1936, 1940, and 1944. Another unexpected finding is that the combined length of the major party platforms from 1912 through 1928 was 50 percent greater than that of those during the years from 1932 to 1948. The explanation for such phenomena as these is not always readily available.

To date the longest platforms of any political party, either major or minor, have been those of the Democrats in 1964, the Communists in 1928, the Democrats in 1960, and the Democrats in 1968. The Communist platform of 1928 heads the list of verbose third party documents, followed in order by that of the American Independent party in 1968, the Socialists in 1960, and the Progressives in 1948. It is highly noteworthy that third party platforms have not proliferated in length as the major party ones have; as a rule third parties do not offer catalogues of handouts for every imaginable group. Since 1892 the Socialist Labor party platforms have run between 1—2 pages in the Porter and Johnson collection, while since 1872 the Prohibition party documents have only increased in length from one to four pages.

Issues and individuals: frequency of citation

Next, one might consider those issues which have been discussed most frequently in major party platforms. In recent years, it would seem two major parties have tried to outdo each other in the number of topics covered in these quadrennial documents. Nevertheless, the typical platform usually allots varying amounts of space to the key issues. Gerald Pomper, who has analyzed the platform commitments of both parties between 1948 and 1964, ranks the order of emphasis as follows: foreign, economic and welfare (tie), government and resources (tie), agriculture, civil rights, defense, and labor.[17]

An examination of the major party platforms for the years 1856 through 1924, though, reveals a somewhat different picture. The half-dozen issues emphasized in Democratic platforms during this period were the tariff, foreign relations, finance, public lands, internal improvements, and pensions, while their Republican counterparts stressed foreign relations, finance, the tariff, immigration, pensions, and the merchant marine. Thus the tariff, finance, and pensions appear on both major party lists; finance should be interpreted here as including banking and currency. The Democrats also tended to be slightly more evasive than the Republicans; they spoke of temperance and polygamy only once. On the other hand, the Democrats did mention slavery more often, but one must remember that the Republicans did not hold their first national convention until 1856.

Admittedly the political process in America did break down at the time of the Civil War, yet throughout American history both major parties have continuously referred to the Constitution in their political platforms, as have some of the extremist parties of the far right and the far left. Aside from the Bill of Rights, the thirteenth, fourteenth, and fifteenth Amendments have received the most mentions, along with the Prohibition Amendment. In the entire corpus of political platforms one also encounters over two dozen references to both the Declaration of Independence and the Monroe Doctrine, but their chronological distribution is by no means identical. There have been only about a half-dozen mentions of the Declaration in the last half-century, while with one prominent exception (the Democratic platform of 1856) drafters ignored the Monroe Doctrine until 1888, at which time this nation had begun to build up a navy and to emerge as a world power. Isolationism was long the official policy of the American government, yet one finds only several references to George Washington's Farewell Address, a rather unexpected and striking neglect.

Nor is the father of our country the most frequently cited statesman in these documents. This honor instead goes to Thomas Jefferson and Abraham Lincoln, to both of whom there are between two and three dozen references. George Washington and Franklin Roosevelt lag far behind with over a dozen mentions apiece, followed by most of the Presidents from Grover Cleveland to Lyndon Johnson. Prior to the time of Cleveland, chief executives such as John Adams, Martin Van Buren, and James Polk were frequently passed over in political platforms; even the controversial Andrew Jackson, along with Jefferson the founder of the modern Democratic party, has received only as many as a half-dozen references, largely by third parties. Throughout American history, the latter have frequently mentioned various chief executives in these documents, with Lincoln being a prime but by no means the only example.

In recent years a progressively larger segment of most political platforms has dealt with foreign policy issues. Aside from such broad concepts as isolationism, internationalism, and imperialism, which we will examine when we shortly contrast major party stands on key issues over the years, there is the matter of which foreign nations have received the most frequent mention. Prior to the Civil War, planks on foreign policy were rather infrequent, but Cuba occasionally was a focal point of attention, as it also was at the time of the Spanish-American War a generation later. During the Gilded Age both parties gave preferential treatment to Ireland and China, but for different reasons; in the competition for the Irish vote, a pre-home rule or anti-British stance was a sine qua non, while from the standpoint of economics the lowly paid Chinese worker threatened to undercut the native American laborer.

Following the turn of the twentieth century, both pro-imperialist Republicans and anti-imperialist Democrats concentrated their attention on the Philippines, and this country remained a focal point of controversy for a generation. The overthrow of the Diaz regime in Mexico just before World War I and the complex series of events that followed also left its mark on American political platforms. With respect to the post-World War II period, the major parties in competing for the Jewish vote have almost invariably taken on a strongly pro-Israel stance, but major and minor party platforms alike have devoted a disproportionate amount of space to Russia, Eastern Europe, Korea, Vietnam, China, and Japan. Curiously, neighboring Canada and Mexico do not rank near the top of the list of most frequent references; most planks dealing with Latin America have been general ones emphasizing either the Good Neighbor Policy and Pan-Americanism or the Monroe Doctrine rather than individual countries. One exception is Castro's Cuba.

At times, too, one encounters references to foreign leaders in these documents, which as a rule are generally favorable. The first such reference in a minor party platform was the Liberty party's greeting to the Irish patriot Daniel O'Connell in 1844; in a major party platform, the Democratic party's tribute to the French Revolutionary leader Lafayette in 1848. Four decades later the Democrats praised the British prime minister William Gladstone and the Irish political leader Charles Parnell. A more unexpected gesture was that of the Prohibition party, which in 1900 quoted the English philosopher Edmund Burke on the definition of a party. During the course of the present century the Communists, Socialist Workers, Socialist Laborites, and the Socialists have frequently referred to European political leaders and thinkers in their platforms; thus the Socialist Workers party in 1960 mentioned such gods of the far left as Marx, Engels, Lenin, and Trotsky. A far more unorthodox coupling was that of the Socialist Labor party, which in 1964 linked the British writer Thomas Carlyle with the American jurist William O. Douglas.

Constitutional revision and political platforms

As for third parties in general, controversy has often focused on how reforms have originated more in minor than in major parties. In this connection David Hinshaw has observed that "Virtually every new policy, accepted late and reluctantly by the major parties, has sprung from the platforms of the minor parties."[18] Perennial Socialist party Presidential candidate Norman Thomas also complained in 1948 that both the Republicans and the Democrats were stealing ideas from his party, but despite these evaluations, the major parties have been more sympathetic to reform than they once were. In this connection Marvin Weisbord has reminded us that "there is hardly a reform of the last sixty years that was not recognized as desirable first by one or both major parties."[19]

With regard to the originality and extent of major party reform proposals, we might turn to the various suggestions for Constitutional revision, as these generally are relatively simple, and lend themselves to systematic examination. A survey of the Constitutional planks in both major and minor party platforms since 1840 reveals that prior to 1896, Constitutional reform was exclusively the property of minor parties.

Among the pre-Civil War abolitionist parties, the Republicans did not espouse Constitutional reform (they did not do so until after 1900). Several reform proposals were offered by the Liberty and Free Soil parties, however, and after the Civil War, the cheap money parties of the Gilded Age made several notable proposals. At least five of these were adopted at a later date. These were (with their initial sponsor in parentheses): the direct election of US Senators, 1913 (Prohibition party, 1872); a federal income tax, 1913 (Greenback party, 1880); woman suffrage, 1920 (Greenback party, 1880); and prohibition, 1919-1920 (Greenback party, 1884). It is apparent from this brief list that a considerable time lag has often ensued between the original proposal in the form of a platform plank and the final ratification of a Constitutional amendment by the states. For example, the anti-Cleveland faction, which seized control of the Democratic party in 1896, adopted a resolution against presidential third terms, but it was not until 1951 that this became a reality—after Franklin Roosevelt had been elected to the office four times.

Following the turn of the twentieth century, both major parties were active in this area, with the Republicans holding a wide lead over the Democrats in the total number of proposals. Other proposed nineteenth-century Constitutional reforms still remain only suggestions. As early as 1844 the Whig party endorsed a single term for the President, while in 1888 the American Party advocated that this single term last six years, rather than four. One of the most popular unfulfilled reforms of the 1800s (and of the 1900s as well) was the direct election of the President (and the Vice President). Among proponents were the Radical party (1864), the Prohibition party (1872), the American National party (1876), the American Prohibition party (1884), and the National party (1896). Unquestionably the most bizarre Constitutional proposals were offered by the newly organized Socialist Labor party in 1892 and 1896. On the prior occasion this radical organization came out for the abolition of the Presidency, the Vice Presidency, and the Senate, with the House of Representatives electing an executive board in their place, subject to its recall. In 1896, it restricted itself to the abolition of the Senate and all upper legislative chambers, and proposed an end to veto power of the executive (national, state and municipal).

Turning to the present century, one discovers as many, if not more, proposed Constitutional reforms in the political platforms of the major parties than in their nineteenth-century counterparts, but with one prominent exception these failed to bear fruit. In 1968 both the Republican and Democratic parties suggested that eighteen-year-olds be allowed to vote; after the US Supreme Court ruled shortly thereafter that Congress did have the right to lower the minimum voting age for federal elections, the states followed suit by adopting a Constitutional amendment extending this reduced minimum age for voting to state elections as well. The minimal time lag here contrasts vividly with that of proposed nineteenth century Constitutional reforms that eventually became realities. With regard to the twenty-first Amendment repealing prohibition, ratified in 1933, the Republicans embraced the eighteenth Amendment as late as 1928 but rejected the Volstead Act, while in 1932 they straddled the fence on the issue. On the other hand, the Democrats, who had long been silent on this topic, attacked the Republicans in 1924 for not enforcing the prohibition laws, and in 1928 reaffirmed this hard-line position, despite the private views of Alfred Smith. In 1932 they reversed field by advocating the repeal of the eighteenth Amendment and the modification of the Volstead Act. The anti-third term stance relative to the Presidency originally taken by the Democrats in 1896 also was abandoned by that party in 1940, when Franklin Roosevelt was re-elected for a third term. In contrast, the Republicans inserted anti-third term planks in their platforms in 1940 and 1944.

Among the pending Constitutional reforms first proposed in this century are (with their original sponsor in parentheses): the direct election of federal judges (Populist party, 1900); the amending of the Constitution by a majority vote of the American people (Socialist party, 1912); a Presidential item veto with respect to appropriation bills (Prohibition party, 1916); the periodical review of Supreme Court justices by the US Senate (American Independent party, 1968); and equal rights for women (Democratic party, 1972). Globally speaking, the Socialists in 1916 proposed that there should be a national referendum on the declaration of war, except in case of invasion. The Prohibitionists in 1920 called for the approval of peace treaties by simple majorities of both houses of Congress. To date only the Socialists (in 1912) have advocated the holding of a Constitutional convention. It should be pointed out, too, that Constitutional reform proposals were more numerous during the Progressive Era and since World War II than they were during the two interwar decades of "Normalcy" and the New Deal; their absence during the 1930s takes on added significance relative to the Supreme Court crisis of 1937. In that year, many pieces of New Deal legislation were declared unconstitutional.

Other reforms and the major parties

When one turns to platform planks dating from the last third of the nineteenth century that advocated restriction of business, encouragement of labor and agriculture, and regulation of economic life in general, it is evident that the minor parties (whose key planks were examined above) approved more than did the major parties. In 1892 the Republicans did give their blessing to the Sherman Anti-Trust Act. As for the Democrats, when they largely took over the Liberal Republican platform in reshuffled order twenty years earlier, they advocated a pro-labor plank, while opposing railroad land grants; in 1896, when the Bryanites gained power, they opposed labor injunctions and fraternizing with bankers. Some of the minor parties offered a more substantial corpus of reform in a single platform.

On the other hand, during the first third of the present century, both the Republicans and the Democrats manifested more enthusiasm for reform. From the Progressive Era one might cite such planks from the Republican platforms as the ones favoring a Department of Commerce and Industries, trust-busting, the Hepburn Act, and a Federal Trade Commission; even from the era of "Normalcy" one might note the planks advocating a national child labor amendment, the grain futures and packer control acts, a Federal Farm Board, and governmental supervision of the radio industry. The Democrats, too, came out for a halt to the use of labor injunctions, the physical evaluation of the railroads, the La Follette Seamen's Act, the Federal Trade Commission Act, an effective child labor law, a Federal Farm Board, and (in 1928) public works during periods of unemployment.

Even before Franklin Roosevelt had assumed the Presidency in 1933 and inaugurated that era of mass reform known as the New Deal, a number of the above proposals offered by both parties had become law. Because they did not require the amending of the Constitution like the last group of reforms just examined, it is not surprising that the time span between the initial proposal and the eventual fulfillment was often much less than a generation. But as far as originality is concerned, it must be admitted that even before the time of the Populists, various third parties had adopted a series of pro-labor and pro-agriculture planks, and had called for the governmental regulation (and even ownership) of the transportation and communication industries. From a technical standpoint, it may be possible to isolate certain planks in the Democratic and Republican platforms in the first third of the twentieth century that had no specific third party predecessor, but when one takes into consideration the general thrust of reform proposals, such an analysis is quite misleading. Since 1933, of course, there has been no continuum of reformist third parties aside from those of the anti-capitalist far left, and thus this type of reform—if only by default—now originates with the major parties.

Bigotry and prejudice in political platforms

Over the years there have been a wide variety of reform planks in party platforms, aside from those groups we have just analyzed as representative of the more important ones. But the bright sunlight of reform also has been accompanied by the dark shadows of reaction. Although it may be a question of semantics as to when a reform is really an anti-reform, many libertarians would regard the two dozen Prohibition party platforms that have appeared during the last century as a supreme example of the latter. Considering party platforms as a whole, however, one might, perhaps, cite an equally representative example of anti-reform: the assorted proposals for various types of discrimination against racial, ethnic, and religious minorities.

During the nineteenth century, the Mormons were a focal point of abuse, especially on the part of the Republicans. As early as 1856 the newly-formed party declared that Congress should prohibit in the territories "those twin relics of barbarism—Polygamy, and Slavery," while in 1884 the Republicans recommended that Congress "divorce the political from the ecclesiastical power of the so-called Mormon church." Equally critical was the Prohibition party, which in 1876 blasted Mormon multiple marriage and recommended the abolition of "these foul enormities, polygamy and the social evil;" in 1884, as the Prohibition Home Protection party, it advocated a Constitutional amendment to forbid polygamy.

In addition, both the Republicans and the Democrats, as well as the National Labor Reform party, the Greenback party, and the Union Labor party, were highly critical of Chinese immigration. It was the National Labor Reform party that was the pioneer here; in 1872 it invoked the "yellow peril" for the first time in a party platform, recommending that the further importation of Chinese workers into the United States should be halted. Even more bigoted were the American party of 1856, whose entire platform was anti-Catholic and anti-foreigner in orientation, and the American party of 1888, which took the positions that immigration should be made more costly and difficult, that no alien should be allowed to hold land, and that language instruction in the public schools should be limited to English. A voice crying in the wilderness was that of the American Prohibition party in 1884, which advocated equal rights for the Indians and the Chinese.

In 1904, for the first and last time, the Democrats included a plank in their platform calling for the extermination of polygamy in the United States. Since that time, party platforms have generally been devoid of the types of discriminatory planks that one encounters in their nineteenth century counterparts, but the platform of the Christian Nationalist party in 1948 was a hymn of hate against the Communists, Jews, and blacks. According to this document, the Marxists and the Zionists, who were in alliance, should be deported; the Negroes, unfortunate victims of slavery being used by various unscrupulous elements, should be colonized or segregated. In 1952, though, the Christian Nationalists modified their platform so as to eliminate the attacks on the Jews and the blacks.

Conversely, the championing of racial, ethnic, and religious minorities by political parties has become more common in this century. Thus the plank on Negro rights found in the lengthy Communist party platform of 1928 was the most complete and progressive set forth by any party up to that time, while in 1944 the Socialist party praised the termination of Chinese exclusion and attacked the Japanese relocation camps on the West Coast. With

respect to the major parties, four years later Democratic liberals
risked a southern walkout by obtaining approval for a minority
plank taking a strong position on civil rights. Since that time there
have been occasions where the Republican plank dealing with this
subject has perhaps been stronger, as in 1956, but generally
speaking it has been the Democrats during the last twenty-five
years who have led the movement for racial equality. Even the
supposedly racist American Independent party platform of 1968
included a plank calling for federal assistance to two "ancient and
noble races"; the American Indians and the Eskimos.

The evasion or omission of controversial issues

While forthright stands on controversial issues may win votes,
they also may lose votes—sometimes more than they win. Thus it
comes as no surprise to learn that there have been occasions when
platform drafters have evaded an issue or omitted it altogether
from the document they formulated, or even offered rhetoric rather
than planks. The Whig party did not even adopt a platform in
1840; in 1844 it devoted one section to a statement of principles, but
its Presidential candidate, Henry Clay, went down to defeat, so
that in 1848 it generally restricted itself to praise for General
Zachary Taylor. Four years later the Whigs offered their most
complete platform to date, and then shortly thereafter ceased to
exist as a major party.

During the present century, that political party most guilty of
wallowing in rhetoric has been the Socialist Labor party, whose
platforms have often avoided specifics like the plague. Yet even the
major parties have been guilty of this sin, too. Gerald Pomper,
who has examined the major party platforms from 1944 to 1968,
has calculated that rhetoric usually constituted about one-sixth of
the total content, although he also admits that it never has taken
up more than a quarter of a document.[20] Pomper also has found
that "Specificity was greatest in the fields of special interest to
identifiable groups of voters: labor, resources, welfare, and agriculture. It was least in such fields as foreign, defense, and
economic policy."[21]

Although it is not always easy to determine when an evasion or
an omission with respect to a specific issue in any given political

platform constitutes a major policy decision on the part of the
platform drafters worthy of retrospective citation and commen-
tary, one does encounter a number of examples both during the
last century and the present one that stand out markedly. In 1844,
for example, the Democratic party came out for the annexation of
Texas and won the election, while the Whig party and the Liberty
party both side-stepped this controversial issue, and lost. On the
other hand, in 1860 Benjamin Butler made an unsuccessful
attempt to gain convention approval for his minority plank
bypassing the slavery issue; had the Democrats approved this, the
party might not have split, and its Presidential candidate might
have defeated Republican nominee Abraham Lincoln. Turning to
the Republicans, in 1856 they failed to include a homestead plank
for the sake of potential Know-Nothing converts fearful of
populating the farms of the West with aliens, but their Presidential candidate, John Fremont, still went down to defeat. In 1880 the
failure of the Republican party to mention Chinese exclusion may
have cost eventual victor James Garfield California and Nevada,
while the omission of any reference to prohibition four years later
may have lost New York and the election for James G. Blaine.

Since 1900 it has been the Democrats who have been guilty of
two of the most glaring omissions. Over the years this party
purposely refrained from mentioning the prohibition issue, but in
1924 it had the daring to criticize the Republicans for failing to
enforce the prohibition laws. Equally noteworthy was the Democratic side-stepping of the monetary issue in 1904 and 1908, after
William Jennings Bryan had split the party during the previous
two elections with his free coinage of silver program; neither
"gold bug" Judge Parker in 1904 nor three-time loser Bryan in
1908 was able to win the Presidency standing on a platform mute
on this question.

Although the next Democratic President, Woodrow Wilson,
was the leading backer of the League of Nations, the Democrats in
1928—four years after Wilson's death and in the wake of two losing
elections—ignored both the League and the World Court. But the
Republicans again triumphed at the polls as a result of issues
other than foreign policy. Significantly, many of the platform
evasions by the latter party have occurred in the diplomatic area:
in 1948 the Truman Doctrine and the Marshall Plan, in 1956 the
deteriorating situation in Egypt, and in 1960 the Castro regime in

Cuba. The Democratic platform of 1936 also failed to mention the Roosevelt administration's recognition of the Soviet Union. As for the election of 1972, the Republicans, hopeful of winning over the labor vote, were silent on the right-to-work laws, while the Democrats, unsuccessfully attempting to ward off a "New Left" image, turned their backs on abortion and marijuana.

Monothematic preoccupations of the third parties

In contrast, far from evading an issue or omitting it, a political party may make a specific plank the focal point of its platform, reducing everything else to a subordinate role. Yet this has happened less frequently than one might expect. Even the first minor party to ratify a platform, the Liberty party, while concentrating on the slavery issue, took the position that "we by no means lose sight of numerous other questions in which all who are to be affected, directly or indirectly, by our Government are deeply interested." Eight years later, in 1848, the Free Soil party came out for a number of reforms not directly related to slavery. Admittedly, the Republican party in 1856 did devote approximately four-fifths of its platform to this question, but it modified its stance, and dealt with a number of other issues four years later on its way to capturing the Presidency. Following the Civil War the cheap money parties frequently approved complex documents, although the platform of the National Silver Republicans in 1896 did focus exclusively on the monetary question.

Even the Prohibition party has sometimes taken stands on a number of different issues. Its first platform, in 1872, supported woman suffrage. In 1896 the "Narrow Gauge" faction, campaigning as the Prohibition party, focused its attention on temperance, but the "Broad Gauge" faction, running as the National party, came out for the free coinage of silver, along with other planks of a Populist nature. A generation later, however, when Alfred Smith was the Democratic Presidential nominee, the Prohibitionists turned their back on reform and approved a platform that manifested an obsession with the temperance issue. In more recent years, the Prohibitionists have returned to more complex platforms, often reshuffling most of the planks from campaign to campaign.

Minority planks and the major parties

On the basis of the information presented here, it is apparent that the content of the political platforms has been of vital importance to the Prohibitionists and the other minor parties. With respect to both the Republicans and the Democrats, it is true that at times the documents they approved have left something to be desired as statements of principle. Nevertheless, if major party platforms were truly meaningless, why would delegates frequently offer minority planks from the floor, and why, on occasion would they walk out of the convention when the majority takes a stance on a certain issue that is distasteful to them? Fortunately for purposes of analysis, the proceedings of the major parties have been published, and in reading them one may relive the great floor debates on the emotionally charged issues of the past. The fact that there have been a larger number of fights at major party conventions over minority planks during the twentieth century than during the nineteenth, together with the previously mentioned data on Constitutional revision and other types of reforms, demonstrates that since 1900 the major parties have treated reform demands with greater tolerance, and even sympathy.

In attempting to break down, for purposes of analysis, the fifty or so minority planks presented over the years at major party conventions, it becomes quickly apparent that an overwhelming majority of them—perhaps as many as three-fourths—deal with domestic rather than foreign policy. From the standpoint of repetition, there were at least several minority planks concerning slavery, money and finance, the tariff, and business regulation from 1840 through 1924, while during the last half-century the most recurrent issues have been the veterans' bonus, prohibition, and civil rights. Looking at foreign policy, one might cite the general League of Nations/Treaty of Versailles issue, as well as the more specific question of Irish home rule, as "repeaters." Even more significant, perhaps, is the fact that in three-fourths of the cases, these minority planks had no sequel. This demonstrates that aside from such highly controversial issues at an earlier date as slavery and the gold standard, and in more recent years as prohibition and civil rights, platform drafters eventually have been able to accomodate most pressing reform demands in one way or another. Otherwise, their proponents might well keep offering them as minority planks.

Presidential candidates and platform pledges

Once the platform is drawn up, the Presidential candidate generally has stood on it. If he is an incumbent running for re-election, he probably has more or less dictated the platform; if not an incumbent, but still the overwhelming front-runner by the time of the convention, he doubtless has placed his stamp upon it. David Hinshaw has opined that "no election was ever won by a good platform or lost by a bad one,"[22] but issues have played a decisive role in a number of campaigns. Many candidates, moreover, emphasize some issues and ignore others, regardless of the platform; thus, in 1884, Republican Presidential nominee James G. Blaine declared that "Formerly, the platform was of first importance. . . . Now the position of the candidate, as defined by himself, is of far more weight with the voters."[23] On the other hand, John Philip Hendrickson, who has studied President Herbert Hoover's re-election campaign in 1932, has discovered a high degree of correlation between the Republican platform and his campaign speeches.[24] Of course, to be both objective and comprehensive, one would have to make a content analysis of the actual speeches of this and every other Presidential campaign, not just rely on the summaries found in *The New York Times* and other places.

There have been a handful of occasions where a platform plank was so unacceptable to the party's Presidential candidate that he openly rejected it. Thus, in 1864 Radical nominee John Charles Fremont attacked that plank calling for the confiscation of the lands of the rebels, while during the same year Democratic standard-bearer George McClellan blasted that labelling the Civil War as "four years of failure." A half-century later, in 1912, Progressive party candidate Theodore Roosevelt opposed a plank favoring a tougher Sherman Anti-Trust Act, but the Resolutions Committee and the assembled delegates overlooked his objections, with the result that TR had this plank deleted from the platform after the convention had adjourned. Then there have been less dramatic instances, as in 1916 when both major party platforms took the position that woman suffrage should be left to the states, but Presidential nominees Woodrow Wilson and Charles Evans Hughes both endorsed a Constitutional amendment during the campaign.

Yet on other occasions, candidates have given their token acceptance to planks obviously at odds with positions they had taken personally. In 1928 Alfred Smith agreed to go along with the Democratic pledge to enforce the eighteenth Amendment and all prohibition laws, while at the same time calling for eventual repeal. And in 1964 Barry Goldwater likewise swallowed that part of the Republican platform committing the party to "full implementation and faithful execution" of the Civil Rights Act of 1964, despite the fact that he had earlier voted against this measure on Constitutional grounds; the Arizona Senator would have preferred the Republicans to restrict themselves to a 250-word statement of principles. In the long run, accomodation has been more frequent than defiance.

Elected Presidents and platform pledges

After the election has taken place and one Presidential candidate has emerged victorious, he is confronted with the responsibility of translating the platform planks into actual deeds. It is quite noteworthy that the two Presidents from the present century, whom historians and political scientists (most of them liberal Democrats) have rated the most highly, have committed a drastic ideological volte face the first several years that they served in office. Woodrow Wilson was forced, because of political considerations, to jettison much of his original New Freedom program in favor of other policies reminiscent of Theodore Roosevelt's New Nationalism. In this connection one might cite an article published in the *North American Review* in 1916 which complained that the Democrats had failed to fulfill platform pledges made four years earlier in such areas as the tariff, the Philippines, the civil service, the reform of the administration of civil and criminal law, Alaska, the Panama Canal tolls, the merchant marine, economy in government, a council of national defense, a single term for the President, and the protection of Americans abroad.[25]

Even more striking was the record of Franklin Roosevelt, who turned the Democratic party away from its traditional commitment to states' rights, towards the creation of a federal leviathan. Despite the opinion of David Hinshaw and Bruno Shaw that the Democratic platform of 1932 was "the best major-party platform, both for thought and expression, in American history,"[26] this relatively brief document did contain a number of planks that came back to haunt FDR in later years. These included the advocacy of a 25 percent reduction in the cost of the federal government, a balanced budget, and the abolition of useless commissions and offices.

Unfortunately for purposes of analysis, prior to World War II the Congressional Quarterly publications were not issued, and what is a difficult task for the student of the post-World War II era becomes a near impossibility for earlier years. Thus John Philip Hendrickson, who has discovered a positive correlation between the legislative record of Republicans in the Seventy-third Congress, the 1932 Republican platform, and the Hoover campaign speeches, also admits that he was unable to reach any definite statistical conclusions.[27] Herbert Hoover, a gifted individual doomed to a perhaps mediocre Presidency by burden of the depression, obviously took platform planks with some seriousness; though not overly enthusiastic about the highly protectionist Hawley-Smoot Tariff of 1930, he signed it nevertheless, because "It was undertaken as the result of pledges given by the Republican Party at Kansas City."[28]

More comprehensive data is available for the post-World War II period. During his second administration, Harry Truman, the surprise victor in the Presidential election of 1948, implemented a number of pledges contained in the Democratic platform. These included establishing a United Nations headquarters in the United States, signing a peace treaty with Japan, extending the Marshall Plan, bringing Israel into the United Nations, providing federal aid for housing, increasing social security benefits, raising the minimum wage, providing fixed farm price supports, repealing margarine taxes, admitting displaced persons into the United States, extending the reciprocal trade acts, and setting up a National Science Foundation. The unimplemented planks included the ones on the repeal of the Taft-Hartley Act, federal aid to education, and civil rights legislation. Yet despite the fact that the same historians and political scientists who rated Wilson and Roosevelt as great Presidents also designated Truman as a near-great, at least until the New Leftists began attacking him for either starting or aggravating the so-called "Cold War," Truman's batting average relative to implementation was not as high as that of some of his successors. Gerald Pomper has found that during the years 1944-1952 (approximately the period that HST served as President) the in-party fulfillment of platform pledges was only around 60 percent, while from 1952 to 1966 it was closer to 80.[29]

These same historians and political scientists also labelled Dwight Eisenhower as only an average chief executive, but one could never deduce this from his record of implementing platform commitments. During a meeting of Republican leaders in 1953, the then President Eisenhower declared that he intended to honor the promises that the party had made at Chicago the previous year; "To my astonishment," he then recollected, "I discovered some of the men in the room could not seem to understand the seriousness with which I regarded platform provisions."[30] Fulfilled planks during the first Eisenhower administration included supporting European integration, concluding the Korean War, publishing the Yalta documents, reducing the civil service, ceding jurisdiction over offshore oil deposits to the states, restricting the TVA, increasing the air force budget, extending social security coverage, opposing federal educational aid, and enacting a Korean GI Bill of Rights. There were failures, too, especially in the areas of full farm parity prices, Taft-Hartley amendments, and civil rights legislation. According to Joseph Freeman, Congress acted favorably during the first two years on thirty-two of the seventy-two provisions contained in the 1952 Republican platform requiring legislative action, while defeating five.[31] Marvin Weisbord also has calculated that "Ike" eventually implemented two-thirds of this document, at least in part; with co-operative Democrats in control of Congress after 1954,[32] Gerald Pomper has opined that the second Eisenhower administration fulfilled platform pledges more faithfully than the first.[33]

Pomper, too, has concluded that the performance record of the eight Eisenhower years compares favorably with that of the eight Kennedy-Johnson years that followed.[34] Of course, under the New Frontier and the Great Society, many new proposals were offered that had not been staples in the Republican platforms in the 1950s.

Again citing Joseph Freeman, during the first two years of the Kennedy administration, Congress acted favorably on 50 of the 104 pledges in the Democratic platform of 1960 requiring legislative implementation, while rejecting no less than 21 others;[35] Seymour Harris was unable to find a single important proposal set forth by JFK that was clearly inconsistent with this document.[36] Yet John Kennedy, despite his charismatic image, obviously was not the master Congressional manipulator that his successor, Lyndon Johnson, was. Following the ascension of LBJ to the Presidency, legislation began to emerge from that body at a more rapid pace, especially after the incumbent's landslide triumph over Goldwater in the Presidential election of 1964 had established overwhelming Democratic majorities in both houses of Congress. His successor as chief executive, Richard Nixon, received less cooperation.

Apart from these analyses of Presidential administrations, studies also have been made of the implementation of platform pledges in various policy areas over varying spans of years during the twentieth century. Victor Profughi, who has analyzed agriculture, labor, tariff, and taxation planks between 1900 and 1960, found that one-third of the Democratic planks and one-fourth of the Republican ones were specific, and that no less than 68 percent of the total planks were ultimately fulfilled. While the Democrats initiated more programs, the Republicans honored a greater percentage of their pledges.[37] As for social security, John Bradley has examined major party planks for the period between 1920 and 1960, and concluded that, "Most of what occurred in social security could be traced to platform proposals, and most of the planks were partly or fully carried out. [But] there were a number of delays and compromises in the performance."[38]

Turning to the post-war period, one also might cite Gerald Pomper's ranking of fulfilled *bipartisan* platform pledges by topic for the years between 1944 and 1966. According to Pomper, the order is, with percentages, agriculture, 100; welfare, 97; resources, 96; foreign, 96; economic, 95; defense, 86; labor, 64; civil rights, 63; and government, 44.[39] For this twenty-two-year span there was some form of fulfillment in approximately 85 percent of the cases where the major parties took similar stands on an issue during the same year.[40]

Because of the several comprehensive studies of a statistical nature that have been made of the fulfillment of platform pledges during the post-World War II period, we will not attempt here to duplicate work done by others. On the other hand, this leaves for analysis an entire century of political platforms from 1840 to 1944, and in the main body of this work we will examine these at some length, Presidential administration by Presidential administration. At the very least, the material presented here demonstrates that in the century prior to World War II, as in the three decades since World War II, most victorious political parties have not placed their platform pledges in mothballs once they have won the Presidential election and taken possession of the White House. Instead, they have made a serious effort to implement most of them.

I. THE 1830s

The Early Years

The modern political platform, as we know it today, is a phenomenon that arose during the era of the second-party system, rather than being a part of the political process since the inception of the republic. Hamiltonians and Jeffersonians, Federalists and Anti-Federalists, aristocrats and democrats—no matter what terminology one uses to describe the great political rivalry that characterized the first half-century of political independence, the fact remains that this struggle was carried on without the benefit of political platforms. One possible exception was the manifestoes of the Workingmen's party of Massachusetts, which began to appear by 1830. Neither were there political conventions; until 1824 the Congressional Caucus, dominated by the Virginia Dynasty, selected the Presidential nominee. Some authorities, though, regard the antiwar Hartford Convention of 1814 as the first interstate political meeting. Of political oratory, of course, there was a copious amount, as there always has been throughout American history.

It was not until 1831 that a political party held a national convention to select a Presidential nominee, and this was not even one of the so-called major parties, but rather the recently created Anti-Masonic party. Originally set up to outlaw secret societies following the mysterious disappearance of one William Morgan of Batavia, New York, who had published a book allegedly exposing the secrets of the Masonic Order, by 1828 this party was backing John Quincy Adams for President against Andrew Jackson, who was a Mason. Exhibiting strength in such states as Vermont, Massachusetts, New York, and Pennsylvania, where there was not a balanced competition for the Presidency, the Anti-Masonic party nevertheless lacked sufficient representation in Congress, both in terms of numbers and of geographical balance,

46

to justify resurrecting the old Congressional Caucus. Consequently, the Anti-Masons convened a national Presidential nominating convention at Baltimore in September 1831, at which they
selected William Wirt of Virginia as their choice for chief
executive. Receiving only the electoral votes of Vermont in the fall
election, the Anti-Masons did not survive the 1830s as a national
party, but at least three members later made their mark on political
history as Whigs and Republicans: William H. Seward and
Thurlow Weed, both of New York, and Thaddeus Stevens, of
Pennsylvania.

Three months later, the National Republicans, who were to be
known as Whigs by 1836, nominated eventual three-time loser
Henry Clay for the Presidency in his second run for that office.
Although this particular gathering did not formulate a political
platform, a committee prepared an address to the people of the
United States after the convention had nominated Clay and the
Vice Presidential candidate. According to Samuel Rhea Gammon,
a modern chronicler of the Election of 1832, addresses to the people
"differed essentially from the present-day platform, first in being
solely a justification of, or sort of apologia for, the actions of the
bodies from which they issued; second in dwelling almost entirely
upon the errors and evils of the opponent's policy, with little or
nothing said, save by implication as to their own constructive
program."[1] Such a general characterization is entirely apt relative
to this particular address to the people, which consisted primarily
of an attack on President Jackson and his administration. Ten
thousand copies were later published and distributed. In its
emphasis on the merits of the Second Bank of the United States
and the threat that Jackson posed to it, this address foreshadowed
the key issue of the 1832 Presidential campaign, which saw Henry
Clay defending and Andrew Jackson attacking this ill-fated
institution, to which the latter was to deal a death blow following
his re-election.

The first true political platform did not make its appearance
until May 1832, when a National Republican convention of young
men met in Washington, D. C., to confirm the nomination of Clay
for President. Consisting of ten relatively short resolutions, this
document constituted a general indictment of the Jackson Administration, both as to domestic and foreign policy. Advocating a
protective tariff and federally financed internal improvements,

two planks in harmony with Clay's nationalist "American System," the platform also condemned the spoils system that Andrew Jackson had brought with him to the Presidency, an aspect of Jacksonian democracy that was a sore spot with the Whig school of historians throughout the nineteenth century. References to the necessity for an independent Supreme Court and Senate constituted a slap at "Old Hickory's" concept of a strong chief executive. The platform also recommended that the King of Holland's proposed settlement of the northeastern boundary question be adopted, but this dispute did not end until ten years later, when Great Britian and the United States signed the Webster-Ashburton Treaty. On the other hand, the platform censured retrospectively the manner in which Jackson had negotiated an agreement with the British reopening the West Indian ports to American trade on the basis of reciprocal privilege. While one committee was drafting these resolutions, another was formulating a similar address to the young men of the United States; following the convention, the delegates visited the tomb of George Washington.

Meeting in Baltimore the same month, the Democrats renominated Andrew Jackson for President, but refrained from drafting either a platform or an address to the people. A committee was appointed to write the latter, but eventually refrained from doing so on the grounds that it was preferable for " . . . the several delegations in this convention, in place of a general address from this body to the people of the United States, to make such explanation by address, report, or otherwise, to their respective constituents of the objects, proceedings and result of the meeting as they may deem expedient."[2] In many ways the most significant act of this convention was the adoption of the two-thirds majority for Presidential nominees, which was to block Martin Van Buren from his party's endorsement in 1844 and "Champ" Clark in 1912, but nevertheless it did not prevent the emergence over the years of such strong leaders as Grover Cleveland, Woodrow Wilson, and Franklin Roosevelt. (FDR eventually had the two-thirds rule abolished in 1936.)

Jackson's victory over Clay by a popular margin of 687,502 to 530,189 and an electoral one of 219 to 49 forced a reassessment of political strategy by National Republican-Whig party leaders, especially because Clay had failed to carry four northern states that

John Quincy Adams had won in 1828. By the beginning of 1835, the anti-Jackson coalition had decided to endorse several regional Presidential candidates in the hope of throwing the Election of 1836 into the House of Representatives, by denying the Democratic nominee a majority in the Electoral College. In pursuit of this strategy, a Massachusetts legislative caucus nominated Daniel Webster in January, and anti-Jackson Democrats in the Tennessee legislature nominated Hugh White during the same month. Still another possibility was General William Henry Harrison, whom the Anti-Masonic party endorsed at Harrisburg, Pennsylvania in December. Under these circumstances, neither a national convention nor a political platform was in order, but the Whig candidates did take ideological stands in their replies to a letter written by Sherrod Williams. The Democrats made their choice just as early; meeting at Baltimore in May they chose the "Red Fox of Kinderhook," Vice President Martin Van Buren, to head the ticket. Grasping at "Old Hickory's" coattails, Van Buren, in his letter of acceptance, pledged himself to "tread generally in the footsteps of President Jackson."[3] The convention refrained from formulating a party platform, but it did appoint a committee that drew up an address to the people, which appeared in the Washington *Globe* on August 26. This Democratic address contained principles similar to later platform planks.

In November 1836, over a year later, Martin Van Buren emerged victorious at the polls, receiving a total of 761,549 popular votes to 736,250 for Harrison, White, and Webster combined. By the time of this election there were competitive parties in every state. Van Buren lost three southern states, but still carried 15 of the 26 states then in the Union; he accumulated an electoral vote majority of 170, despite the fact that a number of Jacksonians did desert him. Unfortunately for Van Buren, his victory was a hollow one. Around the time that he took office the Panic of 1837 erupted, and his Presidency in the eyes of most historians today was only an average one. Were they only able to unite, the Whigs were confronted with a golden opportunity to win the White House in 1840.

II.   1840

Tippecanoe and Tyler, Too

From a party that offered only regional candidates for the Presidency in 1836, four years later the Whig party emerged as a victorious coalition; in the process it waged the first truly modern political campaign, and drew an unprecedented percentage of voters to the polls. Convening at Harrisburg, the site of the 1835 Anti-Masonic national convention, the Whigs passed over the more ideologically oriented Henry Clay, whose support of a protective tariff was suspect, for an aging military hero of the War of 1812, William Henry Harrison. One of the more prominent leaders of the convention was Thurlow Weed of New York, once an anti-Mason, later a Republican. For Vice President, the Whigs chose a candidate identified with states' rights, John Tyler of Virginia, who had broken with Andrew Jackson over the nullification issue at the time that South Carolina had declared the federal tariff null and void within its borders.

Not only did this Whig convention fail to adopt an address to the people, it also failed to draft a platform. This was perhaps wise, in that the speeches presented there were anti-Van Buren and anti-Democratic rather than pro-anything. In commenting on the wisdom in refraining from the adoption of a statement of principles, one Massachusetts delegate observed that, "If the voice of the West rolling down from the mountains and along the valleys of the Atlantic, be not better than all the addresses that ever were issued, then indeed a miracle has been wrought."[1] Still another delegate observed, "Leave the nomination to its own weight."[2] Having turned their backs on a platform, the Whigs nevertheless contributed a significant innovation to the political process through the implementation of the "unit rule," under which the majority of the delegates from a state might commit that state's total vote on some issue or for some candidate. The "unit rule" persisted at Democratic conventions until as late as 1968, when reformers pressured its abolition.

The Democratic convention that met at Baltimore in May 1840 was a picture of contrast to that of the Whigs, both in regard to candidates and platform. Renominating by acclamation the

incumbent President, Martin Van Buren, for another term as chief
executive, the Democrats failed to endorse the incumbent Vice
President, Richard Johnson of Kentucky, thus leaving the choice
of a running-mate to the state electors. Four years earlier Johnson
had made history by becoming the only Vice President ever to be
chosen by the Senate, after having failed to obtain the necessary
simple majority of electoral votes in the general election. Also a
hero of the War of 1812—he claimed to have killed Tecumseh at the
Battle of the Thames—Johnson had become an object of controversy by this time as a result of his alleged liasons with Negro
women. One might well relate the abandoning of him to the
inclusion of a "hands-off" plank on slavery in the platform.

In the opinion of a number of commentators, the Democratic
platform of 1840 was designed to lure John Calhoun and his
supporters back into the Democratic party with its non-inter-
ference with slavery and economy in government planks. Van
Buren, in fact, threatened to veto any act of Congress that would
challenge the "peculiar institution;" this was indeed a dramatic
gesture. On the other hand, the economy in government plank,
which was in harmony with one of the basic tenets of Jeffersonian
democracy, along with the one calling for the strict interpretation
of the Constitution, was to remain a basic part of Democratic
platforms until the time of Franklin Roosevelt, the New Deal, and
increased federal spending. Still other planks carried on the
Jacksonian tradition with their stands against federally financed
internal improvements, the Second Bank of the United States, and
the protective tariff. The plank in favor of liberal naturalization
laws was directed against the anti-foreigner Native American
party of New York City; naturalized Germans and Irish had
contributed to the Jacksonian majority in New York State.

Despite the forthright stands on a wide variety of contemporary
issues, the nine-plank platform was read and passed without
comment, while Isaac Hill of New Hampshire also presented an
address to the people. As Henry Minor, a modern historian of the
Democratic party, has pointed out, the former document was of
more than passing significance: "It is the declaration of Jacksonian principles, and for sixteen years was the political constitution of the party. Readopted in its entirety in 1844, it constitutes
the major part of the party platforms of 1848, 1852, and 1856."[3]
Although Andrew Jackson had completed his two terms as

President and Martin Van Buren failed of re-election as chief executive, the Jacksonian tradition persisted in Democratic politics; it is impossible to fully comprehend the programs of later Presidents, in particular James K. Polk, without reference to "Old Hickory."

While the Whigs were avoiding the slavery issue, and every other issue as well, and the Democrats were adopting a "hands-off" stance towards the "peculiar institution," the moderate anti-slavery and abolitionist forces opposed to William Lloyd Garrison held their first national convention at Albany, New York in April 1840. Subsequent state conventions were held in Ohio and other states of the Northwest. Nominating former slaveholder James Birney of Kentucky for President, the Liberty party professed loyalty to the Constitution; this was in marked contrast to the more extreme views of Garrison, who labelled our fundamental law as "a covenant with death and an agreement with hell."[4] Although third parties in American history frequently have been stereotyped retrospectively in terms of a single issue, the Liberty party proclaimed that, "we by no means lose sight of numerous other questions in which all who are to be affected, directly or indirectly, by our Government are deeply interested." (These were tied in by the reformers to the slavery issue, however.) One of the contributions of the present volume, it is hoped, will be to demonstrate that third party platforms are in fact quite complex, and only on rare occasions are so monolithic that one may summarize them in terms of a lone concept.

If the Whigs campaigned in 1840 without a platform, they more than compensated for this lack of ideological commitment by their effective use of the first great slogan in American Presidential campaigning: "Tippecanoe and Tyler, Too." Nearly a generation earlier a much-younger William Henry Harrison had routed the Indians at the Battle of Tippecanoe, in what has been described as the first battle of the War of 1812. In contrast, the expression "Log Cabin and Hard Cider" had originated as late as May 1840 in an attack on the Whigs published by the Democratic Baltimore *Republican,* which the Whigs quickly turned to their advantage. According to this hostile organ, "upon condition of his receiving a pension of $2,000 and a barrel of cider, General Harrison would no doubt consent to withdraw his pretensions, and spend his days in a log cabin on the banks of the Ohio."[5] But the Whigs, too, often were quite venomous; according to some of their propagandists, "Van, Van is a used up man," an aristocrat who dined with gold spoons at the White House. Aside from the sloganing and mudslinging, public interest was further aroused through the widespread use of many of the devices that one associates with the modern political campaign: placards, emblems, hats, effigies, floats, and rallies.

That fall nearly four-fifths of the eligible voters went to the polls, an incredible advance over the previous high, the 56 percent who participated in the Jackson-Adams contest of 1828. With many voters unfairly blaming him for the Panic of 1837, Van Buren carried only six states, winning 60 electoral votes, while Harrison swept nineteen, amassing a solid total of 234 electoral votes. Admittedly, the popular vote margin was much closer—1,128,702 for Van Buren to 1,275,017 for Harrison—but the disparate coalition that was the Whig party won Congress as well. Having succeeded with General Harrison, as shall be seen, the "military hero" ploy was to remain the key to future Whig Presidential nominations.

III. 1844

54° 40' or Fight

Unfortunately for the aged Harrison, the newly-elected President was to serve only one month in office before dying of pneumonia, apparently contracted at his inauguration. His successor, John Tyler, soon ran afoul of the current Whig leadership with his states' rights principles that led him to reject federally financed internal improvements and a third Bank of the United States. On the other hand, Tyler did go along with the dissolution of Van Buren's Independent Treasury System in 1841 (Polk restored it in 1846), and also signed the Pre-Emption Act of the same year, which pleased the Western "squatters." In the foreign affairs field, the Webster-Ashburton Treaty of 1842 settled the Northeastern boundary question, a subject which the 1832 National Republican convention of young men had mentioned in its indictment of the Jackson administration. Less successful were the attempts to resolve the Texas issue; Secretary of State John Calhoun did sign a treaty annexing the then independent nation in April 1844, but the Senate decisively rejected it. By opposing annexation, Democrat Martin Van Buren and Whig Henry Clay unknowingly dealt a fatal blow to their future Presidential hopes.

The other factor that eventually was to block Henry Clay from the White House was the presence of the Liberty party candidate in the Presidential race. Although James Birney had received only a mere 7,000 votes in 1840, this party renominated him for President at its Buffalo, New York convention in August 1843. Of considerable eloquence was the platform of forty-four resolutions, which were spearheaded by the anti-slavery plank. Observing that "human brotherhood is a cardinal principle of true Democracy, as well as of pure Christianity," this document affirmed that the Liberty party "is the party of 1776," "not a Sectional party, but a National Party." According to the platform, the Liberty party had been organized not merely to achieve the overthrow of slavery, but also to promote equal rights. In an interesting variation on John Calhoun's doctrine of nullification (which South Carolina had applied to the federal tariff), this document took the position that Article 4, Section 2 of the federal Constitution was absolutely null and void with respect to the returning of fugitive slaves. The reasoning employed here was that the latter was in violation of the natural rights philosophy, a philosophy which permeates the Declaration of Independence. Apart from attacking the slave system as a general evil, the platform of the Liberty party also labelled the 250,000 slaveholders of the South (this number was obviously exaggerated) as a privileged aristocracy, and chastized the state governments of the slave states for employing slaves instead of free laborers on public works.

Significantly, the anti-fugitive slave trade resolution had not been a part of the original document, but had been offered as an amendment from the floor by the Reverend John Pierpont of Massachusetts, the grandfather of financier J. P. Morgan. After this amendment had been voted down at the insistence of Salmon Chase of Ohio, it was reintroduced and passed while Chase was absent from the floor. This marked the first floor fight over a platform plank in the history of national party conventions, and it is noteworthy that it occurred at a gathering held by an ideologically oriented "third" party. Still another first was the resolution praising the Irish patriot Daniel O'Connell, the first foreign leader ever to receive favorable mention in a party platform. But conspicuously absent was any specific reference to Texas.

Similarly silent on the Texas question, despite Clay's stand, was the Whig party platform drawn up at Baltimore in May 1844. Nominating the aging Kentucky statesman for his third run for the Presidency, with Peter Frelinghuysen of New Jersey as his running-mate, the Whig convention adopted a platform that personally lauded Clay and Frelinghuysen and indirectly attacked former President Andrew Jackson. The heart of this quite brief document, four paragraphs in length, merits quotation in that it constitutes a succinct summary of contemporary Whig ideology. The second and third principles stated here, it will be noted, were also emphasized in the political platform the young men of the National Republican party had adopted at their Washington convention in May 1832, an indication that in many respects, Whig political philosophy was simply a continuation of that of the National Republicans:

> "*Resolved*, that these principles may be summed up as comprising, a well regulated national currency; a tariff for revenue to defray the necessary expenses of the government, and discriminating with special reference to the protection of the domestic labor of the country; the distribution of the proceeds of the sales of public lands; a single term for the presidency; a reform of executive usurpations:—and generally—such an administration of the affairs of the country as shall impart to every branch of public service the greatest practicable efficiency, controlled by a well regulated and wise economy."

Less evasive were the Democrats, who took the bull by the horns and came out for the reoccupation of Oregon and the reannexation of Texas at their convention, also held at Baltimore in May 1844. After former President Martin Van Buren had fallen short of the two-thirds majority needed to nominate him, the Democrats turned to the first "dark horse" Presidential nominee, James Polk of Tennessee. Polk, who had served as the Speaker of the US House of Representatives and Governor of Tennessee, had the backing of former President Andrew Jackson and historian George Bancroft, and unlike either Van Buren or Clay, favored the annexation of Texas. Again experiencing problems with a Vice Presidential candidate, the Democrats originally selected Silas Wright of New York, but this anti-slavery Van Burenite refused the honor, whereupon the convention nominated George Dallas of Pennsylvania.

Turning to the platform, in opposing the distribution of the proceeds from public land sales to the states, its drafters attacked Jackson's great rival Henry Clay, while in opposing the removal of the Presidential veto (which they claimed had "saved" the nation three times from the Bank of the United States) they manifested their support for "Old Hickory." Largely the work of Robert Walker of Mississippi (although Benjamin F. Butler of New York chaired the Resolutions Committee), this document incorporated those planks that had been adopted in 1840. But the key provision—and one which won the backing of both free and slave state annexationists—was that calling for the reoccupation of Oregon and the reannexation of Texas. The Democrats also laid claim to being the party of the people, in this connection asserting that, " . . . the American Democracy place their trust . . . in a clear reliance upon the intelligence, patriotism, and the discriminatory justice of the American masses." By attacking "Federalism, under whatever name or form, which seeks to palsy the will of the constituent," the Democrats linked the Whigs with a long-defunct party usually identified with the aristocracy. At the final session of the convention, too, a central committee of fifteen was appointed, an early forerunner of the modern Democratic National Committee.

The campaign itself saw the Democrats challenge the Whigs with the slogan "54° 40′ or Fight," a reference to Oregon rather than to Texas (which remained a focal point of public attention); the Whigs offered the retort, "Who is James K. Polk?" During the campaign, Polk defused a "hot" issue by skillfully coming out for a revenue tariff with qualifications in his Kane letter; the Democratic nominee's successful handling of this question con-

trasts vividly with Whig candidate Clay's fatal stance in opposition to the annexing of Texas. Yet in the final analysis, the
Democratic campaign to gain the foreign-born vote by labelling
the Whigs as nativists may have been equally decisive at the ballot
box.

In August President John Tyler, whom a Tyler Democratic
convention had renominated at Baltimore in May, withdrew in
favor of Polk, after his chances of obtaining the annexationist vote
had begun to fade. This furthered the Regular Democratic cause.
In one of the closest elections in American history, Polk edged past
Clay when 15,000 voters in New York cast their ballots for Liberty
party nominee James Birney; this action allowed Polk to carry the
state by a 5,000-vote margin. Although Clay did triumph in
Tennessee, Polk was victorious in fifteen of the twenty-six states,
amassing an electoral vote majority of 170 to 105. The popular vote
was much closer: Polk, 1,337,243; Clay, 1,299,068; Birney, 62,300.
Ironically, the Liberty party defeated its own basic objective by
ensuring the victory of Polk. Texas, in fact, entered the Union via
the joint resolution route as a slave state on March 1, 1845, several
days before Polk took office as chief executive.

IV. 1848

Free Soil, Free Men

Rising to the occasion, James Polk compiled a record as
President far superior to the general run of mediocrities who
occupied the White House between 1840 and 1860; his record has
won him a near-great ranking in at least two polls of American
historians and political scientists conducted since World War II.
Concentrating on four key issues—a tariff reduction, an independent treasury, the reoccupation of Oregon, and the reannexation
of Texas—Polk ran up a perfect score, despite the fact that he did
not enjoy the political leverage that a President who stands for re-

election theoretically possesses. This hardworking Jacksonian, though, barely survived his term in office, so that hypotheses regarding a second Polk administration remain purely academic speculation.

To succeed Polk, the Democratic National Convention at Baltimore in May 1848 selected as its Presidential nominee General Lewis Cass of Michigan, an expansionist who favored squatter sovereignty, a principle which, significantly, was not written into the official platform. Unlike Polk, who eventually compromised and settled for half a loaf on Oregon, Cass pursued Manifest Destiny with a zeal characteristic of midwestern advocates of "54° 40' or Fight." Cass's running mate was the relatively unknown General William Butler of Kentucky. Unfortunately for the Presidential candidate, there were rival slates of delegates from New York, and neither slate was seated after an attempt at compromise had failed. One of these factions, the more conservative Hunkers, eventually pledged their support for the ticket, but the more radical Barnburners, with their anti-administration bias and pro-Wilmot Proviso stance, later rallied to the Free Soil party banner. Their defection was to cost Cass New York and the election. From the standpoint of permanent organization, this convention also witnessed the establishment of the first national committee, consisting of a single member from each state.

In its basic provisions, the Democratic platform of 1848 was a repeat of that of 1844, just as that of 1844 had been a repeat from 1840, although that of 1848 did add a provision that the public debt be paid off. Benjamin F. Hallett of Massachusetts presented this document to the convention. Since Democratic Representative David Wilmot of Pennsylvania had stirred up a hornet's nest two years previously by attempting to ban slavery from every square mile of territory that the United States might acquire from Mexico, it was not surprising that the 1848 Democratic platform would address itself to this general topic. Blasting the abolitionists, this document not only denied that Congress had power to interfere with slavery in the states, but also criticized all efforts to bring the slavery question before Congress. On the other hand, the convention did vote down by a 36 to 216 margin, with Southerners casting all of the aye votes, a resolution offered from the floor that favored noninterference with slavery in the territories. When the entire Florida delegation and two delegates from

Alabama (one of whom was William Yancey) walked off the floor, it marked the first such protest in the history of national Presidential nominating conventions.

On a more positive note, the 1848 Democratic platform lauded the outgoing President, James Polk, for his "principles, capacity, firmness, and integrity," and firmly backed his handling of the Mexican War: "a just and necessary war on our part, in which every American citizen should have shown himself on the side of his country, and neither morally nor physically, by word or by deed, have given 'aid and comfort to the enemy.'" American public opinion, it will be recalled, was sharply divided towards US participation in this conflict. Ironically, in also praising the American soldiers and officers who had fought in the Mexican War, this document extended its blessing to the eventual Whig Presidential nominee, General Zachary Taylor. Turning to other aspects of US foreign policy, the 1848 Democratic platform welcomed the new French republic to the community of nations; in this plank "their" Lafayette was linked with "our" Washington in a reference to the American Revolution. In condemning monopolies and exclusive legislation for the benefit of the few, moreover, this document pledged to sustain and advance Constitutional liberty, equality, and fraternity—a striking echo of the French Revolution.

When the Whigs met in Philadelphia one month later, they passed over 1844 Presidential nominee Henry Clay and General Winfield Scott for Zachary Taylor, who was also a Louisiana slaveholder. The latter aspect of Taylor's career did not endear him to antislavery delegates from New England and Ohio; the convention also voted down a resolution offered by an Ohio delegate affirming the power of Congress to regulate slavery in the territories. For Vice President the convention selected Millard Fillmore of New York, a second-rank political figure who had played a leading role in the drafting of the tariff of 1842.

The platform, if indeed there technically was one, was adopted at a separate meeting held the night of the final day of the session, not at the convention proper. Consisting mainly of a personal testimony on behalf of Taylor—"whom calumny cannot reach"—this document stressed his southwestern origins and conservative principles. It probably had been drawn up originally by the Pennsylvania Whig State Ratifying Convention, rather than by delegates at the national gathering. The empty wording of this platform paralleled the failure of the Whigs eight years earlier even to formulate a statement of principles; they instead relied on a military hero to lead the party to the White House. Ideology had been tried with Henry Clay in 1844, and had been found wanting.

In many respects the most interesting platform formulated by a major party in 1848 was the one the Free Soil party endorsed in August at a national convention at Buffalo, New York (Whig Vice Presidential nominee Millard Fillmore's home town). No less than 465 delegates attended from 18 states. Drawing their strength from Liberty Party members, New England "Conscience" Whigs, and Barnburners, the Free Soilers numbered among their ranks future Republican leaders Charles Sumner of Massachusetts and Salmon Chase of Ohio, and Vice Presidential candidate Charles Francis Adams of Massachusetts, along with the Chairman of the Resolutions Committee, Benjamin F. Butler of New York. Butler had played a similar role at the Democratic convention in 1844; Chase, who had a major voice in the platform's content, also had strongly influenced the Liberty party platform of 1844.

Unlike the more lengthy and monolithic Liberty party platform of 1844, the Free Soilers came out for a number of reforms not directly related to slavery: cheaper postage, more economical national government, popular election of all civil officers, revenue tariff sufficient to reduce the national debt, Congressional funding of river and harbor improvements, and federal homestead legislation. The river and harbor provision was inserted in the aftermath of a Polk veto on the grounds of unconstitutionality of $1,300,000 in projects, and one year after an 1847 River and Harbor Convention at Chicago. Those planks calling for a more economical federal government and a revenue tariff were in line with Democratic thinking, but that advocating the Congressional funding of river and harbor improvements was more consistent with Whig ideology. The homestead plank was later taken up by the Republicans. Not waiting for the campaign itself to evolve, the Free Soilers incorporated their official slogan into the platform as a final plank: "Free soil, free speech, free labor, and free men."

But it was the slavery question that was the focal point of the platform, and here the Free Soilers assumed a stance that many of the extreme abolitionists found unsatisfactory, even though they attacked the Democratic and Whig candidates for having been named "under Slaveholding dictation." In a reference to the Jeffersonian proviso of 1784 forbidding slavery after 1800 in every territory, and the Northwest Ordinance of 1787, this document asserted that at the time of the Founding Fathers it had been the "settled policy of the nation, *not* to *extend, nationalize* or *encourage,* but to limit, localize, and discourage Slavery." Declaring that there should be "No more Slave States and no more Slave Territories," the 1848 Free Soil platform proposed the abolition of slavery in the District of Columbia, affirming that "Congress had no more power to make a SLAVE than to make a KING." Two years later such an act was passed as part of the package constituting the so-called Compromise of 1850. With respect to the West, this document favored the admission of Oregon, California and New Mexico as free states, and condemned the pending fugitive slave law, which Congress also enacted in 1850 while making California a free state. Nevertheless, the Free Soilers also pledged noninterference with slavery in those states where it already existed, and thus in practice adopted a more conservative stance than their Liberty party counterparts had taken four years earlier, in 1844.

Once he had been nominated for chief executive, General Zachary Taylor's occasional public remarks steered wide of ideological commitment. The Whig convention, he observed, "did not fetter me down to a series of pledges which were to be an iron rule of action in all, and in despite of all, the contingencies that might arise in the course of a Presidential term. . . ."[1] Although he was a slave owner, Taylor remained silent on the slavery issue in his most important campaign statement, the so-called "Second Allison Letter." While he privately believed that slavery should not be disturbed in the South, he also was of the opinion that it should not be introduced in the West.

During the course of the campaign two minor parties threw their support to the Free Soilers. Liberty Party Presidential Candidate John Hale of New Hampshire, nominated at New York City in November 1847, eventually endorsed Van Buren, whom the Barnburners later designated as their choice at Utica in June 1848, prior to the Free Soil convention. The election proved to hinge on New York State, though historians rarely stress this fact to the extent that they do relative to that of 1844. In amassing 1,360,101 popular votes, Taylor carried eight slave and seven free states for an electoral vote total of 163, while in attracting 1,220,544 popular votes, Cass won eight free and seven slave states for an electoral vote total of 127. Thus this election was not decided along North/ South lines, like that of 1860. Van Buren received no electoral votes, but his popular vote of 291,263 was almost five times that which Liberty Party nominee James Birney had received in 1844. Van Buren, it might be added, later returned to the Democratic party, but opposed secession. Taylor was to be dead within two years.

V. 1852

The Whigs' Last Hurrah

Like his Whig predecessor in the White House, William Henry Harrison, Zachary Taylor did not survive a full term; like John Calhoun, he died in 1850 during the Congressional debate over the Great Compromise. This also was the year that the Clayton-Bulwer Treaty with England was drawn up, providing for the joint construction of a future Central American canal, another question of importance to the South. The incoming chief executive, Millard Fillmore, is best remembered for signing the Great Compromise on the slavery issue, which won the endorsement of Webster, Clay, Lewis Cass, and Stephen Douglas, but aroused the hostility of Taylor, Calhoun, William Seward, Thomas Hart Benton, Salmon Chase, and John Hale. Among other things, the Compromise of 1850 provided for the admission of California as a slave state, the establishment of Utah and New Mexico as territories without reference to slavery, the passage of a stricter fugitive slave law, and the abolition of the out-of-district slave trade in the District of Columbia. Hopefully a permanent solution to the thorny slavery question, this compromise settlement was fated to last no more than four years before the passage of the Kansas-Nebraska Act in 1854 again muddied the waters.

In 1852 the Democrats convened first, at Baltimore in June. Although the leading candidates for the Presidential nomination included such luminaries as Cass, Douglas, Benton, and James Buchanan, the nomination eventually went on the forty-ninth ballot to New Hampshire "Doughface" Franklin Pierce, a former lieutenant of James Polk. Also without a national following was the Vice Presidential choice, William King of Alabama. Preserving its tradition of continuity, the Democratic platform of 1852 again listed as its basic core those principles first stated in 1840 and reaffirmed in 1844 and 1848, with Aaron V. Brown of Tennessee presiding over the Resolutions Committee. Significantly, this document also drew upon the Kentucky and Virginia Resolutions of 1798, with their emphasis on states' rights, and James Madison's report to the Virginia legislature in 1799. As in 1848, the Democrats again declared the Mexican War just and necessary, but welcomed peace. By endorsing the Compromise of 1850 and opposing further agitation of the slavery question, the Democrats paved the way for the Whigs to follow suit, thus defusing this general problem as an issue in the 1852 campaign. Despite its importance, this document was read through hurriedly before a dwindling and inattentive convention, and passed without comment.

The Whigs, who also met at Baltimore in June, similarly took a large number of ballots (fifty-three) to select their Presidential nominee; they chose Winfield Scott, a Mexican War hero, over the incumbent President, Millard Fillmore, and the dying Senator, Daniel Webster. Like the Democrats, the Whigs turned to the South for their Vice Presidential nominee, naming William Graham of North Carolina. The Whigs also followed the Democratic example, in that they nailed together a platform before nominating a candidate to stand on it; as one delegate asserted, "We want to know who we are, and whether we are all of one party or not. We want to know if our principles are your principles, and your principles ours."[1] Although it was originally decided that each delegation was to vote in accordance with the state's Electoral College representation at the platform committee hearings, Southerners joined forces with Northerners from states with a limited population in an unsuccessful attempt to force a return to the system under which each state cast one vote.

The platform itself, which was devoted to "great conservative principles," endorsed the Compromise of 1850 and opposed further agitation of the "dangerous and exciting" slavery question. Chairing the Resolutions Committee was George Ashmun of Massachusetts. As for the foreign policy field, the Whigs turned to George Washington's "Farewell Address" and to Thomas Jefferson's recommendation that the United States not become involved in entangling foreign alliances. Although this document did support Congressional appropriations for river and harbor improvements, along with a protective tariff, it also endorsed states' rights, the concept that the Federal government was one of limited powers, and economical administration. The first two of these principles were in line with traditional Whig thinking, but the last three were closer to Andrew Jackson than to Henry Clay; one might well interpret their inclusion as evidence of the growing ideological disintegration of the party. Far from accepting this attempt to smooth over differences, it was the Free Soil Whigs from the northern states who led the movement against the platform, casting 66 nay votes to 227 in favor when the convention gave its final approval. One dissenter observed bitterly, "We accept the candidate but we spit on the platform."[2]

Those who were disappointed that both major parties had endorsed the Compromise of 1850 later were given the opportunity to make their views heard when the Free Soil convention assembled at Pittsburgh in August. Though this party is commonly known as the Free Soil party, it is referred to in the platform as the Free Democratic party, while it was sometimes known as the Free Soil Democratic party, or the Independent Democratic party, or simply as the Independent party. John Hale of New Hampshire was its Presidential nominee; Hale also had been the Liberty party's choice in 1847 at New York City. The convention then nominated future Radical Republican George Julian of Indiana as Hale's running-mate.

Quoting the "life, liberty, and the pursuit of happiness" passage from the Declaration of Independence, the Free Soil platform similarly referred to the Lockian trilogy of life, liberty, and property in observing that the Constitution forbids the Federal government from depriving anyone of any of these without the due process of law. To the Free Soilers, like the Jeffersonians, the Federal government was one of limited powers. Unlike the 1848 platform, which concentrated more on the blocking of slavery than on abolishing slavery itself, the 1852 document boldly proclaimed that, "slavery is a sin against God and a crime against man, which no human enactment nor usage can make right; and that Christianity, humanity, and patriotism, alike demand its abolition." Doubtless this passage offended numerous Southerners.

Similarly irritating to Dixie was the plank calling for the American government to recognize the black republic of Haiti, now long independent. At least two of the other foreign policy planks were quite progressive for that day; one called for the self-determination of peoples seeking to establish republican or constitutional governments, while the other recommended the arbitration of disputes between the United States and foreign nations. Aside from the planks dealing with slavery, one domestically-oriented plank demanded that the funds of the general government be kept separate from banking institutions, a provision more in line with Democratic than Whig thinking. Still another plank called for the unimpeded entry of immigrants, a cry that later was taken over by the Republicans. In summary, the Free Soil party platform weighed both the Democratic and Whig parties in the balance and found them wanting: "hopelessly corrupt, and utterly unworthy of confidence."

Forced to choose from a military hero, a Northerner with Southern principles, and an extremist, the American voters opted for the second choice by a relatively close margin in popular votes but by a landslide in the Electoral College. Pierce, carrying twenty seven states, collected 254 electoral votes, while winning 1,601,474 popular votes; Scott, carrying only four states, collected 42 electoral votes, while winning 1,386,578 popular votes, or 46 percent of the total. (The four Whig states were Massachusetts, Vermont, Kentucky, and Tennessee, a rather heterogeneous group.) Hale, who acted as a drain mostly on Scott, carried no states, and his popular vote total of 156,149 was a little over half that which Van Buren had received four years previously as the Free Soil nominee. The Whig failure to win more than four states in the Presidential balloting was compounded by a drop-off in Congressional strength in the South, and in the Middle Atlantic States and Pennsylvania; within four years the party was to be a living corpse, well on the road to extinction, as its predecessor, the Federalist party, had been four decades earlier.

VI. 1856

Bleeding Kansas

Four years after it had placed its stamp of approval on the Great Compromise, Congress gave its consent to the Kansas-Nebraska Act in 1854. This measure, which was a pet project of Senator Stephen Douglas of Illinois, who wanted the proposed transcontinental railroad to pass from Chicago through the central part of the United States, in effect repealed the Missouri Compromise of 1820 with its prohibition on slavery north of 36° 30′ by providing for popular sovereignty in Kansas and Nebraska. It is generally believed that Douglas had already developed Presidential ambitions, and it was only through the backing of the South that he was able to get such a bill past Congress. But in supporting the Kansas-Nebraska measure, Douglas opened a Pandora's box that neither he nor anyone else was able to put the lid on again; opposed by Free Soilers and antislavery Democrats and Whigs, this act played a key role in the formation of the Republican party in 1854. Within two years Kansas had become embroiled in a bitter civil war over the slavery issue.

Were a political solution to be found to the latter, the Whig party was not going to provide it. Two of its greatest leaders, Daniel Webster and Henry Clay, had both died in 1852, and no one had emerged to take their place; by that date, too, it was running out of military heroes to nominate for President. Although originating as an anti-Jacksonian movement, the Whig national platforms rank among the most vague and vapid ever drawn up. Nevertheless, there was a real conflict of opinion among the Whigs on the slavery issue, with the "Conscience" Whigs opposing the "Cotton" Whigs. Unlike the long defunct Federalists, the Whigs were neither a sectional party drawing their strength mainly from New England and Middle Atlantic States, nor an aristocratic one hostile to and distrustful of the masses. On the other hand, the Federalists were probably more united on philosophy, and to survive, a political party does need a basic core of beliefs.

Convening at Cincinnati in June, the Democrats passed over both the incumbent President, Franklin Pierce, and Stephen

Douglas, whose candidacy had been injured by the Kansas-Nebraska agitation, in favor of James Buchanan of Pennsylvania, the aging minister to Great Britain. Buchanan was nominated on the seventeenth ballot after Douglas had withdrawn his name. The possessor of an extensive record, both in Congress and as Secretary of State, the noncontroversial Buchanan was another Northerner, like Pierce, usually regarded as conciliatory towards the southern slaveowners. Both men's names were linked with the abortive Ostend Manifesto, a recent attempt to obtain Cuba for the South. Still another concession to Dixie was the selection of John Breckinridge of Kentucky for Vice President; four years later the Southern Democrats were to nominate Breckinridge as their Presidential candidate.

The Democratic platform of 1856 repeated those basic principles laid down in 1840, with a few additions and in slightly different order. Heading the Resolutions Committee was Benjamin F. Hallett of Massachusetts. Two paragraphs were devoted to an attack on the anti-Catholic and anti-foreigner American party, and "all secret political societies by whatever name they be called." This time there was no reference to the Mexican War, unlike in 1848 and 1852; but the slavery issue received more attention than ever, with this document praising the Kansas-Nebraska Act as well as the Compromise of 1850. A plank calling for a transcontinental railroad was tabled, doubtless because of the States' Righters opposition to federally financed internal improvements, but was eventually included.

After approving the domestic portion of the platform unanimously, the delegates turned individually to five foreign policy planks, which they approved by margins ranging from 239 to 21 (number two) to 180 to 56 (number three). These planks respectively endorsed free seas and free trade (which was in line with traditional Democractic low tariff stands), the Monroe Doctrine, American resistance to British encroachments in Central America, the operations of filibuster William Walker in Nicaragua, and American ascendancy in the Caribbean (which the Ostend Manifesto Buchanan had helped draw up proposed relative to Cuba). Quite clearly, therefore, the foreign policy section of the platform had as southern a flavor as that pertaining to slavery. A final paragraph enumerated the achievements of the Pierce administration.

Far different in orientation was the Republican convention that assembled at Philadelphia in June. One thousand delegates were present, representing every free state, as well as Delaware, Maryland, Virginia, and Kentucky. After considering for the Presidency such luminaries as William Seward, Salmon Chase, and others, the delegates chose John Fremont of California, a forty-three-year-old western "Pathfinder" and son-in-law of Thomas Hart Benton, over the seventy-one-year-old Supreme Court Justice John McLean. Fremont, who had been a Free Soil Democrat, probably was more interested in a transcontinental railroad than the slavery issue; like his Democratic counterpart, Buchanan, he had not been deeply involved in the Kansas-Nebraska question. For Vice President, the Republicans selected William Dayton of New Jersey, an Old Line Whig, with Abraham Lincoln of Illinois placing second in the balloting.

Approximately four-fifths of the platform was devoted to the slavery issue, with special emphasis on the admission of Kansas as a free state. David Wilmot of Pennsylvania chaired the Committee on Resolutions. A considerable part of this section was obviously inspired by the Declaration of Independence, in particular the concept of "life, liberty, and the pursuit of happiness." To quote a key sentence, "Freedom was national; slavery, sectional." In addition, there was a quotation from the Preamble to the Constitution, and a reference to the principles of Washington and Jefferson; the latter is most significant, since it was Jefferson who was the first great leader of what was to become the modern-day Democratic party. Boldly affirming that "it is both the right and the imperative duty of Congress to prohibit in the Territories those twin relics of barbarism—Polygamy, and Slavery," this document coupled the latter two institutions for the first time in the history of American political platforms. The precise wording here, which should be attributed to Ebenezer Hoar, highlighted the possibility that polygamy as well as slavery might enter the territories via the popular sovereignty route. Yet there were no references to the Missouri Compromise, the Fugitive Slave Law, or the status of slavery in the District of Columbia.

Examining this document retrospectively a century or so later, a student of American political platforms, David Hinshaw, observed that it was one of the three greatest ever drawn up.[1] At the time of its formulation, Joshua Giddings, an abolitionist Whig from the Western Reserve of Ohio, maintained that, "I think that it is ahead of all other platforms ever adopted."[2] Not only did this document examine at length the situation in Kansas, but it also unleashed an attack on the Pierce administration with unprecedented fury; having accused the latter of instituting and encouraging "murders, robberies, and arson," it boldly proclaimed that the Republicans would punish the offenders if elected. Turning to the record of the Democratic Presidential nominee, James Buchanan, one plank declared, "That the highwayman's plea, that 'might makes right,' embodied in the Ostend Circular, was in every respect unworthy of American diplomacy."

Aside from the material on Kansas, which was designed to appeal to the Free Soilers, several planks also reflected the traditional Whig preoccupation with federally financed internal improvements in a bid for northern and western votes; among other things, these called for river and harbor improvements and a transcontinental railroad. An attempt by Thaddeus Stevens (who led the McLean forces in Pennsylvania) to inject the nativist issue into the campaign failed, however. One might also attribute the absence of a homestead plank to a desire not to alienate potential Know-Nothing converts fearful of populating the farms of the West with aliens. The entire platform was adopted by voice vote, with only a minor change in wording relative to one plank.

In February, four months before the Democrats assembled, the "Know Nothing" American party met in Philadelphia, with 227 delegates in attendance from every state except Maine, Vermont, South Carolina, and Georgia. For their Presidential choice the "Know Nothings" made the rather curious selection of ex-President Millard Fillmore, who only recently had been in Rome talking with the Pope; a hypothetical parallel would be for some contemporary radical rightist organization to run someone for President who was currently negotiating with the Chinese Communists. Turning to the South for Fillmore's running-mate, the American party picked Andrew Jackson Donelson of Tennessee. The convention took on an even more pronounced southern coloring when a large bloc of delegates from the North (mostly from the Northeast, Pennsylvania, Ohio, Illinois, and Iowa) withdrew after the convention had tabled a motion not to nominate a candidate who was not in favor of the Missouri Compromise.

Perhaps the key phrase in the platform was contained in paragraph three: *"Americans must rule America."* Native-born citizens for office were to be given preference over naturalized ones, and the naturalization laws were to be changed so as to require a continued residence for twenty-one years. Appealing to the Supreme Being (not God), the "Know-Nothings" endorsed the separation of church and state, which long ago had been provided for by the Constitution. Despite the latter plank, the "Know-Nothings" also affirmed, in an oblique reference to the Catholics, that: "No person should be selected for political station (whether of native or foreign birth), who recognizes any alliance or obligation of any description to any foreign prince, potentate or power."

This appeal to the bigots was accompanied by a play for southern votes; states' rights were endorsed, along with the more specific right of each state to regulate its own domestic and social affairs (i.e., slavery). Complaining that the Pierce administration had removed "Americans" and conservatives in principle from office and replaced them with foreigners and ultraists, the American platform announced its "opposition to the reckless and unwise policy of the present administration in the general management of our national affairs." Focal points of attack included the repeal of the Missouri Compromise and the "blundering mismanagement of our foreign affairs," despite the fact that the Ostend Manifesto was pleasing to many Southerners. Ironically, this anti-Catholic, anti-foreigner document concluded with a call for the free and open discussion of the principles contained therein; doubtless the "Know-Nothings" were reacting to the charge that they were guilty of excessive secrecy.

What remained of the once-powerful Whig party assembled in Baltimore in September. Rather than nominate their own candidates, the Whigs gave their assent to the "Know-Nothing" Fillmore-Donelson ticket. The Whig platform was as ambiguous as ever, dispensing with specific planks; expressing their reverence for the Constitution, the Whigs foreshadowed the name of the party that was to replace them in the 1860 Presidential campaign with their admonition "to preserve our Constitutional Union from dismemberment." The Pierce administration was charged with a "culpable neglect of duty" in an indictment more restrained than that of the Republicans, while both rival parties

were attacked for being sectional rather than national in orientation. A personal tribute to Millard Fillmore constituted the final
portion of this document.

The renegade Northern Know-Nothings, who assembled in
New York during June, selected still another ticket, Nathaniel
Banks of Massachusetts for President and General William F.
Johnston of Pennsylvania for Vice President. The former individual, who was the Speaker of the US House of Representatives,
was a friend of Fremont, and accepted the nomination with the
understanding that he would withdraw in favor of Fremont
should the Republicans nominate the latter. Had the Northern
Know-Nothings nominated Fremont first, antislavery Germans
might have deserted the Republican cause. The extremely brief
nine-point platform was presented by Governor Thomas H. Ford
of Ohio, the Resolutions Committee Chairman; its key features
were "Free Territory and Free Kansas," river improvements and
harbors construction, and a transcontinental railroad.

In summarizing the results of the Election of 1856, it might be
said that the Republicans had the most slogans and the Democrats
had the most votes. With "Bleeding Kansas" as their issue and
"Free Soil, Free Speech, Free Men, and Fremont" as their solution,
the Republicans carried eleven free states in amassing 1,335,264
popular votes and 114 electoral ones. They made especially strong
showings in New England, New York, Ohio, Michigan, Wisconsin, and Iowa; had the election been held in September or October,
Fremont might have won. The Know-Nothings attempted to
make political capital out of the untrue accusation that Fremont
was a Roman Catholic, but Fillmore, who was not a bigot, stressed
Whig nationalism rather than American nativism during his
campaign. He won only Maryland in the Electoral College, but
did collect 874,534 popular votes, mostly in the North and the
Border States, 500,000 less than Scott had totalled nationally in
1852. (The latter statistic is misleading, however, in that Fillmore
outpolled Scott in eleven states.)

As for the winner, Democrat James Buchanan, his triumph in
such northern states as Pennsylvania, Indiana, and Illinois proved
decisive. Buchanan carried fourteen slave states and five free ones
on his way to a majority of 174 in the Electoral College; his
popular vote total of 1,838,169 comprised 45 percent of the total, as
compared with 34 for Fremont and 21 for Fillmore. The Democrats

also won comfortable margins in both houses of Congress, after linking the Republicans with the abolitionists. Unfortunately for the nation, though, Buchanan proved no more capable of resolving the dilemma over slavery than Pierce had been; unfortunately for his party, the growing friction between North and South on this issue was to tear the Democrats apart by 1860. The stage was set for the emergence of Abraham Lincoln.

VII. 1860

A House Divided

As the decade of the 1850s neared a close, event after event continued to agitate the slavery question to a fever pitch: "Bleeding Kansas," the Dred Scott decision, Preston Brooks' assault on Charles Sumner, John Brown's raid on Harper's Ferry. With a southern sympathizing President failing to take decisive action, the House of Representatives deadlocked over the choice of a speaker for two months in the winter of 1859-60, a reflection of its internal divisions. Turning to the Senate, the key race during this period was that for one of the Illinois seats; incumbent Democrat Stephen Douglas defeated Abraham Lincoln for this in 1858, in a campaign that featured the seven Lincoln-Douglas Debates. At Freeport, the advocate of popular sovereignty (Douglas) gave his doctrine a new twist: slavery could not exist in the territories, unless the local legislatures passed various measures to protect it. If the Illinois Senator was attempting to find a solution to this thorny issue, another Senator, William Seward of New York, had come to the conclusion that no compromise was possible. Speaking at Rochester on October 25, 1859, Seward opined, "It is an irrepressible conflict between opposing and enduring forces, and it means that the United States will, sooner or later, become either entirely a slaveholding nation or entirely a free-labor nation."[1]

This question also was uppermost in the minds of the 606 delegates who assembled at the Democratic convention at Charleston, South Carolina in April of the following year. This was to prove the only such gathering that convened south of Baltimore or St. Louis prior to the assemblage at Houston, which nominated Alfred Smith for President in 1928. The favorite for the Presidential nomination was Stephen Douglas, whose courting of the South had begun to sour following his enunciation of the Freeport Doctrine; Douglas earlier had lost his position as Chairman of the Senate Territories Committee, owing to growing opposition from the southern leaders of his party. Although the unit rule binding delegates from each state to vote the majority sentiment of the delegation was modified, a change which benefitted Douglas, the two-thirds majority for a Presidential nominee was retained, a decision which later was to block the Illinois Senator from receiving the convention's endorsement. (Van Buren, one will recall, met a similar fate in 1844.) Had the balloting on a Presidential choice preceded the vote on the platform, Douglas still might have been nominated, but his strategists made the fatal mistake of agreeing to tackle the platform first.

To analyze in complete detail the maneuverings over the slavery plank in the platform would literally consume page after page. Perhaps the best contemporary account of it is to be found in William Hesseltine, editor, *Three Against Lincoln: Murat Halstead Reports the Caucuses of 1860*. Aside from the slavery issue, all factions were in agreement that the principles set forth in the Cincinnati platform of 1856 should be reaffirmed. But consensus on the one remaining plank continued to elude the delegates. The majority report, which was narrowly adopted by the Resolutions Committee thanks to a coalition of the southern states, California, and Oregon, advocated the protection of slavery in the territories and the upholding of the Dred Scott decision, while the minority report, whose signatories represented states with a greater total population than those who endorsed the majority one, recommended Congressional nonintervention and adherence to Supreme Court rulings. Still another report, by Benjamin Butler of Massachusetts, attempted to resolve the dilemma by ignoring it completely; Butler was critical of the majority report for protecting the African slave trade, and of the minority one for relying on the Supreme Court. The Butler platform was eventually rejected on the seventh day by a vote of 105 to 198.

After a debate on the platform, which was presented to the convention by William W. Avery of North Carolina, the entire document was recommitted by a 152 to 151 vote, with some crossing of sectional lines in the balloting. When the resolutions emerged again from committee, the delegates substituted the Douglas minority report for the pro-southern majority one by a vote of 165 to 138, in the process triggering a walkout led by "Fire-Eater" William Yancey and other irreconcilables from Alabama, Mississippi, Louisiana, South Carolina, Florida, Texas, Georgia, and Arkansas. The Douglas managers then removed the slavery plank when the Southerners refused to vote. As finally adopted, the Charleston Democratic platform of 1860 reaffirmed the principles contained in its Cincinnati counterpart of 1856 (without specifically enumerating them), and also called for the protection of both native- and foreign-born citizens, endorsed a transcontinental railroad, favored the acquisition of Cuba, and attacked state laws circumventing the Fugitive Slave Act. The last two provisions were obviously included to win the support of the South; the 1856 Cincinnati platform had merely called for American ascendancy in the Gulf of Mexico without mentioning Cuba by name.

Having struggled laboriously to construct this platform, the exhausted Charleston delegates were unable to agree on anyone to stand upon it. The leading candidates apart from Douglas were Robert M. T. Hunter, James Guthrie, and Andrew Johnson. Douglas was able to command the support of a majority of those voting, but no more, and the convention adjourned after fifty-seven ballots without naming anyone to head the ticket, two weeks after it had originally assembled. By the end of the convention most of the northern spectators had gone home, leaving the galleries in control of the Southerners; this factor, along with the ill-will generated over the platform fight, contributed to the inability of Douglas to amass a two-thirds majority.

The Charleston seceders reassembled at Richmond on June 11, but agreed to adjourn until the regulars had gathered at Baltimore on June 18. There, the Southerners walked out again, but the delegates who remained did endorse Douglas for President on the second ballot, with Herschel Johnson of Georgia for Vice President. The platform was retouched, leaving slavery in the territories for disposal by the Supreme Court. Then the Charleston seceders reassembled at Baltimore on June 28. Here 105 delegates from the Charleston convention placed their stamp of approval on the final majority report that had been defeated at Charleston; aside from the slavery question, the planks contained in the Southern Democratic platform were quite similar to those in the Northern Democratic one, although the wording did vary, and the planks appeared in a different order. Like the Charleston platform, the principles contained in the Cincinnati document were reaffirmed without specifically enumerating them. For President, the Southern Democrats nominated John Breckinridge of Kentucky, the current Vice President, and for second place, Joseph Lane of Oregon, a former political lieutenant of James Polk. With the Whig party now dead and the Democrats split asunder, to paraphrase Roy Nichols, American democracy indeed had been disrupted.

Earlier that month, on May 9, remnants of the Whig and American parties had met at Baltimore under the Constitutional Union banner to endorse a ticket of John Bell of Tennessee for President and Edward Everett of Massachusetts for Vice President. (Sam Houston of Texas also was a Presidential possibility.) Bell had been Secretary of War under William Henry Harrison, an Old Whig, slaveholder, and strong Union man, while Everett was to deliver the principal but long-forgotten speech the day of Abraham Lincoln's brief Gettysburg Address. As vague and vapid as some of the Whig platforms of the past, the Constitutional Union statement of principles, drafted under the supervision of Joseph R. Ingersoll, eschewed specifics, instead endorsing "the Constitution of the Country, the Union of the States, and the Enforcement of the Laws." "Experience has demonstrated," began this document, "that Platforms adopted by the partisan Conventions of the country have had the effect to mislead and deceive the people, and at the same time to widen the political divisions of the country, by the creation and encouragement of sectional parties." Benjamin Butler had wanted only to evade one issue at the Democratic convention at Charleston; the Constitutional Unionists converted his approach into universal law.

Confronted with a golden opportunity to nominate the next President, the Republicans did not fumble their opportunity when they met at the Wigwam in Chicago on May 16, with 465 delegates in attendance. Here the front-runner was William Seward of the "Irrepressible Conflict" Speech; had the balloting for President taken place when the convention opened, Seward might have been nominated. Yet this gifted New Yorker was regarded in many quarters as too extreme on the slavery issue, though his antislavery radicalism had taken on a more moderate hue in recent years; his stand on the tariff issue also was unpopular in protectionist Pennsylvania, a pivotal state in the Electoral College. To some delegates, it was more important to have "success rather than Seward," Horace Greeley observing in this connection that 'An Anti-slavery man *per se* cannot be elected."[2]

There were several alternatives to Seward, including John McLean, Simon Cameron, and Salmon Chase, but the individual who was to emerge as the Presidential candidate was Abraham Lincoln, a one-term Whig Congressman from Illinois who had been critical of the Mexican War, and who had unsuccessfully attempted to wrest Stephen Douglas' Senate seat from him in 1858. Lincoln was "available," a Westerner, a symbol of the common man, and a friend of the foreign-born, labor, and the farmers; Judge David Davis, moreover, was able to win over several doubtful states to the Lincoln banner by promises of cabinet positions. Seward did seize the lead on the first ballot, but lost the nomination to Lincoln on the third; the convention then selected a former Democrat, Hannibal Hamlin of Maine, for second place. Unlike Seward, Lincoln had never denounced Southerners, and he had taken a conciliatory position towards Dixie in his Cooper Union Speech on February 27, 1860.

In contrast to the 1856 platform, four-fifths of which dealt with the slavery issue, the 1860 statement of principles devoted less than a third of its contents to the latter. It is instructive to note that when the Free Soil party took a more radical stand in 1852 on the slavery issue than it had in 1848, the vote that its Presidential nominee received fell off to a little more than half of what it had been four years earlier. Had the Republican party followed a similar course, it might have gone down in history as just another third party that failed; Abraham Lincoln probably would not have been elected on an extremist platform. Yet the voices of restraint prevailed, despite the assessment of the New Orleans *Daily Delta* that "The ill-assumed moderation of the platform of the Black Republicans is bosh and nonsense,"[3] and the widely circulated political cartoon that showed Horace Greeley and a Negro carrying Lincoln on a rail: the Republican platform.

The platform itself was the work of a committee of seven, headed by William Jessup of Pennsylvania, and including Horace Greeley, John Kasson, George Boutwell, William Otto, Carl Schurz, and Gustave Koerner. New York newspaper editor Greeley was attending the convention as a delegate from Oregon; Schurz and Koerner were Germans whose presence militated against the inclusion of a nativist plank. Like the 1856 document, there were references to the Declaration of Independence and the Constitution, while in recommending "a return to rigid economy," the Republicans endorsed a basic tenet of the founder of the Democratic party, Thomas Jefferson. Although it made an oblique attack on John Brown, affirmed the right of each state to control its domestic institutions, and made no reference to the "twin relics of barbarism," the platform favored the admission of Kansas as a free state, opposed the reopening of the Atlantic slave trade, and declared that neither Congress nor a territorial legislature had the right to legalize slavery in the territories. (It will be recalled that the 1856 platform had taken the position that Congress should prohibit slavery there.) Clearly the bulk of the 1860 provisions would appeal to moderates, but not to northern abolitionists or southern "Fire Eaters."

Whereas the previous statement of principles had restricted its domestic program to river and harbor improvements and a transcontinental railroad, the document drawn up in 1860 by the Republicans also attempted to capture the western vote with a plea for a homestead law. Buchanan had vetoed such a measure during the course of his Presidency, although Fremont did run a strong race in that section without the Republicans endorsing it in their platform. Then there was the demand for a liberal immigration policy, which was obviously designed to win the votes of the Germans and other ethnic groups. The tariff plank was so worded as not to alienate free-trade Democrats, yet still to retain the support of protectionists in Pennsylvania, New Jersey, and New England. While the 1856 platform had attacked the Pierce administration at length with reference to Kansas, that of 1860 restricted itself to the broader charge that the Buchanan administration had been guilty of a "merciless subserviency to the exactions of a sectional interest." Yet there was nothing vague in the Republican declaration that "we hold in abhorrence all schemes for disunion," the latter being "an avowal of contemplated treason."

What debate there was on the platform—which was adopted unanimously—centered around the Declaration of Independence and the naturalization planks. The former, which was advanced originally by Joshua Giddings of Ohio, long noted for his antislavery views, was at first rejected; it was later included at the urging of George Curtis of the Seward-dominated New York delegation, even though Giddings did not support Seward's candidacy. As for the dispute over the naturalization plank, keynote speaker David Wilmot of Pennsylvania (author of the 1846 Proviso) expressed a desire to omit the phrase "or any state legislation" from the plank opposing any changes in the federal law, but he eventually withdrew his amendment. Wilmot was concerned because this phrase was in conflict with the plank affirming states' rights. One of the chief critics of Wilmot's move was Carl Schurz, who pointed out (perhaps over-optimistically) that 300,000 German-Americans in the northern states had voted for Fremont in 1856. Along with the homestead provision, this plank was the key concern of the German delegates.

The campaign itself proved something of an anticlimax after the conventions, even with four major candidates. In reality, Douglas and Lincoln alone contested for the northern vote, while Breckinridge and Bell alone fought for that of the South. Even though his throat was bad, Douglas engaged in the first nationwide stumping tour that a Presidential nominee had ever undertaken. On the other hand, Bell, whose appeal was to Border State voters and the conservative planters of the South, did little campaigning. Breckinridge similarly made only one major speech, but President James Buchanan secretly aided his cause while publicly affirming that either Douglas or Breckinridge was acceptable. Far more active were the marching clubs and auxiliary organizations: the Wide Awakes (Lincoln), the Little Giants (Douglas), the Bell Ringers, and the Breckinridge National Democratic Volunteers. Within a few months the Wide Awakes had enlisted 400,000 members. Rails split by "Abe the Rail Mauler" were used as symbols by the Republican boosters, a gesture somewhat reminiscent of the "Log Cabin" campaign of 1840; the nominee himself generally remained aloof.

Scattered triumphs in state elections held in Maine, Vermont, Indiana, and Pennsylvania in September and October correctly pointed to a Lincoln victory in November. The final popular and electoral vote totals were, Lincoln, 1,866,352 - 180 (18 free states); Douglas, 1,375,157 - 12 (Missouri and 3 from New Jersey); Breckinridge, 847,953 - 72 (11 slave states); Bell, 589,581 - 39 (3 Border States). In terms of percentages the popular vote breakdown was Lincoln, 40; Douglas, 29; Breckinridge, 18; Bell, 13. Although he finished second in the popular vote, Douglas' vote was so distributed geographically that he limped in fourth in the electoral vote; on this occasion the moderates did not fare well in the Electoral College. Turning to the popular vote, it is significant that Bell and Douglas combined outpolled Breckinridge in the slave states. There was some talk of an anti-Lincoln fusion ticket in a number of places, but even had this been successful, it probably would have cost the Republican nominee only California, Oregon, and New Jersey. Had there been a deadlock in the Electoral College, the House of Representatives might have been unable to resolve it; then the Democratic Senate probably would have picked a pro-southern Vice President like Pierce or Buchanan who then would have ascended to the Presidency by default.

Despite the oft-repeated charge that the Republican party today is a tool of big business, northern capitalists and businessmen were rather unfavorably inclined towards it at this time, partly as a result of its courting the labor vote, although the Republican tariff policy was more pleasing to the industrialists than the traditional Democratic position. Thus one must attribute the Republican plurality in the Presidential race to other types of support: from the small towns and the farms of the North, among the German and Scandinavian voters, and even from some nativists, despite the lack of concessions to them in the Republican platform. Aside from the tariff, Republican campaigners—and it is estimated that 50,000 speeches were made on behalf of the party during the campaign—most frequently emphasized homesteading, which helps explain Lincoln's margin of victory in the western states. In the process of metamorphosis from third party to major party status, the Republicans had already assembled a formidable coalition that was to keep them in the White House for the next quarter-century. And, as we have seen, it was by no means limited to antislavery fanatics, although when the party had been founded only six years earlier, it basically had been a one-issue party. Let us now turn to the implementation of the Republican domestic program during the Civil War.

VIII. 1864

The Great Emancipator

No sooner had it become apparent that the "Black Republican," Abraham Lincoln, had been elected President, than the South Carolina legislature called for a state convention to meet at Charleston. This convention unanimously passed an ordinance declaring that "the union now subsisting between South Carolina and the other States, under the name of the 'United States of America,' is hereby dissolved."[1] By February 1, the other six states of the Lower South had followed suit. Attempts to compromise the widening breach between the North and the South ended in failure; these included the Crittenden Resolution recognizing slavery as legal in territories south of 36° 30′, which was unacceptable to Abraham Lincoln, and the Peace Convention at Washington in February. By the first of the latter month the seceding states had met at Montgomery, Alabama, drafted a constitution, and established a provisional government, with Jefferson Davis as President and Alexander Stephens as Vice President. Thus, when Abraham Lincoln took office as chief executive on March 4, secession was already an established fact, although the Civil War itself did not technically begin until April 12, when the Confederates began attacking the Union-controlled Fort Sumter in Charleston harbor.

The political consequences of the withdrawal of southern delegates from Congress were enormous. Now it was possible for the Republican majority to win enactment for measures whose passage had been blocked during the 1850s: homestead legislation, a transcontinental railroad, and a protective tariff. A national banking act was also enacted, along with a land grant college act, though neither had been Republican planks in either 1856 or 1860. The Democrats were further weakened by the death of Senator Stephen Douglas of Illinois in 1861, and by the splitting of the Union wing of the party into Peace and War Democrats. But the Republicans, too, were divided, as Radicals such as Senator Benjamin Wade of Ohio and Representative Henry Winter Davis of Maryland demanded a harsh line towards the South, while a more moderate element (that included the President) adopted a more conciliatory approach.

The prosecution of the war itself was by no means one uninterrupted triumph for the North; the New York City draft riots of 1863 were a prime example of northern discontent. Lincoln, moreover, was continually undercut by the Radical-dominated Joint Committee on the Conduct of the War, which favored Congressional ascendancy in policy making. In a belated effort to offer a final solution to the racial question, on January 1, 1863, Abraham Lincoln issued his famous Emancipation Proclamation liberating all slaves behind rebel lines. Although he had not stood with the abolitionists at the beginning of the war, Lincoln had come around to the position that such a statement was necessary to win both northern and European support.

It thus was in a general atmosphere of division and uncertainty that a group of radicals convened at Cleveland on May 31, 1864, for the purpose of nominating a President and formulating a platform. Some accounts maintain that as many as 400 delegates were present, but only 158 actually signed the register. While General John Fremont was the favorite of the West, there was strong backing for General Ulysses Grant in the East, and for General George McClellan among the War Democrats. Fremont, the 1856 Republican Presidential nominee, eventually won the nod of the convention, with the second position going to an Easterner, General John Cochrane of New York.

Historians have generally neglected this convention, largely because Fremont eventually withdrew as a candidate, while the disappointing turnout led the Detroit *Union* to the contemporary assessment: "Were the immortal 158 the masses? Truly answer Echo—Them Asses!"[2] Nevertheless, this radical platform has at least several points of interest for the serious student of American politics. Perhaps the most original plank was that calling for the election of the President and the Vice President by direct vote, the first appearance of this concept in a political platform; in endorsing a single term for the President, the radicals merely repeated an 1844 Whig plank, while in advocating the Monroe Doctrine they followed the Democratic precedent established in 1856. (The latter plank was the only one modified by the delegates.) Likewise, the plea for economy in government was in line with the teachings of Jeffersonian democracy, although one also finds this in the 1860 Republican platform. But no precedent was to be found for the plank calling for the confiscation of the lands of the rebels, a plank so extreme that it was rejected not only by the Republican and Democratic platform makers, but even was opposed by the radical Presidential nominee, Fremont.

More conciliatory were the Republicans, who upon assembling at Baltimore in June, adopted the label Union party, a name which they had been using for some time so as to make it easier for War Democrats and other non-Republicans to rally to their banner. Delegates from southern states and territories were seated here, unlike at the forthcoming Democratic convention. Significantly, most radical members of Congress did not bother to attend; it became necessary to transfer the proceedings to an inadequate theatre after dissident elements led by Henry Winter Davis had rented the scheduled meeting-place.

Aside from the incumbent President, the alternate possibilities for first place on the ticket included Fremont, Salmon Chase, and Benjamin Butler, but it was Ulysses Grant who received the only other bloc of votes during the actual balloting. (The final tally stood at 506 votes for the President, with twenty-two Missouri votes going to Grant.) Perhaps the biggest casualty of the convention was the incumbent Vice President, Hannibal Hamlin of Maine, a radical sympathizer and a Lincoln critic; to this day there remains a disagreement among historians relative to the precise role, if any, that the President played in his elimination from the ticket. Hamlin's replacement, Andrew Johnson of Tennessee, had been a US Senator from 1857 to 1862, and military governor of Tennessee from 1862 to 1864. At that time he was acceptable to the radicals, but in later years he was to become their greatest enemy.

Among the more important speeches delivered at this Republican convention was that of the retiring Chairman of the National Committee, Edwin Morgan, who in accordance with a suggestion by Abraham Lincoln, proposed a constitutional amendment to abolish slavery forever. Aiming "a deathblow at this gigantic evil" shortly was to become a platform plank, along with praise for Lincoln's Emancipation Proclamation and support for the use of Negro troops. Even more inflammatory was the keynote address by Robert Breckinridge of Kentucky, a near-relative of John, who asserted that "no government has ever been built upon imperishable foundations which foundations were not laid upon the blood of traitors, the only imperishable cement of free institutions."[3] Despite Breckinridge's bold utterance, *The New York Times* editor Henry J. Raymond's Committee on Resolutions did not even recommend the confiscation of rebel property; the platform drafters, however, did affirm that there was to be no compromise on the war, which was to continue until the South surrendered unconditionally. Significantly, there was no mention at all of postwar Reconstruction in either the Republican or the Democratic platform.

Other planks of a domestic nature called for the encouragement of immigration, a transcontinental railroad, and for economy in government, as the 1860 document had, but this time there was no mention of a protective tariff, of homesteading legislation (recently enacted), or of federally financed river and harbor improvements. A sop to the radicals was the plank which mounted an indirect attack on Postmaster General Montgomery Blair, who shortly thereafter was replaced in the cabinet by William Dennison of Ohio, the permanent chairman of the convention. Conversely, the longest plank, number four, praised Lincoln. The only plank on foreign affairs invoked the Monroe Doctrine against the French presence in Mexico; Napoleon III was pro-Confederate in sympathies, and thus no friend of the Union. Eight years previously, the Democrats had paid lip service to this doctrine in their platform to justify southern imperialism in the Caribbean Basin. In many ways a bold document, this eleven-plank Republican platform of 1860 was adopted unanimously by the delegates.

Having delayed their convention until late August in the hope that military developments would work to their advantage, the Democrats decided at Chicago that they should adopt the war hero approach in making their Presidential choice that the Whigs had employed successfully on two occasions. There were no delegates either from the seceded South or from the territories. The leading candidate for the Presidential nomination was the hero of Antietam, General George McClellan, who sought the Presidency after Lincoln had relieved him from his military command. McClellan, a political novice, who despite later reports to the contrary, really wanted the nomination and thought that he could defeat the incumbent President, triumphed on the first ballot over two northeastern governors, Thomas Seymour of Connecticut and Horatio Seymour of New York, the 1868 convention choice. James Guthrie of Kentucky was the front-runner for second place on the ticket, but he lost out on the second ballot to George Pendleton of Ohio, who had been elected to the House in 1857.

More controversial than the Presidential nominee was the platform, which was drawn up by the Resolutions Committee headed by Kentucky railroad executive James O. Guthrie. The notorious Copperhead, Clement Vallandigham, played a key role during these proceedings; Vallandigham had been arrested and banished behind Confederate lines before escaping to Canada and then returning to the North. One widely circulated report maintained that the platform had been written by Southerners who had met with Northern Democratic leaders at Niagara Falls prior to the convention. Doubtless it was this aspect of the proceedings which led the staunchly Republican Chicago *Tribune* to comment: "Treason to the government has for hours at a time cascaded over the balconies of the hotels, spouted, and squirted, and dribbled, and pattered, and rained on our out of doors listeners and pedestrians."[4]

In its denunciations of the Civil War as "four years of failure," its call for an immediate cessation of hostilities, and its plea that Union prisoners of war be returned, this document bears more than a distinct resemblance to the McGovern-flavored Democratic platform of 1972 during the Vietnam War era. While General Fremont could not accept that section of the radical platform recommending the confiscation of rebel property, General McClellan could not endorse the stand that the Democratic platform took on the war: "I could not look into the face of my gallant comrades of the Army and Navy who have survived so many bloodly battles, and tell them that their labors and their sacrifice of so many of our slain and wounded have been in vain, that we had abandoned the Union for which we have so often perilled our lives."[5] In supporting the continuation of the war, McClellan had the backing of most members of this party. Unlike the Republican document, too, there was no demand for the abolition of slavery in the Democratic platform.

Looking at other aspects of the latter, those who had drafted it largely ignored those principles that had been the cornerstone of every Democratic platform from 1840 to 1860. The introductory remark, "That in the future, as in the past, we will adhere with unswerving fidelity to the Union under the Constitution," might have been taken out of Whig platforms of the past, or that of the Constitutional Union party in 1860. An echo of past Democratic platforms is to be found in several references to states' rights. But one delegate, Long of Ohio, attempted to add to this document the text of Thomas Jefferson's first Kentucky Resolution—which had been mentioned in the Democratic platform of 1852—only to see his amendment referred to committee without the convention taking action on it. On the other hand, complaining that military authorities had directly interfered in recent elections held in Kentucky, Maryland, Missouri, and Delaware, this document did charge that "public liberty and private right alike (have been) trodden down, and the material prosperity of the country essentially impaired." Whether McClellan might have defeated Lincoln with a different platform is debatable; the inclusion of specific planks on issues other than the war and the de-emphasis of the latter might have cost as many votes as they would have won.

The incumbent President entered the campaign by no means assured of victory, even though he was able to balance out the resignations from his cabinet of Salmon Chase as Secretary of the Treasury and Montgomery Blair as Postmaster General. A major crisis arose over the Wade-Davis bill, a measure authored by radicals Benjamin Wade and Henry Winter Davis, which would have required a southern electorate of 50 percent of the eligible voters in 1860; on July 4 Lincoln pocket-vetoed this measure, angering Horace Greeley, and resulting in the issuance of a radical manifesto. Six days before the Democratic convention, Lincoln pessimistically predicted, "This morning, as for some days past, it seems exceedingly probable that the Administration will not be re-elected."[6] But the tide began to turn in Lincoln's favor, as many

soldiers disliked Vallandigham's peace plank, some radicals
disliked McClellan, General Sherman and General Sheridan won
military victories, and Fremont withdrew his third-party candidacy.

On election day, with twenty-five states participating, Lincoln
crushed McClellan in the Electoral College, 212 to 21, while the
Republicans maintained their hold on Congress. Admittedly,
though, the popular vote was much closer, with McClellan
winning about 45 percent of the total, 2,213,665 to 1,802,237.
McClellan carried only Delaware, New Jersey, and Kentucky
(Lincoln's birthplace), although he just missed victory in several
other states. Significantly, the soldiers—who were allowed to cast
their ballots at the front—overwhelmingly favored Lincoln over
the general, 116,887 to 33,748. But as William Cullen Bryant noted
in the New York *Evening Post*, the incumbent President was
popular not only with soldiers, but also with religious individuals
and plain folks as well;[7] it is not without justification that
posterity has labelled the Great Emancipator a man of the people.

IX. 1868

Waving the Bloody Shirt

The moderate, conciliatory approach Lincoln had taken to the
South again found expression in his second inaugural address:
"With malice towards none, with charity for all . . . let us strive on
to finish the work we are in; to bind up the nation's wounds . . . to
do all which may achieve and cherish a just and lasting peace."[1] A
month later Lee surrendered to Grant at Appomattox Courthouse,
Virginia, and an assassin slew Lincoln at a theater in Washington.
The new President, Andrew Johnson, was not a Vindictive, either,
but he was a political bumbler insensitive to public opinion, not a
genius at political manipulation like Lincoln. In August 1866
Johnson called a National Union Convention in Philadelphia,

whose aim was to elect a Congress that would unite Douglas Democrats and conservative Republicans in common cause; unfortunately for the President, this effort proved abortive.

The victorious Radical Republicans, armed with a strategy to keep the South out of Congress to maintain their majority, and to enfranchise the Negro in the South to guarantee Republican victories there, now pushed through Congress a bold program that included the Fourteenth Amendment of 1868 and the First Reconstruction Act of 1867. Against this onslaught Johnson wielded the veto, but in vain. When he allegedly violated the Tenure of Office by removing Secretary of War Edwin Stanton, the House impeached the President and the Senate placed him on trial. Johnson escaped conviction by only one vote, 19 to 35, on May 16, 1868, when seven Republicans voted against their party for his acquittal.

Several days after the conclusion of the impeachment trial the Republicans held their national convention at Chicago. Texas was absent, but the other southern states were present; a dozen or more Negro delegates attended, along with the Confederate governor of Georgia, Joseph Brown. The keynote address was delivered by a prominent German-American, Carl Schurz, who had been a friend of the martyred President and was to become Secretary of the Interior under Hayes. There was only one real possibility for first spot on the ticket: General Ulysses Grant. He had voted for Buchanan in 1856 and favored (but not voted for) Douglas in 1860, but he had become the darling of the Radicals when he turned down an appointment by Johnson to become Secretary of War in January 1867. When Grant was nominated, white doves were released; his acceptance speech was one of the shortest on record. Ben Wade was the front-runner for the Vice Presidential nomination prior to the failure of the impeachment proceedings, but he lost out on the final ballot to Indiana Radical Schuyler Colfax, the Speaker of the House.

As one might have expected, the twelve-plank "National Union Republican Party" platform, drawn up by the Resolutions Committee chaired by Richard W. Thompson of Indiana, enthusiastically endorsed Radical Reconstruction and lambasted President Johnson, "who has acted treacherously to the people who elected him . . . (and) has usurped high legislative and judicial functions." (Plank eight also briefly praised Abraham Lincoln.)

Although favoring the impeachment proceedings, this document did not censure the seven Republican Senators who had supported Johnson on the final vote. With respect to the courting of special interest groups, its call for Civil War pensions for Union soldiers constituted an obvious bid for northern support that remained a staple of Republican ideology for many years to come. Significantly, the Radicals compromised on Negro suffrage; while the platform approved of all loyal (i.e., black) men in the South voting, elsewhere it left the granting of the franchise to the states. To arch-Radical Thaddeus Stevens this was a "tame and cowardly" plank.

Equally noteworthy was the section of this document dealing with financial matters, which opposed Democrat George Pendleton's "Ohio Idea" without specifically mentioning greenbacks. Despite the stereotyped image of the Republican party as the party of the protective tariff, disagreement between low-tariff Westerners and high-tariff Easterners, as well as between importers and manufacturers, led the Republicans to remain as silent on this issue as they had been in 1864. Turning to foreign policy, plank twelve rather vaguely asserted that: "This convention declares its sympathy with all the oppressed people which are struggling for their rights," while plank nine dealing with citizenship and naturalization offered protection to those Irish-Americans who had been involved in the Fenian agitation against the British in Ireland. Two final planks offered by Carl Schurz praised the former rebels who had become loyal, and endorsed the basic principles underlying the Declaration of Independence.

The similarly patriotic Democrats assembled at Tammany Hall in New York City on July 4, with 781 delegates in attendance. Here the leading Presidential possibilities were the incumbent, Andrew Johnson, who had been a Border State War Democrat; George Pendleton of Ohio, the 1864 Vice Presidential nominee; and Horatio Seymour, the former Governor of New York. After the Republicans had nominated Grant for President, Salmon Chase turned his efforts to obtaining the Democratic nomination, but received only a scattering of votes; his daughter Kate bitterly observed that "when the South seceded the brains of the party went with it."[2] Seymour, who was the permanent chairman of the convention, eventually won the nomination, despite the fact that he was a hard-money man. For the second position the Democrats turned to Francis Blair of Missouri, a Union general who had taken the position that the President-elect must declare Reconstruction legislation null and void.

According to the chronicler of the Election of 1868, Charles Coleman, the Democratic platform "as a whole represented the victory of the Western and out-and-out Democratic forces in the party as opposed to the Northern and conservative forces;[3] heading the Resolutions Committee was State Senator Henry C. Murphy of New York. "Unlike the Republican document, here the heroes were President Johnson and Chief Justice Chase. Admitting that slavery and secession were closed questions, this platform advocated the restoration of the South to the Union, political amnesty, and the abolition of the Freedmen's Bureau. Instead of restoring the Union, it complanied, the Radical Republicans had dissolved the Union and "subjected ten States, in time of profound peace, to military despotism and negro supremacy." In turning the latter question over to the states, this document killed the chances of Negroes exercising the franchise in the South without alienating northern humanitarians, by openly endorsing black disenfranchisement.

Less hypocritical was the financial plank, which endorsed George Pendleton's "Ohio Idea" by favoring the payment of the national debt in greenbacks where this was legal; the "Ohio Idea" was as much a debt reduction scheme as an inflationary device. To the historian of the Democratic party, Henry Minor, this was a departure from the old Jeffersonian and Jacksonian hard-money principles[4] With regard to the tariff, the approach adopted after bypassing this issue in 1864 was again the traditional one of a tariff for revenue affording incidental protection, while the call for a reduced army and navy was in line with Jeffersonian economizing. On the other hand, the plank expressing sympathy for labor was a new departure, which was to reach a culmination in the major role that labor played in the New Deal coalition. Like the Republican document, there was an endorsement of the rights of naturalized citizens in an attempt to win the Irish vote; both parties were to "twist the British lion's tail" in the years to come. Despite the fact that the hard-money views of the Presidential nominee, Horatio Seymour, conflicted with the soft-money stand of the platform, the delegates saw fit to adopt it unanimously.

The campaign itself saw the Republicans successfully "waving the bloody shirt" over the conquered South after Congress had agreed in June to admit six "reconstructed" southern states into the Union. Both Seymour and Blair campaigned vigorously for the Democrats, while the Republicans attacked the former's record as wartime governor of New York. In certain respects the Election of 1868 paralleled that of 1864; in both cases the popular vote was relatively close, while the electoral vote was more lopsided. Military hero Grant won twenty-six of thirty-four states for an electoral vote of 214, but his popular vote margin was only about 300,000 out of a total of 5,715,000. His opponent, Seymour, amassed 80 electoral votes, including Louisiana's, in taking 44 percent of the popular vote; popular votes for Grant totalled 3,012,833, for Seymour, 2,703,249.

Despite the fact that considerable attention was paid to the question of whether or not the U.S. federal debt should be paid off in specie or greenbacks, as well as to the tariff issue, it was probably the black voter concerned with Radical Reconstruction who gave Grant his margin of victory. Although one finds conflicting statistics, the probability is that somewhere between 500,000 and 650,000 Negroes voted, and most of them cast their ballots for Grant. The Republicans would also capture various southern states in the next two Presidential elections, but at a terrible price. Between 1876 and 1952 the South gave a significant portion of its vote to a Republican only once, and this was in 1928 when the Democratic nominee was a Catholic opposed to prohibition—Governor Alfred Smith of New York.

X. 1872

Grantism Triumphant

Unfortunately for the nation, Ulysses Grant's military genius as a Civil War general was not matched by his political genius as President. Ranked along with Warren Harding as one of our two worst chief executives by historians and political scientists, Grant's greatest achievements were in the foreign affairs field, most notably the Treaty of Washington in 1871, which settled the outstanding differences between the United States and Great Britain. On the other hand, Grant's abortive effort to annex Santo Domingo (now the Dominican Republic) in 1869 led to a break with the Chairman of the Senate Foreign Relations Committee, Charles Sumner of Massachusetts, and the genesis of the Liberal Republican movement. This diplomatic venture, along with Radical Republican Reconstruction and widespread corruption in the Grant administration, alienated many prominent Republicans, among them Carl Schurz, Gideon Welles, Charles Francis Adams, E. L. Godkin, Horace Greeley, and George Julian. Despite the zeal of the reformers, however, the full extent of political corruption did not become apparent until Grant's second administration, when the depression of 1873 had yet to strike the nation. Thus the incumbent President entered the 1872 campaign still able to pose as the great Civil War military hero that he once was, not as the inept chief executive that he later became.

Long before the two major parties held their national conventions, two minor parties made their first appearance on the political scene, both of them gathering in February to select a ticket and draw up a platform. One of these, the National Labor Reform party, was a forerunner of the Greenback party; it nominated Judge David Davis of Illinois for President and Joel Parker for Vice President. Repudiating the gold standard, 200 delegates who had assembled from seventeen states adopted a platform calling for "a purely national circulating medium based on the faith and resources of the nation." Other planks endorsed amnesty for the South, civil service, and an end to transfer of public lands to corporations.

Aside from these stands, the National Laborites also admitted fear of the "Yellow Peril" for the first time in a national platform, advocating that the further importation of Chinese workers into the United States should be halted. Another labor-oriented plank demanded an eight-hour day for workers employed either directly or indirectly by the government, while still another recommended the abolition of the system of contract labor in prisons. The National Laborites recalled past Whig platforms in their endorsement of a one-term Presidency; on the other hand, they anticipated the Interstate Commerce Commission of 1887 in their demand for railroad rate regulation. Of the remaining planks, one of the more interesting advocated that wars be financed on a pay-as-you-go basis, "and not entailed as a burden on posterity." Despite the original features of the platform, the ticket eventually withdrew and the party collapsed.

Quite dissimilar in orientation was the Prohibition party platform of 1872, adopted in February at Columbus, Ohio, by a convention that nominated James Black of Pennsylvania for President and John Russell of Michigan for Vice President. As one might expect, the focal point of this gathering was the prohibition issue; but the platform was by no means limited to this question. Like the Radicals in 1864, the Prohibitionists favored the election of the President and Vice President (as well as US Senators) by direct vote; like the Republicans later in this period they endorsed a gold standard, while like most parties, both major and minor, they advocated civil service. Other more original planks called for salaries rather than fees for governmental officials, the abolition of the franking privilege, and reduced postage, telegraph, railroad, and water travel rates. Not only did the Prohibitionists favor the extension of public education, they also favored universal suffrage: "the right of suffrage rests on no mere circumstance of color, race, former social condition, sex or nationality, but inheres in the nature of man." Considering the fact that prohibition is generally looked upon as a reactionary reform, it is curious that it was coupled here with a number of other reforms of a more progressive nature.

Far broader in popular appeal were the Liberal Republicans, who assembled at Cincinnati in May at a convention described as "a mixture of a town meeting and barbecue of national proportions," by one commentator.[1] While President Grant wrote off the reformers as "soreheads,"[2] to a more sympathetic observer they were "as honest, intelligent, public spirited a body of men as ever got together for a similar purpose."[3] In the words of "Marse Henry" Watterson, "There were long-haired and spectacled doctrinaires from New England, spliced by short-haired and stumpy emissaries from New York . . . brisk Westerners from Chicago and St. Louis . . . and a motley array of Southerners of every sort."[4] Although some of the delegates attended specifically to advance such causes as a low tariff, civil service reform, and an end to Reconstruction, their principal bond of union was the desire to prevent the re-election of Grant as chief executive.

It is quite probable that Charles Francis Adams would have been the strongest candidate that the Liberal Republicans could have nominated for President, and indeed the Massachusetts reformer led on the first ballot with 203 votes, followed by Horace Greeley, Lyman Trumbull, B. Gratz Brown, and David Davis, in that order. But to the surprise of everyone, the convention turned to Greeley on the sixth ballot after Brown had endorsed him, despite the fact that he was not popular with many reformers or Germans, and despite the fact that his lifelong motto was "anything to beat a Democrat." The convention's choice for Vice President was Border Stater Brown, the man who had made possible Greeley's Presidential nomination.

Stressing the one common bond that united the delegates, the platform featured a massive attack on the Grant administration, not only with reference to its disregard of the law and retention of corrupt men in office, but also vis-a-vis its general inefficiency and mismanagement. This document called for an end to Reconstruction and the introduction of civil service, but failed to take a definite stand on the tariff, which it dumped into the laps of "the people in their Congress[ional] Districts, and to the decision of Congress thereon, wholly free of Executive interference or dictation." Although the Liberal Republicans obviously were quite unhappy with the treatment that the South had received since the end of the war, they nevertheless did accept as settled issues the Thirteenth, Fourteenth, and Fifteenth Amendments. With the transcontinental railroad now complete, the reformers also adopted the stance that the granting of public lands to the railroads should be halted; together with the railroad plank in the National Labor Reform party platform, this marks the emergence of a more critical attitude on the part of political parties towards the railroads. As for foreign policy, the one plank that the Liberal Republicans devoted to this broad subject was as vague as possible. But even though it largely by-passed diplomacy, this document was praised by the *Nation* as the best of its kind to appear in many years.[5]

The Democrats, who met the following month at Baltimore, did little more in their brief, six-hour session than to nominate the Liberal Republican ticket and approve the Liberal Republican platform. No less than 732 delegates were present, with Thomas Jefferson Randolph as the temporary chairman, but many of the old Democratic "war horses" were conspicuously absent. Eighteen state Democratic conventions, including that of New York, had instructed their delegates to adopt a policy of fusion; the adverse publicity resulting from the Tweed Ring scandals in New York City had apparently injured the Democratic cause in the spring elections, and many leaders were of the opinion that only through a coalition with the Liberal Republicans could they avert a massive fall defeat. Greeley was in fact less acceptable to the northern wing of the Democratic party (which was more familiar with him and his views) than to the southern wing, but it was the southern wing that was the more critical when the convention adopted the Liberal Republican platform by a 670 to 62 vote, after adding a short and unimportant preamble and renumbering the planks. The Chairman of the Resolutions Committee was Connecticut newspaper editor Alfred E. Burr. In the opinion of James A. Bayard of Delaware, this document had been "forced down our throats without mastication or digestion."[6]

In fact, the platform was so unpalatable to some Democrats that they regurgitated it; to Bourbons like Alexander Stephens, the choice between Grant and Greeley was one between "hemlock and strychnine."[7] Subsequently, a group of "Straight Out" Democrats met at Louisville in September to nominate a ticket of Charles O'Conor of New York (a Catholic) for President and John Quincy Adams II of Massachusetts for Vice President. Neither accepted this honor, but the "Straight Out" Democrats did appear on the ballots in twenty-three states. Their platform, which was more conservative than the one the regular Democrats had adopted, was as vague as past Whig or Constitutional Union ones had been. One of the more liberal planks constituted an obvious bid for the labor vote: "the interests of labor and capital should not be permitted to conflict, but should be harmonized by judicious legislation. While such a conflict continues, labor, which is the parent of wealth, is entitled to paramount consideration." This document also pronounced a curse on the Baltimore convention that had swallowed the Liberal Republican platform hook, line, and sinker.

Three months earlier the Republicans had assembled in Philadelphia to endorse Ulysses Grant for President on the first ballot.

The atmosphere was dull and the delegates, languid. It took only seventy-nine words to renominate the incumbent chief executive, who had no serious opposition; in his acceptance speech, Grant made the unusually honest admission that "Past experience may guide me in avoiding mistakes, inevitable with novices of all professions and in all occupations."[8] On the other hand, Vice President Schuyler Colfax, who had made quite a few enemies and had been involved in the Credit Mobilier scandal, failed to retain second place on the ticket, after he had toyed with the idea of a Presidential run himself if Grant were to retire. His replacement, Henry Wilson of Massachusetts, was a former shoe manufacturer who had long held antislavery views and was supposedly strong with labor and the Negro. While Colfax was more popular in the West, Wilson enjoyed more support in the Northeast. The outstanding speech of a convention not noted for oratory was probably the one delivered by Senator Oliver Morton of Indiana, in which he attacked both the Liberal Republican defectors and the Ku Klux Klan.

It is one of the great ironies of Gilded Age politics that the worst President of the period would run for re-election on a platform decidedly more liberal than some of its immediate predecessors. Chairing the Committee on Resolutions was G. W. Schofield of Pennsylvania. Unlike the 1868 document, this platform did not equivocate on the question of Negro suffrage in the North, but instead took the position that the Federal government should enforce the Fourteenth and Fifteenth Amendments. The struggle on the part of women for equal rights was "treated with respectful consideration," if not actually endorsed, while a civil service was proposed to "abolish the evils of patronage . . . without practically creating a life-tenure of office." Other proposed reforms included the termination of the franking privilege and the reduction of postal rates. On the other hand, that basic staple of Republican platforms, a high tariff to benefit both industry and labor, again made its appearance after twelve years' absence, along with a pledge to encourage and restore American commerce and ship-building. Despite the fact that the Grant administration's greatest achievements were in the foreign policy area (i.e., the Treaty of Washington), this document curiously devoted very little space to diplomatic matters: "Menacing foreign difficulties have been peacefully and honorably composed, and the honor and power of the nation kept in high respect throughout the world." The platform closed with words of praise for Grant and for Wilson, "an incorruptible legislator and representative man of American institutions."

With respect to the election itself, the outcome was never in doubt. The Radical Republicans were well-heeled financially and manipulated the colored vote, giving a federal appointment to the prominent Negro leader Frederick Douglass; Negroes had enjoyed the right to vote throughout the country ever since the adoption of the Fifteenth Amendment in 1870. Businessmen as well as veterans preferred Grant to Greeley, while a number of Democrats went fishing on election day. The incumbent President did little campaigning, but spent most of his time at Long Branch, New Jersey. As for Greeley, he retired from management of the New York *Tribune* before venturing out on a tour of Pennsylvania, New Jersey, Ohio, and Indiana in September. Greeley, who alienated numerous voters by his odd personal appearance (moon face, crumpled white hat, and untidy clothes), and eccentric beliefs (prohibition, communal living, and vegetarianism), made the mistake of delivering a new speech every day, thus confusing the voters by talking about too many subjects.

Thanks largely to Greeley, Grant's margin of victory on election day, 3,596,745 to 2,843,446 in the popular vote, was greater than that which the winner had enjoyed in recent Presidential contests. Greeley, who amassed 66 votes in the Electoral College to 286 for Grant, carried only six states, all of them in the South. This sad anticlimax to Greeley's brilliant career preceded his death by less than a month; most of his electors cast their ballots either for Thomas A. Hendricks or B. Gratz Brown. Grantism had triumphed, but the President himself was soon to experience dark days.

XI.   1876

The Disputed Election

Six months after Ulysses Grant was inaugurated for a second term as chief executive, the banking firm of Jay Cooke failed, triggering the Panic of 1873 and ushering in an era of economic discontent. Even before the President had been sworn in again, on February 12, 1873, a coinage act known as "the Crime of '73" had terminated coinage of the standard silver dollar and made gold the sole monetary standard of the United States. Grant later did release $26 million in greenbacks following the outbreak of the panic, but when Congress passed a bill on April 14, 1874, to increase the amount of legal tender notes in circulation to the $400 million dollar level, Grant vetoed the measure. Another bill that was signed into law two months later established a $382 million ceiling on the greenbacks, while the Specie Resumption Act of January 14, 1875, called for the resumption of specie payments by January 1, 1879.

Aside from the monetary question, scandal also plagued the second Grant administration. The "Salary Grab" Act of March 3, 1873, had increased the salaries of the President, members of Congress, and other governmental officials; public pressure eventually forced Congress a year later to invalidate the raises that body had granted itself. When the St. Louis *Democrat* exposed the Whisky Ring—a group of revenue officials and distillers who had conspired to cheat the Federal government out of internal revenue taxes—there were 238 indictments returned. One of these, moreover, named Grant's personal secretary, General Orville Babcock, but he avoided conviction after the President intervened. Similarly fortunate was the Secretary of War, William Belknap, who resigned to escape Congressional impeachment after it had been learned that he had profited illegally from the sale of trading posts in the Indian Territory. Adding to Grant's humiliation, the House of Representatives passed an anti-third term resolution in 1875, primarily to discourage the incumbent President from running again in 1876.

With the monetary issue perhaps the most critical one facing the nation at the time, third party reformers called for a Greenback party convention at Indianapolis in May 1876. Although this party was a descendant of the National Labor Reform party of 1872, this was not a labor gathering, nor was it dominated by the Grangers and other agrarian reformers. Instead, the 240 delegates from eighteen states were basically Greenback "true believers;" one James Buchanan, not to be confused with the former President, attended as a delegate, while Ignatius Donnelly, the future orator of the Populist movement, served as the temporary president. After rejecting Judge David Davis as their Presidential nominee on the grounds that he was unacceptable to the East, the convention turned to the eighty-five-year-old Peter Cooper of New York, an iron manufacturer and wealthy philanthropist. Cooper, who early in his career had been a Locofoco friendly to labor, accepted the nomination only after he had become convinced that neither party would act favorably towards the greenback question. As for the Vice Presidency, the leading possibility was an anti-monopolist Senator from California, Newton Booth, but after Booth had declined to accept, the nod went to Samuel Carey of Ohio, a well-known champion of fiat money.

Unlike the National Labor Reform party platform of 1872, the Greenback Party platform of 1876 focused sharply on the monetary issue, bypassing other reforms: "We demand the immediate and unconditional repeal of the Specie-Resumption Act . . . and the rescue of our industries from ruin and disaster resulting from its enforcement." Not only did this document protest the further sale of government bonds in various foreign markets, it also attacked the sale of government bonds to purchase silver to be used as currency; to the true Greenbacker, one must not forget, silver was as "hard" as gold. Later in the convention, after the candidates had been chosen, James Buchanan proposed making the old silver dollar legal tender. Although his motion did carry, his amendment was not included in the official platform that was published.

The Republicans, who assembled at Cincinnati in June, not only had to select a replacement for the retiring chief executive as their Presidential nominee, but also had to overcome a growing feud between New York Senator Roscoe Conkling of the "Stalwarts" and Maine Senator James G. Blaine of the "Half-Breeds"; this rivalry was to wreck both men's chances of winning the endorsement of this convention. Blaine's hopes were further dimmed by the Mulligan Letters expose, which linked the Maine

Senator to the sale of certain railroad bonds, and by the physical collapse that he suffered on the eve of the gathering. Nevertheless, Blaine still might have been nominated had the vote for President been taken at the conclusion of the famous "Plumed Knight" speech. Delivered by the prominent agnostic orator, Colonel Robert Ingersoll, this address demanded that the American people "call for the man who has torn from the throat of treason the tongue of slander—for the man who has snatched the mask of Democracy from the hideous face of the rebellion . . . Like an armed warrior, like a plumed knight."[1]

Ingersoll's speech did have enough of an impact to guarantee the "Plumed Knight" the lead on the first ballot, but on the seventh, the 756 delegates by-passed such candidates as Blaine, Conkling, Benjamin Bristow, and Oliver Morton, to select as their Presidential nominee the relatively unknown governor of Ohio, Rutherford Hayes. In his acceptance speech, Hayes came out for an enlightened southern policy, the resumption of specie payments, and nonsectarian public schools; placing the blame on Congress for the spoils system, he promised to recapture Presidential powers over patronage during the one term that he would serve as chief executive. For the second position on their ticket the Republicans then chose Easterner William Wheeler, who had been the president of the New York state constitutional convention in 1867-68 before going on to serve in Congress. During the balloting the chair established a precedent followed at subsequent conventions by ruling that each delegate could vote his sentiments regardless of state instructions; this in effect terminated Republican adherence to the unit rule, which would long dominate Democratic conventions.

The 1876 Republican platform proved to be one on which Hayes could stand with comfort, since it manifested little enthusiasm for the Greenback heresy. Former Rep. Joseph R. Hawley of Connecticut headed the Committee on Resolutions. Quoting the Declaration of Independence in the vein of past Republican statements of principle, this document affirmed that the United States is a "nation, not a league." By this time most of the southern states had been readmitted to the Union, which increased the danger of widespread Democratic victories there at the polls; accordingly, one plank advocated "the permanent pacification of the Southern section of the Union," a stance in line with Hayes's acceptance speech. Anticipating the onslaught that the Democrats would unleash against Grantism in this campaign, this document bitterly attacked them in language that demonstrated that the bloody shirt was still being waved: "We charge the Democratic Party with being the same in character and spirit as when it sympathized with treason."

With respect to the most original features of the platform, four years after the National Labor Reform party had demanded that the further importation of Chinese laborers into the United States be halted, the Republicans followed suit by calling for a Congressional investigation of the Mongolian question. Memories of 1856 were also invoked in an attack on polygamy. Another plank that appeared in a Republican platform for the first time in 1876 endorsed a Constitutional amendment forbidding the use of public funds for sectarian schools. Prior to endorsing Hayes and Wheeler, this document also assessed the Grant administration in a favorable manner, observing that it "merits commendation for its honorable work in the management of domestic and foreign affairs."

Debate over the platform centered around two main points. Edmund Davis of Texas proposed to substitute an endorsement of the Resumption Act, which was not popular in the West, for that plank calling for "a continuous and steady progress to specie payment." This amendment was rejected. Even more furor was generated by the proposal of Edward Pierce of Massachusetts to strike out the resolution advocating a Congressional investigation of Mongolian immigration. Some Westerners, who regarded this plank as far too weak, reacted vehemently. In the opinion of John Jones of Nevada, the Chinese "have planted themselves like a leprous sore in our midst,"[2] while J. B. Belford of Colorado stated, "the men are thieves and the women are prostitutes."[3] After a bitter debate, the plank was left untouched; Pierce's amendment was voted down, 215 to 532. Those who maintain that white supremacy is a prejudice limited to southern racists might well read the above speeches.

Holding their first convention west of the Mississippi, at St. Louis in June, the Democrats were confronted with a galaxy of Presidential possibilities: General Winfield Scott Hancock, William Allen, Joel Parker, Thomas Bayard, Allen Thurman, and Thomas Hendricks of Indiana, the eventual Vice Presidential candidate. (The delegates also were numerous, there being 983 present.) But the leading Presidential possibility was Governor Samuel Tilden of New York, a former Barnburner and Free Soiler and now a corporation lawyer, who had gained fame by prosecuting the Tweed Ring in New York City and the Canal Ring in New York State. Like Richard Nixon, Tilden was very much concerned with his image, which was also a cold one; not only did he set up a Newspaper Publicity Bureau, but he also polled college students. Despite the opposition of John Kelly of Tammany Hall and Westerners critical of his hard-money stance, Tilden won the Presidential nomination on the second ballot. The ticket was then balanced by choosing Hendricks for the Vice Presidency; he had been the choice of Greenbackers from the farm states for first place.

Tilden's acceptance speech turned out to be three times as long as the platform, a masterpiece of political literature that was largely the work of Manton Marble of the New York *World*, although Resolutions Committee Chairman John A. Meredith of Virginia officially presented it. (Henry Watterson probably wrote the tariff plank.) The resolution attacking the corruption of the Grant administration has been described by Henry Minor as being probably the severest in American or English political literature:[4] "a corrupt centralism which, after inflicting upon ten States the rapacity of carpet-bag tyrannies, has honeycombed the offices of the Federal Government itself with incapacity, waste, and fraud." (The specific crimes of the individual governmental officials were spelled out elsewhere.) Even the plank attacking the protectionist Republican tariff dripped vitriol; to its drafter it was "a masterpiece of injustice, inequality and false pretense." After scolding the Republicans for agitating sectarian strife, the Democrats disposed of the sectarian schools issue by pointing out their long-time advocacy of state-supported public schools.

On the other hand, this document criticized only the resumption clause of the Specie Resumption Act of 1875, rather than attack this measure in its entirety, like the Greenback party. The Democrats even found common ground with the Republicans on the Chinese problem, surpassing them in their demand for a treaty with the Chinese Empire to terminate further immigration. Whereas at the Republican convention the racist language was confined to the debates, here it permeated the platform itself in such passages as one denouncing "the policy which thus discards the liberty-loving German and tolerates the revival of the coolie-trade in Mongolian women for immoral purposes." What debate there was over the platform centered around the plank that called for the repeal of the resumption clause and not the act of 1875 in its entirity: the "soft money" substitute was rejected, 219 to 515, and the platform adopted as written, 651 to 83.

Aside from the Greenbackers, Republicans, and Democrats, the Prohibitionists and American National party also fielded tickets and ratified platforms. The Prohibition party Presidential candidate was General Green Clay Smith of Kentucky; his running-mate was Gideon Stewart of Ohio. Moral reform was the keynote of the Prohibitionists, who desired the abolition of gambling and lotteries, as well as a universal Sunday closing law. Prison reform also was advocated, as well as the arbitration of international disputes; the abolition of the system of contract labor in prisons had been recommended by the National Labor Reform party four years earlier, while the arbitration of international disputes had been endorsed by the Free Soil party in 1852. The Prohibitionists also matched or even outdid the Republicans in their attack on Mormon multiple marriage, calling for the abolition of "those foul enormities, polygamy and the social evil."

A number of reforms were also proposed by the American National party, whose candidates were James Walker of Illinois for chief executive, and Donald Kirkpatrick of New York as his running-mate. Asserting that God is the author of civil government, the American Nationalists adopted a platform resembling that of the Prohibitionists in a number of ways. These included an advocacy of temperance, the observance of the Sabbath, and the teaching of the Bible in the public schools, as well as the direct election of the President and Vice President. The American Nationalists also supported the forfeiture of all charters granted to secret societies.

The key issue of the campaign, however, was embodied in the Democratic motto: "Turn the rascals out;" the solution that they offered for the nation's ills was "Retrenchment and Reform." On the other side of the political fence, the Republicans organized "Boys in Blue" clubs for Hayes and attacked Tilden for his declining health and his war record. The aged Cooper took little if any active part in the campaign, though the poorly financed Greenbackers did hold one big meeting in Chicago. When the results were finally tabulated after the election, it became quickly apparent that the Democrats had captured the popular vote: Tilden, 4,284,000; Hayes, 4,033,000; Cooper, 82,000. Nevertheless, Tilden remained one vote short of an Electoral College triumph, 184 to 165, with 20 votes from Florida, Louisiana, South Carolina, and Oregon in dispute. Tilden had carried New York, New Jersey, Connecticut, Indiana, and the South; Cooper had made his strongest showing in the Midwest and in Pennsylvania.

Although at one time he was only one electoral vote from defeat, Hayes finally emerged victorious after a complex series of events. In January 1877 a fifteen-man electoral commission was set up, consisting of five Senators, five Representatives, and five Supreme Court justices; its political composition of eight Republicans and seven Democrats was reflected in its final ruling awarding the disputed twenty electoral votes (and the election) to Hayes. This series of events could possibly have triggered another Civil War, but the Republicans promised to remove the remaining federal troops from the South if Hayes were allowed to take office. The "deal" also had its economic aspects, inasmuch as northern industrial capitalists desired to invest in the South, and were willing to let the white Southerners have an upper hand over the Negro if this was their price. Hayes won the election, but in the long run the Republicans lost the South; between 1876 and 1952 the South presented a solid Democratic front in Presidential elections. Only in 1928 did the South defect from the faith of their fathers when the Democrats ran a Catholic and a "wet" of immigrant stock, Alfred Smith, for chief executive.

XII.   1880

The GOP versus the General

In statesmanship and ethics the Hayes administration proved to be an advance over that of Grant, though history books generally stress only two major accomplishments of this four-year period:

the withdrawal of the last federal troops from the South in April 1877, and the passage of the Bland-Allison Act over Hayes's veto the following year. This measure provided that the US Treasury was to purchase and coin two to four million dollars worth of silver each month. In still another bill enacted during 1878, Congress voted to maintain $346 million worth of greenbacks in circulation permanently; that fall the Greenback party made its best showing at the polls, collecting over a million votes and electing fifteen members to Congress, including General James Weaver of Iowa. On January 1, 1879, as previously noted, there was a resumption of specie payments, as provided for by an act passed in 1875. Aside from the agitation over the greenback issue, the major focal point of domestic strife was the series of railroad strikes that began on the B&O in July 1877 and led to walkouts on other lines, culminating in riots at Baltimore, Pittsburgh, Chicago, and St. Louis. It eventually became necessary for President Hayes to send troops to Martinsburg, West Virginia and Pittsburgh to restore order, after a number of people had been killed in both places.

Whether Hayes's record as President would have enabled him to capture a second term in the White House, however, is a purely speculative question, since Hayes had committed himself from the first to the role of a one-term chief executive. When the 756 Republican delegates assembled at Chicago in June, therefore, it was to endorse another standard-bearer. A number of candidates were nominated, including William Windom, George Edmunds, Elihu Washburne, and John Sherman, but the leading possibilities were James G. Blaine (supported by the Half-Breeds) and Ulysses Grant (backed by the Stalwarts). Roscoe Conkling's speech on behalf of a third term for the latter proved to be a classic of its kind; in beginning his address Conkling invoked the poetic muse: "And when asked what State he hails from, Our sole reply shall be, He hails from Appomattox, And its famous apple tree."[1]

Grant did lead on the first ballot, but Grant, Blaine, and Sherman proved unable individually to win over a majority of the delegates, and the nomination eventually went on the thirty-sixth ballot to Representative James Garfield of Ohio. Garfield, an original Sherman backer who was "available," had been General Rosencrans's chief of staff during the Civil War; elected to the House of Representatives in 1863, he was an outstanding debater and committeeman able to reconcile opposing factions. Those who were sensitive to omens were reassured when an eagle lit on his house in Washington at the very hour he was picked. Having rebuffed Grant's bid for the Presidential nomination, the convention turned for Garfield's running-mate to a true-blue Stalwart, Chester A. Arthur, an intimate of Conkling who had been Collector of the Port of New York prior to Hayes's removing him.

The Republican platform, which was passed by voice vote, offered some purple patches of rhetoric, but few new ideas. Chairing the Resolutions Committee was Edwards Pierrepont of New York. As usual, the Democrats were lambasted for "the habitual sacrifice of patriotism and justice to a supreme and insatiable lust of office and patronage"; nationalism was upheld at the expense of states' rights, the Constitution being "a supreme law, and not a mere contract." There was an unusual emphasis on statistics vis-a-vis railroad mileage, foreign trade, military pensions, and the public debt, the comparative totals being proof that under Republican rule great progress had been made in a number of fields. Viewing the development of the Solid South as a danger, this document nevertheless reminded the world that it had been the Republicans who had brought slavery to an end: "It transformed 4,000,000 human beings from the likeness of things to the rank of citizens." The outgoing President, Hayes, was also praised for his "purity and patriotism."

What debate there was centered around the merits of the spoils system. Originally there had been no civil service plank, but one was eventually added at the insistence of James Barker of Massachusetts after some haggling. In this connection one delegate from Texas observed, "There is one plank in the Democratic Party that I have ever admired, and this is, 'To the victors belong the spoils'"[2] Even more cynical was the Grant supporter from Pennsylvania who complained that the Democrats "are incrusted like rats in their holes . . . They are full of rebels. . . . I simply want to get them out and make way for our one-legged and one-armed Union soldiers."[3] Some Stalwarts, it would seem, made no pretense at idealism, but instead openly laid their cards on the table.

By far the most progressive convention held that year was that of the Greenback party, which assembled at Chicago in June. Here the factionalism centered around the question of whether or not to enter into a coalition with the Democrats. The delegates had no difficulty in selecting a Presidential candidate, however, James Weaver of Iowa winning the nod on the first ballot. Weaver, who had been elected to Congress in 1878, had been promoted to Brigadier General at the end of the Civil War; he was an orator who favored prohibition and the state regulation of railroads, but never advocated unlimited inflation. In the words of John D. Hicks, the historian of the Populist movement, "His views on the money question would not at a later date have been rejected as extreme."[4] B.J. Chambers of Texas was chosen for the second position on the ticket. Among those who participated in this convention was the anti-Chinese agitator of the California sand-lots, Dennis Kearney, and the noted woman-suffrage leader, Susan B. Anthony; it is quite likely that the Greenback party seriously injured its cause by admitting a number of Socialists to this gathering.

Although the *Nation* found the platform "more remarkable for sonority than novelty,"[5] this document was more extensive than its 1876 counterpart. Surprisingly, there was no denunciation of the Resumption Act, perhaps because it would have been useless to agitate further for its repeal, but there was an attack on "the cruel class legislation of the Republican Party," and on "government of the bondholder, by the bondholder, and for the bondholder." Nor did the Democrats escape censure, as this document lambasted "the action of the old parties in fostering and sustaining gigantic land, railroad, and money corporations and monopolies." Among the reforms proposed here were a graduated income tax, universal suffrage, the abrogation of the Burlingame Treaty permitting unlimited Chinese immigration, the overhauling of Congressional committees, and the regulation of interstate commerce. (The National Labor Reform party had proposed railroad rate regulation eight years before.) There also were a number of labor planks, but the true innovation was the income tax plank.

The Democrats, who met at Cincinnati later that month, were confronted with a half-dozen or more serious Presidential candidates: Thomas Bayard, Allen Thurman, Stephen Field, Thomas Hendricks, Henry Payne, William Morris, and Samuel Randall. Another major possibility, Samuel Tilden, withdrew in favor of Randall during the convention,. The nomination eventually went on the third ballot to another Civil War general, Winfield Scott

Hancock of Pennsylvania, a hero of the Battle of Gettysburg, who had been generally regarded as fair and just while serving as the military governor of Texas and Louisiana. Hancock, it will be recalled, also had been a Presidential possibility in 1876; his acceptance speech in 1880 unfortunately was filled with pious platitudes and naive utterances. Turning to the Middle West for his running-mate, the convention selected William English of Indiana, a millionaire banker with a hard-money record who had retired from the House in 1861. Fireworks at this gathering were provided by the expulsion of the Kelly Tammany delegation from New York City, which had opposed Tilden's nomination in 1876 and threatened to bolt this time if he were again selected as the party's standard bearer.

With respect to the platform, it differed only significantly from that of the Republicans in its endorsement of a revenue tariff, and in its opposition to centralization. Written largely by Henry Watterson, who headed the Committee on Resolutions, this document reached the heights of poetic inspiration in its promise to guard labor from "the cormorant and the commune," while praising the "wisdom, patriotism and integrity" of Tilden. Without mentioning the names of such past leaders as Jefferson or Jackson, the platform proclaimed that "We pledge ourselves anew to the constitutional doctrines and traditions of the Democratic party as illustrated by the teachings and example of a long line of Democratic statesmen and patriots." Congress was praised for reducing the public expenditures $40 million a year, while President Hayes was attacked for his "unprecedented" use of the veto. But the focal point of this document was "The great fraud of 1876-77." Declaring that "This issue precedes and dwarfs every other," the 1880 Democratic platform offered as a solution a "statute which shall make it forever impossible for a defeated candidate to bribe his way to the seat of the usurper by billeting villains upon the people." Quite clearly the bitter taste of the "stolen election" remained in the mouths of the Democrats.

Two other parties selected tickets and wrote platforms in 1880, the Prohibition party and the American National party. The 142 delegates from twelve states, who attended the Prohibition party convention at Cleveland in June, nominated Neal Dow of Maine for President and Henry A. Thompson of Ohio for Vice President. Dow was a lifelong Republican and long-time temperance

crusader who had been a Union Army general before becoming the
mayor of Portland; Thompson was the President of Oberlin
College. While the 1876 Prohibition platform had been quite
extensive, this one limited itself almost exclusively to the temperance issue, but did endorse woman suffrage "as a rightful
means for a proper settlement of the liquor question." Both the
Republicans and the Democrats were attacked for their record on
this issue. On the other hand, a throwback to the Anti-Masonic
party of a half-century earlier was the American National party,
which selected John Phelps of Vermont and Samuel Pomeroy of
Kansas as its ticket. A key plank from its platform reads, "Expose,
withstand, and remove secret societies, Freemasonry in particular,
and other anti-Christian movements, in order to save the churches
of Christ from being depraved."

During this campaign the expression GOP (Grand Old Party)
came to be used interchangably with Republican party, while the
phrase "Old Guard" came to be employed as a synonym for
"Stalwarts." Waving the bloody shirt had begun to lose its
political magic for the Republicans, but the revival of prosperity
and reaping of the largest crops of corn, wheat, and oats in history
aided the GOP. The Democrats probably lost votes by embracing a
revenue tariff, on which issue Hancock was guilty of "wobbling."
Third party candidate Weaver, unlike his aged predecessor
Cooper, made a serious attempt to sway voters; he travelled twenty
thousand miles and delivered a thousand speeches. But Weaver
received only 308,578 popular votes, or about 3 percent of the total.
The popular vote differential between the major parties proved to
be the narrowest in American political history, Garfield edging
Hancock, 4,449,053 to 4,442,035, a margin of only 7,000 votes.
Thanks to his victories in New York and Indiana, Garfield was
able to muster a more decisive majority of 214 to 155 in the
Electoral College. For the first time since 1874 the Republicans
gained control of the House of Representatives; the number of
Greenbackers in Congress dropped off to less than a dozen.
Unfortunately, however, tragedy was to strike the incoming
President within a year, and there was to be another accidental
chief executive, that Stalwart of Stalwarts, Chester A. Arthur.

XIII.   1884

Railroad Bonds and Moral Turpitude

A mere four months after his inauguration, James Garfield was shot at the Washington railroad station by Charles Guiteau, a mentally unbalanced individual who had unsuccessfully sought office and now wanted to make the Stalwart Arthur President. After lingering for several months, Garfield died. To the surprise of nearly everyone, however, Chester A. Arthur did not prove to be another Grant. Cutting his ties with Conkling and pursuing an independent course, the former Collector of the Port of New York saw through Congress measures setting up a nine-man tariff commission, instituting civil service, and laying the groundwork for a first-rate navy. In the foreign affairs field, Chinese exclusion was effected by Congress in 1882, despite Arthur's lukewarm attitude, while American interest in the Congo was encouraged by the chief executive. Arthur's failure to obtain a second term traditionally has been attributed to his inability to build up a strong political following, but information recently made public reveals that the President knew he was a doomed man physically long before the election, and thus did not pursue renomination as vigorously as he might have. Arthur was to die on November 18, 1886, less than two years after leaving the White House.

In 1884 a new third party made its appearance: the Anti-Monopoly party. Assembling in May, representatives from eleven western and six eastern states endorsed the colorful Benjamin Butler of Massachusetts for President, but left the choice of a Vice Presidential candidate to the Greenback party, which had yet to meet. Opposed to monopolies in transportation, money, and communications, the Anti-Monopolists ratified a platform that placed an unusual amount of emphasis on the labor planks. Some of the key provisions of this document recommended a bureau of labor statistics, the arbitration of labor disputes, and an eight-hour day; others favored the election of US Senators by direct vote, the Congressional regulation of interstate commerce, a tariff beneficial to labor rather than capital, and a graduated income tax. (The Greenbackers had advocated the latter four years before.) A final plank constituted a bid for the support of the farmers, whose vote the Greenback party was also attempting to win with their cheap money program.

Meeting at Indianapolis during the same month, the Greenbackers nominated Butler for President, while selecting Alanson West of Mississippi as his running-mate. Like the Anti-Monopoly party, the Greenback party favored tariff reform, but it took the position that financial issues were of greater importance. Aside from the eulogy of Peter Cooper, "that great philanthropist and spotless statesman," new planks recommended constitutional amendments dealing with woman suffrage and the liquor traffic, endorsed the recent Supreme Court rulings on the legal tender question, and came out in favor of shorter terms for US Senators. Whereas the prior platform advocated only the overhauling of Congressional committees, this document vented its wrath against the Senate; to the Greenbackers the upper house was "a body composed largely of aristocratic millionaires, who, according to their own party papers, generally purchased their elections in order to protect great monopolies which they represent." Following the earlier example, there were planks designed to attract labor.

The Republicans, who assembled at Chicago in June, rejected the candidacy of the incumbent President, as well as those of George Edmunds, John Logan, and John Sherman, and instead nominated on the fourth ballot that Republican of Republicans, James G. Blaine of Maine. Since the last election Blaine had served briefly as Secretary of State before being appointed to fill a Senatorial vacancy. Reversing the usual Republican practice of nominating a Midwesterner for President and an Easterner for Vice President, this convention selected John "Black Jack" Logan of Illinois to balance the ticket; Blaine was a Half-Breed, a civilian, and an Easterner, while Logan was a Stalwart, a former Union General, and a Midwesterner. To disappointed reformer E. L. Godkin this gathering was "a mass meeting of maniacs,"[1] and that fall Godkin and others were to bolt the ticket.

That some Republicans refused to support Blaine should be attributed to a lack of respect for the man more than the quite typical platform on which he stood. The Chairman of the Committee on Resolutions was William McKinley, later to be one of the authors of the Tariff of 1890, and afterwards, President. Although he personally was a protectionist, McKinley's document did come out in favor of tariff reform, but not "by the vicious and indiscriminate process of horizontal reduction"; the proposed readjustment of the duties on wool was obviously designed to capture farm votes that might otherwise go to the Greenbackers. Another significant plank advocated the exclusion of Chinese labor, a traditional Republican stance whose deletion in 1880 may have cost the Republicans California and Nevada, but not the election. On the other hand, their failure to deal with the prohibition question in 1884 was to cost Blaine thousands of votes in New York State, and possibly the election itself.

Aside from these provisions, there was the usual Republican blast at polygamy, along with a plea that Congress "divorce the political from the ecclesiastical power of the so-called Mormon church." The one foreign policy plank embraced isolationism and the Monroe Doctrine without specifically mentioning either; still another plank demanded "the restoration of our navy to its old-time strength and efficiency," in effect endorsing President Arthur's shipbuilding program. Significantly, the reaction of the candidate was almost one of disdain: "Formerly, the platform was of first importance. . . . Now the position of the candidate, as defined by himself, is of far more weight with the voters."[2]

With Blaine the Republican Presidential nominee, the Democrats gathered 840 strong at Chicago in July, well aware that they might capture the White House with the right candidate. Passing over such front-runners from past elections as Thomas Bayard, Allen Thurman, and Samuel Randall, the Democrats chose as their standard-bearer on the second ballot Governor Grover Cleveland of New York. A bachelor by choice and a lawyer by profession, Cleveland had previously served as the mayor of Buffalo, where he established a reputation for honesty; in endorsing his candidacy, Congressman Edward Bragg of Wisconsin uttered the immortal words: "We love him for the enemies he has made."[3] Cleveland, like Seymour, Greeley, and Tilden before him, was from New York, and like Tilden he was on bad terms with the Kelly Tammany machine. His running-mate, Thomas Hendricks of Indiana, had also been the Democratic Vice Presidential nominee in 1876. (Since the Civil War the second position on the ticket had been filled either from the Hoosier State or Missouri.) Hendricks, it will be recalled, was the choice of Greenbackers from the farm states for first place in 1876, and thus his monetary views did not harmonize with those of Cleveland, who has become stereotyped as the typical hard-money, gold Democrat of the Gilded Age.

The position that the platform took on the monetary issue was probably closer to that of Cleveland than that of Hendricks: "We believe in honest money, the gold and silver coinage of the Constitution, and a circulating medium convertible into money without loss." Drawn up mainly by John Prentiss Poe of Maryland, a close friend of Senator Arthur Gorman, this document was finalized by the Resolutions Committee headed by Representative William Morrison of Illinois; in the opinion of Frank Kent, a historian of the Democratic party, it was "the most withering and blasting indictment of the Republican party yet framed." [4] Observering that "The Republican party, so far as principle is concerned, is a reminiscence," this document continued with a list of specific grievances against it a la the Declaration of Independence. Fraud was charged with respect to the elections of both 1876 and 1880, while the Republicans were even criticized by the Democrats for accumulating a $100 million surplus. Exhibiting more bravery on the prohibition issue than the GOP, the Democrats flatly came out against sumptuary laws; this stand was consistent with that generally taken by state platforms of the party during the period.

While their foreign policy plank was quite similar to the Republican one, with its references to "an American continental policy" but "entangling alliances with none," the Democrats did attack the Republican party's diplomatic stance towards Great Britain in a bid for the Irish vote. "Republican rule and policy," lamented this document, "have managed to surrender to Great Britain, along with our commerce, the control of the markets of the world"; blasting the Arthur administration, it charged that the Republican party "has squandered hundreds of millions to create a navy that does not exist." From the standpoint of expansion, the Republicans had annexed only Alaska, while the Democrats had obtained Louisiana, Florida, California, and the Southwest. Turning to its heroes and ideals, the platform praised Samuel Tilden for his labors, and reaffirmed the endorsement by its 1856 predecessor of "the liberal principles embodied by Jefferson in the Declaration of Independence, and sanctioned in the Constitution."

Most of the excitement in the debate over the platform was provided by Benjamin Butler, the Anti-Monopoly party and Greenback party Presidential nominee who had received a grand total of zero votes for chief executive in the Democratic balloting. Boasting (with considerable exaggeration) that "I come here as no mendicant, no beggar. I come here representing more than 1,500,000 laboring men,"[5] Butler offered a platform opposing civil service, favoring cheap money, and endorsing a selective protective tariff. There was a recorded vote only on the last item; Butler went down to a crushing defeat, 76½ to 721½. His foray into Democratic politics had proved to be a colossal failure.

Those voters who were repelled by the candidates and/or platforms of both major parties in 1884 were to have the opportunity to make a third choice, not only from the Anti-Monopoly party and the Greenback party, but also from not one, but two, prohibition parties. The American Prohibition party, which endorsed a ticket of Samuel Pomeroy of Kansas and John Conant of Connecticut, came out for the use of the Bible in the schools, the revocation of the charters of secret societies, restrictions on the employment of prison labor and depreciated foreign contract labor, and a revision of those laws relating to patents and inventions. The Prohibitionists likewise advocated equal rights for the Indians and Chinese, the settlement of international disputes by arbitration, tariff reduction, and the abolition of the Electoral College. It will be recalled that while the 1876 Prohibition platform had been quite extensive, that of 1880 limited itself almost exclusively to the temperance issue. This relatively brief 1884 document's stand on behalf of equal rights for the Indians and Chinese obviously was quite at variance with platform planks both major and minor during this period, although most of the other reforms had been suggested previously by other parties.

Of far greater numerical strength was the Prohibition Home Protection party, which selected as its candidates John St. John of Kansas and William Daniel of Maryland at a convention held at Pittsburgh in July. St. John, a former Republican governor of Kansas, had been defeated in 1882 on the prohibition issue. Its platform attacked the Democratic party for opposing sumptuary legislation, as well as personally criticizing the Republican ticket of Blaine and Logan. Aside from endorsing woman suffrage, this document also advocated civil service; it noted that public lands should go to settlers and not to corporations or speculators, while disabled soldiers and sailors should be cared for. Longer than the other Prohibition party platform, this one also contained a smaller number of reforms, since the bulk of it was taken up with the prohibition issue. Constitutional amendments were recommended both to enforce temperance and to forbid polygamy, although there obviously was no connnection between the two.

With a half-dozen parties to choose from, many voters still probably cast their ballots on election day in terms of which major party candidate was the least distasteful to them. One thus had a choice between James G. Blaine and his railroad bonds ("Blaine! Blaine! James G. Blaine! The continental liar from the State of Maine! *Burn this letter.*") and Grover Cleveland and his illegitimate child ("Ma! Ma! Where's my pa? Gone to the White House. Ha! Ha! Ha!") In the opinion of George Mayer, this election was "the dirtiest since 1872 and perhaps the dirtiest in American history."[6] Cleveland's image was further damaged by the revelation that he had bought a substitute during the Civil War to serve in his place; this was in sharp contrast to such military heroes as Grant who became Republican Presidential nominees. But Blaine, too, had his problems. Mugwumps, or reformers, like Curtis, Godkin, Schurz, and Adams bolted to Cleveland, while his long-time enemy Conkling dragged his feet in New York State. In addition, the "Belshazzar's Feast" banquet at Delmonico's of prominent Wall Streeters supporting Blaine led to unfavorable publicity, and the Reverend Samuel Burchard's assessment of the Democrats as the party of "Rum, Romanism, and Rebellion" alienated the Irish vote. As for issues, the tariff probably was the most important one during this campaign, at those moments when the political dialogue rose above the gutter level. Cleveland emphasized civil service, tax reduction, and various labor questions in his two major speeches.

In one of the closest elections in American political history, Cleveland edged past Blaine, 4,911,017 popular votes and 219 electoral votes to 4,848,334 popular votes and 182 electoral votes. Unfortunately for Blaine, the New York State vote proved decisive; Cleveland carried the popular tally by mere 1,149 votes out of a total of 1,125,000. Aside from the other factors working against him there, bad weather in traditionally Republican upstate New York on election day damaged the "Plumed Knight's" cause by holding down the turnout. Butler, who did not wage an active campaign, but was popular with laborers, received 175,370 votes nationwide, 24,000 in his native Massachusetts; St. John, who made forty speeches in New York polled 25,000 of his total of 150,369 votes nationwide there. Butler's and St. John's presence on the ballot doubtless had an effect on the outcome in several states. In any event, the Republican stranglehold on the Presidency had finally come to an end, and the Cleveland Era had begun to dawn on American politics.

XIV. 1888

Sweating Ice Water

Grover Cleveland has been the only American President to serve two nonconsecutive terms. Historians are in general agreement that his first four years were more liberal than his second; in the opinion of Woodrow Wilson, Cleveland really was a conservative Republican, aside from his stand on the tariff issue. There was no tariff reform during his first administration, but Cleveland did devote his annual message to Congress in 1887 to the necessity for lowering duties. He also made an attempt to win the farm vote away from the Greenbackers by signing the Hatch Act of the same year, providing federal subsidies for the establishment of state agricultural experiment stations. But Cleveland, whom many of his admirers loved for the enemies he made, alienated other groups; he infuriated Union Army veterans, for example, by appointing former Confederates to his cabinet, by returning captured battle flags to the South, and by vetoing more special pension bills than any of his predecessors. On the other hand, Great Plains farmers were irked by his rejection of the Texas seed bill appropriating $10,000 for the purchase of seed grain to aid suffering drought victims. With respect to the other features of Cleveland's domestic program, the passage of the Interstate

Commerce Act in 1887 and the continued growth of the navy
might be regarded as pluses, but the enactment of the Dawes
Severalty Act the same year, which broke up the Indian reservations, is generally looked upon as a major error.
There was also considerable activity in foreign affairs. It has
already been noted that Cleveland discouraged the American
involvement in the Congo begun by his predecessor, Arthur; there
was also a rivalry over Samoa among the United States,
Bismarckian Germany, and Great Britain, settled temporarily in
1889. Cleveland likewise attempted to resolve outstanding differences with Great Britain relative to Canada, via the Bayard-
Chamberlain Treaty of 1888, but this went down to defeat in the
Senate later that year at the hands of New England lobbyists and
the fishing interests. This issue had proven both a political and
sectional football. As the Presidential election of 1888 approached,
it was quite clear that the incumbent chief executive had numerous fences to mend.

Turning first to third parties, there was no Greenback party
convention in 1888, as there had been in 1876, 1880, and 1884, but
there were two labor party ones, both of which assembled at
Cincinnati on May 15. Of these the more important was that of the
Union Labor party; here 274 delegates who had gathered from 25
states nominated a ticket of Alson Streeter of Illinois and C. E.
Cunningham of Arkansas. Declaring that "The paramount issues
to be solved in the interests of humanity are the abolition of usury,
monopoly, and trusts," the platform of the Union Labor party
suggested a series of reforms that merely extended the demands of
the Greenbackers without breaking much new ground. Among
these were the governmental ownership of communications and
transportation, a freer monetary system, postal savings banks,
several labor proposals, veterans' pensions, a graduated income
tax, the direct election of US Senators, Chinese exclusion, and
woman suffrage. Here the most original plank was probably the
postal savings one. That calling for the governmental *ownership*
of communications and transportation also represented a step
beyond the Greenback platform of 1884, which, after demanding
the Congressional *regulation* of interstate commerce, advocated
the construction of national railroads, if necessary.

Its rival, the United Labor party, endorsed Robert Cowdrey of
Illinois for President and W. H. T. Wakefield of Kansas for Vice

President, and ratified a platform obviously inspired by New York City "single-tax" advocate Henry George. Aside from endorsing governmental ownership of the railroad and telegraph systems, the United Labor party document came out in favor of the Australian or secret ballot, simplified court procedures, and reduced legal expenses. If only in terms of voter support, it was a less important party than its counterpart.

On the other hand, the Democrats, who met at St. Louis in June, renominated President Cleveland by acclamation, the first time that this had occurred since Martin Van Buren was similarly honored in 1840. As Vice President Thomas Hendricks had died in 1885, there was a need to choose a new Vice Presidential nominee; the nod eventually went to Allen Thurman of Ohio, who had figured as a Presidential possibility at several past Democratic conventions. Thurman, once a Polk Democrat, had served in Congress and as a judge in his native state before winning election to the US Senate in 1868 for the first of two terms. Following the precedent in vogue since the Civil War, the Presidential nominee of the Democrats came from the East, and the Vice Presidential one from the Middle West, though this was the first time that Ohio had furnished the candidate for the second position.

In light of his renomination by acclamation, it is not surprising that Cleveland played a major role in the writing of the platform, in particular the tariff plank, along with the chairman of the Committee on Resolutions, Henry Watterson. (The incumbent President secretly presented his ideas on the tariff to Senator Arthur Gorman.) This document began by reaffirming its counterpart adopted four years previously. As finally drafted, the tariff plank endorsed "the views expressed by President Cleveland in his last annual message to Congress as the correct interpretation of that platform upon the question of Tariff reduction."

With a Democrat now occupying the White House, the 1888 Democratic party platform was more vague on specifics than its recent counterparts had been, and also more moderate in its attacks on the Republicans. Several resolutions, moreover, were added after it had been adopted. One of these, proposed by ex-Governor Leon Abbett of New Jersey in an attempt to capture the Irish vote, expressed sympathy for "the efforts of those noble patriots, who, led by Gladstone and Parnell, have conducted their grand and peaceful contest for home rule in Ireland."[1] Another, which sought to win over the West, blasted the Republicans for denying statehood and self-government to the people of Washington, Dakota, Montana, and New Mexico. This last plank thus made its first appearance in national party platforms; by 1890 six new states had joined the Union under a Republican President. (New Mexico, however, did not become a state until 1912.)

Assembling at Chicago later in June, the Republicans were confronted with a galaxy of would-be Presidential nominees: John Sherman, Walter Gresham, Chauncey Depew, Russell Alger, William Allison, Benjamin Harrison, and that perennial possibility, James G. Blaine. As the convention opened, Sherman's chances of obtaining the nomination seemed as good as anyone's, but Blaine, who was suffering from ill health and felt that his 1884 defeat militated against a second nomination for him, threw his support to Harrison. The latter eventually was selected on the eighth ballot. An Indianapolis lawyer who had been a brigadier general under General William Tecumseh Sherman (John's brother), Benjamin Harrison was an unusually effective public speaker who had won election to the Senate in 1880, but had lost his re-election bid. Perhaps his greatest personal handicap was a chilly personality; "Sherman is too cold," said a Harrison partisan. "Cold!" retorted the Shermanite, "he is a red-hot stove compared to your man. Harrison sweats ice water."[2] After giving its blessing to this Hoosier grandson of William Henry Harrison as its Presidential nominee, the convention turned to Levi Morton of New York, a veteran financier and spoilsman, for his running-mate. Thus the Republicans reverted to their standard post-Civil War practice of selecting a Midwesterner for President and an Easterner for Vice President, after reversing this procedure (and losing) with Blaine and Logan in 1884.

Unlike its Democratic counterpart, the Republican platform contained a number of interesting provisions; William McKinley was again Chairman of the Resolutions Committee. Praising the memory of the dead Abraham Lincoln and the living Philip Sheridan, this document also covered "with wreaths of imperishable remembrance and gratitude the heroic names of our later leaders who have been more recently called away from our councils—Grant, Garfield, Arthur, Logan, Conkling." The key plank renounced fence-straddling and unequivocally endorsed a protective tariff; as in 1884, special attention was paid to the wool industry. Here the Democrats were accused of serving the interests of Europe, while the Republicans were safeguarding those of America. The platform also made a pitch for Union veteran support by noting Cleveland's wholesale veto of pension bills. Still another plank, added at the last minute, expressing sympathy for "all wide and well directed efforts for the promotion of temperance and morality," remedied an omission four years before that doubtless cost the Republicans a number of Prohibition votes. On the other hand, the GOP emulated the Democratic example by favoring statehood for South Dakota, Washington, North Dakota, and Montana, as well as New Mexico, Wyoming, Idaho, and Arizona.

But it was in the field of foreign affairs that the Republican party offered, for the first time since the Civil War, a reasonably comprehensive policy. Not only were the Irish home rulers extended sympathy, but Brazilian emancipators were also offered praise. (Slavery had been ended in Brazil around this time.) Attacking Cleveland's record in the diplomatic field, this platform charged that "the conduct of foreign affairs by the present administration has been distinguished by its inefficiency and cowardice." Despite adherence to the principles contained in the Monroe Doctrine, the Democrats had neither halted the extension of foreign influences in Central America, nor promoted the construction of the Nicaragua Canal. Especially pointed was the attack on the Cleveland administration "for its weak and unpatriotic treatment of the fisheries question, and its pusillanimous surrender of the essential privileges to which our fishing vessels are entitled in Canadian ports. . . ." The defeat of the Bayard-Chamberlain Treaty by the Senate, as noted earlier, occurred during this same year, with the Republicans leading the heavily partisan opposition.

In contrast, domestic considerations predominated at two third-party conventions held that year, aside from the two labor-party conventions previously discussed. The Prohibition party met at Indianapolis in May to endorse a slate of Clinton Fisk of New Jersey for President and John Brooks of Missouri for Vice President, and to recommend in its platform the abolition of the saloon. As in 1884 there were a number of planks on issues other than prohibition, including one condemning both the Republicans and Democrats for denying statehood to the people of

Dakota Territory. However, the Prohibition party stance on the tariff was closer to that of Cleveland than that of the Republicans.

Quite different in character was the American party, a forerunner of the American Protective Association, whose members gathered at Washington in August. Here 126 delegates were present, with those from New York and California playing a decisive role; James Langdon Curtis of New York won the Presidential nod, James Greer of Tennessee the Vice Presidential one. The key provisions of the American party platform, which recall those of the American party a generation earlier, emphasized the need for the restriction of immigration. Not only would the latter be made more costly and difficult, but no alien would be allowed to hold land. (California was to achieve this objective at the state level in 1913 with the passage of the Webb Act.) There also were demands for the separation of church and state, and the taxation of church-owned property. Curiously, the Americanists played down the heated tariff question, declaring that "the assumed issue 'Protection' vs. 'Free Trade' is a fraud and a snare." Perhaps the most original "anti-reform" the American party advocated was the limitation of language instruction in the public schools to English; the most original true reform, a sole six-year term for the President.

Shrewdly exploiting Cleveland's stand on the tariff issue, the Canadian fisheries, and military pensions, the Republicans built up a huge campaign fund. To make matters worse for the incumbent chief executive, the so-called Murchison letter was made public several weeks before the election; here the British Minister to the United States, Sackville-West, endorsed Cleveland's bid for re-election, in the process driving away numerous Irish-American voters who had defected from Blaine in 1884 after the "Rum, Romanism, and Rebellion" speech. But Cleveland could count on the solidly Democratic South, while a White House marriage and the passage of time had more or less defused the illegitimate child issue of 1884. Nor was the "Hoosier iceberg" enough of a military hero or a charismatic personality to offer a palatable alternative to Cleveland. Building upon his southern base, Cleveland actually outdistanced Harrison in the popular vote, 5,540,050 to 5,444,337, but Republican triumphs in New York and Indiana enabled Harrison to capture the Electoral College 233 to 168. This time the Prohibitionist candidate (Fisk) received a quarter of a million votes, while the Union Labor party nominee (Streeter) collected nearly 150,000. In a sense, the will of the people had been thwarted, but there was no talk of revolution as there had been in 1876; not since that time, though, has the winner of the popular vote been denied the Presidency, as was Cleveland's fate in 1888.

XV. 1892

Old Grover Again

Benjamin Harrison's Presidency, if not a brilliant one in the eyes of historians, was at least an eventful one. During 1890 the Dependent Pension Act, the Sherman Antitrust Act, the Sherman Silver Purchase Act, and the McKinley Tariff became law. Of these measures, the Dependent Pension Act proved to be most politically advantageous to the Republicans; the number of pensioners increased from 676,000 to 970,000 between 1891 and 1895, while the annual appropriation had risen from $81 million to $135 million by the time that Harrison left office. With respect to the Sherman Antitrust Act, it was too weakly worded to be truly effective, while the ill-fated Sherman Silver Purchase Act helped bring on a panic before Cleveland pressured Congress into repealing it in 1893. Even more disastrous was the McKinley Tariff. As a result of its passage, by the end of 1892 the federal treasury surplus had become a deficit, and the Republicans suffered a crushing loss of seats in the Congressional election of 1890. The Congress at that time was to become known as the "Billion Dollar Congress," because it was the first body in history to approve annual expenditures in excess of this amount. Despite these actions, Congress did refrain from enacting the Force Bill, a measure providing for the supervision of Federal elections by the National government, which was obviously directed against the solidly Democratic South.

In the foreign affairs field, James G. Blaine finally had the opportunity, when serving his second term as Secretary of State, to preside over the first Pan-American conference in 1889. The same year also witnessed the signing of the tripartite agreement among the United States, Bismarckian Germany, and Great Britain, relative to Samoa. Harrison's scheme to annex Hawaii, though, remained unfulfilled during his Presidency, and Cleveland threw cold water upon it after assuming office for the second time in 1893.

Following the last Presidential election, agrarian, "cheap" money, and labor groups held a series of conventions: at St. Louis in December 1889; at Ocala, Florida, in December 1890; at Cincinnati in May 1891; and at St. Louis in February 1892. In July of the latter year, 1,300 to 1,400 accredited delegates met at Omaha to nominate a President and write a platform; among those in attendance were such noted Populist leaders as Ignatius Donnelly of Minnesota, "Sockless Jerry" Simpson and Mary Ellen Lease of Kansas, and Thomas Watson of Georgia. After Walter Gresham of Illinois, a federal circuit court judge, had in effect disqualified himself by requesting a unanimous nomination, the convention named as its standard-bearer James Weaver of Iowa. Weaver, who had been the 1880 Greenback party nominee, was in fact more conservative than some of the other Populist leaders; his main rival was James Kyle of South Dakota, the candidate of the radicals and silverites. The ticket was completed with the choice of General James Field of Virginia for Vice President.

Although Richard Hofstadter makes reference in his standard work, *The Age of Reform,* to "the daring or the originative force of the Populists of the 1890s,"[1] the fact remains that their 1892 platform was little more than a restatement of past demands by agrarian and labor reformers, and "cheap" money proponents. The lengthy preamble, in fact, had been presented at the February convention by Ignatius Donnelly, a noted orator; it made reference to "a nation brought to the verge of moral, political, and material ruin." Perhaps the most original plank was the one calling for the adoption of the initiative and referendum, but the most famous one recommended the free and unlimited coinage of silver at the ratio of 16 to 1. Nevertheless, the influence of the Greenbackers was felt in this document, while Alexander Campbell, "The Father of Greenbackism," received a standing ovation from the delegates.

Aside from these planks, most of the others had a distinctly warmed-over flavor: the governmental ownership and operation of all transportation and communication lines, a graduated income tax, a postal savings system, the direct election of US Senators, a single term for the President, the secret ballot, the prohibition of alien land ownership, and various labor reforms. "We seek to restore the government of the Republic," asserted this document, "to the hands of 'the plain people,' with which class it originated." Whatever its antecedents may have been, however, the cumulative effect of the platform was such as to lead one unsympathetic observer to describe it as "that furious and hysterical arraignment of the present times, that incoherent intermingling of Jeremiah and Bellamy."[2] The delegates entered into a wild demonstration upon its adoption.

The Republicans, who had met at Minneapolis the previous month in blistering heat, endorsed the incumbent President, Benjamin Harrison, for re-election, despite the fact that many party leaders were indifferent or even hostile to his candidacy. James G. Blaine was also considered as a standard-bearer, but he was in the last year of his life; William McKinley was likewise Presidential timber, despite the fact that the tariff bill bearing his name had brought political ruin to the Republicans. Less fortunate was the incumbent Vice President, Levi Morton, who did not actively seek renomination, and who had irritated Harrison with his Senate rulings. Morton was replaced on the ticket by another New Yorker, Whitelaw Reid, owner of the New York *Tribune,* and more recently, Minister to France. Probably the most noteworthy address delivered at this convention was that of eighty-three-year-old Colonel Richard Thompson of Indiana, who observed that the Democrats were proposing to destroy the McKinley Tariff Act "piecemeal, like rats gnawing at the ropes of a ship and seeking to sink it, while the great craft moves onward and bids defiance to the storm."[3]

The platform was more or less a carbon copy of that of 1888, a typically orthodox document, but this time former Governor Joseph Foraker of Ohio headed the Committee on Resolutions. Although the platform did endorse a protective tariff, thus ignoring the 1890 election returns, it also declared in favor of commercial reciprocity; both the Sherman Anti-Trust Act and the Force Bill met with its approval. Unlike the Populists, the Republicans straddled the fence on the currency issue, and refused to endorse a gold standard. There were again planks designed to attract prohibitionists, veterans, and Irish home rulers, along with a protest against the persecution of Jews in Russia. Another new twist was the resolution favoring "efficient legislation by Congress to protect the life and limbs of employees of transportation companies engaged in carrying on inter-State commerce." The plank lauding the World's Columbian Exposition at Chicago was hardly a controversial one, and that praising the Harrison administration ("Under it the country has enjoyed remarkable prosperity") showed more restraint than similar utterances in past documents.

While the Republicans were nominating Harrison, the Democrats were giving their blessing to Cleveland, at Chicago. Since leaving the White House, "Old Grover" had associated himself with a Wall Street law firm that handled much of the legal work involving the House of Morgan; in the stormy world of New York State politics a rivalry had emerged between Cleveland and Democratic Governor David B. Hill. Although it proved necessary for a New Jersey delegate to nominate him, Cleveland won the nomination of his party over Hill with little difficulty. For the second position the convention turned to a midwestern bimetallist, Adlai Stevenson of Illinois, the grandfather of the Democratic Presidential nominee of the 1950s.

Invoking the past, the platform drawn up by St. Louis newspaper editor Charles H. Jones's Resolutions Committee began by paying homage to Jefferson, as well as to "the long and illustrious line of his successors in Democratic leadership, from Madison to Cleveland." The Sherman Silver Purchase Act was attacked as a "cowardly makeshift," a stance in line with Cleveland's pro-gold sympathies; the Populist takeover of the Democratic party was still four years down the road. The unenacted Force Bill was similarly lambasted, a quite logical step in view of the heavily Democratic South. There was the usual plank against Chinese immigration, but that endorsing "all legitimate efforts to prevent the United States from being used as the dumping ground for the known criminals and professional paupers of Europe" marked a new stance. Since the Civil War, it must be remembered, there had been a growing influx of immigrants from southern and eastern Europe, neither Protestant in religion nor Anglo-Saxon in race. With respect to foreign affairs, not only did the Democrats sympathize with the Jews under persecution in Russia, but also with the Lutherans. Another plank recommended the early construction of the Nicaraguan Canal.

What debate there was on the platform centered around the tariff plank. The original one straddled this issue, but it eventually was replaced by a stronger one at the insistence of Henry Watterson, long a prominent leader at Democratic conventions. Here the roll-call vote was a decisive 564 to 342 in favor of the substitute. In its final version this plank boldly proclaimed, "We denounce the McKinley tariff law enacted by the Fifty-first Congress as the culminating atrocity of class legislation. We denounce the Republican protection as a fraud, a robbery of the great majority of the American people for the benefit of the few." Yet the Democrats by no means endorsed free trade, since the platform also contained a slam at reciprocity. An attempt, too, was made by Thomas Patterson of Colorado to so amend this document as to endorse the free coinage of silver, but his motion was defeated by voice vote without further ado.

In contrast, the big debate at the Prohibition party convention at Cincinnati in June was over the monetary issue. Here John Bidwell of California was nominated for President and James Cranfill of Texas for Vice President. Though to the *Nation* the platform was "one of the most striking marks of the progress of political intelligence that have recently been presented,"[4] the Prohibitionists sidestepped a stand on the free coinage of silver, defeating both the majority and minority planks on this topic. On the other hand, the majority report favoring a "defensive" tariff was adopted over the minority one advocating a protective tariff. Other noteworthy provisions of this document included attacks on the speculation in margins and on the cornering of grain, and on "the competition of both the [major] parties for the vote of the slums."

Still another third party to hold a Presidential nominating convention in 1892 was the Socialist Labor party, which assembled in New York City. Its ticket of Simon Wing of Massachusetts for President and Charles Matchett of New York for Vice President polled only twenty thousand-odd votes in the election, as contrasted with over a million votes for the Populist slate, but an examination of its platform reveals a series of proposals that far surpassed those of the Populists in originality. Perhaps the most radical of these was the one providing for the abolition of the Presidency, Vice Presidency, and the Senate; the House of Representatives was to elect an executive board in their place, subject to its recall. Other planks recommended the abolition of capital punishment, the recall of all public officers, and the governmental renumeration of inventors. Less original was the rhetoric: "Our despotic system of economics is the direct opposite of our democratic system of politics." Aside from the Socialist theorizing, there also was a reference to the Declaration of Indepencence.

With the election approaching, strikes at Homestead, Pennsylvania, and Coeur d'Alene, Idaho, worked against the Republicans. This time it was the Democrat, Cleveland, who had the largest financial war chest in history; "Old Grover's" unswerving position on the gold standard had won him solid backing from conservative eastern financiers and businessmen. The Republicans were still suffering, too, from the political repercussions of the McKinley Tariff of 1890, while Harrison's cold personality also cost them votes. To compound their difficulties, Whitelaw Reid's New York *Tribune* was in the midst of a protracted labor dispute, but Democratic New York Governor David Hill remained lukewarm to Cleveland, further adding to the political turmoil in New York State. Throughout the nation as a whole, there was considerable apathy towards both major party nominees.

Although Cleveland improved his showing at the polls in November by only 14,000 votes over 1888, Benjamin Harrison suffered a fatal drop-off of approximately a quarter-million. The final totals were Cleveland, 5,554,414 popular votes and 277 electoral votes; Harrison, 5,190,802 popular votes and 145 electoral votes; Weaver, 1,027,329 popular votes and 22 electoral votes; Bidwell (the Prohibitionist) 271,058 popular votes. Aside from their victory in the Presidential race, the Democrats also secured control of both houses of Congress, the first time since 1858 that they had accomplished this feat. But the most significant aspect of the balloting was not the five million-plus votes apiece that Cleveland and Harrison received; it was the one million votes which Populist Weaver attracted. Four years later the Bryanites were to take over the Democratic party, sweeping aside Cleveland and the "gold-bugs," and thus irreversibly transforming the course of American political history.

XVI.   1896

The Cross of Gold

Grover Cleveland entered the White House in 1893 riding the crest of three successive popular vote triumphs in Presidential races. He left there in 1897, having been repudiated by his own party; not only was his second administration more conservative than his first, but it also was more crisis-torn. When Cleveland finally was presented by Congress with a new tariff, the somewhat protective Wilson-Gorman proposal of 1894, Cleveland ranted at "party perfidy and party dishonor," but nevertheless allowed the bill to become law. After the Panic of 1893 broke out, Cleveland pushed a measure repealing the Sherman Silver Purchase Act of 1890 through Congress, much to the disgust of the western silverites; he further alienated the latter by turning to J. P. Morgan for aid in stemming the drain on the Treasury gold reserves. When the American Railway Union boycotted Pullman cars in 1894, moreover, Cleveland sent in federal troops to restore order, over the protests of Governor John Peter Altgeld of Illinois. That same year Coxey's army of unemployed workers marched on Washington, demanding a public works relief program. Given these circumstances, it was not surprising that the Republicans won control of both houses of Congress in the Congressional election of 1894.

Turning to foreign affairs, Cleveland did undercut Hawaiian annexation in 1893 after taking over as chief executive following Benjamin Harrison, but he also put some teeth into the Monroe Doctrine by standing up to the British at the time of the Venezuelan boundary crisis of 1895. Richard Olney, who had been the Attorney General at the time of the Pullman Strike, was now Secretary of State; in his note to the British, Olney proclaimed. "Today the United States is practically sovereign on this continent, and its fiat is law upon the subjects to which it confines its interposition."[1]

But the key issue in the Election of 1896 was the free coinage of silver at the ratio of 16 to 1, and this "battle of the standards" tore apart not only the Republicans and the Democrats, but even the Prohibitionists. The "Narrow Gauge" faction nominated a slate of Joshua Levering of Maryland for President and Hale Johnson of Illinois for Vice President; after pledging allegiance to Almighty God as the Rightful Ruler of the Universe, this group devoted the remainder of its platform solely to prohibition. In contrast, the "Broad Gauge" faction, assembling as the National party rather than the Prohibition party, gave its blessing to Charles Bentley of Nebraska and J. H. Southgate of North Carolina. Unlike the 1892 National Prohibition party platform, which sidestepped the monetary issue without taking a stand, this document came out openly for the free coinage of silver at a ratio of 16 to 1; more vague was the tariff plank, which advocated that "import duties should be levied as a means of securing equitable commercial relations with other nations." Populist influences were noticeable in new planks recommending that the President, Vice President, and US Senators be elected by direct vote, and that the initiative, referendum, and proportional representation be adopted.

The Republicans were the first major party to meet, at St. Louis in June. Here the leading candidate was Governor William McKinley of Ohio, the one-time tariff expert of the House of Representatives; McKinley was the candidate of the brilliant political manipulator, Cleveland industrialist and financier, Marcus Hanna. Another leading candidate was Speaker of the House Thomas Reed of Maine, who favored a gold standard and was popular in the East. Although there were other Presidential possibilities as well, including Matthew Quay, Levi Morton, and William Allison, McKinley won the nomination with ease on the first ballot , after endorsing the gold standard and renouncing a policy of straddling. He proved to be the last Civil War participant that the Republicans were to nominate for the highest office in the land. To the skeptical *Nation*, "McKinley's absence of settled convictions about leading questions of the day, and his want of clear knowledge of any subject, make him emphatically the round man in the round hole";[2] this assessment was perhaps unfair, in light of his tariff views. After Reed had rejected the Vice Presidency, Hanna and the convention political bosses gave their nod to the relatively undistinguished Garret Hobart, the Governor of New Jersey.

Although Senator-elect Joseph Foraker of Ohio was again the chairman of the Resolutions Committee, Speaker Reed's supporters and friends dominated the platform writing. Praising "the matchless achievements of the thirty years of Republican rule," this document lambasted the Cleveland administration for its "record of unparalleled incapacity, dishonor and disaster." The Wilson-Gorman Tariff, which hardly pleased Cleveland, was to the Republicans "sectional, injurious to the public credit and destructive to business enterprise." Here the sugar producers were singled out as innocent victims. Equally outspoken was the monetary plank, which placed the Republicans more squarely on the side of gold than any other platform drawn up since the Civil War; the free coinage of silver was to be permitted only by international agreement, and past efforts in the latter direction had not proved successful.

Anticipating the rise of America to world power status, the foreign policy planks were more numerous than usual. In addition to the customary plea for a Nicaragua Canal, there was a demand for the annexation of the Hawaiian Islands and the purchase of the Danish (i.e., Virgin) Islands. Recent massacres and related atrocities that had taken place in Armenia were deplored, as was the treatment of American residents in Turkey and the destruction of American property there. Even more significant was the plank advocating Cuban independence: "We watch with deep and abiding interest the heroic battles of the Cuban patriots against cruelty and oppression, and best hopes go out for the full success of their determined contest for liberty." Another first was the recommendation that the citizens of Alaska should have representation in Congress.

By taking a firm stand in favor of a gold standard instead of endorsing bimetalism, the platform drafters precipitated a walk-out of several dozen silverites led by long-time Republican Henry Teller of Colorado, later the sponsor of that amendment forbidding the United States to exercise sovereignty over Cuba. Teller offered a minority plank advocating the coinage of silver at 16 to 1, which lost by the lopsided margin of 818½ to 105½. Teller's speech, like Bryan's at the upcoming Democratic convention, was dramatic, but unlike Bryan's address, proved futile; in his own words, "I cannot before my country and my God, agree to the provision that shall put upon this country a gold standard, and I will not."[3] Despite his poor showing in the actual vote, the fact remains that only one delegate west of the Missouri favored a gold plank, so that at least in sectional terms Teller's stand was a representative one.

Teller was later to surface again at the Democratic convention in Chicago on July 7, where he was a Presidential possibility along with Horace Boies, Richard Bland, and William Jennings Bryan. The latter two individuals had helped frame "The Appeal of the Silver Democrats" over a year earlier, which advocated the free coinage of silver at the ratio of 16 to 1. At this convention the free silver faction was decidedly in control: the Clevelands and the Olneys played only a subordinate role. Since the debate on the platform came before that on the candidates, Bryan was afforded the opportunity to mesmerize the convention in a defense of the majority report, and he did so in his immortal "Cross of Gold" Speech—unquestionably the most remarkable address ever delivered at a national nominating convention. In one of his less charitable moments, Republican Joseph Foraker observed that like the River Platte Bryan was "six inches deep and six miles wide at the mouth,"[4] but the "Great Commoner" could have had his party's Presidential nomination on the first ballot had the voting taken place immediately. Instead, there was an interval, and it took five ballots for the former two-term Nebraska Congressman to overcome Bland's initial lead. The convention's choice for the second position also proved quite interesting: Arthur Sewall of Maine, a banker, industrialist, and corporation director who nevertheless was a silverite. Like Bryan, he won on the fifth ballot.

By the time the candidates had been chosen, as noted above, the platform had been written by the Resolutions Committee headed by Senator James K. Jones of Arkansas. Despite the fact that it did depart from past Democratic tradition by endorsing the free coinage of silver at the ratio of 16 to 1, and attacking gold monometallism as a British policy, the 1896 document by no means embraced the whole parcel of Populist reforms. Unlike the section dealing with money, that examining the tariff reflected more orthodox Democratic attitudes. On the other hand, although it did invoke the name of Jefferson, it also failed to praise the record of the Cleveland administration, an omission with few parallels in American political history. In fact, its stand against the use of injunctions against labor constituted an attack on Cleveland and Olney relative to their handling of the Pullman Strike, since its condemnation of "trafficking with banking syndicates" represented an indictment of Cleveland's dealings with J. P. Morgan. It takes little imagination or effort to interpret

the unprecedented anti-third term plank as an attempt to discourage Cleveland from again seeking the Presidency. Another
target was the Supreme Court, which the previous year had
declared a federal income tax law invalid.

Despite their differences, it is often overlooked that in 1896 there
were quite a few similarities between the two major party
platforms. Following the lead of the Republicans, the Democrats
approved a plank recommending that Alaska be granted a delegate
in Congress, along with one expressing sympathy with the people
of Cuba "in their heroic struggle for liberty and indepencence"; as
David Hill pointed out during the debate on the platform, the
Republican and Democratic documents resembled each other in
their stands on pensions, the territories, and civil service. The
Democrats, however, paid far less attention to foreign affairs than
did the Republicans, as they made no mention, for example, of an
international agreement on silver.

The debate on the platform was long and tumultuous, punctu-
ated with applause and boos. "Pitchfork Ben" Tillman of South
Carolina, the leadoff speaker for the majority report and a long-
time foe of Cleveland, made the memorable observation in
response to his critics that: "There are only three things in the
world that can hiss—a goose, a serpent, and a man."[5] Tillman
later in his address introduced a resolution denouncing the
Cleveland administration as undemocratic and tyrannical, but he
eventually withdrew this after the convention had failed to amend
the platform in praise of it. Despite the excitement aroused by
Tillman's speech, it paled to insignificance when compared with
Bryan's defense of the majority report. Far from being an
impromptu effort, Bryan's speech had been long in preparation;
according to one observer, he had mentioned before delivering it
that it would gain him the nomination. This address closed with
the immortal cry, ". . . you shall not press down upon the brow of
labor this crown of thorns. You shall not crucify mankind upon a
cross of gold."[6] But a closer reading of Bryan''s speech reveals
several other points of interest: the concept that rural attorneys,
crossroads shopkeepers, farmers, and miners were businessmen;
the idea that its farms were more vital to America than its great
cities; the linking of Wall Street with Great Britain in a conspiracy
against free silver.

After the convention had rejected an amendment embracing

gold more firmly, 303 to 626, and another one praising the Cleveland administration, 357 to 546, it then adopted the majority report, 628 to 301. Significantly, the Clevelandites did not bolt, despite the indignities they suffered; nevertheless, 178 "sound money" men refused to vote either for the platform or for the candidate, with the result that Bryan and Sewall received a two-thirds majority only of those actually voting. Yet even had the "gold bugs" blocked Bryan or Bland by casting ballots against them, they had no truly strong candidate of their own, nor could they have nominated one, in any event.

Meeting at St. Louis in July, the National Silver Republicans, led by Senator Henry Teller of Colorado, expressed their dissatisfaction with the regular Republican gold plank by endorsing the Democratic candidates, Bryan and Sewall. Attacking the domination of America by the money power—"a power more destructive than any which has ever been fastened upon the civilized men of any race or in any age"— they embraced the free coinage of silver at a ratio of 16 to 1: "We are in favor of restoring to the people of the United States the time-honored money of the Constitution-gold and silver, not one, but both-the money of Washington, Hamilton, Jefferson, Monroe, Jackson, and Lincoln." Whereas third-party platforms frequently deal with a galaxy of issues, this one focused exclusively on the monetary question.

That very same day (July 22) the Populists also assembled in St. Louis. Nominating for President the "Boy Orator of the Platte," Bryan, the convention delegates maintained their separate identity from the Democrats by selecting for Vice President Thomas Watson of Georgia, an ex-Congressman and country editor. Bryan had announced publicly that he would not accept the Populist nomination unless Sewall was picked as his running-mate. Aside from Bryan, the leading Presidential possibility was S. F. Norton, the relatively unknown editor of a Populist newspaper in Illinois. Turning to the Resolutions Committee, its chairman was General James Weaver, the 1892 Presidential nominee; the drafters noted their allegiance to the previous platform, declaring that the financial question was "the pressing issue," and recommending the free coinage of silver at a ratio of 16 to 1. "The influence of European moneychangers," observed this document, "has been more potent in shaping legislation than the voice of the American people."

Despite the claim of Senator Marion Butler of North Carolina
that the Democrats had committed "petty and grand larceny by
stealing the People's platform almost in its entirity,"[7] an examination of the two documents suggests that it was the Democrats who
were the pioneers. This is particularly true of the resolutions
attacking the Supreme Court for its voiding of the income tax law,
and the Cleveland administration for its military intervention in
the Pullman Strike. Another plank not found in past Populist
platforms expressed sympathy for the Cuban people in their quest
for political freedom and independence, but this merely imitated
similar Republican and Democratic planks adopted in 1896. One
vocal reformer, Jacob Coxey, also failed in his attempt to persuade
the Resolutions Committee to endorse public works programs for
the unemployed. Because of its derivative character, therefore, one
must challenge the widespread notion that most of the new ideas
during this period originated with the Populists; if anything is
obvious from the analysis presented thus far, it is that the
Populists were vastly overrated as political innovators.

While the Clevelandites did not actually bolt the Democratic
convention, as the Tellerites had walked out of the Republican
one, they did convene at Indianapolis in September to nominate
an independent slate and ratify a separate platform. Delegates
from forty-one states and three territories were present. In a
brilliant piece of ticket-balancing the delegates chose for President
John Palmer of Illinois, a former Union general, and for Vice
President Simon Buckner of Kentucky, a former Confederate
general. The National Democratic platform, which was prepared
in advance by Senator William Vilas of Wisconsin and others,
came out for a gold standard and a revenue tariff, praised
Cleveland, and depreciated attacks on the Supreme Court. After
condemning the Chicago platform, the National Democrats
charged that the Republicans were wrecking the nation with their
high tariff, while the Populists were ruining it with their silverite
agitation. Stressing "traditional" Democratic principles, this
document concentrated almost entirely on domestic affairs, aside
from a plank favoring the use of arbitration in the settlement of
international disputes.

By far the most radical convention to meet in 1896 was that of the
Socialist Labor party, which sat at New York City on July 4. Its
ticket consisted of Charles Matchett of New York for President and

Matthew Maguire of New Jersey for Vice President; Matchett had been the Vice Presidential candidate in 1892. Instead of recommending the abolition of the Presidency, Vice Presidency, and the Senate, like it had done four years previously, this platform restricted itself to the abolition of the Senate and all upper legislative chambers, and of the veto power of the executive (national, state, or municipal). Other than this, though, its list of recommended reforms coincided with those drawn up for 1892.

The focal point of the campaign was Bryan, who made 600 speeches to five million people in twenty-nine states during fourteen weeks. Even Republican William Allen White observed retrospectively, "It was the first time in my life and in the life of a generation in which any man large enough to lead a national party had boldly and unashamedly made his cause that of the poor and the oppressed."[8] Although Bryan did embrace the free silver cause, he did not go along with the Populists in demanding federal paternalistic legislation; nor, despite his admitted powers as an orator, was he a profound thinker capable of forging a new political ideology. But the Republicans, backed by a huge campaign fund, were able with considerable success to paint Bryan as an anarchist and revolutionist who was fomenting class conflict and encouraging violence and bloodshed.

With respect to the other major candidate, McKinley, he stayed at home in Canton, Ohio, waging a "front porch" campaign on behalf of the "full dinner pail," with a protective tariff and the gold standard his key themes. Both McKinley and Hanna had a creditable record vis-a-vis labor, and the Republicans intimidated the laboring man with threats of closed factories if Bryan won. There was no need to intimidate the incumbent President, Cleveland, who privately asserted that the Bryanites had committed a crime against the Democratic party worthy of the penitentiary. The Palmer ticket provided a convenient way out for his supporters who could not back Bryan because of free silver and who could not support McKinley because of the protective tariff; one disgrunted party member observed, "I am a Democrat still— very still."[9]

In an election that matched the agrarian West and South against the moneyed East, Bryan ran the strongest of his three Presidential races, but lost to McKinley, 6,467,946 popular votes to 7,035,638, and 176 electoral votes to 271. The Prohibitionist, Levering, edged

Palmer for third place, 141,676 to 131,529. Not only did the Republicans win every county in New England and every northern state east of the Mississippi, but they held on to the old Granger states as well: Illinois, Wisconsin, Iowa, and Minnesota. New York, which had gone Democratic in 1892 by 46,000 popular votes, went Republican in 1896 by 268,000; Bryan had once referred to the East, and to New York in particular, as "the enemy's country."[10] The Republicans, moreover, swept the ten largest cities, retained control of Congress, and for the first time in their history achieved an absolute majority in the popular vote. (It must be remembered that quite a few of the post-Civil War elections were relatively close, and there were several third-party entries in the field aside from the two major ones.) Nevertheless, the fact remains that a change of 14,000 votes in a half-dozen states would have produced a Bryan majority in the Electoral College.

XVII. 1900

Imperialism Vindicated

The first McKinley administration was blessed by a revival of prosperity, a development which quite naturally proved a political asset to the Republicans. As they promised in their 1896 platform, there was a return to protection with the Dingley Tariff of 1897; three years later the Gold Standard Act of 1900 dealt a fatal blow to the 16 to 1 philosophy. But it was in the foreign relations field that the McKinley administration truly made its mark on history. The Spanish-American War of 1898 led to US acquisition of colonies in the Philippines, Guam, and Puerto Rico, while an independent Hawaii voluntarily joined this nation the same year. In 1899 Samoa was divided between America and Germany. Thanks to its growing Pacific empire, the United States was in a stronger position to preserve inviolate its Open Door Policy towards China, as the twentieth century dawned. At home the silverites continued to agitate for the implementation of their pet panacea, but a new, equally vocal school of anti-imperialists arose following the acquisition of an overseas empire. The Treaty of Paris ending the Spanish-American War passed the Senate by a narrow 57 to 27 margin; fortunately for the expansionists, William Jennings Bryan had decreed that the colonial question should be fought out during the Election of 1900, and not on the floors of Congress. Unlike in 1896, therefore, foreign affairs were a focal point of the campaign.

There were two Socialist conventions in 1900, those of the Social Democratic party and of the Socialist Labor party. The first of these was at Indianapolis in March, and it nominated a slate of Eugene Debs of Indiana for President and Job Harriman of California for Vice President. Perhaps the most radical innovation it its platform was the call for public ownership of all gold, silver, copper, lead, coal, as well as all oil and gas; this marked a drastic step beyond the earlier proposal that all railroads, telegraphs, and telephones be nationalized. As for labor legislation, not only was it to be national, but also international in scope where possible, and was to include national accident, unemployment, and old-age insurance prophetic of the Social Security Act of 1935. Then there was the Socialist Labor party convention, which assembled in June at New York City. Having selected Joseph Maloney of Massachusetts as its Presidential candidate, it turned to Valentine Remmel of Pennsylvania for his running-mate, and adopted the first half of its 1896 platform as its 1900 platform. Absent this time were the twenty-one specific resolutions that had been a key part of the 1896 document.

Another party that split into two warring wings in 1900 was the Populists, with the anti-fusion Middle-of-the-Road faction contending against the Fusion faction that backed the Democratic slate. The former met at Cincinnati in May to endorse Wharton Barker of Pennsylvania for President and Ignatius Donnelly of Minnesota for Vice President. An examination of its platform reveals few points of interest, other than that federal judges be directly elected by the people in addition to the President, Vice President, and US Senators. In length this document was only one-quarter that of the Populist platform of 1896, unlike its Fusion faction counterpart in 1900, though it did reaffirm the Omaha platform of earlier Populist days.

More united were the Republicans, who assembled at Philadelphia in June to renominate William McKinley for President by a unanimous vote. The big fight was over the Vice Presidency; the incumbent, Garret Hobart, had died the previous year. By this time Spanish-American War hero Theodore Roosevelt had been elected governor of New York, and state political boss Thomas Platt, angered by his semi-independence, successfully maneuvered him into Hobart's position in an attempt to be rid of TR. Another powerful Republican figure, Senator Matthew Quay of Pennsylvania, made an unsuccessful attempt to reduce the strength of the southern delegations in upcoming conventions.

There was no debate on the platform, but the Resolutions Committee, chaired by Senator Charles Fairbanks of Indiana, did make a number of changes in the original sketch prepared by Postmaster-General Charles Smith with the approval of President McKinley. (A plank dealing with Congressional legislation relative to Puerto Rico was eliminated.) To no one's surprise, the finished product embraced both the gold standard and the protective tariff without mentioning an international agreement on silver, as in 1896. There was the usual plank recommending liberal pensions to army and navy veterans and their families, which in the opinion of Republican party historian William Myers "were steadily becoming a greater scandal and reproach";[1] there also was the usual civil service plank, a rather hypocritical gesture, in that the McKinley administration had actually undermined the merit system. Yet the domestic planks did support some reforms, including the extension of Rural Free Delivery service and the establishment of a Department of Commerce and Industries.

Refraining from overtly preaching a doctrine of imperialism and expansion, this document asserted that the American people "have conducted, and in victory concluded, a war for liberty and human rights. No thought of National aggrandizement tarnished the high purpose with which American standards were unfurled. It was a war unsought and patiently resisted, but when it came, the American Government was ready." With respect to the Philippines, the American government had suppressed an "armed insurrection" there, but there was no call for a large standing army, despite the efforts of numerous Republicans in Congress to create one. McKinley's handling of the Samoan treaty and

Hawaiian annexation was also praised, while the construction of an isthmian (not a Nicaraguan) canal was again recommended; the need to find markets for farm surpluses was noted, especially in the Orient.

A far different interpretation of American domestic and foreign policy permeated the Democratic convention at Kansas City in July. There was less of an attempt than in 1896 to humor the demands of the Populists and Silver Republicans, although William Jennings Bryan was again the Presidential nominee. Bryan's race in 1896 had been a quite creditable one, but he received the party's nod four years later more or less by default, since McKinley's seeming invincibility at the polls discouraged potential Democratic rivals. Rather than balance the ticket with an Easterner, as they had done with Sewall in 1896, the Democrats turned to a former Vice President, Adlai Stevenson of Illinois, for the second position. Stevenson thus was on different occasions the running-mate of both Cleveland and Bryan. David Hill of New York might have had the Vice Presidential nomination if he so desired, but by withdrawing his name he paved the way for Stevenson.

The lengthy Democratic platform of 1900 differed most markedly from its predecessor in the extra attention it paid to foreign affairs. Senator James K. Jones of Arkansas was the Chairman of the sharply divided Resolutions Committee. Attacking the Dingley Tariff as "a trust breeding measure," this document also lambasted the Gold Standard Act of 1900, and endorsed the free coinage of silver at the ratio of 16 to 1. Most members of the Committee on Resolutions would have preferred to have the convention approve in general the document ratified in 1896, without specifically mentioning silver, but Bryan would have none of this subterfuge, and threatened unless his demands were met to force a convention debate and to reject the Presidential nomination. Despite his undoubtedly sincere threat, the Resolutions Committee upheld Bryan by only one vote. One domestic plank new to Democratic platforms reflecting Populist ideology was the call for the direct election of US Senators.

With respect to foreign policy, the Democratic platform was strongly anti-imperialistic, declaring that imperialism was the "paramount" issue of this campaign: "We assert that no nation can long endure half republic and half empire, and we warn the

American people that imperialism abroad will lead quickly and inevitably to despotism at home." Taking a position diametrically opposite to that of the Republicans, the Democrats attacked the "greedy commercialism" of McKinley's Philippine policy, and labelled as "criminal aggression" his war against the Filipino insurgents. In opposing militarism this platform favored the National Guard over a large standing army; it supported the acquisition of overseas territories only when they might become states later. Unlike the Republicans, the Democrats condemned the McKinley administration's handling of the Boer War and the "ill concealed Republican alliance with England." Nor did the Democrats endorse the Republican Caribbean policy, especially that towards Puerto Rico, Cuba, and Nicaragua. Although the delegates unanimously adopted the platform, this Democratic document was still anathema to some contemporary journalistic observers. To *Gunton's Magazine,* for example "Nothing worse in finance was ever suggested,"[2] while to *Harper's Weekly,* "Mr. Bryan's platform is a threat."[3]

While the National Democratic party composed of followers of Cleveland and the gold Democrats did not hold a convention in 1900, instead adopting resolutions affirming the Indianapolis platform of 1896, both the Fusion faction of the Populist party and the Silver Republicans held conventions where they endorsed Bryan for President, but ratified separate platforms. At its Sioux Falls gathering the Fusion faction of the Populists followed the lead of the Democrats by embracing free silver and attacking imperialism; it added Washington and Lincoln to Jefferson and Jackson in invoking a quartet of heroes. (Reference also was made to the "Lincoln greenback.") Among the more original planks of this document were those attacking the use of the military against the striking Coeur d'Alene miners, and differentiating among Mongolian, Japanese, and Malaysian immigration in a plea for restrictions on oriental immigration.

On the other hand, the Silver Republicans paid particular homage to Lincoln at their Kansas City meeting, but also favorably mentioned Washington and Jefferson. Their platform contained no truly new planks, being instead a mixture of free silverism, Populism, and anti-imperialism. Among the more memorable passages was one pointing out that past American Congresses had expressed sympathy towards revolutionary uprisings on the part of the French, the Greeks, the Hungarians, the Polish, the Armenians, and the Cubans, but had not done so in the case of the Boers. Imperialist Westerners, like Teller, clashed with anti-imperialist Easterners; thus the Filipino plank straddled the issue, rather than condemn the McKinley administration outright.

Unlike 1896, there was only one Prohibition party ticket in the field during 1900. Meeting at Chicago in June, the delegates endorsed a slate of John Woolley of Illinois for President and Henry Metcalf of Rhode Island for Vice President. The Prohibition party platform, which was much longer than its 1896 counterpart, focused almost entirely on the liquor question, but contains a great deal of prose quotable if only because of its extremist *Weltanschauung*. "So long as the saloon debauches the citizens and breeds the purchasable voter," observed this document, "money will continue to buy its way to power." For the first time in the history of American political platforms, Edmund Burke was quoted, but with respect to his definition of party rather than his views on prohibition. The anti-imperialist argument also received a new twist in a reference to the deleterious effect of American-produced liquor on the citizens of Alaska, Hawaii, the Philippines, and Cuba. McKinley was written off as a failure as President, not because of his views on the tariff, gold, or imperialism, but because of "his conspicuous example as a wine-drinker at public banquets and a wine-serving host in the White House." Today, observed the platform, there were only two real parties relative to the liquor traffic: the Perpetuationists and Prohibitionists.

With the exception of Henry Clay, perhaps no other major political leader in American political history had the unfortunate knack of selecting the wrong issue at the wrong time as did William Jennings Bryan. In making imperialism the paramount issue in the Election of 1900, Bryan failed to excite voters more interested in Republican prosperity and the "full dinner pail"; he eventually turned to the trusts as a more appealing topic during the course of the more than 600 speeches which he delivered. Successfully keeping the explosive Chinese situation out of the campaign, the Republicans compared the anti-imperialists with the Filipino guerillas; Mark Hanna observed relative to overseas economic contacts, "If it is commercialism for the Republican party or the American people to look beyond the borders of our own country to find markets for our surplus products, then I am for commercialism."[4] An imperialist stance, in fact, probably helped the Republicans at the ballot box in the Far West. Generally speaking, this campaign proved less inflammatory than that four years before, with the eastern newspapers and business interests solidly arrayed against Bryan. The latter did run a respectable race in 1900, but he failed to equal his performance in 1896. The totals for the two major party candidates were: McKinley, 7,219,530 popular votes and 292 electoral votes; Bryan, 6,358,071 popular votes and 155 electoral votes; as Roosevelt did most of the Republican speech-making, the contest in effect was one between Bryan and TR. Lagging far behind were the Prohibitionist Woolley (209,166), the Socialist Debs (94,768), and the Populist Barker (50,232). Ironically, McKinley, who had just won re-election as President, was to have his political career cut short within a year by assassination, while Bryan, the two-time loser, was to survive still another Presidential defeat before ending his public career at the Dayton, Tennessee, evolution trial in 1925.

XVIII. 1904

Alton Who?

On September 6, 1901, Leon Czolgosz, an anarchist, shot President William McKinley during a reception at the Pan-American Exposition at Buffalo, New York. McKinley lingered on for eight days, and then died. His death catapulted into the White House the dynamic Theodore Roosevelt, much to the displeasure of Marcus Hanna, Thomas Platt, and other old-line Republican political bosses. Confronted with a Republican Congressional leadership dominated by such conservative figures as Joseph Cannon in the House and Nelson Aldrich in the Senate, TR also had to preside over a party that ideologically was split along sectional lines, with the western wing the more liberal. Nevertheless, Roosevelt's first administration was highlighted domestically by such achievements as the filing of the Northern Securities Company suit, the intervention in the Pennsylvania anthracite coal strike, the signing of the Newlands Act providing for federal irrigation projects, the establishment of a Department of Commerce and Labor, and the passage of the Elkins Act outlawing rebates to railway shippers.

While TR's domestic program, often referred to as the "Square Deal," had its moments of excitement, it was more than matched by his foreign policy, frequently described as "Big Stick" diplomacy. When the Colombian Senate failed to give its assent to a canal treaty in 1903, Roosevelt gave his blessing to a revolt in Panama culminating in independence. TR also promulgated his own interpretation of the Monroe Doctrine, the so-called Roosevelt Corollary. After England and Germany had made threatening gestures towards Venezuela in the winter of 1901-1902 over the latter's failure to pay its debts, TR had the United States take over the Dominican Republic's finances in 1904 to forestall a possible European intervention. As chief executive, it was clear, Roosevelt was no figurehead.

Following the example set in 1900, the Socialists fielded two separate tickets and ratified two separate platforms in 1904. Meeting at Chicago in May, the Socialist party nominated Eugene Debs of Indiana for President and Benjamin Hanford of New York for Vice President. While the Social Democratic platform of 1900 had included twelve "immediate demands," the Socialist platform of 1904 buried its specific proposals near the beginning of section five. A national party referendum later endorsed this document by the overwhelming vote of 5,776 to 549. Then there was the Socialist Labor party, which fielded a slate of Charles Corregan of New York and William Cox of Illinois at its July gathering in New York. Like its 1900 counterpart, the 1904 Socialist Labor platform was sheer rhetoric, devoid of concrete demands.

Senator Marcus Hanna of Ohio died in February 1904, and his passing removed the only real threat to Theodore Roosevelt's renomination. There was an undercurrent of resentment against TR during the June Republican gathering at Chicago, but he nevertheless won his party's Presidential nomination by a unanimous vote; in praising Roosevelt, Frank Black observed, "He is not conservative, if conservatism means waiting till it is too late."[1] The ticket was balanced geographically and ideologically by the choice of Charles Fairbanks, an Indiana conservative, for Vice President; the selection of Speaker of the House Joseph Cannon to be permanent chairman of the convention was generally interpreted as another bow to the "Old Guard" faction. Aside from the interest generated by convention business proper, a flurry of excitement also occurred when the convention learned of Secretary of State John Hay's telegram to the American consul to Morocco, declaring, "We want either Perdicaris alive or Raisuli dead,"[2] Raisuli was a native chieftain who had kidnapped Perdicaris, allegedly a naturalized American citizen. Since negotiations were already underway to secure Perdicaris's release, the publication of this message seems in retrospect a theatrical gesture to emphasize TR's decisiveness.

The Republican platform in 1904 was also shaped to a considerable degree by party conservatives, with Senator Henry Cabot Lodge of Massachusetts chairing the Committee on Resolutions; to the *Nation* it was a case of "a bold and forthright candidate standing upon a mixture of trickery and hypocrisy."[3] As in 1900, there was a firm endorsement of both the gold standard and the protective tariff. From the standpoint of domestic reform, perhaps the most interesting plank was that dealing with the trusts: "Combinations of capital and labor are the results of the economic movement of the age, but neither must be permitted to infringe upon the rights and interests of the people." Roosevelt, it must be remembered, was the first Republican (or Democratic) President to engage actively in trust-busting. One paragraph that the *Outlook* criticized as "a great blunder"[4] advocated a proportional reduction in the representation in Congress and in the Electoral College of those states which had "unconstitutionally limited" the elective franchise; over the last decade and a half Louisiana, Mississippi, Alabama, South Carolina, North Carolina, and Virginia had disenfranchised the Negro. "I think," observed TR, "it is the only insincere plank in the platform."[5]

The Republican document, too, paid a great deal of attention to foreign affairs, praising the Roosevelt administration's policies towards the Philippines, China, Puerto Rico, Cuba, and Panama. As expected, one paragraph towards the end eulogized William McKinley; more unprecedented were those extolling the merits of

TR, the longest such passage to date in the history of political platforms. Describing Roosevelt as possessed of "a clear hand, a brave heart, and earnest patriotism, and high ideals of public duty and public service," this document noted with approval TR's record both with regard to foreign and domestic affairs.

Meeting at Springfield, Illinois, on July 4, the Populist party selected as its Presidential candidate the 1896 Vice Presidential nominee, Thomas Watson of Georgia. His running-mate was Thomas Tibbles of Nebraska. The platform reaffirmed the Omaha statement of principles and subsequent party declarations without breaking much new ground; curiously, it paid homage not to past or present Populist leaders, but rather to the memory of Abraham Lincoln, citing him to the effect that labor is prior to capital. One passage that could easily have become a slogan was: "It is better for the Government to own the railroads than for the railroads to own the Government," but the demand for the nationalization of railroads had appeared in Populist platforms as early as the Omaha statement of principles.

Two days after the Populists assembled at Springfield, the Democrats gathered in St. Louis to nominate a ticket and write a platform. With respect to Presidential possibilities, Grover Cleveland was too old and David Hill too battle-scarred; two-time loser William Jennings Bryan eventually swung his weight behind Senator Francis Cockrell of Missouri. The nomination, however, went to Judge Alton Parker of New York on the first ballot. Parker was a relatively unknown, pro-gold, Cleveland Democrat who outdistanced his closest competitor, newspaper publisher William Randolph Hearst, by the decisive margin of 679 to 181. Since Bryan had failed to carry the North and the East in his two Presidential runs, Democratic strategists had concluded that it would be desirable to return to a northeastern Presidential nominee; Bryan himself was opposed to Parker, but refrained from bolting the party. For the New Yorker's running-mate the Democrats turned to ex-Senator Henry Davis of West Virginia, an octogenarian with little to recommend him as a candidate other than his ability to make a large campaign contribution.

In accepting the nomination Parker declared, in a letter made public to the delegates, "I regard the gold standard as firmly and irrevocably established, and shall act accordingly, if the action of the convention today shall be ratified by the people."[6] This time, however, there was no mention in the platform of the free coinage of silver at the ratio of 16 to 1 as there had been in 1896 and 1900, but, owing to Bryan's efforts, neither was there a plank endorsing the gold standard, as there was in the 1904 Republican platform. Far from being a trivial omission, the Democratic failure to take a stand on the monetary question in 1904 is one of the "great evasions" in the history of platform writing; the Chairman of the Committee on Resolutions who avoided this issue so adeptly was Senator John Daniel of Virginia.

Having frequently attacked past Republican Presidents during the Gilded Age for a lack of leadership, the Democrats in 1904 adopted an entirely different approach, lambasting Theodore Roosevelt for "executive usurpation of legislative and judicial functions," and charging him with conduct in office that was "spasmodic, erratic, sensational, spectacular, and arbitrary." The Democrats also took full credit for the Newlands Act. There was the customary indictment of the protective tariff, but this time couched in more memorable phraseology than usual: "We favor a revision and a gradual reduction of the tariff by the friends of the masses and for the commonweal, and not by friends of its abuses, its extortions, and its discriminations." Perhaps the most unusual domestic plank was the one calling for the extermination of polygamy in the United States and recommending the complete separation of church and state in political affairs, a stance far more typical of past Republican platforms than Democratic ones.

With regard to imperialism, this document invoked George Washington, John Adams, and Thomas Jefferson in attacking recent American colonial policy, but foreign affairs took up far less space than domestic affairs. Significantly, in endorsing a Panama Canal, there was no criticism of TR's isthmian dealings. One new plank did advocate a more liberal trade arrangement with Canada, a proposal that was to give a later Republican President, William Howard Taft, more trouble than he had bargained for when he attempted to implement it.

The previous month, in June, the Prohibition party met at Indianapolis to select as its Presidential candidate, Silas Swallow of Pennsylvania, and as his running-mate, George Carroll of Texas. Unlike in 1900, there was no attempt to blame the US government for encouraging the consumption of alcoholic beverages in various territories and nations abroad; this time there was a list of specific reforms in areas other than prohibition at the end of the document rather than a rambling discourse on the merits of prohibition interspersed with various demands. Perhaps the most interesting plank was the last, which called for the reform of divorce laws, the abolition of polygamy, and the crushing of prostitution.

When the campaign unfolded, it became quite apparent that Theodore Roosevelt was more liberal on most economic and social questions than Judge Parker, but the Morgans and the Harrimans nevertheless backed TR. Why? According to the New York *Sun*, "We prefer the impulsive candidate of the party of conservatives to the conservative candidate of the party which the business interests regard as permanently and dangerously impulsive."[7] Bryan did give nominal support to the ticket, but a considerable number of his followers probably voted for the Populist or the Socialist(s) candidates; Parker drew his support at the polls almost exclusively from Cleveland Democrats and Southern Democrats. The key issues of the campaign included Roosevelt's imperialistic policies towards Panama and the Philippines, Republican ties with big business, and the antitrust question, which Parker wished to handle under the common law.

Taking only 38 percent of the popular vote, Parker went down to a crushing defeat at the hands of TR, while the Republicans maintained control of both houses of Congress. Roosevelt outdistanced Parker by a three-to-two margin in the popular vote, 7,628,834 to 5,084,401, and by a 2½ to 1 margin in the electoral vote, 336 to 140; TR took every northern and western state, with the Republicans carrying Missouri for the first time. Parker, who ran a conventional and ineffective campaign, did well only in the South. To sum up the third parties, the Socialist candidate Debs polled 402,460 popular votes, the Prohibitionist candidate Swallow 259,257, and the Populist candidate Watson 114,753. At the moment of his victory, Theodore Roosevelt, the first "accidental" President to succeed himself, announced that he would not be available in 1908 for what would have amounted to a 3rd term: "under no circumstances will I be a candidate for or accept another nomination."[8] In the years that followed, when Taft fumbled and faltered as chief executive, Roosevelt came to regret that brash utterance, and by 1912 he was ready to challenge Taft for the leadership of the Republican party.

XIX. 1908

Bryan Goes Down a Third Time

Unlike Cleveland, TR's second term as chief executive proved more liberal than his first, though again there was no action on tariff reform, revision, or reduction. During 1906 alone the Hepburn Act providing for stricter railroad regulation, the Pure Food and Drug Act, and the Meat Inspection Act were signed into law, despite a lukewarm response on the part of eastern conservatives. On the other hand, when the Panic of 1907 broke out following the suspension of the Knickerbocker Trust Company in New York, Roosevelt allowed U. S. Steel to acquire the Tennessee Coal and Iron Company, with the understanding that this merger would not lead to an antitrust suit. Another result of this panic was the passage of the Aldrich-Vreeland Act the following year, which set up a National Monetary Commission with Nelson Aldrich as chairman. There also was a White House Conservation Conference in 1908, a meeting that reflected one of TR's great interests.

In the foreign affairs field, jingoist Roosevelt ironically won the Nobel Peace Prize in 1905 for helping to settle the Russo-Japanese War. A more thorny issue was the presence of the Japanese in California, and their segregation in the San Francisco schools, leading to the Gentlemen's Agreement of 1907, under which Japan promised to curtail severely emigration to the United States. In 1906 the United States also participated in the Algeciras Conference on Morocco; towards the end of his second term, TR sent the bulk of the US navy on a world cruise, while work began in earnest on the Panama Canal.

The Populists were first to hold a national convention in 1908; they assembled at St. Louis in April to nominate a ticket of Thomas Watson of Georgia for President and Samuel Williams of Indiana for Vice President. Watson, it will be recalled, had been the previous standard-bearer of the party. In 1908 the Populists again continued their practice of reaffirming the Omaha platform of 1892, as the Democrats had done prior to the Civil War relative to their platform of 1840. Unlike the 1904 document, though, which had invoked the memory of Lincoln, this statement of principles also praised Washington's Farewell Address and the state papers of Jefferson. Aside from the plank opposing gambling in futures, most of the truly new planks concerned labor; the Populists endorsed public works in time of depression for unemployed workingmen, advocated an employer's liability act, and raged against "criminal carelessness" in the operation of mines. In a Biblical reference rare in political platforms, but typical of Bryan, the "syncophants of monopoly" were compared with Judas Iscariot. There was no mention at all of foreign affairs, not even a token endorsement of anti-imperialism.

When the Republicans assembled at Chicago two months later, there was an undercurrent of sentiment for drafting Roosevelt for a third term, but on the first ballot TR was able to impose on the convention his choice for the nomination, William Howard Taft. Among the other Presidential possibilities were Robert La Follette, Joseph Cannon, Charles Evans Hughes, and Charles Fairbanks. Taft, a three-hundred pounder, had been Governor General of the Philippines and Secretary of War; he did not actively seek the Presidency to the extent that most other successful candidates have. For his running-mate the convention selected Representative James "Sunny Jim" Sherman of New York, a decision that might be interpreted as a concession to the anti-Roosevelt wing of the party. Significantly, the most prolonged demonstration during this convention—even longer than that precipitated by Bryan's Cross of Gold Speech—was touched off by Senator Henry Cabot Lodge's reference to TR as "the most abused and most popular man in the United States today."[1]

Senator Albert Hopkins of Illinois was selected to head the Committee on Resolutions, which brought in a platform that glorified Lodge's close friend, Roosevelt, to the skies: "The highest aspirations of the American people have found a voice." In differentiating the Republican party from the Democratic one, this document levelled the charge of socialism against the latter, which was to become a daily accusation during the era of the New Deal. To maintain, however, that the Republican platform stood in reactionary contrast to its Democratic counterpart in 1908, would be quite inaccurate, since the former not only endorsed the Aldrich-Vreeland Act and the Hepburn Act, but also recommended a stricter enforcement of antitrust legislation, and an expansion of the conservation program. There were a number of declarations in favor of labor reform; nevertheless, that upholding the use of labor injunctions incurred the wrath of both the AFL and the National Association of Manufacturers. The call for tariff "revision" by means of the maximum and minimum principle was in line with Taft's support of reduced rates, but the declaration that "protected industries" should enjoy a profit made its appearance here in a Republican platform for the first time.

With respect to foreign policy, one plank lauded the growth of Latin American commerce, along with the Pan-American movement, while another praised the ratification by the US Senate of eleven Hague conventions and twelve arbitration treaties. In line with past utterances, there also was an endorsement of American policy towards Cuba, Puerto Rico, Panama, and the Philippines; considering TR's vigorous Big Stick diplomacy, a proportionately small amount of space was devoted to his achievements in this area. In an overall evaluation W. B. Fleming satirized "The Republican Platform Unmasked" for the *Arena*,[2] but the *Outlook* praised the literary skill of this "always clear and occasionally eloquent document," "free from evasions, truisms, and platitudes."[3]

Taking a step which anticipated the split of the Republican party four years later along liberal/conservative lines, the Resolutions Committee member from Wisconsin (Henry Cooper) presented a minority report that encompassed many of the demands of the La Follette wing. These included the direct election of US Senators, the physical valuation of the railroads, and the publicizing of campaign expenditures; to the Wisconsinite the majority report also had taken an unsatisfactory stand with respect to tariffs, injunctions, and trusts. What debate there was on the minority report centered around an exposition by Cooper of his views, although the majority made no real effort to challenge the ideas contained in this document. Three minority planks were voted on separately, with the direct election of US Senators losing by a 114 to 980 margin in the best showing of the three; later, the convention adopted the majority report without a roll call. In attacking the minority report, some regulars cried: "Take it to Denver"; Denver was to be the site of the Democratic convention.

As in 1900 and 1904, there were two Socialist conventions. The Socialist party met at Chicago in May before the two major parties had convened, and the Socialist Labor party assembled at New

York City in July after the Republicans and Democrats had gathered. The Socialist party again nominated its 1904 slate of Eugene Debs of Indiana for President and Benjamin Hanford of New York for Vice President. Aside from the usual call for the governmental ownership of railroads, telegraphs, telephones, steamships, mines, quarries, oil wells, forests, and waterpower, there was an unprecedented demand for "The collective ownership of all industries which are organized on a national scale and in which competition has virtually ceased to exist." Equally innovative were the recommendations that the US Supreme Court be stripped of its power to declare acts of Congress unconstitutional, and that the US Constitution be amended by majority vote of the American people. Ten months after the November election, though, a national referendum of party members favored the deletion of that section of the platform advocating collective ownership of "all the land," by a vote of 5,382 (for) to 3,117 (against). In contrast to the Socialists, the Socialist Labor party again formulated a platform composed of generalities in endorsing August Gillhaus of New York for President and Donald Munro of Virginia for Vice President.

Turning their backs on their 1904 strategy of nominating a New Yorker for chief executive, the Democrats, meeting at Denver in July, gave their blessing to William Jennings Bryan for the third time. Bryan received 888½ votes out of 994 on the first ballot; two other names presented to the convention were those of John Johnson and George Gray. Compared with 1896 and 1900, there was less open hostility towards Bryan on the part of the Clevelandites and the "gold-bugs," since his earlier demand for the free coinage of silver at the ratio of 16 to 1 was no longer a viable issue. For the third time, too, Bryan failed to turn to the Northeast for the Vice Presidency, but instead endorsed as his running-mate John Kern of Indiana.

While Bryan was more acceptable to party conservatives the third time around than he had been previously, the platform was not as irritating to the Clevelandites and the "gold-bugs" as those of 1896 and 1900 had been, due to the fact that Oklahoma Governor Charles Haskell's Committee on Resolutions avoided extremism. Following the precedent set in 1904, it was again silent on the monetary question. Unlike the Republican document, there was a call for tariff reduction rather than tariff revision, while the plank

opposing the use of labor injunctions proved acceptable to
Samuel Gompers and other labor leaders. The Democratic document also included a demand for publicizing campaign contributions (a plank the Republican delegates had rejected) along with a
plea that corporations not be allowed to donate money to
campaign funds. Another Republican "reject" that made an
appearance here was an endorsement of the physical evaluation of
the railroads. The passage indicting the Republican party for the
Panic of 1907 was surprisingly mild; significantly, the Republicans had dismissed the panic in their platform as a mere
"financial disturbance" that had been overcome.

In a striking departure from custom, Republican President
Theodore Roosevelt was even praised by the Democrats with
respect to his conservation measures, "the enforcement of which
Mr. Roosevelt has vainly sought from a reluctant party," although
elsewhere he was lambasted by them for advocating "the establishment of a dynasty." (This was of course with reference to TR's
selecting Taft as his successor.) In increasing the number of
officeholders, Roosevelt had added 23,784 federal employees to the
payroll during the past year alone, in contrast to the total of 10,279
that Cleveland and McKinley had tapped for governmental
service. A special target of abuse was Speaker of the House Joseph
Cannon, who earned five caustic paragraphs under the heading:
"Arbitrary Power—The Speaker." It was, however, to be a liberal
Republican, Representative George Norris of Nebraska, who
would lead the successful movement several years later to reduce
Cannon's powers.

Turning to foreign policy, this document was less wordy than
its 1900 and 1904 counterparts, but with reference to the Philippines it again condemned "the experiment in imperialism as an
inexcusable blunder." There also were planks favoring closer
Pan-American relations and the reservation of the public lands of
Hawaii for bonafide settlers. The conclusion to this platform bore
a striking resemblance to the Republican document, in that the
two parties were contrasted: "The Democratic Party stands for
Democracy; the Republican party has drawn to itself all that is
aristocratic and plutocratic."

A week after the Democrats had assembled, the Prohibition
party met at Columbus, Ohio. Here Eugene Chafin of Illinois
received his party's Presidential nomination, with Aaron Watkins

of Ohio as his running-mate. Dispensing with much of the
rhetoric that had consumed past Prohibition party platforms, the
overwhelming bulk of this short document was taken up by a
fourteen-plank platform, only the first two of which dealt with the
prohibition issue. Quite a few of the planks were new to
Prohibition party platforms, but were commonly found in those
of other parties during the Progressive Era; these included
graduated income and inheritance taxes, postal savings banks and
the guaranty of deposits, the regulation of all corporations doing
an interstate business, an employer's liability act, the prohibition
of child labor, and various conservation measures. Perhaps the
most original plank recommended a court review of Post Office
Department decisions.

During 1908, too, a new third party made its appearance on the
scene: the Independence party. This party, which was an outgrowth of the Independence League led by publisher William
Randolph Hearst, was formed by the latter and his followers in an
attempt to supersede the Democratic party; Hearst, it will be
recalled, had placed second to Judge Parker during the Democratic balloting for President in 1904. Rather than nominate
Hearst, though, the Independent party selected as its ticket
Thomas Hisgen of Massachusetts for President and John Temple
Graves of Georgia for Vice President. At the Chicago convention,
Judge Samuel Seabury did make an attempt to bring up Bryan's
name, but this was cut short without a debate.

Although it attacked both the Republican and the Democratic
parties, the platform also asserted, "Our object is not to introduce
violent innovations or startlingly new features." This assessment
was in fact a quite accurate one, as there is little in this document
that does not appear in the reform planks of other parties during
this period, although there is practically nothing on foreign
policy and no indictment of imperialism. One of the more
original planks favored the suppression of the bucket shop and a
prohibition of the fictitious selling of farm products for future
delivery. Reaffirming the Declaration of Independence "as the
fountainhead of all political inspiration," the Independence party
platform also invoked the principles of Washington, Lincoln, and
Jefferson. A significant editorial reaction was that of the *Arena*,
which found this document far superior to its Republican and
Democratic counterparts, yet criticized Hearst for not founding
this party four years earlier.[4]

Perhaps the most conspicuous feature of the campaign was Roosevelt's absence; the incumbent President instead devoted himself to his duties as chief executive. Bryan again proved the most talkative candidate, inaugurating a nonstop, sixty-day tour of the country on August 20. A year previously Bryan had advocated the governmental ownership of the railroads, an old Populist demand which he had never embraced, and the Republicans subsequently hammered away at this as another proof of Bryan's socialistic tendencies. Other campaign issues were the Philippines, tariff reduction, the guaranty of bank deposits, campaign contributions, and labor. His past currency stand to the contrary, Bryan nevertheless received far more enthusiastic backing from Cleveland Democrats and from Tammany Hall in 1908 than he had during his two prior Presidential runs. Taft, though, was able to win the support of both the "Old Guard" and Progressive wings of his party, as well as to obtain the backing of independents and non-Republican reformers; his affable personality proved attractive to many voters, and the election results demonstrated that he could win without TR incessantly campaigning for him.

Sweeping the North and the West, but by smaller margins than Roosevelt, Taft sent Bryan down to his worst defeat, 7,679,006 popular votes to 6,409,106, and 321 electoral votes to 162. Like in 1904, the Socialist and Prohibitionist candidates finished respectively third and fourth, Debs polling 420,820 votes and Chafin 252,683. The Independence party nominee, Hisgen, the Populist nominee, Watson, and the Socialist Labor nominee, Gillhaus, each received less than 100,000 votes, with Watson's poor showing marking the death knoll for the Populist party as an active force in Presidential elections. The Republicans, aside from capturing the White House, also maintained control of both houses of Congress. Unfortunately for the GOP, Taft's triumph was to prove a rather hollow victory: within four years the Republican party was to be as badly torn as the Democratic party had been a half-century before.

XX. 1912

Strong As a Bull Moose

As chief executive, Taft was to prove far less politically adept than TR, and far less progressive than Roosevelt would have wished him to be. Yet a retrospective examination of the Taft administration reveals achievements far more in line with the political thinking of TR and La Follette than of Aldrich and Cannon, including the ratification by the states of a Constitutional income tax amendment. Under "trust-busting Teddy," forty-four antitrust suits were started; under Taft, the total number was doubled rather than halved, with the Supreme Court handing down rulings against Standard Oil and the American Tobacco Company in 1911. Roosevelt, though, became irritated when the Taft administration filed a suit for dissolution against the U. S. Steel Corporation as a result of its absorption of the Tennessee Coal and Iron Company during the Panic of 1907. Elsewhere on the domestic scene, the Mann-Elkins Act strengthening the ICC and the Postal Savings Bank Act were both signed into law by Taft in 1910.

Middlewestern Insurgents, however, opposed the Payne-Aldrich Tariff of 1909, which Taft characterized at Winona, Minnesota, as the best bill of its type the Republican party had ever passed. The next year, House of Representatives reformers, led by George Norris of Nebraska, stripped Speaker Joseph Cannon of his power to appoint the Rules Committee, against the wishes of Taft and without his support. Taft also sided with his Secretary of the Interior, Richard Ballinger, in the latter's famous quarrel with Gifford Pinchot, the Chief of the US Forest Service, thus angering conservationists. Such gestures as these by Taft tarnished the President's Progressive image.

With regard to foreign policy, Taft largely jettisoned TR's Big Stick policy in favor of "Dollar Diplomacy" towards Latin America and the Far East, though he did send the marines into Nicaragua in 1912. He also succeeded in persuading Congress to enact a reciprocity agreement with Canada over the objection of midwestern farmers, but Canadian Liberals seized upon this issue to discredit and defeat the Conservatives in the Canadian national

election of 1911. As President, it was clear, the judicially-minded
Taft at times was not at home.

In 1912 it was the Socialists who assembled first, the Socialist
Labor party at New York in April and the Socialist party at
Indianapolis in May. The Socialist Labor party ticket consisted of
Arthur Reimer of Massachusetts for President and August
Gillhaus of New York for Vice President. As usual, the platform
was devoted to rhetorical discourse; affirming that "The programme of the Socialist Labor Party is *revolution*," it nevertheless
took the position that "the Socialist Labor Party is the constitutional method of political action."

In contrast, the Socialist party nominated Eugene Debs for
President and former mayor Emil Seidel of Milwaukee for Vice
President, and gave its blessing to a series of very specific demands
prefaced by a more general introduction. Planks added since 1908
included ones calling for the termination of the monopoly
ownership of patents, the abolition of all Federal district courts
and the US Circuit Court of Appeals, and the elimination of the
veto power of the President and his selection by the Electoral
College. There also was a provision favoring a Constitutional
convention. Victor Berger did endorse a plank that called for tariff
reduction, but this was challenged and eliminated as irrelevant to
the Socialist movement. After the Progressive party had formulated its platform later that year, William Ghent, secretary to
Congressman Berger, complained that "it begins its career with
the brazen theft of half the working program of the Socialist
party,"[1] but the *Independent* noted that many proposed reforms
were the common property of more than one political party.[2]

Renominating its slate of 1908, the Prohibition party gave
Eugene Chafin of Illinois its Presidential nomination and Aaron
Watkins second place on the ticket at its Atlantic City gathering in
July. The Prohibition platform also imitated its immediate
predecessor by dispensing with rhetoric and listing a dozen or so
specific demands. Of these perhaps the most original was the one
advocating that the President be limited to a single six-year term;
the other planks merely repeated with occasional variations the
demands contained in past documents. On this occasion God was
specifically mentioned "as the source of all governmental authority," while there was only one plank (albeit a lengthy one)
advocating prohibition.

Before turning to the Republican party convention at Chicago in June, it is necessary to recall the developing schism within the Republican party during the Taft administration. This eventually led to the establishment of the National Progressive League at Washington on January 21, 1911, by Insurgents led by Senator Robert La Follette of Wisconsin, whose basic aim was the promotion of popular government and progressive legislation. On October 16 this organization endorsed La Follette for President. The La Follette boom, though, was to falter early in 1912, when the Wisconsin Progressive broke down while delivering an intemperate harrangue at Philadelphia in February; that same month Theodore Roosevelt announced that he would accept the Republican Presidential nomination if it were offered to him. During the preconvention period, TR received a total of 1,157,397 primary votes to 761,716 for Taft and 351,043 for La Follette, winning the Presidential preference primaries in six states. (Roosevelt also carried four state conventions.) He thus approached Chicago maintaining with considerable justification that he was the preferred choice of Republicans throughout the land.

Unfortunately for TR, at the convention the Republican National Committee, which was controlled by Taft, excluded most of the Roosevelt delegates in contested cases. The incumbent President subsequently won renomination easily on the first ballot, amassing 561 votes to 107 for TR and 41 for La Follette, but this victory becomes less impressive when one considers that 344 other Roosevelt delegates abstained from voting. Sherman also was renominated for Vice President, but he died on October 30, before the voting took place. Although the Rooseveltites technically did not bolt the Republican convention, they assembled separately the same day that the regulars nominated Taft, and called upon TR to assume the leadership of a third party. Roosevelt had already established a precedent by becoming the first avowed candidate to appear at a national convention before the actual balloting.

In view of the Progressive defection, an examination of the Republican platform for 1912 is mandatory so as to determine whether it reflected the political philosophy of Roosevelt and La Follette, or that of Aldrich and Cannon. As one might expect, certain parts of the document had a Taftian flavor, owing to the work of former Vice President Charles Fairbanks of Indiana and his Committee on Resolutions. Taft had delayed statehood for Arizona because of the provision in that state's constitution permitting the recall of judges, and the platform thus opposed the recall of judges as "unnecessary and unwise"; Taft also felt that woman suffrage should be left to the states, so there was no plank endorsing a national Constitutional amendment. On the other hand, Taft had never favored a Federal Trade Commission in the past, and this document included such a plank. The protective tariff and the gold standard made their usual appearance, but there was no section dealing with labor, nor was there any reference to the Aldrich-Vreeland Act as there had been in 1908, although the Republicans did promise currency reforms. One of the most unusual features of this document was its ignoring of foreign policy, aside from the Philippine policy, "a national obligation which should remain entirely free from partisan politics," and the International Court of Justice. There also were words of praise for Presidents Lincoln, McKinley, Roosevelt, and Taft, despite the fact that TR would soon bolt the party and challenge the incumbent President.

Although they had been rebuffed in 1908, the Wisconsin Progressives again presented a minority report encompassing many of the reforms passed over by the regulars, but these thirty demands were tabled and the platform was adopted by a vote of 666 to 53, with 343 Rooseveltites present and not voting. Attacking the "Money Trust" which "can make and unmake panics" and the Aldrich currency plan (on which the majority report was silent), the minority report placed great reliance on a new Federal Trade Commission as the answer to the regulatory problem. Primaries to nominate the President, Vice President, and members of Congress also were endorsed as a substitute for the convention system; the amending of the Constitution by a majority vote throughout the nation and in a majority of the states was recommended. With respect to the functioning of Congress, the minority report came out in favor of making all committee hearings public and setting up a legislative reference bureau, and suggested that it might become necessary to apply the recall to Representatives and Senators. The one foreign policy plank constituted a direct slap at Taft's "Dollar Diplomacy," which "has reduced our State Department from its high plane as a kindly intermediary of defenseless nations into a trading outpost for Wall Street interests, aiming to exploit those who would be our friends."

With the Republican party on the verge of splintering, the Democrats approached their convention at Baltimore in June aware that they might be nominating the next President of the United States. The leading candidates were Speaker of the House Beauchamp "Champ" Clark of Missouri, Governor Woodrow Wilson of New Jersey, and Representative Oscar Underwood of Alabama. Clark held an initial lead, even achieving a majority vote, but never reached the necessary two-thirds level; no Democratic Presidential hopeful in seventy years had come so close to the nomination without actually obtaining it. The nod eventually went on the forty-sixth ballot to Governor Woodrow Wilson of New Jersey, the former president of Princeton University who had turned against the political bosses of that state and had seen through the legislature an impressive body of Progressive measures. Bryan often is given credit for Wilson's nomination, but in truth a rather complex series of political maneuverings featuring individuals other than Bryan led to that event. For the Vice Presidential position the convention selected Governor Thomas Marshall of Indiana, most remembered for his observation: "What the country needs is a good five-cent cigar."[3] Marshall balanced the ticket both geographically and ideologically.

The Democratic platform of 1912, drawn up by a Resolutions Committee headed by Senator John Kern of Indiana, proved to be entirely acceptable to the Presidential nominee, aside from the planks calling for a single term for the chief executive and the exemption of American ships from Panama Canal tolls. (There also was an endorsement of Presidential preference primaries.) Unlike the Republican document, it blamed the high cost of living on the protective tariff; unlike the Republican one, it condemned the Aldrich currency plan. Again silent relative to the merits of gold versus silver, this platform took the customary Democratic stance in favor of a tariff for revenue and the abolition of monopolies. One of this document's more unusual features was the quoting, verbatim, of the 1908 planks on labor, a device rarely encountered in political platforms.

With respect to foreign affairs, the expression "inexcusable blunder" was again applied to our Filipino policy, which had been the focal point of the anti-imperialist crusade since 1900. A more original plank lauded the Democratic members of the House and the Senate for the role they had played in terminating the Russian treaty of 1832; during this period there had emerged a growing number of protests in this country as a result of various episodes of Russian anti-Semitism. Homage was also paid to Thomas Jefferson and "a long and illustrious line of Democratic Presidents" (which would include Grover Cleveland), but not to long-time party leader William Jennings Bryan. Yet Bryan found this platform to be "the most progressive ever presented to the country."[4]

More cut-and-dried with respect to the selection of a Presidential nominee, but just as exciting in other respects, was the Progressive party convention at Chicago in August. This group was overwhelmingly Republican in political affiliation. Proclaiming that he felt "as strong as a bull moose," from which phrase was derived the symbol of the party, Roosevelt reached oratorical heights matched only by Bryan and a few others in his impassioned utterance: "We stand at Armageddon and we battle for the Lord."[5] After annointing TR as its Presidential candidate, the convention turned to the Progressive governor of California, Hiram Johnson, for the Vice Presidential nomination. This proved to be, therefore, one of the rare instances in the history of national political conventions where the delegates chose first-raters for both places on the ticket.

Despite the highly emotional atmosphere of the Progressive party convention, in terms of content the platform the delegates produced stands as one of the most remarkable ever drawn up. The woman suffrage plank was written by Jane Addams, the labor one by John Mitchell, and the conservation and waterways plank by Gifford Pinchot. David Hinshaw, who rates it as one of the three greatest statements of principle, has characterized it as "a document that rises to statesmanship like a phoenix from the dead ashes of the political embers of its day";[6] in the opinion of George Mowry, "Altogether it was perhaps the most radical platform any major party had yet presented to the electorate."[7] On the other hand, Amos Pinchot felt that it hedged on every important issue except conservation.[8]

Invoking the names of Thomas Jefferson and Abraham Lincoln at the beginning, this document pronounced a curse on both established major parties before setting forth "A Covenant with the People." An examination of the various planks, however, reveals few items that had not appeared previously in the political platforms of the major and minor parties during the Progressive Era. Nevertheless, its emphasis that reform should be national in orientation and its attack on the Democratic endorsement of states' rights clearly sets it apart. Perhaps the most reactionary plank was that favoring the Republican protective tariff concept over the Democratic one of a tariff for revenue; yet this also condemned the Payne-Aldrich Tariff of 1909 and the Canadian Reciprocity Act of 1911, two measures passed during the Republican Taft administration. As a whole, this document manifested an almost complete preoccupation with domestic affairs, avoiding the debate between the imperialists and the anti-imperialists, although it did encourage the development of friendship and commerce with Latin America.

What debate there was over this document centered around its antitrust provisions. Theodore Roosevelt, who had turned thumbs down on planks opposing the exportation of raw material and favoring the socialization of lawyers, vetoed on grounds of unenforceability a recommendation by the Resolutions Committee that a plank be included favoring a tougher Sherman Antitrust Act. Without the knowledge of TR and party financier George Perkins, though, the Resolutions Committee failed to delete this plank, and the convention later voted to adopt the majority report, including this plank, before the Roosevelt forces were aware what was happening. Following the convention, TR ordered that the Sherman provision be deleted, over the objections of many members of the party.

Given this lineup of parties and candidates, it is not surprising that the campaign was an exciting one. Theodore Roosevelt's "New Nationalism," which he had first enunciated two years earlier, stood in marked contrast to Woodrow Wilson's "New Freedom"; the incumbent President was the most conservative candidate of the three, though his record as we have seen was by no means devoid of Progressive touches. Wall Street split three ways—with Taft receiving the least support. TR, who unlike Wilson attacked Taft personally, spent much of his time denouncing the theft of delegates at the Republican convention, while Wilson hammered away at trusts, bossism, and the tariff, rather than emphasize foreign policy. The incumbent President's cam-

paign was the least active of the three. On October 14 a crazed anti-
third termer shot Roosevelt, but TR managed to finish his speech
before collapsing, and survived to live another seven years.
The Republican split guaranteed a Wilson victory. Nevertheless, the Democratic nominee's popular vote majority was the
largest in history up to that time; he won only a minority (41.9
percent) of the popular vote. The popular vote totals were Wilson,
6,286,214; Roosevelt, 4,126,020; Taft, 3,483,922; Debs, 897,011;
Chafin, 206,275; Reimer, 29,075. Taft carried only Vermont and
Utah, while Roosevelt, who was the strongest in the Middle West
and the Far West, triumphed in six states. The remaining forty
states were won by Wilson, twelve by a majority vote, and Wilson
defeated TR in the Electoral College 435 to 88, with Taft receiving
a mere 8. While the Democrats won control of Congress, the
Progressives captured only a dozen seats—a sure indication that
this party would be hard-pressed either to challenge the two major
parties in 1916, or to survive as a permanent organization.

XXI. 1916

He Kept Us Out of War

As President one of the most important aspects—if not the most
significant feature—of Woodrow Wilson's first administration
was the abandonment of his original New Freedom for a program
much closer in spirit to Theodore Roosevelt's New Nationalism.
The Underwood-Simmons Tariff of 1913 was enacted into law
with only minor changes, but in the case of the Federal Reserve Act
of 1913, the Federal Trade Commission Act of 1914, and the
Clayton Antitrust Act of 1914, Wilson's proposals were drastically
modified. The last of these measures included a section protecting
labor. Another group which benefitted were the farmers; in this
connection one might cite the Smith-Lever Act of 1914, the Federal
Farm Loan Act of 1916, and the Warehouse Act of 1916. A leading

Progressive appointment was that of Louis D. Brandeis to the US Supreme Court in January of the latter year. Other key pieces of legislation included the La Follette Seamen's Act of 1915, a model workmen's compensation measure for federal employees (1916), the Keating-Owen Child Labor Act of 1916, and the Adamson Act of 1916, creating an eight-hour day on interstate railroads.

Turning to foreign affairs, William Jennings Bryan, who had helped Wilson obtain the Democratic Presidential nomination, served as Secretary of State for two years; before resigning at the height of the *Lusitania* crisis, Bryan successfully negotiated twenty-one "cooling-off" treaties with foreign nations. Wilson's interventions in Haiti in 1915 and in the Dominican Republic in 1916 were in the spirit of Theodore Roosevelt's Big Stick diplomacy, but he also inaugurated a policy of "Moral Diplomacy" by refusing to recognize the Huerta regime in Mexico. Indeed, Wilson's first administration was highlighted by a series of crises involving Mexico, including incidents at Tampico and Vera Cruz in 1914, Pancho Villa's raid on Columbus, New Mexico, and General John J. Pershing's Mexican expedition in 1916. Another key diplomatic episode was the repeal in 1914 of the exemption of American coastwise shipping from the payment of tolls for the use of the Panama Canal. But even more important was the reaction of the United States to the outbreak of war in Europe during the summer of 1914. Wilson adopted a policy of neutrality, and even made an unsuccessful attempt to persuade the warring powers to agree to a negotiated peace, but both his second Secretary of State (Robert Lansing) and his intimate adviser Colonel Edward House proved to be more hawkish than either Wilson or Bryan.

Generally speaking, the Socialists were not happy with European developments, since most of them regarded the war as one between capitalist nations, from which the working class would suffer rather than benefit. The Socialist party did not even hold a convention in 1916, but it did nominate by a mail referendum Allen Benson of New York for President and George Kirkpatrick of New Jersey for Vice President. Their platform contained few new domestic planks of consequence, although unlike its 1912 counterpart it specifically mentioned the Panic of 1907, and criticized Taft and Wilson for failing to bring back "good times." Far more remarkable were the half-dozen "measures to insure peace": the repeal of all laws and appropriations increasing the

US Army and Navy; Congressional responsibility for the devising of foreign policy and the conduct of diplomatic negotiations; a national referendum on the declaration of war except in cases of invasion; the abolition of the Monroe Doctrine as a tool of the capitalist class; immediate independence for the Philippines; and a congress of all neutral countries to mediate between the belligerents. According to this document, our imperialist policy towards Mexico would eventually lead to American involvement in a world war. In contrast, the Socialist Labor party, which nominated Arthur Reimer of Massachusetts and August Gillhaus as its ticket at New York City in April, again formulated a platform composed of generalities which ignored the war issue, and in fact was half the length of its 1912 counterpart.

Foreign policy, however, was a key issue at the Republican convention at Chicago in June. A number of Presidential possibilities made their appearance on the first ballot—Charles Evans Hughes, Elihu Root, Albert Cummins, Theodore Burton, Charles Fairbanks, Theodore Roosevelt—but the nod eventually went to Hughes on the third ballot as the candidate most acceptable to all factions. Hughes, who had not taken part in the 1912 donneybrook, had investigated insurance companies prior to becoming governor of New York; at the time of his nomination he was serving as an associate justice of the US Supreme Court. He did not actively campaign for the nomination, but Taft did support him. For Vice President the convention turned to Charles Fairbanks of Indiana, who had served in that capacity during the second Theodore Roosevelt administration. TR himself, who had hoped to receive both the Republican and Progressive Presidential nominations in 1916, was passed over by the former because of his belligerency and irregularity.

Roosevelt's friend, Henry Cabot Lodge, still representing Massachusetts in the US Senate, did serve as the chairman of the Resolutions Committee, whose product loftily proclaimed: "We believe in American policies at home and abroad." Hughes had little, if any, influence on its content. The platform was particularly critical of Wilson's foreign policy, and indeed the diplomatic planks shattered precedent by preceding the domestic ones; this was in marked contrast to 1912, where the foreign policy planks played only a minor role. With reference to the European War, the 1916 document favored the "maintaining of a strict and honest neutrality," and lambasted the Wilson administration for not protecting the rights of American citizens. The Mexican plank was equally critical of the President, but there was no criticism of the TR-style interventions by Wilson in Haiti or the Dominican Republic.

The domestic planks are of lesser interest. The platform did label the Underwood-Simmons Tariff as "a complete failure in every respect," and attack the Rural Credits Act proposed by the Wilson administration, while applauding Taft's attempt to establish a "simple businesslike budget system." Like the Democrats, the Republicans left the enfranchisement of women to the states. One of the more original planks recommended Congressional legislation or even a Constitutional amendment placing the nation's entire transportation system under federal control.

The usual Wisconsin minority report again made its appearance, and again the convention rejected it decisively. Attacking un-American and undemocratic secret diplomacy, this document, like the Socialist platform, advocated a national referendum on the declaration of war. Despite the fact that Taft was no longer President, there again was a repudiation of "Dollar Diplomacy." More innovative was the call for the abolition of the private manufacture of munitions in favor of the governmental production of them; this scheme antedated by two decades the Nye Committee's investigation of the munition makers, or "merchants of death." The other domestic planks more or less constituted an extension of their 1912 counterparts, although the minority report did endorse the La Follette Seamen's Act of 1915.

On the very day that the Republicans assembled in Chicago the Progressives met separately in the same city. Both conventions appointed committees to meet with each other and attempt to reach a mutual understanding, but these failed. Had the Progressives nominated Theodore Roosevelt for President before the Republicans had selected their candidate, the latter may have been forced to go along with this choice; instead, the Progressives gave their blessing to TR after the Republicans had endorsed Hughes, and Roosevelt then withdrew in favor of the latter. This embittered many delegates, who eventually turned to Wilson rather than the Republican nominee. The Progressive national committee did approve Hughes later that month, although an Indianapolis conference of the party repudiated this step early in August. While

Roosevelt campaigned for Hughes, the Progressive Vice Presidential nominee, Democratic Governor John Parker of Louisiana, threw his support to Wilson.

The Progressive and Republican platforms proved to be quite similar in a number of ways, though Henry Cabot Lodge was unable to persuade his fellow Republicans to accept the universal service proposal contained in the Progressive document. The preparedness plank was described by the *Literary Digest* with reference to its Republican counterpart as "at once more specific and more radical, and naturally more Rooseveltian."[1] Unlike in 1912, the few social reforms mentioned in the latter were confined to a single paragraph; an attempt was made to insert a prohibition plank, but this failed. Domestic planks that specifically paralleled Republican stands included the tariff, child labor, workingmen's compensation, the conservation of natural resources, rural credits, the regulation of business, and civil service. With respect to foreign affairs, the Progressives took the position that "the American tradition of isolation has been ended," and attacked the Wilson administration's record vis-a-vis Mexico and the protection of American citizens on the high seas. (Admittedly the Republican Mexican plank was more vitriolic.) Like the Republican platform, there was no mention either of hyphenated Americans or of Germans. In the opinion of the *Review of Reviews*, this document was "briefer and better phrased" than its Republican and Democratic counterparts;[2] to Paul U. Kellogg writing in the *Survey* "It is an editorial, a brief, a preachment of militant, self-reliant, self-righteous nationalism."[3]

The Democrats assembled in St. Louis one week after the Republicans had met at Chicago. For the first time since 1896, William Jennings Bryan did not play a major role in the proceedings, either as a Presidential nominee, a king-maker, or a forceful proponent for some cause. (Bryan, it will be recalled, had quit as Secretary of State the previous year.) The Presidential and Vice Presidential nominations proved to be a mere formality, as Woodrow Wilson won easily on the first ballot, 1092 to 1, while Thomas Marshall won an equally impressive victory. On the last occasion that an incumbent Democratic President had sought renomination, in 1888, Grover Cleveland had likewise won his party's nod by acclamation.

The Democratic platform was described by Key Pittman of
Nevada during the debate as "the greatest platform of achievements and enunciations of principle since the Declaration of
Independence,"[4] while to the *Nation* it was "of a quality in
substance and form, far above that usually encountered in these
documents."[5] Senator William J. Stone of Missouri served as
Chairman of the Committee on Resolutions; there was a struggle
in that body over the woman suffrage plank—Wilson preferred it
to be stronger than its Republican counterpart—but the committee nevertheless voted to leave it to the 48 states. To no one's
surprise, such key measures of the first Wilson Administration as
the Federal Reserve Act, the Federal Trade Commission Act, and
the Underwood Tariff were endorsed, as was the La Follette
Seamen's Act, which the President only grudgingly allowed to
become law. Of especial interest was the lengthy farm plank. With
respect to new domestic reforms, one might point to the call for the
eventual creation of a national budget for the Federal government,
and to the advocacy of an effective child labor law. This time,
though, there was no mention of the recommendation made four
years earlier advocating a single term limitation on the President,
since Wilson was a candidate for re-election. A more sinister plank
was that dealing with Americanism, with its implied condemnation of hyphenated Americans and Germans.

As for foreign affairs, this document, as usual, endorsed
Filipino independence, linked Wilson's Mexican policy to the
Monroe Doctrine, and advocated the establishment of a world-
wide association of nations. It is of no little significance that the
platform referred to "the splendid diplomatic victories of our great
President," in concluding that "Woodrow Wilson stands to-day
the greatest American of his generation." Conspicuously absent
was any endorsement of Bryan's arbitration treaties. Once this
document was before the convention, an attempt was made to
include a plank favoring Irish independence, but this failed; a
minority report leaving woman suffrage to the states was also
rejected by a vote of 888½ to 181½, with the South backing it more
strongly than any other section. The *Independent* found the
Democratic platform quite similar to the Republican one, but
preferred the latter on those issues where there was a genuine
difference of opinion: the tariff, the Philippines, the control of
business, the regulation of transportation, the merchant marine.[6]

It was the Prohibitionists who held the last national convention in 1916, at St. Paul in July. Their ticket as approved by this gathering was J. Frank Hanly of Indiana for President and Ira Landrith of Tennessee for Vice President. Hanly had once been a Republican Congressman and governor in his native Indiana. In terms of sheer number of words, this platform was at least four times as long as its 1912 counterpart. After taking its usual stand in favor of prohibition and reminding its readers that the Prohibition party had come out in favor of woman suffrage as early as 1872, this document turned to defense and diplomacy. Lambasting the "wasteful military programme of the Democratic Republican parties," it endorsed the World Court scheme and attacked universal military training, as well as private profits in munitions manufacturing. With respect to hemispheric affairs, it observed that "Mexico needs not a conquerer, but a good Samaritan," and followed the Democratic precedent by affirming the Monroe Doctrine in this connection.

While the 1912 platform had recommended that the tariff issue be turned over to a commission, that of 1916 favored a reciprocal trade agreements program. Like the Democratic document, there was a plank dealing with Americanism, but somewhat briefer and milder in character. Among the more significant domestic reforms proposed were the adoption of a national budget system and a Presidential item veto with respect to appropriation bills; the extensive farm program included a call for governmentally-owned and operated grain elevators and cotton warehouses. Labelling both established major parties as the Conservative party of the United States, the Prohibition party described itself as the "only great Progressive Party," and this was perhaps the most progressive platform in the party's history. To the *Review of Reviews,* the Prohibitionists were "the original party of progressivism," despite their obsession with demon rum.[7]

In the months that intervened between the conventions and the election, Wilson did little active campaigning, making perhaps a speech once a month from his residence. His supporters, though, obtained considerable political mileage out of the slogan, "He kept us out of war"; other issues in the campaign included the tariff, Mexico, and the railroads. Although Wilson by this time had alienated much of the Irish-American and German-American vote, he attracted a large segment of the women's vote, particularly in the West where women could vote in some states. The Olympian Hughes evaded some issues and straddled others, but he did win the backing of the Hearst press; on the other hand, he antagonized railroad labor by denouncing the Adamson law, which the President had recently signed along with other labor legislation. Even worse, Hughes's campaign managers may have cost him the Presidency by failing to arrange a meeting with Senatorial candidate Hiram Johnson while both were staying at the same hotel in California. That November Johnson carried California by 300,000 votes, but Hughes lost the state (and the election) to Wilson by 3,773 votes.

Since the Republicans carried all the eastern and midwestern states except Ohio on the day of reckoning, Hughes had gone to bed thinking that he was the next President. But Wilson matched his triumphs in the South with victories in the West that were not reported until the next day, and narrowly edged out Hughes in the Electoral College, 277 votes to 254. The margin in popular votes was wider: Wilson, 9,129,606; Hughes, 8,538,221; Benson 585,113; Hanly, 220,506; Reimer, 13,403; impeached New York governor William Sulzer also ran on the American party ticket, with a pledge to "redeem America from rum rule and Roman rule."[8] Despite the presence in the race of two prohibition candidates, Wilson carried ten of the twelve states with women suffrage, and twenty of the twenty-five with prohibition. The Democrats also retained control of both houses of Congress. Unfortunately for the re-elected President, six months later the country was at war; like FDR in 1940 and LBJ in 1964, the peace candidate shortly thereafter had to eat his own words.

XXII.   1920

The Smoke-Filled Room

Reinaugurated as chief executive in March, Wilson was proposing war to Congress the following month. American entry into World War I stifled the further passage of domestic legislation, although the New Freedom was by that time complete. The Smith-Hughes Act, which had been signed into law prior to the close of Wilson's first term, did provide for federal grants-in-aid to the states for the promotion of agricultural and trade education. In the foreign policy field, during the last year of the first Wilson administration, the United States competed an agreement with Denmark transferring the Virgin Islands to the US. The war itself unfortunately led to the suppression of free speech; Socialist Presidential candidate Eugene Debs was tried and convicted under the Sedition Act of 1918, and an era of witch-hunting was inaugurated by Attorney General A. Mitchell Palmer. Another highlight of the war years was the adoption by Congress of the Prohibition Amendment late in 1917. After the customary number of states had ratified this early in 1919, it went into effect a year later after Congress had passed the Volstead Act over the President's veto.

More progressive measures dating from the last year of Wilson's second term included the Esch-Cummins Transportation Act, widening the powers of the Interstate Commerce Commission, and the Water Power Act, setting up the Federal Power Commission. During 1920 the nineteenth Amendment universalizing woman suffrage also went into effect. Although Wilson had called for the election of a Democratic Congress in 1918, the Republicans had triumphed at the polls, a development which resulted in his arch-foe Henry Cabot Lodge of Massachusetts becoming chairman of the Senate Foreign Relations Committee. There ensued a tragic series of episodes which saw Wilson going to Paris to negotiate peace, the US Senate hardening in opposition to the Versailles settlement, and Wilson suffering a physical breakdown during a national tour in the fall of 1919. Despite his martyrdom, the Senate never ratified this treaty or approved the League of Nations.

During the spring of 1920 the Socialists, whose opposition to World War I has already been noted, held their two conventions at New York City, both in May. W. W. Cox of Missouri won the Presidential nod of the Socialist Labor party, with August Gillhaus of New York his running-mate. The platform reaffirmed former declarations, which were just as general as those found in this document, but it differed from its 1916 counterpart in its mention and condemnation of World War I. "A capitalist deadlock of markets," it observed, "brought on in 1914 the capitalist collapse popularly known as the World War."

On the other hand, the Socialist party selected the imprisoned Debs again as its candidate, but strangely failed to lament his martyrdom in its platform; Seymour Stedman of Ohio won the convention's backing as his running-mate. The platform, however, did attack the Espionage Act and other repressive measures adopted by the Wilson administration in more general terms, while espousing several new domestic reforms. These included the governmental ownership of insurance companies, the registering to vote of migratory workers, and a progressive property tax .

To the Socialists the Treaty of Versailles was "an infamous pact formulated behind closed doors by predatory older statesmen of European and Asiatic imperialism." One section of the platform, devoted strictly to foreign affairs, recommended the voiding of claims resulting from loans to the Allies, the dissolution of the "mischievious organization" known as the League of Nations, the conclusion of peace with the Central Powers, the diplomatic recognition of Soviet Russia and independent Ireland, and said the American government should cease protecting US investments abroad. The Socialists did favor an international parliament, democratically elected and based upon the recognition of equal rights and the principle of self-determination, but their bitterness against the Wilson administration was so great that they were unable to accept the League of Nations.

More unpredictable were the Republicans, who assembled the following month in Chicago, with 984 delegates in attendance. With respect to the Presidential aspirants, Taft and Hughes were losers, Lodge and Root were too old, and TR—(who might have been nominated otherwise)—was dead. The two leading contenders were the Rooseveltian General Leonard Wood, who was disliked by the Old Guard, and Governor Frank Lowden of Illinois; Senator Hiram Johnson of California was another progressive alternative. There was some popular demand for Herbert Hoover, who had served under Wilson, but his political managers were unable to transform this support into convention votes. After Wood and Lowden had been damaged by the making public of their campaign expenses, the convention deadlocked before turning on the tenth ballot to Senator Warren Harding of

Ohio, a conservative regular and political conciliator who was owner and editor of an Ohio newspaper.

Most accounts of this convention picture Harding's choice as being made by the party bosses in a smoke-filled hotel room early in the morning, although this is probably a myth. These leaders, however, were unable to dictate their choice for the Vice Presidential nomination, Irvine Lenroot of Wisconsin. Instead, the delegates turned on the first ballot to Governor Calvin Coolidge of Massachusetts, who had won national publicity through his smashing of the Boston police strike; this marked the first such challenging of the bosses since the Republicans nominated James Garfield for President forty years previously. Among the more noteworthy speeches at the 1920 convention was the keynote address of Henry Cabot Lodge, which the New York *Evening Post* described as a "Hymn of Hate" against Wilson.[1]

Three times as long as its 1916 counterpart, the Republican platform was the work of a committee headed by Senator James Watson of Indiana. The *North American Review* opined, "never before in the history of American politics had such efforts been made to elicit the will of the party."[2] As was the case in 1916, foreign relations were treated before domestic affairs. Blasting the Democrats for "Unpreparedness for War" and "Unpreparedness for Peace," this document pledged the Republican party "to end executive autocracy and restore to the people their constitutional government." With respect to Wilson's "Moral Diplomacy" and Fourteen Points, the Republicans made the accusation that his foreign policy was lacking in principle and conceptualization. Among the specific focal points of this attack were the President's Mexican diplomacy, the proposed American mandate for Armenia, and the League of Nations. The latter issue caused the Republican platform writers a serious problem, but Elihu Root was able to come up with a formula satisfactory to both internationalists and irreconcilables, which endorsed an "agreement among the nations to preserve the peace of the world." According to this document, the covenant that Wilson had signed at Paris violated the principles of Washington, Jefferson, Monroe, and every Presidential administration for more than a century.

Turning to domestic affairs, the GOP took credit for such measures as the Transportation Act and the Woman Suffrage Amendment, but lambasted Wilson for his veto of the executive budget. There also was a belated attack on the Panama Canal Tolls Act of 1914. The right of labor to bargain collectively was recognized, but the "government initiative" against strikes that followed the great wave of walkouts in 1919 was also endorsed, as was the prohibition relative to strikes against the government. Another plank, which gave lip service to free speech, also denounced resistance to the law, the violent overthrow of the government, and "alien agitation." Because of such antiprogressive provisions, one analyst has labelled this platform as perhaps the most conservative one adopted by the Republicans in two decades;[3] to Norman Hapgood it was "reactionary" and "cowardly,"[4] while to Edward Devine it was "long and tedious and badly written."[5]

A Wisconsin minority report was again offered, as at the more recent Republican conventions, but this was much shorter than usual, being less than two printed pages in length. Like the majority report, it attacked the League of Nations and the Treaty of Versailles, that "would make us a party to the enslavement of Egypt and India, the rape of China and the ruthless oppression of Ireland."[6] Instead, it favored a League for Peace. The free speech plank was more liberal than that of the majority report, since it endorsed the repeal of the Espionage and Sedition Acts. Universal military training and the stationing of American troops overseas in time of peace were also condemned. With respect to domestic reforms, one might cite such new demands as the repeal of the Esch-Cummins Railroad Law, and governmental acquisition of the stock yards and packing plants. Of particular interest was the call for a St. Lawrence Seaway. Unfortunately for the Wisconsinites, the motion to substitute the minority report for the majority one did not even receive a second. Oscar De Priest of Illinois then introduced a separate resolution which advocated uniform national voting qualifications, a step designed to keep southern whites from preventing Negroes to vote, but the convention turned this down and adopted the majority report instead.

When the Democratic delegates assembled at San Francisco late in June, there was another sharp battle over the Presidential nomination, during which Wilson remained neutral. The leading possiblities included Wilson's son-in-law and former Secretary of the Treasury, William Gibbs McAdoo, witch-hunting Attorney General A. Mitchell Palmer, Governor James Cox of Ohio,

Governor Alfred Smith of New York, and even the aging Bryan. Despite the fact that he had married one of Wilson's daughters, McAdoo was unable to parlay his support into a nomination, and the nod went on the forty-fourth ballot to Cox, who like Harding, was an Ohio newspaper executive. Of special interest was the convention's choice by acclamation for Vice President: the thirty-eight-year-old Franklin Delano Roosevelt, who like his cousin Theodore had served as Assistant Secretary of the Navy. A dozen years later he would usher in a brand new era in American politics.

According to David Burner, the Democratic platform in 1920 was "perfunctory and defensive."[7] Many publications commented on the similarities between it and the Republican one; these included the Springfield *Republican,* the *Outlook,* and the Philadelphia *North American.*[8] In any event, it was the longest platform the party had approved to date, so long that it took Resolution Committee Chairman Carter Glass of Virginia two solid hours to read it to the convention. To the surprise of no one—and it was acceptable to Wilson, whom it praised—this document endorsed the Versailles Treaty and the League of Nations, attacking the US Senate in general and Henry Cabot Lodge in particular. Other planks came out in favor of Irish and Armenian independence, and expressed sympathy to the peoples of China, Finland, Poland, Czechoslovakia, Yugoslavia, and Persia, who recently had established representative governments.

With respect to the domestic scene, the farm and labor planks were quite long, particularly the former, and there was an endorsement of the Federal Highways. Act of 1916. Like the Republican platform, though, it avoided mentioning prohibition; Wilson did formulate the draft of a resolution advocating liberalization of the Volstead Act, but the "dry" Glass failed to present this at the committee hearings. Elsewhere this document endorsed the St. Lawrence Seaway, as had the Republican minority (not majority) report. Assuming that the best defense is a strong offense, it defended the somewhat questionable record of the Wilson administration on free speech: "No utterance from any quarter has been assailed, and no publication has been repressed, which has not been animated by treasonable purposes." The platform also made reference to the lavish use of money by certain Republican Presidential aspirants. It is not surprising, therefore, that it was attacked in such Republican newspapers as the

Pittsburg (Kansas) *Gazette-Times* ("a Wilson platform throughout, and tricky accordingly") and the Albany *Evening Journal* ("a mess of verbiage . . . necessarily mendacious praise of the Wilson Administration.")[9]

Here, too, there was a minority report, offered by Bryan, who remained a formidable speaker. The "Great Commoner" favored a League, but with reservations, since this was the only realistic approach; he also advocated a Constitutional amendment providing for the ratification of treaties by a majority vote in the Senate. The domestic planks offered by Bryan included an endorsement of prohibition, a national bulletin devoted equally to each major party, criminal liability for corporate officials, state trade commissions, the prevention and publicizing of profiteering, and co-operatives. (He opposed universal military training.) The dry plank was voted down 155½ to 929½, the others by voice vote. Conversely, Bourke Cockran presented a plank on behalf of the "wets," which was opposed by Bryan, that would give the states the right to fix the alcoholic content of cider, light wines, and beer. This one lost 356 to 726½. Still another resolution on behalf of a soldier's bonus law was rejected on a voice vote; there was a plank in the majority report relative to aid for disabled soldiers. A substitute for the Irish self-government plank also failed 402½ to 676½.

Their cause triumphant, the Prohibition party met at Lincoln, Nebraska, in July to nominate Aaron S. Watkins for President, with D. Leigh Colvin as his running-mate. In its platform it expressed "its thanks to Almighty God for the victory over the beverage liquor traffic which crowns fifty years of consecrated effort"; attempts by this vested interest to nullify the Prohibition Amendment were "treasonable." Rather than praise the Republicans and Democrats for enacting prohibition, this document blasted them for not including prohibition in their platforms. One of the more original domestic planks attacked profiteering. With respect to foreign affairs, the Prohibitionists came out in favor of the League of Nations, while not objecting to reasonable reservations, and the approval of peace treaties by simple majorities of both houses of Congress. This document closed by proudly proclaiming that the party "has never sold its birthright for a mess of pottage."

A new third party that made its first appearance on the national political scene was the Farmer-Labor party, which assembled at Chicago to endorse P. P. Christensen of Utah for President and Max Hayes of Ohio for Vice President. Blasting the "money-masters" and "their puppets in public office," this document advocated "100 per cent Americanism": free speech, the election of federal judges, universal suffrage, and the initiative, referendum, and recall. Other proposed domestic reforms included the governmental ownership of railroads, mines, natural resources, and banks, and a sharply graduated income and inheritance tax. Significantly, the labor plank was much longer than the farm plank. The foreign policy planks had an anti-imperialist flavor, attacking dollar diplomacy and US colonial policy, and endorsing peace with Mexico and the recognition of Finland and Russia. Instead of coming out in favor of the League of Nations, this platform expressed its approval of "a league of free peoples." As is apparent, few if any of these reforms were really new; in the opinion of John Spargo, they paralleled Socialistic demands.[10]

According to the ailing Republican political boss Boise Penrose of Pennsylvania, the key issue of the campaign was "Americanism." Republican nominee Harding, who wisely waged a front-porch campaign, called for a return to "Normalcy," and a slackening of domestic reform and a retreat from international obligations. Woodrow Wilson desired to make the Treaty of Versailles and the League of Nations the focal point of the campaign, and both Cox and FDR did campaign vigorously on behalf of these; in contrast, Harding adopted a "straddling" pose, which proved acceptable to both Republican internationalists and irreconcilables. Among the other issues were campaign contributions, prohibition, Irish independence, the cost of living, nativism, and Red-baiting. Making a rather uncharacteristic endorsement of a new department of public welfare, Harding also courted agriculture and business.

With women voting for the first time nationwide in a Presidential election, Warren Harding achieved one of the greatest landslides in popular votes ever recorded: 16,152,200 to 9,147,353 for Cox and 919,799 for Debs. But owing to the Democratic Solid South, Harding defeated Cox in the Electoral College by a margin of only 404 to 127, a ratio that was not unprecedented. Christensen and Watkins also made modest showings in the popular vote; the former received 265,411, the latter 189,408. The Republicans retained their strangle hold on Congress, winning the House by a lopsided margin , and dooming possible American entry into the League. By the next Presidential election, however, both Wilson and Harding would be dead, and the country would be "keeping cool with Coolidge."

XXIII. 1924

Keeping Cool with Coolidge

Warren Harding has long been ranked with Ulysses Grant among the worst Presidents, although in recent years a wave of revisionism has set in which has inspired at least several historians to rate his administration more highly. Harding's abbreviated term as chief executive, in fact, was by no means devoid of achievements. One might cite in this connection such measures enacted during the first year of his administration as the Budget and Accounting Act, the Veterans Bureau Act, the Packers and Stockyards Act, and the Grain Futures Act. A more traditional Republican measure was the highly protective Fordney-McCumber Tariff of 1922; other pieces of legislation enacted in 1921 and in 1924 (when Coolidge was President) placed restrictions on immigration from southern and eastern Europe. But it was in the foreign affairs field that one is to find the best-known achievements of the Harding Administration: the Washington Disarmament Conference of 1921-2, and the treaties with Germany and Colombia.

With respect to the "darker side" of his administration, Harding's death on August 2, 1923, mercifully removed him from the political scene just prior to the exposure of a large number of scandals. His successor, Calvin Coolidge, served only a little over a year in office before standing for election at the polls. This brief period did witness the formulation of the Dawes Plan for scaling down German reparations, and the termination of the U. S.

occupation of the Dominican Republic. On the home front, Coolidge vetoed a Soldiers Bonus Act, as had Harding; this time, however, Congress overrode the President, much to the delight of the veterans.

During the course of the 1924 Presidential campaign, the Socialist party, rather than nominate a candidate of its own, endorsed the Progressive party standard-bearer, Senator Robert La Follette of Wisconsin. Instead of drawing up a platform, it published a declaration of principles. More orthodox in its actions was the Socialist Labor party. Assembling at New York City in May, it selected a ticket of Frank Johns of Oregon for President and Verne Reynolds of Maryland for Vice President. The platform that the Socialist Laborites adopted merely reiterated that ratified four years previously, with only a minor variation in wording here and there, so there is no point in analyzing it point by point.

While the Socialist Labor party thought in terms of an America of the distant future, the Prohibition Party faced this campaign with its basic objectives already a historical reality. Perhaps the most significant innovation that emerged from its June convention at Columbus, Ohio, was the nomination of a woman, Marie Brehm of California, as the Vice Presidential running-mate of Presidential candidate Herman Faris of Missouri. The platform was largely a rehash of previous ones, but it did substitute an endorsement of the International Court of Justice for that of the League of Nations found in its 1920 counterpart. Another section linked the Harding scandals with demon rum: "the inevitable consequences of the moral bankruptcy of a political party which, perpetuating the old liquor regime, is dependent upon the wet vote for its margin of plurality." Complaining that discriminatory election laws had rendered more difficult the establishment and survival of third parties, this document also struck a new note by demanding their repeal.

Unlike that held four years before, the Republican party convention, at Cleveland in June, proved to be a rather cut-and-dried affair. Calvin Coolidge did not win his party's Presidential nomination unanimously, but he did amass a total of 1,065 ballots, in the process dwarfing the efforts of Robert La Follette and Hiram Johnson, who received a total of 44 votes combined. The speech nominating Coolidge, one of the longest on record, pursued three main themes during its platitudinous course: the

Man, the American, the Human Being. William Borah could have had the Vice Presidential nomination, but he refused to allow his name to be proposed; Frank Lowden then received his party's nod, only to decline this honor in a dramatic gesture. The convention next turned to General Charles Dawes of Illinois, the first Director of the Budget, an active campaigner who was weak with labor, but strong with the German-Americans.

Although General Jacob Coxey caused a flurry of excitement when he appeared at the convention to plead for the abolition of interest and for a currency based on need, he was no more successful in placing his stamp upon the platform than the Wisconsin La Follette Progressives had been. The head of the Resolutions Committee was Ambassador to Mexico Charles B. Warren of Michigan. Praising Warren Harding's role in the Washington Disarmament Conference as his greatest achievement, this document pictured this "true patriot" and "great leader" as "a public servant unswerving in his devotion to duty." Calvin Coolidge was also lauded for his "practical idealism in office." The foreign relations plank followed the President's wishes by endorsing American membership in the World Court, but not in the League of Nations; it also recommended that disarmament be extended to include land forces, submarines, and poison gas. Opposition was voiced elsewhere to the cancellation of war debts.

After blaming the recession of 1921 on the Democrats, the Republicans pointed with pride to the steps they had taken towards reducing taxes, the public debt, and governmental expenditures. Since it was in line with traditional Republican thinking, the Fordney-McCumber Tariff won the blessing of the platform-drafters. The labor plank endorsed the President's child labor amendment, while the agricultural one praised the grain futures and packer control acts; there was, however, no reference to the Ku Klux Klan, an issue which sharply divided the Democrats, or of Coolidge's veto of the soldiers bonus legislation. Far from evading the issue, the Republicans met the Harding scandals head-on by espousing conservation and proclaiming such misdeeds nonpartisan: "Dishonesty and corruption are not political attributes." In addition, this platform came out in favor of the immigration restrictions written into law during the last four years, taking the position that these would protect both the American citizen and the alien against economic competition.

The Wisconsin minority report was presented by Henry Cooper, who reminded the unenthusiastic convention that twenty six of the thirty one demands that his group had set forth since 1908 had been written onto the statute books. Contrasting the unlimited prosperity of the great corporations with the ruin and bankruptcy experienced in agriculture, this document also attacked both the Mellon tax plan and the Fordney-McCumber tariff; it also took a harder line on the Harding scandals than the majority report, and came out for a veteran's bonus. One new Constitutional reform that it proposed was allowing Congress to repass a law over a judicial veto. The eleventh plank, which was the only one to deal specifically with diplomatic issues, attacked the "mercenary system of degraded foreign policy," while also suggesting that the Versailles Treaty be revised in accordance with the terms of the armistice. Despite the high batting average of the Progressives in getting their demands enacted, their minority report again went down to defeat on a voice vote.

No convention of a major party during the present century has witnessed a more acrimonious struggle over the nomination of a President and the writing of a platform than the Democrats experienced in 1924, when they met at New York City in June. Here, William Gibbs McAdoo, the candidate of the rural South and West, the "drys," and the nativists, confronted Alfred E. Smith, who represented the urban North and East, the "wets," and the immigrants. Neither was able to command the necessary two-thirds majority required for nomination, nor were such other candidates as the anti-Klan Oscar W. Underwood able to unite the two warring factions behind them. After a week of fruitless balloting, the weary delegates turned on the 103rd ballot to John W. Davis of West Virginia, a Morgan lawyer who had also served as Solicitor General and as Ambassador to Great Britain. Senator Thomas Walsh of Montana, who chaired a committee that investigated the Harding scandals, could have had the Vice Presidential nod had he desired it, but he declined this honor. Instead, the delegates attempted to balance the ticket ideologically and geographically with Governor Charles Bryan of Nebraska, William Jennings's brother. No more apt illustration of the old adage that "politics make strange bedfellows" could be offered; Davis and Bryan had little in common other than that they were both Democrats, and the party thus doomed itself to presenting a divided image to the American public even before the campaign had begun.

While William Jennings Bryan referred to the platform offered by the Resolutions Committee, presided over by Homer Cummings of Connecticut, as the best one the Democratic party had ever written, another one-time Presidential nominee, James Cox, attacked it as "a foolish platform given us by Hearst, Bryan, and McAdoo." The Springfield *Republican* found it perhaps the most conservative Democratic platform in a generation,[1] and the *New Republic*, devoid of progressive features.[2] After praising the Wilson adminstration, it vigorously lambasted the record of Harding and Coolidge: "Never before in our history has the government been so tainted by corruption and never has an adminstration so utterly failed." Its specific targets included the Fordney-McCumber Tariff and the Mellon tax plan. There was even a plank which attacked the Republicans for failing to enforce the prohibition laws, even though the Democrats had avoided mentioning this issue in their past platforms as if it were contaminated.

Although this document did not specifically condemn the Ku Klux Klan, one plank did "deplore and condemn an effort to arouse lame duck sessions of Congress and advocated the development of aviation; after two decades of flying, platform drafters finally had begun to take notice of man's conquest of the skies. Turning to foreign affairs, the platform endorsed world disarmament, and came out in favor of a national referendum on the League of Nations, while again favoring both it and the World Court. There also was an attack on the Lausanne Treaty relative to Armenia and a greeting to the Republic of Greece.

In the most closely contested platform fight in the history of American national political conventions, supporters of the majority report managed to defeat a minority plank specifically condemning the Ku Klux Klan by the incredibly narrow margin of 542-3/20 to 541-7/20. Although it was generally favored by Northeasterners, it was opposed by Bryan and most of the McAdoo delegates; the three-time Presidential nomineee observed that "if our party is turned aside from its transcendent duty as champion of the rights of the masses, another party can take our place."[3] In supporting the minority plank, former Secretary of State Bainbridge Colby referred to the Klan as "this poisonous, this alien thing in our midst, abhorrent to every American."⁴ To Colby and other proponents of the substitute, this action by the convention was an unforgivable step placing political expediency above lofty ideals.

With emotions at such a fever pitch, it is not surprising that bitterness also marked the debate on a plank offered by Newton Baker of Ohio, endorsing the League of Nations but not advocating a national referendum. This went down to defeat by a better than two-to-one margin, 353½ to 742½; both the Irish and the Klan voted against it. During this debate Key Pittman of Nevada struck a rather low blow at Wilson's former Secretary of War with his attack on "The speaker who spoke before here, with his wild burst of oratory, with the tears in his eyes and his broken-down, slobbering body across this rail."⁵ Not to be outdone, Baker himself had referred to Henry Cabot Lodge not as a person but as a "malevolent institution."⁶ Fortunately, there was no riot during these debates.

More united in principle was the Conference for Progressive Political Action, generally referred to as the Progressive party, which met at Cleveland on the Fourth of July. In accordance with his wishes, the Progressives endorsed rather than nominated Robert La Follette for President; to the aging Wisconsin reformer, the CPPA was an independent party, not a third party. La Follette eventually won the backing of the Farmer-Labor party, the Socialist party, the American Federation of Labor, and the Railway Brotherhoods. The Vice Presidential nominee of the Progressive party was Burton Wheeler of Montana, who unlike Republican La Follette, was a Democrat. He was chosen by his party's national committee rather than by the national convention.

The platform, which was written mostly by La Follette, might be described as dovetailing Populist and Progressive planks with pacifist and isolationist ones. According to the *New Republic*, it had a decided agrarian flavor.⁷ It was far shorter than the Republican or Democratic ones in an age when these documents were becoming increasingly verbose; in many ways it was quite similar to the minority platform voted down at the Republican convention. The foreign policy plank was even a verbatim transcription, with its call for "a revision of the Versailles Treaty in accordance with the terms of the armistice." Despite its unqualified endorsement of freedom of speech, press, and assemblage, there was no attack on the Ku Klux Klan. This omission doubtless was not the result of a desire not to offend Progressive Ku Kluxers, since most members of this organization were either Democrats or Republicans. While Washington Pezet observed at the time in the *Forum* of the Progressives that they were "a *potpourri* of undigested malcontents,"[8] Kenneth MacKay concluded retrospectively of the document which they drew up that it "can stand comparison with such able—and rare—statements of policy as the Democratic platform of 1932."[9]

A week later the Communist party held its first national convention, at which it selected as its Presidential candidate William Foster of Illinois, and as his running-mate Benjamin Gitlow of New York. The platform was directed at the workers and farmers; the exploiters were specifically identified as the Garys, Morgans, Rockefellers, Fords, McCormicks, and other great capitalists. Although this document did mention the Harding scandals, it also made reference to profiteering during World War I "with the connivance of government officials." "Strikebreaker" Coolidge and "Morgan-Rockefeller lawyer" Davis were pictured as tools of the "capitalist-dictatorship," while La Follette was categorized as "the representative of little business against big business."

Among the specific domestic reforms it proposed were the creation of a mass farmer-labor party, the nationalization of industry under the control of the workers, unemployment compensation, abolition of injunctions against labor, release of all political and class war prisoners, land for the users, and nationalization of transportation. The two foreign policy planks attacked U.S. policy towards Haiti, the Dominican Republic, and Central America, colonialism in the Philippines, and the Dawes Plan, and endorsed the recognition of the Soviet Union by the American government. The historian might cite some obvious parallels between these planks and those found in the platforms of the Socialist and Socialist Labor parties, but the Communists here attacked the Socialists as well as the Progressives for the "betrayal" of the Farmer-Labor party of 1920.

For the first time in a Presidential election radio played a major role in 1924. The voters, though, remained apathetic, owing in part to a revival of prosperity, and again in part to a declining interest in the question of American global involvement. La Follette, Bryan, Davis, and Dawes eventually attacked the Ku Klux Klan during the campaign, but "Silent Cal" remained taciturn. With only a half of the qualified voters bothering to go to the polls, the result was an overwhelming victory for Coolidge—and "keeping cool"—over Davis and the divided Democrats: 15,725,016 popular votes and 382 electoral votes to 8,385,586 and 136. The anti-Coolidge popular vote, however, totalled over 13 million. Third party nominee La Follette amassed 4,822,856 popular votes and ran ahead of Davis in half the states west of the Mississippi, even though the Republicans had pictured the former as a radical and a Socialist. With prohibition now a reality, the vote for their Presidential candidate dropped off from the 200,000 range typical of past elections to a mere 57,551; the Socialist Labor party and Communist party nominees lagged even further behind.

Although polling techniques were not truly scientific at this time, one might examine a survey which the *Outlook* conducted by mail of voter sentiment on various issues prior to the national conventions.[10] Partisan divisions of opinion were most apparent relative to the tariff question and the League of Nations, but on many issues Democrats and Republicans stood in substantial agreement, as in their support of the Mellon tax plan, prohibition, immigration restrictions, and the child labor amendment. Republican men and women apparently disagreed with each other less than Democratic men and women, but the Democratic platform was found was more in line with Democratic public opinion than in a similar survey of Republicans. With respect to sectional attitudes, the South was the most sympathetic to the League of Nations and the Ku Klux Klan; yet more Southerners opposed than favored the Klan, and more supported than condemned a federal antilynching law. If only accurate to a degree, these results indicate that public opinion on the great issues of the day during Presidential election years may be a bit more complex than opposing planks in major party platforms would indicate.

XXIV. 1928

Rum, Romanism, and the Happy Warrior

Calvin Coolidge's second term as President, as we have just pointed out, was more or less a continuation of his first, with few if any abrupt shifts in ideology. Cleveland's second administration may have been more conservative, and TR's more liberal, but "Silent Cal" did not veer from his predetermined course. Thanks to revenue acts passed in 1926 and 1928, personal income and inheritance taxes were reduced; these measures were in line with the fiscal philosophy of Secretary of the Treasury Andrew Mellon. On the other hand, Coolidge vetoed the McNary-Haugen Farm Relief bill in 1928, although he did sign a Flood Control Act appropriation for Mississippi Valley projects, along with the White-Jones Merchant Marine Act encouraging private shipping.

With respect to foreign affairs, the US Senate endorsed American membership in the World Court in 1926, but one reservation which it attached relating to advisory opinions proved unacceptable to court members. American participation in the Geneva Disarmament Conference the following year led to no real accomplishment, while the Kellogg-Briand Peace Pact of 1928 failed in achieving its stated objective of outlawing war. Turning to this hemisphere, Coolidge sent US troops into Nicaragua in 1927, while during the same year Ambassador to Mexico Dwight Morrow reached an understanding with officials there relative to the Mexican expropriation of American oil properties. The following year the Clark Memorandum was drawn up repudiating the Roosevelt Corollary to the Monroe Doctrine.

Had he so desired, Coolidge could have had his party's Presidential nomination in 1928 and probably would have defeated his Democratic opponent. But on August 2, 1927, while vacationing in the Black Hills of South Dakota he issued the cryptic statement: "I do not choose to run."[1]

Unlike in 1924, the Socialist party nominated a Presidential and Vice Presidential candidate and approved a platform. With Eugene Debs now dead, the delegates who had assembled at New York City in April turned to Norman Thomas of New York, an Ohio-born Presbyterian minister who had founded *The World*

Tomorrow and edited *The Nation,* as their choice to head the ticket; Thomas was to be the Socialist Presidential candidate for another two decades. James Maurer was chosen as his running-mate. The platform contained little new domestically, although for the first time there was a section on farm relief. As one might expect, Sacco and Vanzetti's trial, conviction, and execution were described as "legalized murder."

Of greater interest were the foreign policy planks, which attacked the debt settlement with fascist Italy, and lambasted recent US policy towards Latin America, especially President Coolidge's "infamous little imperialist war in Nicaragua." Although it had categorized the League of Nations in 1920 as a "mischievous organization," in 1928 it instead suggested that this body be made all-inclusive and democratic, in which even the United States should join. In contrast, the Socialist Labor party, in endorsing Verne Reynolds for President and Jeremiah Crowley for Vice President, ratified a platform overflowing with generalities, which advocated no specific domestic reforms and ignored foreign affairs. This document, though, was twice as long as the documents the party had approved in 1920 and 1924.

Another party whose orientation was in the same general direction as these two organizations was the Farmer-Labor party, which had backed Robert La Follette for President in 1924 after nominating a candidate of its own in 1920. Its Presidential candidate in 1928 was Frank Webb. The platform, which was shorter than that of 1920, consisted of twenty planks and did not include a preamble. There are few new departures to be found here, although the agricultural plank did endorse the equalization principle calling for the dumping of farm surpluses abroad; there was far less emphasis on labor than there had been eight years previously. One foreign policy plank attacked US intervention in Nicaragua, China, and Mexico. The call for independence for the Philippines merely echoed past demands of this and other parties, but the recommendation of civil government for the Virgin Islands struck a new note.

With Calvin Coolidge out of the running for another term as chief executive, the Republicans assembled at Kansas City in June to select a new standard-bearer. One possible candidate, Frank Lowden of Illinois, diminished his chances by tying his nomination to Republican support for the McNary-Haugen plan. The front-runner, Iowaborn Herbert Hoover of California, was not looked upon with enthusiasm by the President or Secretary of the Treasury Andrew Mellon, and had lost to favorite-son candidates in Presidential preference primaries in such states as Illinois and Nebraska. Nevertheless, Coolidge's Secretary of Commerce capitalized upon his fame as an engineer and humanitarian to seize the nomination on the first ballot, when he tallied 837 votes to 74 for Lowden and 64 for Carl Curtis of Kansas. The latter, who was then serving as Senate Majority Leader, had originally taken the position that he would decline the Vice Presidential nomination; disregarding his reluctance, the convention nevertheless tapped him. Thus for the first time in American political history a major party nominated its candidates for President and Vice President from states west of the Mississippi.

The Committee on Resolutions was also headed by a Westerner, Senator Reed Smoot of Utah, whose name would be immortalized two years later upon the passage of the highest tariff in American history, the Hawley-Smoot Tariff. After taking the usual step of endorsing "without qualification" the incumbent administration, the platform affirmed that "the record of the United States Treasury under Secretary Mellon stands unrivalled and unsurpassed." Perhaps the most controversial domestic plank was the one that rejected the McNary-Haugen scheme for farm relief in favor of the establishment of a federal farm board. With respect to prohibition, this document endorsed the eighteenth Amendment, but ignored the Volstead Act. The tariff plank offered no surprises, generally approving the Fordney-McCumber Act of 1922, while other ones praised lower taxes and debt reduction. More original was that calling for the governmental supervision of the emerging radio industry.

Without being more specific, the platform gave its blessing to "a foreign policy based upon the traditional American position," still opposing American membership in the League of Nations. According to it, the US government had adopted a "firm and friendly" policy towards Mexico, while our Nicaraguan policy "absolutely repudiates any idea of conquest or exploitation"; China was "that unhappy nation" where we had been forced to intervene. In addition, this document came out in favor of the Kellogg-Briand Pact and of international arbitration, but these were less controversial stands.

This time the Wisconsin minority platform was offered by Robert La Follette, Jr., who had succeeded his father in the US Senate in 1925 upon the latter's death. It was signed by delegates from eight states. Perhaps its most unusual feature was its advocacy of the McNary-Haugen bill, although it also supported the liberalization of the Volstead Act and steeper income taxes for the wealthy, and opposed the landing of American troops on foreign soil. The delegates were more friendly to La Follette than their counterparts had been to other spokesmen for dissent in the past, but the convention took no action on this minority platform. Instead, it rejected by a 807 to 277 margin a plank offered by Earl Smith of Illinois which endorsed the spirit of the McNary-Haugen bill without mentioning it by name or spelling out provisions. Another plank repealing the eighteenth Amendment that Nicholas Murray Butler proposed was tabled by a voice vote.

The Democrats assembled later the same month at Houston, a site selected as a concession to southern predilections. William McAdoo had announced in December 1927 that he would not be a candidate for the Presidency, while Thomas Walsh, the investigator from Montana who was both a "dry" and a Catholic, also withdrew his name from consideration. This left the path clear for Governor Alfred Smith of New York, one of the few Democratic officeholders in the North during that decade to win re-election with regularity; placing his name in nomination as he had in 1924, Franklin Roosevelt referred to Smith as "the Happy Warrior."[2] Smith, a Catholic, a "wet," a Tammanyite, and the city-bred son of immigrants, won his party's endorsement on the first ballot, owing to some changed votes at the end of the roll call. To balance the ticket, the delegates turned to the Senate Minority Leader, Joseph Robinson of Arkansas, a Southerner, a "wet" and a Protestant. According to one writer, "The Democratic donkey with a wet head and wagging a dry tail left Houston."[3]

Senator Key Pittman of Nevada, who had so vehemently blasted Newton Baker's minority plank on the League of Nations four years previously, served as the chairman of the Resolutions Committee. Following the pattern set by its Republican counterpart, this body experienced the greatest difficulty in domestic affairs relative to the prohibition and agricultural planks. Although the document they formulated did not endorse the McNary-Haugen plan, it declared that "farm relief must rest on the basis of an economic equality of agriculture with other industries," and advocated the establishment of a Federal Farm Board. "Drys" were pleased with the pledge to enforce the eighteenth Amendment and all prohibition laws, but Smith, in supporting this, also called for the eventual repeal of the eighteenth Amendment. Deviating somewhat from tradition, the tariff plank was milder than most found in past Democratic platforms; there was no specific condemnation of the highly protective Fordney-McCumber Tariff. One might cite as among the more innovative features the radio plank with its call for governmental supervision and control, and the demand for a scientific plan on the basis of which the government would make appropriations for public works during periods of unemployment.

The foreign policy section, which ignored the war debt question, not surprisingly condemned the Republicans for interfering in the internal affairs of Mexico and Nicaragua, but also took a more unexpected stance by attacking the relatively successful Washington Disarmament Conference, along with its less fruitful sequel at Geneva. Unlike in 1924, this time there was no mention either of the League of Nations or of the World Court; there was, however, an endorsement of the Kellogg-Briand Pact. While words of praise were offered such past Democratic leaders as Thomas Jefferson and Grover Cleveland, the most touching eulogy was that intoned over Woodrow Wilson, "who in his life and in his official actions voiced the hopes and aspirations of all good men of every race and clime." During the course of the debate, Governor Dan Moody of Texas proposed a minority plank taking a stronger stand on prohibition than the majority report, but he withdrew this without a vote taken on it. To former Governor Nellie Tayloe Ross of Wyoming, the platform was "clear and concise,"[4] but to the *World's Work* it was a "crazy quilt."[5]

The Prohibition party itself met at Chicago the following month (July), sharply divided as to whether it should back Hoover and Dawes or field a separate ticket. The delegates eventually nominated William Varney of New York for President and James Edgerton of Virginia for Vice President, with the understanding that they would withdraw at a later date if asked to by the party's executive committee. With respect to the platform, the Resolutions Committee submitted a lengthy one to the national convention, but that body rejected this in favor of a briefer statement that gave the Prohibition party credit for pioneering in the sponsorship of two reforms that had become a part of the Constitution: prohibition and woman suffrage. The seven demands that constituted the final part of this document ignored other domestic issues and foreign policy to concentrate on preventing "the threatened calamity of the election of the wet Tammany candidate." Despite the fact that in the past they had been as vocal in their denunciation of the Democrats and the Republicans as the latter had been of each other, the Prohibitionists sanctimoniously depreciated "the custom of political parties in their platforms charging all sins and shortcomings to each other."

While the Prohibitionists concentrated on one issue, the Communists, at their May convention at New York City, embraced a galaxy of issues in nominating William Foster of Illinois for President and Benjamin Gitlow of New York for Vice President. The platform the delegates adopted was the longest one any party had endorsed up to that time, and almost as long as the longest one any party to date has sanctioned. Prophetically declaring that a second world war was inevitable, this document also made the accusation that this nation was then in the grips of an economic depression. In terms of structure, it consisted of a series of eighteen statements of philosophy, all but the first and last of which were followed by a series of specific demands. The more original of these included public kitchens to provide free meals for all the unemployed and their families, a death knell for company unions, the ousting of John L. Lewis as the head of the United Mine Workers, the ending of religious and "jingoist" instruction in the public schools, and the repeal of legislation prohibiting the teaching of evolution.

In certain respects the section on Negro rights was the most complete and progressive set forth in any platform to date; this demanded the voiding of all "Jim Crow" laws and the granting of complete equality. As for prohibition, in advocating the repeal of the Volstead Act, the Communists gave this old issue a new twist by a call for "Energetic propaganda against alcoholism as one of the more malignant soul diseases under capitalism." This document also was the first in American history to complain about the disenfranchisement of eighteen-to-twenty-one-year-olds. Especially negative was the foreign policy section, which attacked

US intervention in Nicaragua, China, and Mexico, American colonialism, extraterritorial rights overseas, the Kellogg-Briand Pact, the Dawes Plan, the World Court, and the League of Nations. One more positive recommendation favored the election of officers by rank-and-file soldiers and sailors.

With Smith as the Democratic nominee, Hoover correctly felt from the beginning that he was the front runner, and campaigned accordingly. Although he side-stepped Smith's Catholicism, he did attack the Democratic platform as state socialism; Hoover was by no means charismatic as an orator, but he did not alienate his audience to the extent that Smith did with his East Side accent. The Republican candidate proved to be popular with the German voters, due to his role in World War I relief, and he did not lose many votes to Smith on the farm issue, which he called the "most urgent economic problem in our nation today."[6]

Disenchanted by Smith's Catholicism and "wetness," five southern states voted for a GOP nominee for the first time since 1876, as nationally the Republicans endorsed "A Chicken for Every Pot." Hoover, with 21,392,190 popular votes and 444 electoral votes, easily outdistanced Smith, whose totals respectively were 15,016,443 and 87, while the Republicans maintained control of both houses of Congress; the Socialist Thomas made the best showing of the third party candidates, amassing 267,720 popular votes, while the Communist Foster lagged far behind with 48,770. The only northern states that Smith carried were Rhode Island and Massachusetts, in both cases probably for the reason that he was a "wet." Yet it was "the Happy Warrior" who, in a losing cause, battled Hoover on even terms in the large cities outside of Dixie, and thus loosened the strangle hold that the Republicans had long held there. Smith, therefore, paved the way for Franklin Roosevelt's victory four years later, and the forging of a new Democratic majority coalition that was to control the Presidency for two decades.

XXV.   1932

FDR, the Forgotten Man, and the New Deal

A half-year after he took office as chief executive, the roof caved in on Herbert Hoover when the stock market began its monumental collapse in October, ushering in the greatest depression in American history. Before this crash Hoover had signed into law the Agricultural Marketing Act, which established a Federal Farm Board; this went out of business in 1933, after spending more than $180 million in a futile effort to support agricultural prices. The following year Hoover reluctantly signed into law the highest tariff ever enacted, the Hawley-Smoot Tariff. These attempts to win the votes of special interest groups did not prevent the Republicans from experiencing a setback at the polls in the Congressional election of 1930, the first such loss they had suffered in fourteen years. Hoover was less sympathetic to the veterans, vetoing a bonus bill in 1931 that Congress later passed over his veto; there was a "Bonus March" of disgruntled ex-servicemen on Washington in the summer of 1932, which led to an eventual confrontation with Federal troops. Although Hoover at first was of the opinion that recovery from the depression was as much a private as a public matter, by 1932 he was signing into law such measures as the Reconstruction Finance Corporation Act, the first Glass-Steagall Act, and the Federal Home Loan Bank Act.

Turning to the foreign affairs field, the Young Plan of 1929 reduced the amount of reparations due from Germany, while the Debt Moratorium of 1931 suspended payments for one year on both interallied debts and reparations. With the Great Depression encompassing the entire world, the collection of these sums became increasingly difficult. The United States also participated in the London Disarmament Conference of 1930, which was a partial success, and the Geneva Disarmament Conference of 1932, which was an outright failure. On the other hand, a moral victory was achieved by Secretary of State Henry Stimson in his attempt to uphold the territorial integrity of China in the wake of the Japanese establishment of a puppet state in Manchuria.

The outbreak of the Great Depression quite naturally afforded the more radical political organizations a golden opportunity to proclaim that capitalism was finished and that a new era lay ahead. One of these, the Socialist Labor party, assembled at New York City late in April to endorse a ticket of Verne Reynolds of New York for President and John Aiken of Massachusetts for Vice President. Significantly, the platform this convention ratified made reference to the impact of the economic collapse throughout the world as well as on the United States. After noting that the Socialist Labor party had "ceaselessly pointed out the inevitable doom of the capitalist system," it boldly proclaimed that: *"This state of social dissolution is now upon us."* But, as usual, there were no specific proposals for reform.

The Socialist party assembled in May at Milwaukee. Norman Thomas was again its Presidential nominee, with James Maurer of Pennsylvania his running-mate. Far from recommending a slash in the Federal budget as the Republicans and Democrats did, the Socialist party platform came out for a Federal appropriation of $5 billion for immediate relief, and of $5 billion for public works and roads, reforestation, slum clearance, and better housing. One of the more original aspects of this document was a proposed worker's rights amendment to the Constitution, embracing the Socialist program. With respect to the global scene, it recommended the creation of one or more international economic organizations on which labor was adequately represented. Although the platform declared that "there can be no permanent peace until Socialism is established internationally," the preamble restricted itself to a discussion of the impact of the depression on the United States. Two months later the League for Independent Political Action, which met at Cleveland in July, threw its support to the Socialists as the best choice among those parties then in the field.

Even more extreme was the platform the Communist party drew up at the time its convention was nominating a ticket of William Foster of New York for President and James Ford of Alabama for Vice President. (Ford was a Negro.) Unlike the document ratified in 1928, this one was far briefer, and was in many respects a summary of the former. Mostly philosophical in nature, it endorsed a half-dozen specific reforms: unemployment and social insurance financed by the state and employers; the termination of Hoover's "wage-cutting" policy; emergency relief and tax exemption for the farmers; equal rights for Negroes; and the ending of capitalist terror and imperialist war. The last section called for the establishment of a United States of Soviet America.

In contrast, an endorsement of the status quo was the basic concern of a dull and dispirited group of Republican delegates that met at Chicago in June to renominate Herbert Hoover for President. Hoover received 1,126½ out of a possible 1,154 votes on the first ballot; his chief "rival," former Senator Joseph France of Maryland, obtained a mere four votes after running up a meaningless string of victories in uncontested primaries. A more serious possibility, Dwight Morrow, had died the previous year, while James Coxey of Coxey's Army fame won the Ohio Presidential preference primary over France. Charles Curtis was again the Vice Presidential nominee. Since the Hoover administration had generally reflected traditional Republican principles in its policies and actions, for the delegates to repudiate it would have been an act of political suicide.

James Garfield of Ohio, the son of the martyred President, presided over the Resolutions Committee, whose product contained few, if any, surprises. Pledging a sharp reduction in governmental expenditures and a balanced budget, it contrasted the Republican record with that of the Democrats. The now-Democratic House of Representatives was the focal point of attack in this connection: "Individualism running amuck has displaced party discipline and has trampled under foot party leadership." The Democrats were specifically criticized for favoring pork-barrel legislation, the issuance of fiat currency, the manipulation of commodity prices, the guaranty of bank deposits, and the squandering of the public resources. In contrast, President Herbert Hoover was "a leader—wise, courageous, patient, understanding, resourceful," who had done as much as any man could have done to counteract the effects of a world-wide depression.

Pointing out that Great Britain had been forced to go off the gold standard, this document favored keeping it, and recommended the convening of an international monetary conference. There also was an endorsement of the exorbitantly protective Hawley-Smoot Tariff, which was supposedly a great blessing to farmers as well as to industrialists, and of the ill-fated Federal Farm Board and the Reconstruction Finance Corporation. In 1932, for the first time, the St. Lawrence Seaway was favorably mentioned by name by the Republicans, although it had been alluded to as early as 1924. More ambiguous was the prohibition plank, which was a masterpiece of fence-straddling: "We do not favor a submission limited to the issue of retention or repeal, for the American nation never in its history has gone backward, and in this case the progress which has been thus far made must be preserved, while the evils must be eliminated." The Chicago *Tribune* found this a "declaration of political bankruptcy—and futile as it is fraudulent,"[1] while the *Nation* opined, "It is doubtful if a more cheaply dishonest plank was ever embodied even in the Republican platform before."[2]

With respect to foreign affairs, in favoring a "just balance between Japan and China" this document took a surprisingly soft line towards the former, especially in light of the so-called Stimson Doctrine. While in 1928 the Republicans had opposed American membership in the League of Nations, this time they noted with reference to the Far Eastern dispute that the US has "acted in harmony with the governments represented in the League of Nations." There also was a separate section calling for American membership in the World Court, in accordance with the desires of Harding, Coolidge, and Hoover; still another plank endorsed the accomplishments of the London Disarmament Conference, and noted American participation in its successor at Geneva. In the opinion of the *Review of Reviews* the platform as a whole was "an unusually clear and well-expressed document,"[3] but the *World Tomorrow* was doubtful whether any other Republican platform had exceeded that of 1932 "in buncombe, evasion, duplicity, and insincerity."[4]

What debate there was centered around the highly controversial prohibition plank. Hiram Bingham of Connecticut sponsored a minority substitute which recommended that Congress propose a Constitutional amendment repealing prohibition, with the understanding that should this be ratified every effort would be made to promote temperance and abolish saloons. In the course of his defense Bingham observed: "We adopted the 18th Amendment in order to help win the war. We must repeal it in order to help win the depression."[5] Another defense of the minority plank by Ambrose Kennedy of New York took the rare step of quoting in Latin the Roman poet Horace's observation that the mountain has labored and brought forth a mouse. But economic arguments and Latin quotes failed to ensure victory for the minority substitute, as Hoover and the South favored the majority plank; the final tally, though, was relatively close, 460-2/9 [for] to 690-9/36 [against] (The vote in the Resolutions Committee had been 17 to 35.) It is significant that James Garfield, who was the Chairman of the Resolutions Committee, was booed so vigorously in the course of his defense of the majority plank that he had to stop speaking. After the above roll-call vote was taken, the majority report as a whole was approved by voice vote.

Later that month the Democrats also assembled at Chicago, truly confident of victory for the first time since 1916. The front-runners for the Democratic Presidential nomination included the 1928 candidate, Alfred Smith; the Speaker of the House of Representatives, John Nance Garner; the conservative, states-rights governor of Maryland, Albert Ritchie; and the current governor of New York, Franklin Delano Roosevelt. The latter emerged as the leader on the early balloting, winning the support of a majority of the delegates, and obtained the nomination on the fourth ballot when Garner and William McAdoo threw their support to him. Garner was then offered, and accepted, second spot on the ticket. Roosevelt, who broke tradition by flying to Chicago before he had been officially notified of his selection, set the keynote for the campaign and for the next dozen years of American politics by telling the delegates: "I pledge you, I pledge myself, to a new deal for the American people."[6]

As noteworthy as the Presidential candidate was the platform, officially drafted by a committee presided over by former Senator Gilbert Hitchcock of Nebraska, but conceived in large part beforehand by Wilson's Attorney General, A. Mitchell Palmer. To Karl Schriftgiesser this was "one of the few really great platforms ever presented at a national convention,"[7] while to David Hinshaw and Bruno Shaw it was "the best major-party platform, both for thought and expression, in American history."[8] Only 1,727 words in length, it certainly was short; less known is the fact that the Resolutions Committee experienced such difficulties in finalizing a draft that it was unable to report until the evening of the third day. Nor did this document take stands opposite from its Republican counterpart on every issue, although the Democrats differed from the GOP in their advocacy of unemployment and old-age insurance legislation at the state level, and of measures enabling farmers to obtain a return on their products in excess of cost.

Unlike the Republicans, the Democrats laid the blame for the depression at the door of the Harding, Coolidge, and Hoover administrations: "the chief causes of this condition were the disastrous policies pursued by our government since the World War." A number of the proposed remedies that the Democrats set forth to remedy this condition were to come back and haunt FDR after he had launched the New Deal; these included a 25 percent reduction in the cost of the Federal government, a balanced budget, and the abolition of useless commissions and offices. The pledge for "a sound currency to be preserved at all hazards" also ran contradictory to the Roosevelt administration's removal of the United States from the gold standard, while the call for an international monetary conference was not in harmony with FDR's undercutting of such a gathering at London.

On the other hand, the New Deal did represent a consummation of such planks in the 1932 Democratic platform as those calling for reciprocal trade agreements, various restrictions on holding companies, and the regulation of stock exchanges and the full publicizing of stocks. There also was a demand for various banking reforms, but no specific endorsement of the deposit guaranty scheme, in accordance with the wishes of Roosevelt, who did not want to project a radical image to the banking community. As one would have expected, this document attacked the Federal Farm Board, not the greatest of Republican achievements, but ignored the Reconstruction Finance Corporation. Despite pressure from Huey Long, FDR forbade mention of a veterans' bonus. One of the more forthright planks came out openly for the repeal of the eighteenth Amendment, while another recommended the immediate modification of the Volstead Act; to H. L. Mencken, writing in the Baltimore *Evening Sun*, these resolutions marked "the death-bed of Prohibition."[9] Relatively little attention was paid to foreign policy, however, and the League of Nations was ignored, if not attacked. Nevertheless, the platform did endorse the World Court, the Kellogg-Briand Pact, and the Monroe Doctrine, and opposed the cancellation of war debts, a subject on which the Republicans failed to take a stand.

While Governor "Alfalfa Bill" Murray of Oklahoma offered an eight-point minority platform, and a half-dozen other individuals presented separate minority planks, the focal point of the debate was prohibition. Cordell Hull's minority plank left this question up to state conventions, declaring that the majority report had made it a partisan issue; both Alfred Smith and Albert Ritchie spoke in favor of the latter, while FDR also supported repeal. The minority plank was then overwhelmingly defeated on a roll-call vote, 213¾ to 934¾. Aside from this issue, William McAdoo offered a minority plank calling for bank deposit guaranty legislation, a reform that had only narrowly lost in the Resolutions Committee, but his proposal went down to defeat on a voice vote. There apparently was some sentiment for "Alfalfa Bill's" call for an immediate payment of the veterans' bonus, but both this and his demand for the governmental coining of both gold and silver suffered the same fate as McAdoo's scheme. The one minority plank the convention adopted was offered by Caroline O'Day of New York; this recommended: "Continuous responsibility of government for human welfare, especially for the protection of children."[10] It won on a voice vote.

With its short-lived triumph in jeopardy, the Prohibition party assembled at Indianapolis in July to endorse a ticket of William Upshaw of Georgia for President and Frank Regan of Illinois for Vice President. The platform was much longer and more detailed than that adopted in 1928, and devoted surprisingly little space to prohibition; one plank did recommend that all representatives of the US government overseas should observe the eighteenth Amendment. Recognizing that "the country finds itself in the midst of the most severe depression in its history," this document advocated the establishment of an economic council composed of leaders in the fields of economics, agriculture, labor, finance, commerce, and industry to propose various remedies. One of the more original domestic planks favored the governmental censorship of motion pictures. There was little on foreign policy, aside from an endorsement of American membership in the World Court.

The Farmer-Labor party, which made its last appearance in the 1932 campaign, met at Omaha several days later. Its Presidential nominee (and original Vice Presidential candidate) was Jacob Coxey of Ohio, who already had run in that state's Presidential preference primary as a Republican; its first choice, Frank Webb, had resigned to accept the Liberty party nomination. The platform, which represented a departure from tradition in that many of the planks were only a sentence long, giving it a telegraphic appearance in spots, set forth a series of remedies for the depression in its first two sections. These included the abolition of the Federal Reserve System, the free coinage of silver, a public works program, flood relief, price floors under agricultural products, a moratorium on the foreclosures of mortgages, prohibitions against gambling in securities and commodities, unemployment insurance, a cash soldier bonus, and old-age pensions.

Other planks called for a ten-year limit on patents and the outlawing of holding companies and chain stores. This document was extremely limited on foreign policy, although it did advocate independence for the Philippines, and recommend that the United States should stay out of the League of Nations and the World Court.

Because of the Depression, it is likely that any Democratic nominee could have defeated Hoover, but Roosevelt campaigned in thirty-seven states and spoke frequently. As a radio orator, FDR far surpassed the incumbent President. Roosevelt had earlier abandoned his long-standing support for the League of Nations in a successful attempt to win the backing of powerful newspaper publisher William Randolph Hearst, but foreign policy played only a secondary role in this campaign. That spring, prior to receiving his party's Presidential nomination, FDR, in a compassionate moment, had spoken of "the forgotten man at the bottom of the economic pyramid."[11] During the campaign itself he made several recommendations that anticipated the New Deal legislative program, including a domestic allotment scheme for agriculture and a public power program. More ambiguous was his fence-straddling stance on the tariff; in attacking deficit financing while advocating social welfare and unemployment relief, Roosevelt placed himself in a near-impossible position with respect to credibility. Perceptively realizing that Roosevelt's policies might well constitute a radical departure from the American tradition, Hoover warned that should his Democratic rival triumph, "the grass will grow in streets of a hundred cities, a thousand towns; the weeds will overrun the fields of millions of farms."[12]

But this threat proved to no avail. FDR carried 2,721 out of the nation's 3,050 counties, an unprecedented number, in a landslide victory; continuing the trend begun by Smith, he won every large city except for Philadelphia, where the Vare machine was entrenched. Such prominent Senators as Johnson, La Follette, and

Norris defected to the Democratic cause. Roosevelt ran up a three-
to-two edge over Hoover in the popular vote, 22,809,638 to
15,758,901, and a lopsided majority in the Electoral College, 472 to
59. Hoover carried only six states, all of them in the Northeast:
Maine, Vermont, New Hampshire, Connecticut, Pennsylvania
and Delaware. The Democrats also won unquestioned control of
both houses of Congress. Turning to the third party candidates,
Norman Thomas amassed 881,951 votes; the totals for the others
ranged from 102,785 for the Communist Foster down to 7,309 for
the Farmer-Laborite Coxey. If America was to undergo a revolution—and to many the New Deal was a revolution—it was to be a
Constitutional one, not one of the violent sort.

XXVI. 1936

Landon-Knox Falling Down

Any effort to summarize briefly the domestic legislation that
was enacted during Franklin Roosevelt's first administration
would obviously be an impossible undertaking. One might
speculate at length as to whether the New Deal was merely an
extension of the Progressive movement, or whether it marked a
break with the past. According to one scheme of periodization, the
years 1933-35 featured recovery, 1935-38 reform, and 1938-41
stagnation, but one might note a number of specific exceptions to
this chronology. Supported by overwhelming Democratic majorities in both houses of Congress, FDR pushed numerous reforms
through that body during his first three months in office, the so-
called "Hundred Days." Some of these measures were so hastily
drawn up that the US Supreme Court later invalidated them on
Constitutional grounds. A list for 1933 alone would include the
Emergency Banking Relief Act, the Economy Act, the CCC
Reforestation Relief Act, the denial of the convertibility of gold,
the Federal Emergency Relief Act, the Agricultural Adjustment

Act, the Tennessee Valley Authority, the Federal Securities Act, the second Glass-Steagall (FDIC) Act, and the National Recovery Administration. The prohibition amendment also was repealed during this year.

So extreme a departure did these measures seem from established political practice to many observers that in August 1934 an anti-New Deal coalition of industrialists, financiers, corporation lawyers, and conservative Democrats joined forces to set up the Liberty League. But the Roosevelt administration nevertheless improved its margins in both houses of Congress during the Congressional election of 1934. A list of those measures enacted into law during 1934 and 1935 would include the Municipal Bankruptcy Act, the Securities Exchange Act, the Communications Act, the Silver Purchase Act, the Federal Farm Bankruptcy Act, the Emergency Relief Appropriation Act, the National Labor Relations Act, the Social Security Act, the Public Utility Holding Company Act, and the Bituminous Coal Stabilization Act. Despite this deluge of new laws, a number of radical critics arose in opposition to the New Deal, including Francis Townsend, Huey Long, and Charles Coughlin; Roosevelt "defused" these critics by implementing their better ideas, and in the process further alienated the political right.

Turning to foreign relations, the first Roosevelt administration was highly isolationist in orientation. Unquestionably the focal point of FDR's foreign policy was Latin America, where the Roosevelt administration continued the policies begun by Herbert Hoover with its Good Neighbor Policy, abrogated the Platt Amendment (Cuba) in 1934, and participated in the Montevideo and Buenos Aires conferences. At the very beginning of his tenure in office, FDR helped to undercut the gold standard by failing to support the London Economic Conference; this action dealt a serious blow to international cooperation and tended to poison American relations with Europe. On the other hand, the Roosevelt administration did recognize the Soviet Union after the United States had diplomatically ignored the new Communist state for sixteen years. But US relations with Europe remained minimal. Between 1934 and 1936 the Nye Committee investigated the alleged responsibility of the munition makers for American involvement in World War I; in 1935 and 1936 Congress passed the first two in a series of Neutrality Acts, after the Johnson Debt Default Act of

1934 had forbade loans to any foreign government in default to the
United States. If America was to be drawn into some future
European conflict, it would not be for lack of attempts to avoid it.

Confronted as they now were with a Presidential administration
whose policies contrasted sharply with those of the Harding-
Coolidge-Hoover era, the more radical American political parties
were faced with the dilemma of whether or not they should
endorse the New Deal. When the Socialist Labor party assembled
at New York City in April to approve a ticket of John Aiken of
Massachusetts for President and Emil Teichert of New York for
Vice President, its platform had long been so vague that there was
no problem, had this party chosen to evade taking a stand.
Nevertheless, after formulating a document composed mainly of
platitudes, the Socialist Labor party did attack the New Deal:
"Every reform granted by capitalism is a concealed measure of
reaction, exemplified by the NRA, AAA, TVA, CCC, WPA, etc."

A month later the Socialist party, which traditionally had been
more specific in its demands, gathered at Cleveland. Again
nominating Norman Thomas of New York for President, the
convention selected George Nelson of Wisconsin as his running-
mate; the basic theme of its platform was that the New Deal had
failed as the "Old Deal" had. Complaining about the suppression
of civil liberties and the development of fascistic trends in
America, this document attacked the Civilian Conservation Corps
and the National Youth Administration, but it also favored the
continuance of Works Progress Administration projects at union
wages, and an immediate appropriation of $6 billion to provide
federal relief for the unemployed. Aside from an onslaught against
militarism, there was little on foreign policy; the Socialists did
recommend the maintenance of friendly relations with Soviet
Russia, but did not praise FDR for extending diplomatic recognition.

The Communist party met at New York the following month.
Earl Browder of Kansas was its Presidential nominee, with James
Ford of New York as his running-mate. "Democracy or Fascism,
progress or reaction—this is the central issue of 1936," proclaimed
the Communists in their platform. After placing the party on
record in favor of the establishment of a national Farmer-Labor
party, this document attacked the Republican party for being a
tool of Wall Street and Franklin Roosevelt for compromising. As

for the "secretly formed Union party of Lemke and Coughlin," it
was "the creature of Landon, Hearst, and the Liberty League,"
with a platform similar in many respects to the Republican one.
Despite the accusation that the New Deal had failed, the Communist party recommended that the Works Progress Administration
and the National Youth Administration be extended. Of these
three parties the Communists unquestionably had the most
extensive foreign relations plank, with their key proposal being
that the League of Nations institute financial and economic
sanctions against Hitlerian Germany, Fascist Italy, and imperial
Japan, with the backing of the United States.

Faced with the unpleasant prospect of confronting FDR again,
the Republicans met at Cleveland in June. Although they could
have nominated Herbert Hoover for the third time, they instead
selected as their standard-bearer on the first ballot Governor Alfred
Landon of Kansas, an oil millionaire who had been elected in 1932
and re-elected in 1934. Landon, who received 984 votes to 19 for
Senator William Borah of Idaho, generally had avoided the
primaries, partly because he did not want to appear as the rich
man's candidate, partly because he lacked the funds to engage in
multistate campaigning. Senator Arthur Vandenberg of Michigan
was offered the second spot on the ticket, but he declined this offer;
Landon then turned to Colonel Frank Knox, a Chicago newspaper publisher and a former Bull Mooser, as his running-mate.
Knox, who was to adopt an "Old Guard" stance during the
campaign, nevertheless employed the language of the TR Progressives in his correspondence with Landon.

Of greater interest than the candidates was the platform, whose
stance towards the New Deal had many significant implications.
Despite the fact that Cincinnati civil reformer Charles Taft
coordinated the drafting of planks, party conservatives controlled
the Resolutions Committee, chaired by Herman M. Langworthy,
a Kansas lawyer; William Allen White, who was Landon's
representative on this body, was unable to get reinstated Landon's
views on labor, monetary matters, and civil service, after the Old
Guard had inserted its planks into this document. On the other
hand, William Borah, who was a lesser Presidential possibility,
placed his stamp of approval on those planks dealing with
isolationism, antimonopoly, and currency. While the platform
opened with the statement "America is in peril," followed by a

declaration of grievances a la the Declaration of Independence, the main body of this document recommended the modification of certain aspects of the New Deal, along with the dismantling of other parts. There unquestionably was a greater emphasis on state action than was to be found in the Democratic platform, though there was a stress as well on self-help. It is also important to note that the Republican platform took the position that the New Deal was a violation of Democratic pledges, just as thirty-six years later the Republicans pictured the McGovern candidacy as a betrayal of Democratic principles.

With respect to specifics, this document recommended that the responsibility for relief be returned to nonpolitical local agencies, and that the New Deal version of Social Security be abandoned for an alternate system. The labor plank indirectly attacked the Wagner Act, while the anti-AAA farm plank offered to "protect and foster the family type of farm." Turning the tables on the Democrats, the Republican endorsement of a balanced budget and an end of deficit spending mirrored those planks in the 1932 Democratic platform which FDR had chosen to ignore. Another plank, though, had a decidedly "me too" flavor in that it advocated the federal regulation of the marketing of securities and the interstate activities of public utilities. Probably the most typical plank to be found in this document was that dealing with the tariff; this demanded the repeal of the reciprocal trade agreements program and charged that the New Deal "secretly has made tariff agreements with our foreign competitors." A "furthermore" section attacked the New Deal for being anti-Negro.

Despite the fact that the Republicans did oppose the further devaluation of the dollar and favored international currency stabilization, there was no call for a return to the gold standard as such in accordance with the wishes of Borah, who represented a pro-silver state in Congress. Nor was there any mention of the Good Neighbor Policy or of recent neutrality legislation, perhaps for the reason that both were acceptable to most Republicans, although there was a recommendation that the war debt be collected. But as the *Nation* observed with considerable justification, "The real platform is hatred of Mr. Roosevelt."[1]

In contrast, the Democrats assembled at Philadelphia later in June, confident of victory. To no one's surprise, Franklin Roosevelt was renominated for President and Garner for Vice Presi-

dent, without opposition. FDR, who in 1932 had been the
champion of Southerners, Westerners, farmers, and the middle-
class "forgotten man," by 1936 had become the spokesman for the
urban masses and organized labor. Thus it was not unexpected
when Roosevelt in his acceptance speech attacked "economic
royalists" in affirming that "This generation of Americans has a
rendezvous with destiny."[2] Perhaps the most significant act of this
convention, though, was the abolition of the two-thirds majority
for Presidential and Vice Presidential nominees, a rule that had
deprived Martin Van Buren of his party's Presidential nomination
in 1844 and "Champ" Clark in 1912. Henceforth, would-be
candidates would need assemble only a simple majority of
delegates, as always had been the case with the Republicans.

The Democratic platform was drafted almost entirely by three
men: the President, Judge Samuel Rosenman, one of his intimate
advisors, and Senator Robert Wagner of New York, the Chairman
of the Resolutions Committee. As one would have expected, it
represented an endorsement of the Roosevelt administration and
of the New Deal; to *Business Week*, "Everything in the Democratic
platform and the official illuminations of it points towards social
and economic nationalization."[3] In its final version this document
went so far as to promise to rid our land of kidnappers, bandits,
and "malefactors of great wealth," a passage which obviously was
designed to arouse class antagonisms. The preamble imitated the
Declaration of Independence in that the expression: "We hold this
truth to be self-evident" occurs no less than six times.

From the philosophical standpoint, perhaps the most remarkable feature of this document was the derogatory coupling of the
Republican party with states' rights; states' rights long had been a
basic staple of Democratic ideology, ever since the days of
Jefferson. In this connection the platform declared that "pressing
national problems" "cannot be adequately handled exclusively by
48 separate State legislatures, 48 separate State administrations,
and 48 separate State courts," but also affirmed that "We have
sought and will continue to seek to meet these problems through
legislation within the Constitution." The latter passage constituted an apparent rebuff to the Supreme Court for voiding
certain New Deal measures. With respect to foreign policy, this
document followed the Republican example by touching on this
area only briefly; here the Democrats endorsed the Good Neighbor

Policy, the spirit of the Kellogg-Briand Pact, neutrality, and the reciprocal trade agreements program. Like the Republicans, however, there was no mention of recognizing the Soviet Union, nor of the St. Lawrence Seaway, while the Democrats ignored the World Court instead of attacking it.

Shortly before the Democrats assembled, Representative William "Liberty Bill" Lemke of North Dakota, a Republican, had announced that a new Union party would field a ticket of himself for President and Thomas O'Brien of Massachusetts (a Democrat) for Vice President. Protestant Lemke, who was supported by the "radio priest," Father Charles Coughlin, was an agrarian radical; to H. L. Mencken, "Lemke [was] not a human being at all, but a werewolf."[4] As for the now forgotten O'Brien, he was a Boston Irish Catholic lawyer who had served as a counsel to unions, as well as district attorney. Thus at least from the standpoint of party, religion, and geography the ticket was balanced, perhaps more so than most national tickets have been.

A group of delegates assembled at Cleveland in August to endorse the Lemke-O'Brien slate and to ratify a platform. This document, which was rather brief and consisted of fifteen planks, attacked the New Deal in principle without mentioning either it or the two major parties by name. It was so drawn up as to appeal to the supporters of Coughlin, Dr. Francis Townsend, and Gerald L. K. Smith, who had inherited a part of the late Huey Long's following. Nevertheless, the Union party platform did not specifically embrace the Townsend program of old-age pensions, while it also omitted half the basic principles of Coughlin's National Union for Social Justice, including the nationalization of key resources. It did, however, reflect the "radio priest's" cheap money, antibanker outlook; to David Bennett it was "a potpourri of the monetary panaceas of the time."[5]

Although plank fourteen called for a limitation on the annual income of any individual and a limitation on the total value of a gift or an inheritance, plank thirteen instructed Congress to protect private property from confiscation through unnecessary taxation. Other special interest groups whom the Union party sought to aid were the farmers, laborers, aged, and small industrialists. The currency plank made no mention specifically of gold, silver, or paper, but there was an indirect endorsement of the protective tariff. With respect to foreign policy, this document did recommend an adequate defense, but discouraged overseas military adventures; embracing isolationism, it asserted in its very first plank that: "America shall be self-contained and self-sustained— no foreign entanglements, be they political, economic, financial or military."

Still another third party in the field was the Prohibition party, which convened at Niagara Falls in May to nominate Dr. D. Leigh Colvin of New York for President, with Claude Watson of California as his running-mate. The preamble to the platform lambasted the New Deal for leaving "our gravest problems unsolved," in particular attacking the "bipartisan conspiracy" which had brought about the repeal of the eighteenth Amendment. The Prohibitionists, however, did not condemn the New Deal in toto; they took credit, in fact, for being the first party to endorse old age pensions. Aside from prohibition, the longest domestic plank dealt with the currency issue. Here this document recommended that the special privilege of issuing currency should be withdrawn from the Federal Reserve Banks, and that a sound currency redeemable in bonds should be substituted for the present irredeemable paper money. Another new plank declared against lotteries and gambling. There was even less on foreign policy than there had been in 1932, with a one-sentence plank favoring the promotion of world peace through arbitration.

The campaign proved a disaster for the Republicans. Landon, who was only a mediocre radio speaker, concentrated on the midwestern farm vote, at times out-New Dealing the New Dealers; the more conservative Knox, on the other hand, generally adhered to the Old Guard line. Admittedly such prominent Democratic leaders as Alfred Smith, John Davis, and Bainbridge Colby supported the Republicans, while the latter spent heavily on behalf of Landon, but these efforts proved to no avail, despite the fact that approximately 75-80 percent of the country's newspapers publicly endorsed the Kansas governor. In contrast, Franklin Roosevelt enjoyed the support of Labor's Nonpartisan League, the National Progressive Conference, the Minnesota Farmer-Labor party, and the people, North, South, East, and West. Waging class warfare, he identified the Republican party with the privileged few. Union Party candidate William Lemke did break with tradition by conducting the first extensive airplane campaign, travelling thirty thousand miles; even with Father Coughlin's backing, however, Lemke proved unable to arouse public opinion on his behalf.

Rolling up one of the great landslides in American political history, FDR crushed Landon, 27,751,612 popular votes to 16,681,-913, with Lemke trailing badly with 891,858; the Socialist Thomas polled 187,342 popular votes, the Communist Browder, 80,181. In the Electoral College, too, FDR humiliated his opponent 523 to 8, with the Kansas governor carrying only Maine and Vermont. It was the greatest electoral victory since 1820, and the greatest ever in any Presidential contest in which there were two or more separate tickets. The Democrats also maintained their lopsided majorities in the House (331 to 89) and in the Senate (76 to 16) over the Republicans. If the New Deal was indeed heresy, the American people had overwhelmingly embraced it.

XXVII. 1940

The Third Term

The second Roosevelt administration differed from the first in that there was a slowdown in domestic reform and an increase in international involvement. Re-elected by a landslide in 1936, FDR almost immediately challenged the Supreme Court with a court-packing bill; despite heavy Democratic majorities in both houses of Congress, this proposal never became law, thanks largely to the hostile attitude of the American people. The following year, in 1938, the last major pieces of the New Deal legislation were written into law: the Second Agricultural Adjustment Act and the Fair Labor Standards Act. During the Democratic primaries of that year Roosevelt attempted to purge such conservative Senators as Millard Tydings of Maryland and Walter George of Georgia, but these efforts boomeranged as the court-packing effort had. It was during 1938 that Republicans and Southern Democrats finalized their alliance in Congress that blocked passage of further New

Deal domestic legislation, and which persists today. In the fall elections, too, the Republicans registered their first Congressional gains since 1928.

Turning to foreign affairs, the Ludlow Amendment providing for a national referendum on declarations of war failed to pass Congress in 1938, although that body did enact another Neutrality Act the following year, as Adolf Hitler precipitated World War II by invading Poland. During the summer of 1940, as the Netherlands, Belgium, and France were falling before the German military machine, the United States began extending aid to Great Britain, while the Act of Havana made the Monroe Doctrine multilateral. That fall the Selective Training and Service Bill held the attention of the country. With the Presidential election of 1940 nearing, the Japanese threat began to loom even larger, especially after that nation negotiated a three-power pact with Germany and Italy.

Between the Presidential elections of 1936 and 1940, the Russians and Germans had reached an understanding which paved the way for the division of Poland between them. To the Socialists who assembled at Washington, D. C., in April, this Russo-German pact of August 23, 1939, was highly odious. Again nominating Norman Thomas for President, with Maynard Krueger of Missouri as his running-mate, this party in its platform made reference to "the tragedy of Russia" and "the brutal regimentation of agriculture employed by Stalin." As one would have expected, the "ruthless brutality" of Hitler also was anathema to the Socialists, although there was no mention of fascist Italy or the Japanese warlords. With respect to the home front, this document did praise New Deal efforts in the areas of social insurance, minimum wage legislation, collective bargaining, and public power projects, but maintained that the Socialists had demanded these first. Instead of attacking the CCC and the NYA, as in 1936, there was a call for their expansion. Unlike the Democrats and the Republicans, who preached military preparedness at the same time that they adopted a generally noninterventionist stance, the Socialists lamented "armament economics and the hope of wartime profits."

Similarly critical was the Socialist Labor party, which gathered at New York City later that month to nominate John Aiken for President again, and Aaron Orange for Vice President. "American involvement in the European war is inescapable," asserted its platform, since "Capitalism means war" and "War referendums, pacifism, and antiwar resolutions are futile, childish gestures." The Socialist Labor platform again stuck to generalities, making only a glancing reference to the New Deal in connection with national defense.

In contrast, the Communist party, whose ticket as in 1936 was Earl Browder and James Ford, praised Soviet Russia, while lambasting other nations indiscriminately, at their June convention. In this connection the platform made reference to "The predatory war unleashed by the imperialist ruling classes of Berlin, London, Paris, Rome and Tokyo," as well as to "the warmongers of Wall Street" who "are striving to strengthen their imperialist positions in China and aim towards control of the Dutch East Indies (Indonesia) in struggle for mastery of the Pacific." This latter charge is especially noteworthy in light of the fact that it was the Japanese, not the Americans, who were attempting to conquer the Far East militarily. On the other hand, to the Communists the land of socialism and peace was the Soviet Union, against which the "bogus" Socialist party and other political parties in the United States were leading a "holy crusade." Turning to the domestic scene, this document made the amazing claim that the Roosevelt administration had abandoned the New Deal and embraced the Liberty League, in the process surrendering to the economic royalists. Like in 1936, however, there also was a recommendation that the WPA and NYA be extended, as well as the CCC.

Of the two major parties, the Republicans met first, at Philadelphia in June. There were at least several serious contenders for the party's Presidential nomination: Thomas Dewey, Robert Taft, Arthur Vandenberg, and . . . Wendell Willkie. The front-runner was the thirty-eight-year-old crime-busting New York City District Attorney, Dewey, but he proved no more able to put together a majority coalition of the delegates than Taft or Vandenberg. Instead, the convention turned on the sixth ballot to a true dark-horse candidate, Wendell Willkie of Indiana; Willkie was a former Democrat who only recently, as President of Commonwealth and Southern, had fought the New Deal over the Tennessee Valley Authority. (Harold Ickes described him as "Just a simple, barefoot Wall Street lawyer.")[1] Backed by the Luce magazines, the Scripps-

Howard newspapers, and the New York *Herald Tribune*, Willkie was more of an internationalist than an isolationist, who domestically was opposed to the weak points of the New Deal rather than the latter as a whole. As his running-mate, the delegates turned to Senator Charles McNary of Oregon, the Senate Minority Leader, before departing to the hustings in anticipation of battling FDR for a third term.

The Republican platform, which the delegates adopted unanimously, began by quoting the preamble to the Constitution, and then attacked the Roosevelt administration in a parody of the Constitution. Because of the great difficulty in phrasing national defense and foreign policy sections, there was a long delay before the Resolutions Committee, presided over by Oklahoma isolationist Herbert K. Hyde, reported this document; 1936 Presidential nominee Alfred Landon served as the chairman of the subcommittee dealing with these two areas. One deleted plank would have proclaimed World War I a failure. Just before the convention, Republicans Henry Stimson and Frank Knox (the 1936 Vice Presidential nominee) had agreed to join the Roosevelt administration respectively as Secretary of War and Secretary of the Navy, and it was only with some difficulty that a formal resolution calling for their expulsion from the party was sidetracked.

Thanks in part to pressure from angry isolationists such as Representative Hamilton Fish of New York, the national defense section of the platform opened with a firm proclamation that: "The Republican Party is firmly opposed to involving this Nation in foreign war"; plagiarizing the editorial position of the isolationist Chicago *Tribune*, it also affirmed that: "The Republican Party stands for Americanism, preparedness and peace." The New Deal was then assigned full responsibility for both our unpreparedness and the danger of American involvement in war. Within this same plank, however, the Republicans seemingly rejected isolationism by declaring that: "We favor the extension to all peoples fighting for liberty, or whose liberty is threatened, of such aid as shall not be in violation of international law or inconsistent with the requirements of our own national defense." It is little wonder, therefore, that such a perceptive critic as H. L. Mencken would observe that this statement had been "so written that it will fit both the triumph of democracy and the collapse of democracy."[2]

Less controversial were the domestic planks, which were quite similar to those contained in the 1936 platform. In essence they attacked the New Deal as a philosophy of government ("Confusion has reigned supreme"), but supported many of the specific reforms that it had initiated. The currency plank was stronger than it had been in 1936, in that it embraced gold, and lambasted both the Thomas Inflation Amendment of 1933 and the Silver Purchase Act of 1934. Another new plank contained an attack on "the appointment of members of . . . un-American groups to high positions of trust in the national Government"; one might interpret this as an indirect endorsement of the House Committee to Investigate Un-American Activities, headed by Democratic Representative Martin Dies of Texas, that had been set up in 1938 to investigate Nazis, Communists, and fascists. There also was an anti-third term plank in anticipation of F. D. R.'s candidacy, "To insure against the overthrow of our American system of government."

When the Democrats met at Chicago the following month, it was by no means certain that Franklin Roosevelt would accept a third term for President. During the course of the convention, a letter was made public from the President expressing no great desire for renomination, but leaving it up to the delegates to cast their votes in accordance with their wishes. The result was a stampede for FDR, who received 946 votes on the first ballot to 72 for Postmaster-General James Farley and 61 for Vice President John Nance Garner, two former political intimates who had broken with him on the third term issue. With Garner out of the running for a third term as Vice President, the convention turned with some reluctance to Secretary of Agriculture Henry Wallace of Iowa; Democratic strategists had hopes that Wallace would attract the midwestern farm vote. Four years later, however, leftist Wallace's presence in the administration had become so odious to many party leaders that it became necessary to remove him from the ticket in favor of Harry Truman.

Like in 1936, the Chairman of the Resolutions Committee was Senator Robert Wagner of New York. The platform which the Democrats formulated was highly positive in nature, free of direct attacks on the Republicans; this time there was no emphasis on national government at the expense of state government, as there had been four years previously. Although a group of isolationist

Senators, headed by Burton Wheeler of Montana, David Walsh of Massachusetts, Pat McCarran of Nevada, Bennett Clark of Missouri, and Edwin Johnson of Colorado, threatened to bolt the convention, the foreign affairs plank was as ambiguous as the Republican one in its simultaneous embracing of isolationism and internationalism. After bluntly asseting that "war, raging in Europe, Asia and Africa, shall not come to America" and that "We will not participate in foreign wars . . . except in case of attack," this document advocated a vigorous program of national defense and even aid to the Allies under certain conditions.

The two domestic sections of the platform contained little new, and aroused little controversy. That on economic efficiency stressed agriculture, labor, business, and electric power; relative to the latter there is a reference to "The nomination of a utility executive by the Republican Party as its presidential candidate." There were no less than eleven subheadings under the welfare of the people section, with the most space being devoted to the subject of unemployment. When the platform was before the convention there was no attempt to introduce a minority resolution more vigorously endorsing isolationism, but Congressman Elmer Ryan of Minnesota did propose an anti-third term amendment, which the convention rejected by a voice vote. Such a plank, it will be recalled, had been included as a part of the platform forty years earlier in an attempt to embarrass the incumbent President, Grover Cleveland.

Earlier that year, in May, the Prohibition party had gathered at Chicago to nominate Roger Babson of Massachusetts for President, with Edgar Moorman as his running-mate. The relatively brief platform catalogued a series of evils threatening America, including the liquor traffic, harmful narcotics, commercialized gambling, indecent publications, debasing moving pictures, deceptive radio broadcasting, and political graft. With respect to political reforms, this document proposed debt and tax reduction, the conservation of natural resources, aid to farmers, businessmen, workers, consumers, worthy youth, and the aged, as well as equitable immigration and tariff policies. There was, however, only a passing reference to "maintaining friendly relations and providing adequate defense." The Prohibitionists also called for "a union of church people and others who stand first for righteousness, into a Third Party": the NEW Prohibition party.

The outcome of the election of 1940 hinged upon more than one issue. Aside from personal love or hatred for FDR, there was the third term question, the New Deal, and the foreign situation. Willkie's nomination largely "defused" the last as an issue, since he was far more of an internationalist than such would-be Republican candidates as Taft and Vandenberg; to Roosevelt the choice of Willkie was a "godsend . . . because it eliminated the isolationist issue from the campaign and reassured the world of the continuity of American foreign policy."[3] Willkie's Wall Street connections doubtless hurt him, as did his change of party, while his voice also broke during the strenuous campaigning. In contrast, FDR toured defense installations and spoke for preparedness, playing the role of President as well as that of politician. Yet he did deliver a speech at Cleveland in which he spoke of an America liberated from poverty and monopoly.

Although the Democratic slogan "Better a third termer than a third rater" was obviously unfair to Willkie, the American people in the final analysis decided that it was better not to change horses in the middle of the stream. Willkie, though, did make a most creditable showing, far better than that of Hoover and Landon against the Democratic nominee. Carrying ten states with 82 electoral votes, this convert to Republicanism amassed 22,305,198 popular votes, as compared with Roosevelt's total of 449 electoral votes and 27,244,160 popular votes. The third parties made their weakest showing in years, with only Norman Thomas receiving as many as 100,000 popular votes, and the Prohibition and Communist nominees receiving approximately half that. But, as had been the case in 1916 and would again be the case in 1964, the victorious "peace" candidate would find himself in the near future leading his nation into war; Pearl Harbor lay only thirteen months distant, and with it American involvement in World War II.

XXVIII. 1944

America During Wartime

In the year that followed Franklin Roosevelt's re-election to a third term, developments both in Europe and Asia drew the United States closer and closer to war. Recommending lend-lease for the Allies, FDR proclaimed the "four freedoms" in a speech delivered on January 6, 1941: freedom of speech and expression, freedom of worship, freedom from want, and freedom from fear.[1] Two months later Congress enacted legislation implementing lend-lease. After Germany had declared war on Russia during June, Roosevelt and Winston Churchill met on August 14 to formulate that joint statement of principles known as the Atlantic Charter. Four days later the draft was extended, after having passed the House by only one vote. That fall relations with Japan continued to worsen; on December 7 the Japanese attacked Pearl Harbor, suddenly drawing America into World War II, and terminating the great debate in this country.

From then until the end of the war little new domestic legislation of consequence was enacted, but then, the New Deal for all practical purposes had been completed by 1938. The Republicans did make significant gains in the Congressional election of 1942, picking up forty-six seats in the House and nine in the Senate. By the end of the war such pre-war isolationists as Arthur Vandenberg of Michigan had moved over to the internationalist camp, and a GOP advisory committee meeting at Mackinac Island in 1943 after considerable soul-searching endorsed postwar international cooperation. There probably was less domestic repression during World War II than there had been during World War I; nevertheless, the US government did relocate West Coast Japanese by Executive order. On the other hand, Congress displayed more gratitude to members of the armed forces than it had during the earlier conflict, since it enacted a "G. I. Bill of Rights" in 1944, even before the war was over.

With the United States and the Soviet Union now allies, the Communists did not formulate a platform or run a Presidential candidate in 1944. As it had done on every occasion since 1928, the Socialist party picked Norman Thomas as standard-bearer at its

June convention at Reading, Pennsylvania; Darlington Hoopes was its Vice-Presidential choice. The Socialist platform was critical both of appeasement and unconditional surrender, taking the position that the Roosevelt administration "is prolonging this war and inviting the next by underwriting with the lives of our sons the restoration and maintenance of the British, Dutch and French empires in the Far East, and the Balkanization of Europe between Moscow and London." As conditions for peace the Socialists recommended the self-determination of peoples and the organized co-operation of nations. Domestically this document praised the termination of Chinese exclusion by Congress during World War II, while attacking the Japanese relocation camps; it is significant that neither major party mentioned the latter in their planks dealing with minorities. Far more general was the platform of the Socialist Labor party, which assembled at New York City in May to nominate Edward Teichert for President and Arla Albaugh for Vice President. Proclaiming that "What the New Deal failed to do . . . war did," the platform described World War II as "the greatest crisis ever to face civilized man," blaming it on the pre-war struggle among the capitalist powers.

When the Republicans met at Chicago on June 26, they had legitimate hopes of toppling the ailing Roosevelt from power, based upon their impressive showing in the Congressional election of 1942. Their previous standard-bearer, Wendell Willkie, had suffered a fatal defeat in the Wisconsin Presidential preference primary, while Robert Taft chose to run for re-election to the Senate from Ohio rather than campaign for first place on the ticket. Although there were a number of other possibilities, including former Governor Harold Stassen of Minnestoa, Governor John Bricker of Ohio, and even General Douglas MacArthur, the obvious front-runner on the basis of the primaries was Governor Thomas Dewey of New York. The youthful but cold Dewey, who was perhaps the best speaker of any of the Republicans to run against Roosevelt, received 1,056 votes on the first ballot to one for General MacArthur, after Governor Bricker had withdrawn. When Governor Earl Warren of California refused to consider the Vice Presidency, it was offered to Bricker, a conservative, like Taft, but a lesser figure. Dewey's acceptance speech emphasized the persistence of unemployment, and Democratic quarrels, squabbles, and feuds.

Prior to the Republican convention, the 1940 Republican Presidential nominee had in fact written a complete platform that he transmitted to the Committee on Resolutions headed by Senator Taft. His opposition to a return to states' rights in certain respects aligned him with Roosevelt rather than against him, while Willkie also took advanced stands on such issues as civil rights and social security that alienated conservatives. In the words of the *Nation*, Willkie had been "dipping into the discarded black bag of Dr. New Deal (retired)."[2] Although he did attack FDR's foreign policy for having produced "dislike, distrust, and loss of prestige for the United States,"[3] he also blasted the Republican foreign relations plank as ambiguous, despite the fact that it was far more internationalist in orientation than any other GOP plank in memory. Since he was not a delegate, Willkie did not have the opportunity to introduce his platform from the convention floor; it is highly significant that no delegate acted as his spokesman in this connection, either. For a similar example of repudiation, one must go back four decades to the shameful humbling of Cleveland by the Bryan forces in 1896.

The final version of the Republican platform, as expected, attacked New Deal centralization and inefficiency. Apparently the most protracted debate in the Resolutions Committee was over the tariff issue, which this group resolved with a compromise plank. Asserting that "Four more years of the New Deal policy would centralize all power in the President," this document charged that "under the New Deal American economic life is being destroyed." Rather than criticize the Wagner Act of 1935 per se, the Republicans complained about its "continued perversion" by the New Deal. The veterans' plank was a vigorous one, although it was not quite as strong as that of the Democrats, while the plank dealing with racial and religious intolerance attacked the treatment of Negroes in the armed forces, and recommended the establishment of a federal Fair Employment Practices Commission. Like in 1940, there was an anti-third term resolution.

The most politically significant diplomatic plank was that calling for the opening of Palestine to unrestricted Jewish immigration and land ownership, and for the establishment of Palestine as a free and democratic commonwealth. (Also sensitive to the Jewish vote, the Democrats were to include a similar plank in their platform.) With respect to this hemisphere, there was a

Republican endorsement of Pan-American solidarity and a "genuine" Good Neighbor Policy, but also a criticism of the Roosevelt
administration for the "the reckless squandering of American
funds by overlapping agencies." FDR also was attacked for
neglecting to feed the starving children of the Allied powers and
the Nazi-dominated nations; in this connection the platform
recommended the immediate extension of relief and other forms of
assistance to the peoples of the liberated countries. Turning to the
future, the Republicans advocated "responsible participation by
the United States in post-war co-operative organization among
sovereign nations," a clear-cut abandonment of isolationism.
Although there was little criticism of the Roosevelt administration's handling of the war, with victory only a year away, near the
end of this document there was an unfavorable mention of the
Pearl Harbor reports.

The following month the Democrats gathered at Chicago. Most
party leaders were aware that the President might be dying, but
polls showed that he was the only Democrat who could win; thus,
FDR announced that as a "good soldier" he would accept
renomination. Roosevelt won renomination easily on the first
ballot, receiving 1086 votes to 89 for Senator Harry Byrd of
Virginia, the spokesman for the southern conservatives. A more
difficult operation was the removal of Vice President Henry
Wallace from the ticket. Roosevelt announced that he would have
voted for this controversial figure had he been a delegate, but left it
up to the delegates to weigh the pros and cons of the situation.
This loophole proved sufficiently large for an anti-Wallace
majority to pass through, and on the second ballot the convention
turned to Senator Harry Truman of Missouri, a New Dealer but
more conservative than Wallace. Truman had attracted widespread attention during World War II by his investigation of the
national defense program. The deposed Wallace was eventually
made Secretary of Commerce, thus returning to the cabinet which
had served as his steppingstone to the Vice Presidency.

Like its 1932 predecessor, the platform was somewhat on the
terse side, beginning with the broad affirmation that "The
Democratic Party stands on its record in peace and in war"; in the
words of *Time*, it was so brief and so general that it "could offend
no man or woman, and could be written on a postcard.[4] The head
of the Resolutions Committee was Rep. John McCormack of

Massachusetts. Setting forth as their basic objectives a commitment to expedite victory, to establish and maintain peace, to
ensure full employment, and to provide prosperity, the Democrats
openly took credit for saving the free enterprise system, as well as
for awakening the nation to the dangers confronting it as war
loomed. Although this document quite naturally recited the
achievements of the New Deal, buried halfway through it was a
call for "the amendment or repeal of any law enacted in recent
years which has failed to accomplish its purpose." It also omitted
any reference to the currency and public debt issues. Turning to
the future, there was a firm promise to the veterans that their cause
would be given first priority on the postwar agenda.

More specific in their internationalism than the Republicans,
the Democrats endorsed the Atlantic Charter, the "four freedoms,"
the United Nations, and an international court of justice. The
Jewish plank, which was quite similar to that of the Republicans,
advocated the opening of Palestine to Jewish immigration and
colonization on an unrestricted scale, and the setting up of a free
and democratic Jewish state. In closing, the platform extended "its
affectionate greetings to our beloved and matchless leader and
President, Franklin Delano Roosevelt," offering the hope and
prayer "That God may keep him strong in body and in spirit to
carry on his yet unfinished work." One minority plank was
proposed by Roland Bradley of Texas calling for an international
air force, but this was rejected as superfluous by the delegates on a
voice vote.

The Prohibitionists, even though they were fighting for a lost
cause, did establish a precedent of sorts during this campaign by
holding their convention the previous year, at Indianapolis in
November. Their Presidential nominee was Claude Watson of
California, his running-mate, Andrew Johnson of Kentucky. The
platform, like its 1940 counterpart, emphasized domestic issues
rather than foreign policy. Adopting a stance diametrically
opposite from that the Democrats had taken in 1936, this document affirmed, "The support of state government in all its
constitutional rights is the current bulwark against tyranny and
dictatorship." There was a call for a single Presidential term of six
years, and for the abolition of the "increasingly expensive
paternalistic bureaucracy." The one paragraph on foreign policy
did advocate that the United States should co-operate and collab-

orate with other nations in some type of world organization, but that in the tradition of George Washington's Farewell Address we should enter into military alliances with none. The platform closed with a lengthy analysis of the liquor problem, which among other things, had been "delaying, if not endangering, the success of our war effort."

This campaign in many respects proved more frustrating to the Republicans than any other in memory. Dewey, although he could not publicly state that the President was a dying man, made veiled expressions of concern over his health; since military victories had defused the war as an issue, the Republican nominee emphasized New Deal shortcomings. Willkie, who never really endorsed Dewey, died a month before the election, but prior to his passing had attacked both parties with respect to international co-operation and racial inequality. A touch of humor was interjected into the campaign by FDR, who in a speech to the Teamsters, defended his "little dog Fala" against Republican attacks.[5] Roosevelt did not campaign strenuously, aside from one ap-pearance in New York City, where he braved a heavy rain while riding slowly in an open car. It was here that he strongly endorsed the United Nations.

When the ballots had been counted, it became apparent that Roosevelt had won a clear-cut victory; nevertheless, his popular vote margin of 25,602,505 over Dewey's 22,006,278 was the smallest since 1916, when Wilson narrowly defeated Hughes. As for the Electoral College, the results were more lopsided, with Roosevelt carrying thirty-six states with 432 electoral votes, and Dewey twelve states with 99. Cincinnati was the only city with a population of over five-hundred thousand to support the Re-publican nominee, who did quite well in the rural areas and small towns of the North. The popular vote totals for the third party candidates stood: Thomas, 80,158; Watson, 74,758; Teichert, 45,336. Reversing the trend established in 1942, the Democrats maintained control of both houses of Congress; the Political Action Committee of the CIO claimed that its support helped to elect seventeen candidates for the Senate and 120 for the House. In victory FDR declared that his future domestic program would remain "a little left of center,"[6] but his death was to remove him from the political scene five months later, with the Pacific war still raging and the atomic bomb untested.

XXIX.   1948

The Great Upset

Three months after being inaugurated for a fourth term as chief
executive, President Roosevelt died, catapulting Vice President
Harry Truman into the Presidency. Aside from the fact that he was
not as prominent as FDR, and thus lacked widespread public
support, Truman had to face a by no means friendly Congress,
where the Republican-Southern Democratic coalition persisted;
in the off-year election of 1946 the Republicans achieved their
greatest triumph at the polls since the Hoover era. Consequently,
Truman was not able to get through Congress much of his
program of domestic reform, the so-called Fair Deal. Perhaps the
most significant piece of legislation passed by this body during his
first term, the Taft-Hartley Act of 1947, was enacted over his veto
and the bitter opposition of labor leaders. Other than this,
Truman's domestic record was highlighted by such relatively
noncontroversial measures as the Legislative Reorganization Act
of 1946 modifying Congressional procedure, the Presidential
Succession Act of 1947 revising the law of 1886, and the law setting
up the Hoover Commission to streamline the executive branch of
the government. HST also issuued a loyalty order in 1947 calling
for an investigation of employees serving in the latter, thus
waging a "cold war" against the Communist menace at home as
well as abroad.

Harry Truman's place in history as President , in fact, rests
largely on his handling of foreign affairs. Although when he took
office as chief executive he focused his attention on crystallizing
American support for the United Nations, shortly thereafter he
began to concentrate his efforts on the Russian threat to European
security. Admittedly the "New Left" school of historians has
recently taken HST to task for aggravating, if not causing, the
"cold war," but following the close of his Presidency, many
historians and political scientists, in assigning Truman a near-
great ranking, emphasized his diplomatic innovations. One
might cite as representative in this connection the Truman
Doctrine, establishing a protective umbrella over Greece and
Turkey, the Marshall Plan, providing for the economic recon-

struction of Western Europe, and the Berlin airlift of 1948—49 in response to a Communist blockade.

Unlike 1944 and like 1940, Russia in 1948 was again looked upon as America's enemy rather than friend, and this metamorphosis had its impact on the political platforms of both the major and minor parties, including those of the left. Saving the Progressive party for later analysis, we will examine first those of the Socialists, the Socialist Laborites, the Socialist Workers, and the Communists. The latter refrained from nominating a Presidential candidate, instead throwing their support to the Progressive party nominee, Henry Wallace. An examination of these four platforms reveals many points of interest, both in regard to similarities and differences.

Meeting at Reading, Pennsylvania, in May, the Socialist party selected Norman Thomas as its Presidential nominee; Thomas had recently authored an article in *Look* complaining that the Republicans and Democrats had been pilfering Socialist ideas.[1] Its choice for the second position was Tucker Smith. While the Socialists favored the repeal of the Taft-Hartley Act relating to labor, they also advocated the passage of the Taft-Ellender-Wagner housing bill. The racial equality plank expressed sympathy for the West Coast Japanese as its 1944 predecessor had, along with more traditional references to Negroes and other groups. In suggesting the elimination of the House Committee on Un-American Activities, this document called for the defeat of any legislation that would drive the Communist party any further underground.

Nevertheless, in the section of this document dealing with foreign policy, the Socialists took the position that "The major, but by no means the only threat of war, lies in the aggression of the Soviet empire and the international communist movement." While they attacked the Yalta agreements and Henry Wallace, they also were critical of the military phase of the Truman Doctrine, though they did praise the European economic recovery program. One of the more original planks called for the internationalization of the Panama and Suez Canals, the Danube River, and the Dardanelles and Gibraltar Straits. Other specific recommendations concerning foreign affairs included the admission of four-hundred-thousand refugees into the US, the withdrawal of American troops from occupied countries as soon as possible, and

American support for a self-governing Jewish state in Palestine. Advocating a democratic federal world government as the ultimate objective, the platform also endorsed the abolition of the Security Council veto at the United Nations.

Like in 1944, Edward Teichert was the Socialist Labor party Presidential nominee, but this time Stephen Emery was his running-mate. The platform adopted in May at New York City was as general as usual, but the mention of atomic bombs, guided missiles, and germ warfare struck a new note. Of special interest was the "plague on both your houses" attitude towards the United States and the Soviet Union. Unusually pointed, too, was the specific indictment of the "labor-shackling" Taft-Hartley Act. To the Socialist Laborites the crucial issue of the age was "Capitalist Despotism or Socialist Freedom," and their ultimate objective was to establish a "Free Socialist Republic of Peace, Plenty, and International Brotherhood."

Pro-Russian was the Communist platform adopted at New York City in August, with its attack on Wall Street and "the bipartisan Truman-Dewey atomic diplomacy and a call for a halt to the cold war. Among the suggested reforms in American foreign policy it proposed were an end to the draft and the huge military budget, an end to further military aid and intervention in China, Korea, and Greece, the breaking of diplomatic and economic ties with Franco Spain, and a repudiation of the Marshall Plan and the Truman Doctrine. Quite correctly the Communists noted that the restoration of American-Soviet friendship was the key to world peace; with Russia a member of the United Nations, the platform took a positive stand on the latter organization. The key domestic planks included a call for the repeal of the Taft-Hartley Act, the abolition of the House Un-American Activities Committee, and the establishment of a national Fair Employment Practices Commission. Of the Progressives it observed: "It is not a Socialist or a Communist Party and we are not seeking to make it one."

In 1948, for the first time, the Trotskyite Socialist Workers party formulated a platform, while nominating Farrell Dobbs for President at New York City in July. Its official heroes were Marx and Engels, Lenin and Trotsky, Debs and Haywood. This document paralleled its Communist counterpart in its attack on the Taft-Hartley Act, the Mundt bill, and the House Committee on Un-American Activities, but it parted company in its criticism of the Stalinists and "the unashamed champion of decaying capitalism," the Progressive party. Franklin Roosevelt and Henry Wallace were attacked for carrying "the infamy of a Jim Crow Army to every quarter of the globe." Turning to foreign policy, the anti-United Nations Socialist Workers recommended a national referendum on war, the withdrawal of all troops from foreign soil, and the complete independence of the colonial peoples. The party's fundamental objective in the 1948 campaign, as set forth here, was "the mobilization of the masses for a Workers and Farmers Government."

Of the major parties, the Republicans assembled first, at Philadelphia in June, confident that they would nominate the next President of the United States. This was the first widely-televised national convention. The candidate of the Old Guard conservatives and isolationists was Senator Robert Taft of Ohio, but there were doubts as to whether he could win, while former Governor Harold Stassen of Minnesota was another strong possibility, until his narrow defeat by Governor Thomas Dewey of New York in the Oregon primary dimmed his chances. Dewey, who led on the first ballot, won nomination on the third; this marked the first time in history that the Republicans had renominated a loser. Representative Charles Halleck of Indiana, who had thrown his support to Dewey, was under the impression that he had been promised the Vice Presidential nomination, but he was too isolationistic and conservative for the New York governor. Instead, the Dewey forces turned to Governor Earl Warren of California, a liberal and internationalist who was popular with both Republicans and Democrats.

Senator Henry Cabot Lodge of Massachusetts, who served as chairman of the Resolutions Committee, openly favored a document that was both brief and broad. The Republican platform, if only because of Democratic attacks, was forced to endorse the record of the eightieth Congress, which "in the face of frequent obstruction from the Executive Branch, made a record of solid achievement," including the Taft-Hartley Act. (The latter is described as a "sensible reform.") Nevertheless, this document also advocated a number of proposals that the eightieth Congress had not enacted, including civil rights legislation, public housing, an increased minimum wage, and aid to displaced persons, while ignoring federal aid to education and a fair employment practices commission. Among the more innovative proposals set forth in this document was a plea for a revision of the method of electing the President and Vice President that would more accurately reflect the popular vote.

Turning to foreign affairs, the Republicans advocated both the strengthening of the United Nations and "the rooting out of Communism wherever found." Although there was no specific mention of either the Truman Doctrine or the Marshall Plan, there was a reference to "the most far-reaching measures in history adopted to aid the recovery of the free world on a basis of self-help and with prudent regard for our own resources" as one of the accomplishments of the Republican eightieth Congress. This claim obviously irked the Democrats, and the *Nation* called it "the mask of a guilty conscience."[2] With respect to specifics, there was an endorsement of the Western Hemisphere Defense Pact, a reiteration of American friendship with China, and a greeting to the independent state of Israel. On the whole this document, to quote Lodge, did not reflect "the usual party line."[3] Moreover, it received wide praise in newspapers not usually pro-Republican.

In contrast, when the Democrats met at Philadelphia in July, the over-all atmosphere was one of gloom and defeatism; an attempt to persuade Dwight Eisenhower, then head of Columbia University, to run for President had proved abortive. With no other real alternative remaining, the delegates renominated Harry Truman for President on the first ballot, Truman receiving 947½ votes to 263 for Senator Richard Russell of Georgia, the Southern conservatives' entry. (Only thirteen Southerners, in fact, voted for Truman, all of them from North Carolina.) Senator Alben Barkley of Kentucky, the Senate Minority Leader who had given a rousing keynote speech, then was offered the Vice Presidential nomination after Supreme Court Associate Justice William Douglas and Russell both had refused to be considered. Like Truman, Barkley was a Border Stater, and thus the ticket lacked geographical balance. The southern delegates also offered a resolution to restore the old two-thirds rule that had been abandoned at the insistence of FDR in 1936, but this failed to pass. To many observers, this 1948 Democratic convention was the worst managed in years.

Senator Francis Myers of Pennsylvania was the chairman of the Resolutions Committee; the document which this group produced generally conformed to White House desires. In evaluating the over-all thrust of the platform, one might cite as a typical statement its opening words: "the destiny of the United States is to provide leadership in the world towards a realization of the Four Freedoms." While it understandably attributed such achievements as the United Nations, the Truman Doctrine, and the Marshall Plan to Presidential leadership, it also credited the Democrats with helping the Allies before Pearl Harbor, despite the fact that Democratic Congresses had passed the various pieces of neutrality legislation. No less than six paragraphs were devoted to Israel; there also was a Polish plank at the insistence of HST.

To the surprise of no one, the domestic policies section of this document was highly critical of what Harry Truman frequently described as the "do-nothing" Republican eightieth Congress; one focal point of attack quite naturally was the Taft-Hartley Act, which that body had passed over the President's veto. Among those liberal reforms the eightieth Congress was accused of thwarting were the expenditure of $300 million for federal aid to education, and the entry of four hundred thousand displaced persons from abroad into the United States. The eightieth Congress was also blamed for the high cost of living. In asserting that "We reiterate our pledge to expose and prosecute treasonable activities of antidemocratic and un-American organizations," the Democrats laid themselves open to the accusation of "red-baiting"; HST, it must be remembered, issued a loyalty order three years before Senator Joseph McCarthy began his anti-Communist crusade, although his approach to subversion differed markedly from that of the Wisconsinite.

Unquestionably the most controversial aspect of the platform was the civil rights plank. President Truman had wanted the relatively moderate 1944 plank repeated in hopes that it would be acceptable, if not pleasing, to both conservatives and liberals, but the Americans for Democratic Action contingent led by ex-Congressman Andrew Biemiller of Wisconsin and Mayor Hubert Humphrey of Minneapolis would not settle for a compromise. Paraphrasing HHH, the time had come to walk out of the shadow of states' rights and into the sunlight of human rights.[4] Nevertheless it is quite likely that many northern delegates would not have voted for the Biemiller minority plank, had it not been for the fact that three southern minority planks also were offered on the civil rights issue, each advocating a strong states' rights interpretation.

Although the first southern substitute was defeated 309 to 925, and the other two on a voice vote, the Biemiller amendment was adopted by a vote of 651½ to 582½, with the Confederate and Border States and most of the small states throughout the nation opposed. As a result of the adoption of this more liberal plank as a substitute for the original, thirty-five delegates from Mississippi and Alabama bolted the convention, with Birmingham Police Commissioner "Bull" Connor as their leader. These later were to form the nucleus of the Dixiecrat convention delegates, who challenged the Democratic regulars by adopting their own platform and nominating their own Presidential candidate at Birmingham later that month. Although Senator Russell was the first choice of this new States' Rights party, he declined to run as its Presidential nominee. Thereupon the 500 delegates, many of them from Alabama and Mississippi, but others from California, Indiana, and Maryland as well, turned to Governor J. Strom Thurmond of South Carolina as their standard-bearer. (Thurmond, then a Democrat, later became a Republican Senator from that state.) Another governor, Fielding Wright of Mississippi, was picked as his running-mate; both candidates were recommended rather than nominated by the convention. The keynote speaker was former Governor Frank Dixon of Alabama, while former Governor "Alfalfa Bill" Murray of Oklahoma and the racist minister, Gerald L. K. Smith, were in attendance. Absent, however, were such Democratic pillars of the Senate as Russell, Walter George, and Harry Byrd.

The relatively brief platform quoted its Democratic predecessor of 1840 in espousing states' rights. Stressing adherence to that document, the Dixiecrats chastized both the executive and judicial branches of the goverment for their actions relative to tidelands oil, public schools, primary elections, restrictive covenants, and religious instruction. With respect to the recent Democratic convention, this platform charged that it was "rigged to embarrass and humiliate the South," and that the substitute civil rights plank was an "infamous and iniquitous program"; it also stressed the past loyalty of the South to the Democratic party, and embraced the democratic ideals of such revered statesmen as Thomas Jefferson, Andrew Jackson, and Woodrow Wilson. Despite its bold stand for the segregation of the races, though, the failure to include a white supremacy plank upset Gerald L. K.

Smith. But the simultaneous display of both the American and the Confederate flags left no doubt about the delegates' sentiments.

The newly-formed Progressive party also met at Philadelphia in July, in one of the most controversial third-party conventions in modern American history. There was no question as to who would constitute the ticket, since the 3,400 delegates unanimously nominated Henry Wallace for President, and the "singing cowboy", Senator Glen Taylor of Idaho, for Vice President. Wallace, who had observed at Chicago in December the previous year, "We have assembled a Gideon's army,"[5] took the position that President Harry Truman (who had fired him as Secretary of Commerce) had betrayed the New Deal and was moving towards an armed confrontation with Russia. A black lawyer from Des Moines, Charles Howard, delivered the keynote speech. In the opinion of David Saposs, "Surcharged with fervent emotionalism, it resembled more a gathering of the faithful of an unconventional revivalistic sect than a political convention."[6] Yet not everyone was "turned on" by the Progressive proceedings.. The Alsops found the convention "a dreary and sometimes nauseating spectacle,"[7] while H. L. Mencken was so critical in his accounts of the gathering that an unsuccessful attempt was made to introduce a resolution censuring him.[8]

Despite the fact that he had the nomination sewed up long before the convention opened, Henry Wallace did not dictate the platform, let alone play a major role in its shaping. The chairman of the Resolutions Committee, one-time New Dealer and later governor of Puerto Rico, Rexford Tugwell, had prepared a moderate version in Chicago, while its secretary, former CIO general counsel and ex-Communist Lee Pressman, had formulated a militant one in New York City. Public hearings apparently had little impact on the drafting, though the Resolutions Committee did engage in a extensive debate. According to Fred W. Perkins, a Scripps-Howard staff writer in the employ of the New York *World Telegram*, fifty of the seventy-two members of this body had at least one Communist front connection.[9]

During the course of the Resolutions Committee debate, the phrase peace, progress, and prosperity was changed to peace, freedom, and abundance. Vito Marcantonio demanded a Puerto Rican independence plank, which Tugwell opposed, with the result that Wallace had to draft a compromise; the Presidential nominee left his greatest imprint on this document in the plank advocating world government. The original draft favored Macedonian independence until it was recalled that the Macedonian Communists were supporting Yugoslavia against Russia; Pressman then announced the deletion of this plank to the delegates, without explanation. Even before it reached the convention floor, therefore, the platform had been the focal point of protracted discussions.

In a tribute to its political idols, the finished document mentioned Jefferson, Jackson, Lincoln, Douglass, Altgeld, Debs, La Follette, Norris, and FDR, while pledging allegiance to both the Constitution and the Declaration of Independence. Such a listing of prominent names and state papers, though, fails to blur the clear fact that many of the foreign policy recommendations were indeed in line with Communist thinking at the time. These included a Soviet-American agreement, the repudiation of the Marshall Plan and the Truman Doctrine, a US pullout from China, the dismantling of America's atomic stockpile, and the abandonment of US military bases abroad. On the other hand, the domestic sections represented an extension of the Populist-New Deal-Fair Deal tradition, in conjunction with economic planning, rather than a call for America to embrace Communism, socialism, or some other radical political ideology. The "freedom" section of the platform thus advocated an end to discrimination, the right of political association and expression, and democracy in the armed forces, while the "abundance" section offered various types of assistance to such interest groups as labor, agriculture, small business, women, young people, and veterans.

Aside from the protracted deliberations of the Resolutions Committee, there was 7½ hours' debate on the convention floor. No less than seventy-five individuals spoke or tried to speak. Of the rejected amendments reintroduced by their sponsors, two were adopted and six defeated; one of the former called for the abolition of the colonial system, the other for Jewish and Arab solidarity on Israel. Some Pennsylvania delegates found the plank on industrial socialization too mild, as they desired to nationalize coal and steel, but their proposed amendment, which was unacceptable to Wallace, went down to a decisive defeat. But the high light of the platform debate on the convention floor was the rejection on a very close voice vote of the so-called Vermont resolution which, though

critical of current American diplomacy, refused "to give blanket
endorsement to the foreign policy of any nation," i.e., Russia.[10] In
the opinion of Curtis P. MacDougall, the defeat of this veiled anti-
Soviet resolution "might possibly have been the turning point in
the fortunes of the New Party,[11] and it unquestionably furnished
ammunition to those who were labelling the Progressive party a
Communist front.

Equally controversial, but in a different manner, was the
Christian Nationalist party platform, adopted in August at St.
Louis, which was probably the most racist document of its type
ever drawn up in the United States. On it stood the party's
Presidential nominee, the Reverend Gerald L. K. Smith, and its
Vice Presidential choice, Henry Romer. Generally speaking, the
platform was a hymn of hate with the Communists, Jews, and
Negroes its prime targets: the Marxists and the Zionists, who were
in alliance, should be deported; the Negroes, unfortunate victims
of slavery who were being used by some unscrupulous elements,
should be colonized or segregated. This mass removal of undesira-
bles would solve another problem by making houses available to
those currently in need of them, while a severe curtailment of
immigration would prevent the further entry of the former. Even
where it was not openly expressed, the widespread anti-Jewish
bias of this document was reflected in the recommendations that
the atomic bomb should be transferred from the hands of the
Lilienthal committee to the military establishment, and that the
control of the money system might be shifted from private
banking houses (many of which of course were Jewish) to the
hands of Congress. More progressive were the domestic planks
calling for assistance to the aged, the infirm, labor, agriculture,
and veterans, although the labor plank did describe the uniform
union scale as a Marxist system.

Since the United Nations was "a Jewish-Communist instru-
ment for the destruction of the sovereignty of all nations," the
United States should avoid it like the plague, instead adopting a
policy of constructive nationalism in the spirit of George Washington's Farewell Address. Also singled out for censure were the
Marshall Plan, the Truman Doctrine, the new Jewish state of
Israel, and the "satanic" Morgenthau plan for Germany; viewed
in a more favorable light were Nationalist China and Franco's
Spain. Especially vicious was the section on "war criminals,"

which bluntly asserted: "It is a matter of common knowledge that prior to and during World War II men in high office, including the late Franklin D. Roosevelt, committed crimes against our people which tax the imagination of even the most enlightened." Correctly anticipating that their brainchild might meet with criticism, the drafters of this document warned that: "evil and materialistic forces will oppose the fulfillment of this Platform with every power at their command."

Less inflammatory was the Prohibition party platform, adopted at Winona Lake, Indiana, in June 1947; as in 1944, Claude Watson was the party's Presidential nominee, but this time Dale G. Learn of Pennsylvania was the second-place choice. This document was in essence a reshuffling of various planks contained in its 1944 predecessor, in some cases with exactly the same wording. One new domestic plank, which was included for the benefit of ex-service men, declared that every American family should own its own home, should it so desire. A little more attention was paid to foreign policy than four years before, with the pertinent planks asserting that the United States should assume a role of global leadership, there should be international control of atomic energy, and there should be no peacetime military conscription.

In this, the last national Presidential campaign before television conquered America, Harry Truman "whistle-stopped" across the United States in a seemingly hopeless cause, as the Gallup and other polls showed Thomas Dewey far in the lead. The overconfident Dewey pulled his punches, engaging in what his critics often have described as a "me too" campaign. Fortunately for the Democrats, too, most Dixie Bourbons failed to back Thurmond, fearful that such an act would jeopardize Southern Democratic control of Congressional committee chairmanships, while charges of Communist domination eroded Progressive chances for an impressive showing. HST further proved his decisiveness by issuing an executive order terminating segregation in the armed forces, and by recalling the eightieth Congress in special session and challenging it to act on the Republican platform. Key issues of the campaign included the record of this Congress, farm price supports, the Taft-Hartley Act, Communism in government, the Berlin crisis, and US policy towards the new Jewish state of Israel.

Pulling off the greatest upset in modern American political history, the President defeated his Republican challenger 303 to

189 in the Electoral College, bettering him by over 2 million popular votes, 24,105,812 to 21,970,065. Truman did lose New York, Maryland, and Michigan to Dewey because of Wallace, but the Progressive party nominee did not carry a single state himself in amassing 1,157,172 popular votes; on the other hand Thurmond, who drew 12,000 more voters than Wallace, won in Louisiana, Mississippi, Alabama, and South Carolina for a total of 39 electoral votes. The other third-party entries fared even more poorly, with only Thomas and Watson passing the 100,000 mark in popular votes. Equally significant was the Democratic takeover of both houses of Congress from the Republicans, by a majority of twelve in the Senate and ninety-three in the House of Representatives. Another loser was the pollsters, who morosely retired to their tents, hopeful that they could escape the fate of the now-defunct *Literary Digest* that had predicted a Landon victory over FDR in 1936.

XXX. 1952

Communism, Corruption, and Korea

Even with a Democratic Congress working with him, Harry Truman proved no more able to implement the bulk of his Fair Deal program during his second administration than he had been during his first, since the old Southern Democratic-Republican coalition held firm against him. Whereas in 1947 the Taft-Hartley Act was passed over his veto, in 1951 the McCarran Internal Security Act was enacted in a similar manner; this provided for the registration of Communist and Communist-front organizations, and HST's failure to sign it led to the charge that he was soft on reds. The previous year Republican Senator Joseph McCarthy of Wisconsin had begun his four-year crusade against Communists in government, while Democratic Senator Estes Kefauver of Tennessee had initiated his expose of crime. Although the latter did not affect the Truman administration directly, irregularities centering around the Reconstruction Finance Corporation, the Internal Revenue Service, and surplus war materials led to talk about "that mess in Washington." The President failed to act decisively in the wake of these revelations, but in 1952 he did seize the steel industry rather than invoke the Taft-Hartley Act, only to have the Supreme Court declare this action unconstitutional.

More fruitful were HST's efforts in the foreign affairs field. In 1949 the United States approved the North Atlantic Treaty, while in 1951 it signed the Japanese peace treaty and military pact, the tripartite security treaty (ANZUS) with Australia and New Zealand, a mutual assistance pact with the Philippines, and the West German peace treaty. Yet the focal point of controversy during the second Truman administration was none of these agreements, but rather the Korean War, which broke out in the summer of 1950 followed by rapid American intervention, and continued through two years of armistice negotiations until the summer of 1953. During the winter of 1950-51, there was a "great debate" on the subject of American foreign policy between isolationists and interventionists, while in April 1951, HST fired General Douglas MacArthur after the officer had threatened Communist China with a naval and air attack. It was little wonder, then, that the Republicans settled upon "Communism, Corruption, and Korea" as one of their slogans during the 1952 Presidential campaign.

For the first time since 1928, the Socialist party nominated a candidate other than Norman Thomas for President, endorsing instead Darlington Hoopes at its June convention. Its choice for the second position was Samuel Friedman. The domestic planks of the platform contained little new, although there was an equating of the McCarthy anti-Communist crusade with the Truman adminstration's loyalty program. Curiously, one finds no specific mention of the Korean War. Among those objectives set forth by the Socialists in the foreign policy area were the strengthening of the United Nations and the Socialist International, in conjunction with world development, brotherhood, and freedom.

In contrast, the Socialist Labor party openly attacked the conflict in Korea as "a senseless War to all but the capitalists and Russian imperialist interests that profit from it." Like in 1948, there was an indictment of the "labor-shackling" Taft-Hartley

Act, an island in a sea of generalities. One of the more unusual features of this document was the quoting of Abraham Lincoln's statement that "The dogmas of the quiet past are inadequate for the stormy present" as a justification for the establishment of the Socialist Republic of Peace, Plenty and International Brotherhood. At the May convention that approved this platform the Socialist Laborites nominated Eric Haas as their standard-bearer, and 1948 Vice Presidential candidate Stephen Emery as his running-mate.

Even more vocal relative to Korea was the platform of the Socialist Workers party, which again endorsed Farrell Dobbs for President in July, with Mrs. Myra Tanner Weiss its choice for his running-mate. Advocating that the United States should get out of Korea and recognize the new Chinese Communist regime, this document declared, "To keep the boom going requires war scares and wars, small ones in Korea, or a bigger war later against China, the Soviet Union and the countries of Eastern Europe." Like in 1948, the Social Workers were careful to distinguish between Communism and "Stalinism," with the latter being described as "an aid not a foe of capitalist reaction." Domestically, there was a criticism of the McCarran-Walter "Race-Hate" Act passed over President Harry Truman's veto in 1952; this allowed the Attorney General to deport immigrants with Communist and Communist-front affiliations even after they had become American citizens. Still another object of castigation was the McCarran "Concentration Camp" Internal Security Act. Following the example set by the Socialists, the Socialist Workers charged that "The Democratic administration under Truman is the real inspirer of Republican witch-hunter McCarthy." While there was the expected attack on the Taft-Hartley Act, there also was a complaint to the effect that HST had broken more strikes than any other President.

Despite the fact that they had thrown away their chances of victory four years previously, the controversy surrounding the Korean War and the continuing decline in Truman's popularity led Republicans correctly to believe that their chances of victory were excellent. Although there were several other Presidential possibilities, including Harold Stassen, Earl Warren, and Douglas MacArthur, the contest by the time they assembled at Chicago in July had narrowed to a choice between Senator Robert Taft and

General Dwight Eisenhower; Taft was the candidate of the conservatives, neo-isolationists, and the Middle West, while "Ike" was that of the Dewey wing moderates and internationalists centered on the Eastern Seaboard. Taft may have entered the convention with as many, if not more pledged delegates than Eisenhower, but his doom was sealed when that body ruled against him in the credentials fight involving Georgia, Louisiana, Mississippi, and Texas. Eisenhower, who had returned from Europe only in June, was nominated on the first ballot, after Stassen threw him his support at the end of the roll call. The Eisenhower forces then rejected Taft's choice for the Vice Presidency, Senator Everett Dirksen of Illinois, a conservative neo-isolationist who had publicly insulted Dewey, selecting instead the youthful Senator from California, Richard Nixon, who had attracted national attention with his slashing political campaigns and his role in the Hiss case.

The platform was an uneasy compromise that proved acceptable to both Taft and Dewey supporters, although the *Nation* was of the opinion that it represented "virtually total capitulation to the extreme right wing of the party"[1] and the *New Republic* found it "distorted in its charges, dishonest in its promises."[2] The chairman of the Resolutions Committee was Senator Eugene Millikin of Colorado, another Taft ally, but the foreign policy section followed much of a recent article in *Look* by John Foster Dulles, an Eisenhower supporter who was to become Secretary of State.[3] Clarence Budington Kelland's philosophical preamble began with a statement reminiscent of Jean Jacques Rousseau: "We maintain that man was not born to be ruled, but he consented to be governed." Despite these intellectual beginnings, however, there followed a slashing attack on twenty years of Democratic rule, unlike the 1948 platform, which was more positive in tone; if the warring factions of the Republican party were able to agree on anything, it was that the Truman administration should be replaced.

Citing specifics, this 1952 document accused the Democrats of promoting socialism, shielding traitors in high places, and engaging in corrupt practices, while it also described the proposed Brannan Plan for agriculture as a fraud. Conversely, the record of the Republican eightieth Congress was again praised, and the retention of the Taft-Hartley Act was advocated, along with a balanced budget and a reduced national debt. Perhaps the most controversial domestic plank was the one dealing with civil rights; in that it did not mention a Fair Employment Practices Commission, it marked a retreat from the 1948 document. A minority resolution was almost presented from the floor challenging this plan, but this was withdrawn at the last minute. Another controversial provision that helped swing Texas into the Republican column that fall was the demand that the tidelands oil be awarded to the states, a pledge in which Senator Richard Nixon took particular interest.

Even more hardhitting were the foreign policy planks. Accusing the Truman administration of plunging the United States into the Korean War without obtaining the approval of Congress, the platform also condemned HST for abandoning China and eastern Europe to Communism. In the latter connection it pledged the liberation of those nations behind the Iron Curtain, a promise which proved rather embarrassing to the Republicans when the Eisenhower administration failed to fulfill it, as in the case of the Hungarian revolt of 1956. With respect to the policy of containment, it was "negative, futile and immoral," according to the Republicans; the Democrats had no foreign policy, but instead "swung erratically from timid appeasement to reckless bluster." Despite the fact that Eisenhower embraced McCarthy rather gingerly, no less than four paragraphs dealt with the loyalty issue, and these were far more in line with the thinking of McCarthy than that of his critics.

Aside from the Communist threat, that issue which received the most attention in the foreign policy section was an independent state for the Jewish people in Israel, which the Republicans supported. Turning to national defense, the Truman administration was criticized for allowing waste, while an unusual emphasis was placed upon air power; the expression "retaliatory striking power," however, was eliminated from the final draft at the insistence of "Ike." Although Senator Taft did not approve of a considerable number of the diplomatic planks, the neo-isolationists refrained from triggering a floor fight on foreign policy. As for the platform as a whole, despite criticisms by Oregon's maverick Senator Wayne Morse,[4] it was "broad enough to cover the diverse elements of the party, vague enough not to offend minority or special interests, and denunciatory enough to provide phrases for the campaign ahead," in the words of *The New York Times*.[5]

Two weeks later the Democrats assembled at Chicago. On March 30, HST had announced that he would not be a candidate for re-election, and thus for the first time since 1932 the race for the Democratic Presidential nomination was thrown wide open. Crimebusting Senator Estes Kefauver led in the primaries, but he had incurred the wrath of the big city bosses; among the other possibilities were Richard Russell, the candidate of the southern conservatives, and Senator Robert Kerr of Oklahoma. Kefauver did lead on the first two ballots, but on the third one the nod went to Governor Adlai Stevenson of Illinois, Harry Truman's choice for the nomination. Perhaps the most reluctant Presidential candidate since James Garfield, the grandson of Cleveland's Vice President was a middle-of-the-roader with a background in law, who had served in both the Navy and State Departments. The convention then endorsed John Sparkman of Alabama for Vice President by acclamation. A threatened southern bolt failed to materialize after the convention had permitted delegates from Virginia, South Carolina, and Louisiana to vote, despite their refusal to take an oath to support the party's nominees that November.

Like in 1944, Representative John McCormack of Massachusetts headed the platform committee, whose product advocated the foreign and domestic policies of the New Deal and the Fair Deal in line with an earlier White House draft. By calling for the maintenance of prosperity, the Democrats showed that they were still running against Herbert Hoover; among Congressional measures specific objects of attack included the Taft-Hartley Act and the McCarran-Walter Act. With respect to new governmental projects, Henry Hazlitt observed in *Newsweek* that the platform "reaches new heights of vicarious generosity."[6] Another significant feature was that the section on agriculture was longer than any other relating to domestic matters, promising, unlike the Republicans, to maintain both rigid farm supports and crop controls.

Turning to the loyalty issue raised by Senator Joseph McCarthy, the Democrats took the bull by the horns, declaring that their program "has served effectively to prevent infiltration by subversive elements and to protect honest and loyal public servants against unfounded and malicious attacks." There again was a bitter dispute over the civil rights plank, especially relative to discrimination in employment; former Solicitor General Philip Perlman and others fortunately managed to engineer a compromise that proved acceptable to most of the delegates, both North and South. Highly pleasing to many Southerners was the fact that for the first time since before the New Deal there was a reference to "the Jeffersonian principle of local control" in the section on Constitutional government.

In the area of foreign policy, the Democrats endorsed "peace with honor." While they placed their stamp of approval on the Truman Doctrine and the Marshall Plan again, they likewise gave their blessing to the North Atlantic Treaty Organization, Point Four, and the Pacific security pacts. Like in 1948, this document took a pro-Israel stance, while also pledging aid to the Arab states to further their economic development and raise their living standards. Finally, in answering Republican charges, it promised that central and eastern Europe would not be abandoned to the Communists.

After the delegates had voted to adopt the platform, a Kefauver supporter attempted to introduce a minority resolution calling for a commission to investigate crime and corruption. This proposal obviously was out of order. The delegates from Georgia and Mississippi also requested that their states be recorded as opposed, since the delegates had approved the platform by a voice vote rather than on a roll call. Thus every controversy was by no means resolved to everyone's liking at the Democratic convention.

With Henry Wallace no longer available as a Presidential candidate, in July the dying Progressive party instead endorsed Vincent Hallinan for President, and Mrs. Charlotta Bass for Vice President. Hallinan was also the nominee of the American Labor party. The preamble to the platform opened: "Cease Fire in Korea at Once—No Ifs, Ands or Buts. The American people want peace." Despite the widespread charge four years previously that the foreign policy planks of the Progressive party platforms followed the Communist line, their 1952 counterpart remained critical of the "Truman-Dulles cold war," while praising the Roosevelt-Willkie policy of One World. One passage linked American mistreatment of Koreans abroad with American mistreatment of Negroes at home; the section on minority rights stressed blacks,

Mexicans, and Puerto Ricans. Domestic objects of attack included the Taft-Hartley, Smith, and McCarran Acts, McCarthyism, and McCarranism. Taking credit for the Brannan Plan as a part of the 1948 Progressive platform, this document blasted the Truman administration for its "shameful betrayal" of this scheme.

On the other hand, the Christian Nationalist party moderated its platform so as to eliminate the attacks on Jews and Negroes which had highlighted the 1948 document. Their unwilling Presidential nominee in 1952 was General Douglas MacArthur, with the "California McCarthy," Jack Tenney, as his running-mate; this party, which was on the ballot in some states as the Constitution party, attracted the support of the extreme right wing of the GOP. Criticizing the movement towards increasing federal centralization and state socialism, the platform declared, "It is unnecessary here to indict the present administration for all of its tragic blunders." The foreign policy section was especially critical of the American failure to halt Russian advances in both eastern Europe and the Far East, and took the position that in the case of Korea "our leaders lacked the courage to fight to a military decision, even though victory was then readily within our grasp." Nevertheless, one also finds in this document the accusation that the United States had taken sides in international disputes which were none of our business and had meddled in other nations' domestic problems. This was probably with reference to the American tendency to favor Israel at the expense of the Arab States. Correctly observing that the present age had been characterized by a universal sentiment of nationalism, the platform expressed its allegiance to the symbols of the cross and the flag.

As it had done prior to the previous election, the Prohibition party met in Indiana a year early, at Indianapolis in November 1951. There it nominated Stuart Hamblen as its Presidential candidate, and Dr. Enoch A. Holtwick as its Vice Presidential nominee. Of approximately the same length as the 1948 platform, the 1952 platform dealt with fewer issues; it largely repeated the language of the previous document, with the planks offered in a different order. One specific new reference was to the revelations made by the Senate Crime Investigating Committee, these sinful misdeeds being the result of the rapid decline in the moral standards of America that followed in the wake of the repeal of the eighteenth Amendment. Of the Korean War, there was no mention.

Eisenhower quickly made his peace with Taft, and captured the imagination of the American people with his promise to go to Korea if elected. Ike's "Great Crusade" helped to negate the "me too" accusation that had been directed against Dewey earlier; on a lower level, Republican sloganeers accused the Democrats of "Communism, Corruption, and Korea," with Senators McCarthy and Jenner engaging in red-baiting. Other issues included Nixon's slush fund, tidelands oil, high prices and taxes, and excessive governmental spending. While Eisenhower had to contend with the Old Guard of the Republican party, Stevenson had to defend the record of the Truman administration. An outstanding speaker whose objective was "to talk sense to the American people,"[7] the Democratic Presidential nominee conducted a high-level campaign sometimes sprinkled with humor against "Ike," who was running as a military hero. Stevenson did attract the "eggheads," or intellectuals, while maintaining the support of most labor leaders, but he lost most of the farm vote, and many southern leaders remained neutral or even openly supported Eisenhower. Governor Allen Shivers of Texas was an outstanding example of the latter.

With television playing a greater role than it ever had in a Presidential campaign, "Ike" decisively defeated Stevenson, 33.9 million popular votes to 27.3; both candidates received the highest popular vote for a winner and loser in American history. Making the first serious inroads into Democratic strength in the South since Hoover, Eisenhower carried Tennessee, Virginia, Florida, and Texas on his way to a 442 to 89 landslide victory over Stevenson in the Electoral College, where Stevenson won only nine states. The Progressive nominee Hallinan received 140,123 popular votes, approximately one-seventh the total of Wallace four years previously, while MacArthur limped home with 17,205, 3,000 less votes than Hoopes. The Republicans also gained control of both houses of Congress by a narrow margin. Twenty years of Democratic rule was at an end, but "Ike" was not to return to the isolationism and "Normalcy" of the pre-New Deal decade; for better or for worse, big government and international obligations were here to stay.

XXXI. 1956

I Like "Ike" Again

As chief executive Eisenhower was to prove a less dynamic leader than either Roosevelt or Truman. He cooperated with Congress rather than coerced it, especially after the Democrats regained control of that body following the 1954 Congressional elections; thereafter Senate Majority Leader Lyndon Johnson and Speaker of the House Sam Rayburn played a key role in guiding his program through Congress. "Ike" was probably the last President to rely heavily on his cabinet, the original version of which has been described as consisting of eight millionaires and a plumber. Key White House assistant Sherman Adams likewise was highly influential in the decision-making process. Aside from this diffusion of responsibility, another factor that tended to reduce Presidential power was the fact that Eisenhower, who was sixty-two years old when he took office, saw his health deteriorate by the end of his first term; he suffered a heart attack in September 1955, and underwent an ileitis operation in June 1956. Nevertheless, "Ike" did run for re-election, being the only Republican who had solid prospects for victory.

With respect to the key domestic measures of the first Eisenhower administration, one might point to the approval of the St. Lawrence Seaway, the establishment of the Department of Health, Education, and Welfare, the passage of the Federal Aid Highway Act, the implementation of a flexible supports farm program, and the return of the tidelands oil to the states. Summing up his domestic philosophy, Eisenhower once observed that the government should be liberal with respect to public needs, but conservative in matters of finance. Although the Supreme Court declared segregation in the public schools illegal in 1954, "Ike" did not move decisively to enforce this decision at first. Later that year red-baiting Senator Joseph McCarthy was condemned by the Senate, highlighting his rather precipitous fall from power, after he had incurred the emnity of the President and Republican moderates. The Democrats attempted to make a major scandal out of the Dixon-Yates contract establishing a private generating plant at West Memphis, Arkansas, but the government eventually cancelled this.

On the diplomatic front, the Republicans proved unable either to dismantle the "Iron Curtain" and liberate eastern Europe, or to pull down the "Bamboo Curtain" and restore Chiang Kai-shek to power on the mainland of China. Not only did "Ike" refuse to allow the United States to become involved deeply in the Indochinese civil war at the time of the French defeat and withdrawal in 1954, but he also joined with the Russians to oppose the British, French, and Israeli attack on Egypt following Nasser's seizure of the Suez Canal. On the other hand, the United States gave at least unofficial support to the overthrow of a Communist-sympathizing regime in Guatemala. Turning to written agreements, the American government during these years signed the SEATO pact, the Austrian peace treaty, the protocol ending the occupation of West Germany, and a new Panama Canal treaty. Another victory for the Eisenhower administration was the rejection by the Senate in 1954 by one vote of the Bricker Amendment, which would have limited the power of the President to make executive agreements, and restricted the scope of treaties. To support his foreign policy "Ike" also unveiled a "New Look" in military policy, which reduced the manpower level of the armed forces and placed greater reliance on atomic weapons; two of his more innovative proposals included "atoms for peace" and a mutual "open skies" inspection, which the Russians rejected at the Geneva summit meeting of 1955.

In June 1956 the Socialist party endorsed its next-to-last Presidential candidate, Darlington Hoopes, with Samuel Friedman as his running-mate as in 1952. Observing that "The American people have already adopted many socialist measures," the platform gave a plausible explanation for the party's increasing decline at the polls in recent Presidential elections. Although the Socialists did attack a policy of "creeping socialism when capitalism fails," they also recognized that social ownership is not necessarily governmental ownership; in addition, they declared that it would be no improvement to substitute one irresponsible state bureaucracy for another, singling out the Tennessee Valley Authority as superior to the post office in this regard. Television and new advertising techniques also were censured, in so far as they denied minority parties access to the people because of their expense, while the US Supreme Court decisions relative to segregation were applauded. The foreign policy section emphasized the importance of abolishing every form of colonialism, racism, and imperialism, and of encouraging democratic socialism in Asia and racial justice in Africa, rather than a reliance by this country on military aid and defensive pacts. Hoping to prevent another world war, the Socialists advocated a World Federation of Cooperative Commonwealths.

The Socialist Labor party, which in May again nominated Eric Haas for President, while selecting Mrs. Georgia Cozzini for Vice President, adopted a document which reaffirmed its previous platform pronouncements. Taking a position somewhat similar to the Socialists, this platform called for the elimination of bureaucrats as well as capitalists; not only did the former control the "Iron Curtain" countries, but they also were displacing the latter in the West. Instead, power should be given to the workers. With respect to its pantheon of heroes, the Socialist Laborites included Karl Marx and Daniel De Leon, but not the recently deceased dictator, Joseph Stalin. Pessimistically assessing the future, this document observed that "Capitalism today can postpone economic breakdown only by plunging the whole world into a veritable hell of hydrogen-bomb destructiveness and deadly radioactivity."

Still another radical party, the Socialist Workers, again endorsed Farrell Dobbs as its Presidential nominee in September, proposing an "unbeatable" alliance of industrial workers, small farmers, agricultural laborers, and blacks. As in 1952, Mrs. Myra Tanner Weiss held down the second position. Going beyond both the Socialists and Socialist Laborites in some of its demands, the Socialist Workers' platform called for a confiscatory 100 percent tax on all incomes over $25,000 a year, together with complete tax exemption for all those under $7,500. It also attacked the Communist party for "playing Democratic Party politics," and praised the Montgomery bus boycott that the Reverend Martin Luther King, Jr., had led earlier in the year. The foreign policy section, although quite critical of the now-deceased Soviet dictator Stalin also took the position that the Kremlin bureaucracy was continuing his basic policies. The newly installed governments of Iran and Guatemala were described as mere puppets of Wall Street, while the national movements in Cyprus, Algeria, and Egypt were lauded, along with the Communist regime now controlling mainland China. Among the specific recommendations set forth

in this document were a national referendum on declarations of
war, the withdrawal of all troops from foreign soil, the halting of
all nuclear weapon tests, and the abolition of all military
alliances.

For the first time since 1888, the Democrats met before the
Republicans, at Chicago in August. Estes Kefauver again made a
strong showing in the primaries, but he failed to accumulate
enough delegate strength to win, so he threw his support to Adlai
Stevenson before the balloting began. Governor Averill Harriman
of New York, who was the candidate of former President Harry
Truman, remained in the race, but received only 200 votes on the
first ballot to 905½ for Stevenson. Stevenson then placed the Vice
Presidential nomination into the hands of the convention rather
than dictate the choice himself. In an exciting, closely-contested
balloting Kefauver edged past Senator John Kennedy of Massachusetts; Kennedy, however, obtained national exposure, which
served as a launching-pad for his successful 1960 Presidential bid.

Like the 1952 Republican platform, its 1956 Democratic counterpart largely represented an indictment of the party in power:
"our National Government cannot be trusted to the hands of
political amateurs, dominated by representatives of special privilege." Each section of it was read to the assembled delegates by a
different individual. Linking Eisenhower with Harding,
Coolidge, and Hoover, this document placed full responsibility
for the Republican record of "Confusion and Complacency" on
"Ike." Aside from its attack on the "scandalous" behavior of
Eisenhower's appointee as governor of the Virgin Islands, the
platform also pointed with scorn at the Dixon-Yates contract, the
Al Sarena timber scheme, and the low-level Hells Canyon Dams;
in contrast to the Republicans, the Democrats came out in favor of
90-100 percent parity payments for farmers, but failed to mention
the controversial Brannan plan. As for innovations, the Democrats established a precedent for both major parties by setting a
quantitative economic goal of a $500 billion national economy as
of 1960. Yet the civil rights plank, which was challenged from the
floor, merely asserted that Supreme Court decisions relative to
segregation "have brought consequences of vast importance to
our Nation as a whole and especially to communities directly
affected," without demanding federal legislation to implement
equality. To party strategists, Eisenhower's popularity militated
against a party split on this touchy issue.

The foreign policy section likewise was highly critical of "Ike." Making reference to the "wreckage of American world leadership under a Republican Administration," it attacked the Dulles policy of "brinkmanship" and the "second-best defense" supporting it. The Democrats quite correctly pointed out that the Republicans had failed to free the Communist satellites or to unleash Chiang Kai-shek against the Chinese mainland, or even to repudiate the wartime agreements drawn up at Yalta and elsewhere; they also blamed the Suez crisis on the Republicans, despite the fact that Eisenhower's handling of this situation was to win him votes at the polls that November. "Ike," in fact, was even attacked relative to his "open skies" proposal, and his "atoms for peace" program.

Following the pattern of events four years earlier the civil rights plank did not prove satisfactory to some liberals, but this time the convention voted down an attempt by Robert Short of Minnesota and others to insert a stronger plank. John McCormack of Massachusetts, who again headed the Resolutions Committee as he had in 1944 and 1952, took the position that the 1956 civil rights plank was stronger than in 1952; former President Harry Truman also spoke on behalf of the majority report, praising the platform in general as the best ever. On the other hand, such prominent party leaders as Herbert Lehman, G. Mennen Williams, and Paul Douglas were unable to accept its stance on this issue. Admittedly the majority report did call for the party to eliminate illegal discrimination in the area of civil rights, but the proposed substitute went a step further in pledging federal legislation to secure the latter and to implement the Supreme Court antisegregation decisions. By adopting the more moderate majority plank the delegates left the party "powerfully united and egregiously evasive," in the words of Roscoe Drummond;[1] to the *New Republic* it was a "department-store approach" that "tries to display something for everybody."[2]

If there was excitement at the Democratic convention over the Vice Presidential nomination and the civil rights plank, there was little if any drama at the Republican convention at San Francisco in August. With the renomination of Dwight Eisenhower a foregone conclusion, interest centered on whether Richard Nixon would receive the Vice Presidential nomination again. But despite an attempt by Harold Stassen to substitute Governor Christian Herter of Massachusetts for Nixon, after much thought, "Ike" gave his blessing to the incumbent, who won renomination by a unanimous vote.

The Republican platform was the work of a Resolutions Committee headed by Senator Prescott Bush of Connecticut. Reflecting Eisenhower's domestic philosophy, the opening section declared: "In all those things which deal with people, be liberal, be human. In all those things which deal with people's money, or their economy, or their form of government, be conservative." Again quoting the President, it observed: "Government must have a heart as well as a head." Unlike the Democrats, the Republicans came out in favor of flexible parity payments to farmers, and of partnership among federal agencies, the states, and private enterprise relative to public power. With respect to the civil rights plank, it was as liberal, if not more so, than its Democratic counterpart, affirming that "with all deliberate speed" segregation in the public schools must be "progressively eliminated." According to this document, more progress had taken place in the civil rights area relative to exclusive federal jurisdiction than in any similar period during the past eighty years. There also was a passing endorsement of the St. Lawrence Seaway and the return of the tidelands oil to the states.

In a departure from the past, members of the cabinet read appropriate parts of this document, with only Secretary of State John Foster Dulles absent. Lauding the Eisenhower administration for ending the Korean War, there was a reference to "our lack of preparedness which had brought it about," an obvious attack on Harry Truman and the Democrats. Unlike 1952, the statements calling for the liberation of captive peoples were muted; on the other hand, the endorsements of foreign aid and reciprocal trade were more vigorous than they had been four years earlier. The platform also affirmed that American citizens could not lose their constitutional rights because of a treaty or an international agreement, despite the defeat of the Bricker Amendment in 1954 with the blessing of the Eisenhower administration. As one might have predicted, the President's "atoms for peace" and "open skies" proposals were praised as notable achievements, together with the liberation of Austria, Iran, and Guatemala from Kremlin control. But with respect to the recent Suez Canal crisis, this document remained significantly silent. The platform was approved without any public opposition.

Repeating the practice they had adopted during the last two Presidential elections, the Prohibitionists assembled a year early in Indiana, at Camp Mack in Milford, during September 1955. Their ticket was Dr. Enoch A. Holtwick and Edwin M. Cooper. Rather than innovate, they merely shuffled the planks in their platform, adding some new material here and there. The economic aid to foreign nations declaration was of special interest because of its progressive character, stressing as it did technical assistance to the "Third World." With respect to the extension of democracy at home, the Prohibitionists came out for the direct election of the President and Vice President; home rule for the District of Columbia; immediate statehood for Alaska and Hawaii; eventual complete internal self-government for Puerto Rico, the Virgin Islands, Guam, and Samoa; and full citizenship for all Indians. There was, of course, the usual extended discourse on the alcohol problem.

Although it published a declaration of principles rather than a platform, there was also a convention held at Memphis in mid-September attended by 317 delegates representing half of the states. This gathering endorsed the independent candidacy of T. Coleman Andrews of Virginia for President and Thomas Werdel for Vice President. Calling itself the "National Conservative Movement," the convention refrained from forming a third party; it was obvious, however, that it was set up as a vehicle for extreme right-wing and states' rights enthusiasts for whom Eisenhower was too liberal.

During the campaign proper the President continued to receive his usual adulatory press coverage, while both major parties spent quite heavily in arousing little interest. Crying "Nixon, Dixon, and Yates," the Democrats refrained from attacking Eisenhower directly, instead picturing him as an ailing front for Nixon and the other "red-baiters." Stevenson, whose campaign was less lofty and more political than it had been in 1952, did come out for an international ban on the testing of nuclear devices and an end to the draft, but swung few votes his way by this stand. Even the Suez crisis that reached its peak just before the election apparently helped "Ike." Improving on his decisive 1952 margin, Eisenhower defeated Stevenson in the popular vote 35,590,472 (57 percent) to 26,022,752 (42 percent), and in the electoral vote 457 to 74. The Democratic nominee carried only Missouri, Arkansas, Mississippi, Alabama, Georgia, North Carolina, and South Carolina. Among the third-party entries, only Andrews topped the 100,000-vote mark. But despite the Presidential debacle, the Democrats continued to control both the House and the Senate; for the first time since 1848 a winning Presidential candidate had failed to carry with him at least one house of Congress. "Ike" was popular, yes, but his coattails were not very long.

XXXII. 1960

The Great Debate

In his second term Dwight Eisenhower exercised more power than he had during his first four years in office, despite the fact that he was in his late sixties. Assistant to the President Sherman Adams was discredited as the result of a scandal, while Secretary of State John Foster Dulles was removed from the scene when he died of cancer in 1959. Domestically, the passage in 1957 of the first civil rights act since 1875 caused a furor, as did "Ike's" dispatch of troops to Little Rock the former year to integrate the schools. The Labor Management Reporting and Disclosure Act of 1959, more commonly known as the Landrum-Griffin Act, also aroused the wrath of some union leaders, along with the attempted passage of right-to-work laws in various states. With many farmers opposed to the Eisenhower administration's policy of lowered price supports for farm products, the outbreak of a recession in 1958 created a political atmosphere that enabled the Democrats to win margins of fifteen seats in the Senate and forty-eight in the House during that fall's Congressional elections.

But it was not only in the domestic area that Eisenhower was confronted with various problems. In 1957 the Russians launched their first successful space satellite, or "sputnik"; as a result, the United States inaugurated a crash program to improve the schools. Three years later, the Russians shot down an American spy pilot, Gary Powers, in the U-2 incident, and cancelled a projected visit by "Ike." Elsewhere, the outbreak of anti-American riots in Japan resulted in a similar cancellation of plans for an Eisenhower trip, while an angry mob nearly lynched Vice President Richard Nixon in Caracas during his 1958 trip to Latin America. Thus it really should have come as no surprise that public opinion polls taken overseas just before the 1960 Presidential election revealed that the American image abroad was slipping. But if the later indeed was the case, "Ike" still was by no means passive in his conduct of foreign affairs. In 1958 the United States sent troops in to Lebanon after the Eisenhower administration had taken the position a year before that America would permit no further Communist victories in the Middle East. Revolts in the Congo and Laos led to the installation of regimes with which the United States could form a working relationship, but in the case of pro-Communist Cuba, the American government broke off diplomatic relations with Castro just before "Ike" left office. It was this 1959 Cuban takeover which in retrospect looms as Eisenhower's greatest failure in the diplomatic field.

Gathering at Washington in May, the Socialist party formulated its last and longest political platform, while refraining from nominating a Presidential candidate; unfortunately for its supporters, a more detailed exposition of its political philosphy failed to halt its slide into political oblivion. "Contrary to popular myth," this document proclaimed, "Socialists do not favor 'big government,' " Endorsing the Montgomery bus boycott and the student sit-in campaign, it accused the Northern Republicans and Southern Democrats of rendering civil rights legislation enacted in 1957 and 1960 ineffective. Other objects of attack included the Landrum-Griffin Act, the war-oriented educational push resulting from the successful launching of the Russian sputnik, and capital punishment. Turning to foreign policy, two key planks called for the admission of Communist China into the United Nations and the granting of self-determination to Algeria. Aside from the platform proper, there also were three independent resolutions dealing with foreign aid , Latin America, and Mexican farm laborers. Less specific was the Socialist Labor party , which again nominated Eric Haas for President in May, and Mrs. Georgia Cozzini for Vice President. In its platform it established socialism and survival versus capitalism and catastrophe as the overriding issue of the 1960 campaign, painting a gloomy picture of the nuclear horrors that awaited mankind unless the forces of reason and sanity emerged victorious.

More significant ideologically was the platform of the Socialist Workers party, for which Farrell Dobbs again ran as the Presidential candidate, and Mrs. Myra Tanner Weiss as the Vice Presidential nominee. (Dobbs was selected in August.) With Stalin dead now for seven years, the Trotskyite Socialist Workers has assumed a more friendly stance towards Russia, seeing that nation and China, rather than America, as representing the road to progress. The US government was censured not only for refusing to help Egypt build the Aswan dam, but also for its growing hostility towards Castro, its military intervention in Lebanon, and its "war pact" with Japan. Significantly, the platform failed to condemn the Russian invasion of Hungary in specific terms, although there is a passing reference to the uprising there. Key domestic provisions included a call for the repeal of the Landrum-Griffin Act and right-to-work laws, and an endorsement of the Negro sit-ins. Praising such heroes of the radical movement as De Leon, Haywood, Debs, Marx, Engels, Lenin, and Trotsky, the Socialist Workers declared that the three key problems confronting mankind were the saving of the world from the threat of nuclear destruction, the wiping out of hunger and poverty, and the winning and maintaining of equality and democracy.

As in 1956, the Democrats assembled before the Republicans, at Los Angeles in July. Two-time loser Adlai Stevenson remained a Presidential possibility, but even Minnesota Senator Eugene McCarthy's magnificent speech for him proved insufficient to win Stevenson the nomination. The front-runner at Los Angeles was the youthful John Kennedy of Massachusetts, the first serious Catholic contender for the nomination since Alfred Smith, a generation earlier; Kennedy had given his candidacy a boost by defeating Senator Hubert Humphrey, also of Minnesota, in the Presidential primary in heavily Protestant West Virginia. JFK, it will be recalled, had challenged Tennessee Senator Estes Kefauver for the Democratic Vice Presidential nomination in 1956 before winning re-election to the Senate two years later, by an unprecedented 875,000-vote margin; he captured a number of Presidential primaries in 1960. Another leading possibility was Senate Majority Leader Lyndon Johnson of Texas, who unlike Kennedy had avoided the primaries. Johnson did obtain 409 votes on the first ballot, but Kennedy nevertheless won the nomination with 806. LBJ then was offered (or demanded) the Vice Presidential nomination in a maneuver that remains something of a mystery even today. To some observers, JFK picked the latter as his running-mate because he felt (quite correctly, as it turned out) that Johnson would help him carry the South; to others, Kennedy made the offer as a good will gesture, hoping and expecting that it would be rejected. The convention ultimately gave its blessings to the politically astute Texan, despite some rumblings of discontent in liberal quarters.

Representative Chester Bowles of Connecticut, later to serve John Kennedy as Undersecretary of State, presided over the Resolutions Committee, whose work reflected the views of JFK. Between 1956 and 1960 the Advisory Council to the Democratic National Committee had issued a series of position papers, and the writers of the platform frequently relied on these in drafting their lengthy document. The issue in 1960, as in 1776, proclaimed the opening, was "The Rights of Man." Making pointed reference to the recessions of 1953—54 and 1957—60, "Ike's" tight money policy, and the general Republican failure to balance the budget or reduce the national debt, the Democrats charged that under Eisenhower the rate of growth of the economy had slowed down to about one-third that of the Soviet Union. In the latter connection this document called for a 5 percent annual growth rate that would furnish the government with many billions in additional income tax revenue. Republican farm policies were blamed for causing farmers' income to drop 30 percent, while the Landrum-Griffin Act was lambasted in company with the Taft-Hartley Act and right-to-work laws. There also was an attack on administered prices in the iron and steel industries, along with a hint that there would be a restoration of price controls.

With respect to new social programs, the Democrats endorsed a governmental program of medical care for the aged; here they differed sharply from the Republicans, with their stress on the private sector. On the other hand, the cities were to be restored over a ten-year period, and a cabinet position dealing with urban problems created. Anticipating the Goldwater moral crusade of 1964, the Democrats also complained , "We have drifted into a national mood that accepts payola and quiz scandals, tax evasion

and false expense accounts, soaring crime rates, influence ped-
dling in high Government circles, and the exploitation of sadistic
violence as popular entertainment." In one of its more poetic
moments, the Democratic party was pictured as the party of hope
and the Republican party that of memory, employing the terminology of Ralph Waldo Emerson.

The national defense and foreign policy sections of this
document likewise were critical of the Republicans, who were
accused of allowing this nation to slip from a position of global
pre-eminence. "No political platform promise in history," it
declared, "was more cruelly cynical than the Republican effort to
buy votes in 1952 with false promises of painless liberation for the
captive nations. The blood of heroic freedom fighters in Hungary
tragically proved this promise a fraud." There also were com-
plaints about the mishandling of the U-2 espionage flights and the
misjudging of Japanese public opinion. Nevertheless, despite a
pledge to defend Formosa as well as Berlin, the platform charged
that the Republicans had concerned themselves too much with the
military aspects of the Communist threat. Emphasizing the non-
Communist underdeveloped nations of Asia, Africa, and Latin
America, the Democrats linked the Jeffersonian tradition that
underlay their party's early years with the rising expectations of
the Third World. A section devoted to the "Image" of America
likewise reflected their concern with the decline of US prestige
abroad, while the plank on foreign trade was perhaps the most
uncompromisingly liberal one in modern political history.

Unquestionably the most controversial plank in this platform
was that relating to civil rights. The strongest in the party's
history, it made reference to discrimination in voting, education,
the administration of justice, housing, employment, and restaurant facilities, and pledged to enforce the Civil Rights Acts of 1957
and 1960. Calling for every school district affected by the Supreme
Court decision to submit at least a first step compliance by 1963,
the one hundredth anniversary of the Emancipation Proclamation, this plank also recommended that Congress revise its rules so
as to prevent future filibusters on civil rights legislation. Here,
perhaps more than anywhere else in this document, the liberal
views of the northern urbanites predominated; nevertheless, there
was no mass exodus of Southerners as there had been in 1948,
despite the fact that the convention rejected a minority plank

supported by ten southern delegations requesting that the delegates strike out the passage dealing with civil rights.

Sampling various reactions to this document, Henry Hazlitt in *Newsweek* proclaimed, "What we have, in sum, is a pledge to impose a total welfare state."[1] To *Barron's*, "It offered something for everybody, but precious little for all America."[2] Admittedly *Time* found it "probably the most coherent blueprint for Utopia ever to come out of a convention,"[3] but Norman Thomas, in observing that it was "utopian to a degree that we Socialists never were ,"[4] threw considerable light on why his party died.

At their Chicago convention later in July, the Republicans nominated Vice President Richard Nixon for President on the first ballot, after his main rival, Governor Nelson Rockefeller of New York, had withdrawn following an agreement by the two on the platform. Nixon then selected as his running-mate the American Ambassador to the United Nations, Henry Cabot Lodge of Massachusetts, who had lost his Senate seat to John Kennedy eight years earlier. Lodge was chosen because of his experience in the field of foreign affairs. Perhaps the most stirring speech of the convention was the keynote speech delivered by Representative Walter Judd of Minnesota, a doctor who once lived in China and who was a fervent anti-Communist.

Charles Percy of Illinois, a youthful Illinois industrialist, was the chairman of the Resolutions Committee. Percy earlier had headed the Republican Committee on Program and Progress, which in 1958 had issued reports under the title, *Decisions for a Better America*; he thus had a considerable influence on the platform, as did various members of the White House staff, who drew up their own document. Unlike the Democrats, the Republicans demanded an end to racial barriers in unions, and called for a termination of feather-bedding. The health plank did pledge the free distribution of the Salk polio vaccine, but emphasized the private sector. Stung by Democratic charges that the tax legislation they had enacted in 1954 had benefited the rich man, the Republicans pledged additional reductions in taxes, with particular attention to lower- and middle-income families. There also was a departure from traditional Republican principles in the assertion that expenditures should be covered by revenues, except in times of war or *economic adversity*, a statement that marked the first step towards Republican acceptance of Keynesian doctrines.

Still another innovation was the provision for the veto by the President of specific items in appropriation bills.

Turning to foreign policy, the platform advocated the stands of the Eisenhower administration relative to such "hot spots" as Berlin, Formosa, and Lebanon. Although there was a reference to "The brutal suppression of the human rights and the religious traditions of the Tibetan people," there was no specific plank dealing with the Castro regime. It was also pointed out that the Republicans had admitted into this nation thirty-two thousand refugees from Hungary, and it was recommended that the annual number of immigrants should be doubled. "Since 1954," this document proclaimed, "no free nation has fallen victim behind the Iron Curtain." Yet it only went so far as not to condone the subjugation of the peoples of eastern Europe to Communist rule, expressing the hope and belief that one day they would again rule themselves; this plank stands in marked contrast to the strident trumpetings of its 1952 predecessor. On a more positive note, there was a call for "appropriate regional groupings to work out plans for economic and educational development" that reflected the thinking of Nelson Rockefeller.

The two most controversial sections in the platform were those dealing with civil rights and national defense. After Governor Rockefeller had demanded stronger planks in these and other areas, he and Vice President Nixon met at the former's New York City apartment to hammer out a fourteen-point compromise, with Nixon making most of the concessions in a effort to obtain party harmony. To Barry Goldwater this was a political Munich;[5] to the Chicago *Tribune*, it was Grant surrendering to Lee.[6] The platform committee later swallowed most of the Rockefeller-Nixon joint manifesto, despite the fact that the fourteen points diverged somewhat from the philosophies and practices of the Eisenhower years. Blaming the Democratic controlled Congress for watering down the civil rights legislation of 1957 and 1960, the final version of the platform credited the Republicans with having done more in this area during the previous eight years than had been accomplished in the past eighty years. Its specific recommendations included the enforcement of voting rights and desegregation in the public schools. In an attempt to pacify Southerners, who were led by future Senator John Tower of Texas, there was no specific mention of sit-ins; with LBJ as the Democratic Vice

Presidential nominee, Nixon apparently was pessimistic about his chances of winning Dixie. (Barry Goldwater later claimed that a more moderate civil rights plank would have guaranteed a Republican victory.)

As for the national defense plank, it was rewritten with "Ike's" approval after a three-way Rockefeller-Percy-Eisenhower telephone conversation. There was the expected statement that under Eisenhower and Nixon the United States had forged a military machine second to none, and the expected attack on the Democrats for alleged neglect vis-a-vis the Polaris submarine and the ballistic missile. Yet in asserting and pledging that "There is no price ceiling on American's security," this document in effect turned its back on Ike's "New Look" in military policy, with its reduced budget, a de-emphasis on conventional forces, and reliance on nuclear weapons. Despite the fact that the Rockefeller-Nixon manifesto had upset both Eisenhower and Goldwater, there was no floor fight over the platform; had Nixon not capitulated, there might have been one, with disastrous effects on Republican chances in New York and the Northeast.

The National States Rights party nominated Governonr Orval Faubus of Arkansas for President in March against his wishes, with Admiral John Crommelin as his running-mate. That party did not formulate a platform, but the Prohibition Party, which endorsed Dr. Rutherford Decker and Professor E. Harold Munn, Sr., at Winona Lake, Indiana, in September 1959, did ratify such a document. Twice as long as its 1956 counterpart, the Prohibition platform included new planks in several areas. There was a call, to cite one example, for the indefinite suspension of the testing of nuclear weapons on a multilateral basis. Domestically, the Prohibitionists endorsed the work of the Office of Education in collecting and disseminating educational information, but opposed any sort of direct federal aid to education; relative to public health, they warned against unnecessary commitments for alleged insanity and "those programs of mass medication" which might be unconstitutional. As usual, the most space was devoted to the prohibition issue.

In 1960, however, issues probably were less decisive than images in determining the will of the electorate. By his impressive showing against Vice President Nixon in the first of four nationally televised Great Debates, Senator Kennedy proved that he was indeed a formidable opponent. JFK also "defused" the religious issue in a manner acceptable to most. His Catholicism may have cost him votes in the rural and Protestant South and West, but it also may have won him votes in the urban industrial states dominating the Electoral College. Aside from the Catholics, Kennedy also enjoyed heavy Negro and Jewish backing. Nixon proved unable to transfer "Ike's" charisma to himself, while his past record of political attacks alienated some voters; nevertheless, the Vice President managed to hold his own against Kennedy during the campaign, thanks in part to his great political skill. Among the other issues which played at least a minor role in this campaign were declining American prestige abroad, Quemoy and Matsu, the economic recession, and national stagnation. (JFK suggested relative to the latter that it was necessary "to get this country moving again.")[7]

In the closest Presidential election since 1884, Kennedy edged past Nixon by slightly over 100,000 votes out of a record total of 68.8 million. JFK ran well in the Eastern Seaboard states and the Deep South, but narrowly carried Texas and Illinois amidst changes of vote frauds. Nixon, who actually won more states than Kennedy did, came out on the short end of a 303 to 219 division in the Electoral College, with 15 unpledged electors in Alabama and Mississippi and one Nixon elector in Oklahoma casting their ballots for Virginia Senator Harry Byrd. The most impressive third-party showing was that of the National States Rights party, which amassed 227,881 popular votes. As was the case during the last six years of Eisenhower's Presidency, both houses of Congress remained Democratic. John Kennedy thus became our youngest elected President, yet three years later he was to be dead at the hands of an assassin, thus continuing the tradition that every President elected at twenty-year intervals since 1840 has died in office.

XXXIII. 1964

All the Way with LBJ

Our youngest elected President served a little over a thousand days, but during his term as chief executive failed to push much of his New Frontier program through Congress, despite the fact that he was the first Democratic Senator to go directly from that body to the Presidency. Most of the achievements of the Kennedy administration, therefore, were in the foreign relations field; these included the setting up of the Peace Corps and the signing of a nuclear test ban treaty. After the Bay of Pigs invasion of Cuba by a band of CIA-trained exiles proved a fiasco in the spring of 1961, JFK reached the height of his popularity by standing up to the Russians at the time of the Cuban missile crisis in the fall of 1962. Nikita Khrushchev, who had met with Kennedy at Vienna shortly after the latter had taken office, apparently had concluded that the new President would back down in a confrontation with the Russians. Aside from his handling of this potentially explosive episode, JFK will perhaps be remembered most for the inspirational style that he brought to the Presidency; one might cite in this connection the famous passage from his inaugural address: "ask not what your country can do for you: Ask what you can do for your country."[1]

When Kennedy was assassinated on November 22, 1963, however, he was replaced by an entirely different political type, Vice President Lyndon Johnson. LBJ, whose Texas background prejudiced him in the eyes of many members of the eastern establishment, nevertheless had proved himself a master manipulator as Senate Majority Leader. Capitalizing on the outburst of public sympathy following Kennedy's death, Johnson guided through Congress such measures as the Civil Rights Act, the Economic Opportunity Act, the Mass Transit Act, the Water Research Act, and the Wilderness Act as part of his Great Society program. While JFK had proclaimed in his inaugural, "Let us begin,"[2] LBJ declared in his first speech to Congress: "Let us continue."[3] Yet Johnson's reaction to a Communist attack on American ships in the Gulf of Tonkin off Vietnam, leading to a Congressional resolution giving him broad powers to take retaliatory action, marked a departure from past US policy towards southeast Asia, in that it heralded a period of escalation that was to divide this nation and destroy LBJ politically.

Now that the Socialist party was defunct, the radical left electorate in the United States had remaining to it only two possible vehicles for political action: the Socialist Labor party and the Socialist Workers party. The former organization, which assembled in May to endorse Eric Haas as its standard bearer for the fourth time, with Henning Blomen as his running-mate, formulated a platform that included the cryptic observation "Everything seems pregnant with its contrary." In an obvious swipe at LBJ's Great Society, there was an attack on "phony antipoverty wars." The closing section of this document quoted both Supreme Court Justice William O. Douglas and the Scottish essayist and historian Thomas Carlyle.

In contrast, the Socialist Workers party, which nominated a black man, Clifton de Berry, for President in January, ratified a platform that began by quoting Lyndon Johnson's State of the Union message when he spoke of "one-fifth of all American families with income too small to even meet their basic needs." (Edward Shaw held down the second position.) Rather than endorse the Great Society, though, this document continued with section headings such as "Bleak Future," "Token Rights Bill," and "Congressional Inquisitions." Turning to foreign policy, there was an indictment of those bipartisans who "back to the hilt military overlords in South Vietnam"; there likewise was a reference to the "criminal Bay of Pigs invasion," along with a complaint that "Washington's anti-Cuba policy was carried to the very brink of general nuclear war in the 1962 missile crisis." Among the prescriptions offered by the Socialist Workers for a better America were the teaching of Negro and African history in the nation's schools, and the establishment of independent labor and Negro parties. All in all, there was a total of ten planks.

Similarly extremist in orientation, but in the opposite direction, was the Republican convention that met at San Francisco in July. For a generation the ultra-conservative "Old Guard" wing of the party had failed to dictate a Presidential nomination; instead, control of the party had rested with the more liberal eastern wing, which had selected what the "Old Guard" regarded as "me too" candidates: Wendell Willkie, Thomas Dewey, Dwight

Eisenhower. (The nomination of Richard Nixon four years previously had represented a compromise between the two factions.) This time it was Governor Nelson Rockefeller of New York, a key figure in the 1960 platform fight, who was the choice of the Willkie-Dewey-Eisenhower wing. Rockefeller, however, narrowly lost the California Presidential preference primary to Senator Barry Goldwater of Arizona, and the latter entered the convention as the favorite. There was a last-minute attempt to substitute Governor William Scranton for Rockefeller, but one or more of Scranton's aides injured his chances by sending a highly insulting letter to the Arizona Senator. His forces in control, Goldwater easily won his party's Presidential nomination on the first ballot.

The Arizona conservative, who had refused to make even minor concessions on the platform, made reconciliation with the liberal wing even more difficult by the famous observation in his acceptance speech that "extremism in the defense of liberty is no vice" and "moderation in the pursuit of justice is no virtue."[4] For his running-mate he selected Representative William Miller, the Republican National Chairman, a right-wing member of Congress from upstate New York, and a bitter anti-Johnson partisan; lost in the turmoil was the fact that Miller, like John Kennedy, was a member of the Catholic faith. Aside from the Arizona Senator's acceptance speech, probably the outstanding address to the convention was that of former President Dwight Eisenhower. Much to the pleasure of the delegates, "Ike" said they should not let themselves be divided by "those outside our family, including sensation-seeking columnists and commentators . . . who couldn't care less about the good of our party."[5] Officially attending the convention in the capacity of a television commentator for ABC, Eisenhower had refused to join the stop-Goldwater bandwagon and endorse an alternate candidate, but his brother, Milton, did nominate the Pennsylvania governor, William Scranton.

The stamp of the right-wing was also on the platform, which at nine thousand words was somewhat shorter than its 1960 counterpart, and bore the inscription "For the People." It still was too long for Barry Goldwater, who would have preferred a brief and vague statement of principle.[6] Representative Melvin Laird of Wisconsin, a politically gifted conservative, headed the Resolutions Committee on Republican Principles that had formulated a

Declaration of Republican Principles and Policy. Other sources of the platform included the recommendations of the Critical Issues Council headed by Milton Eisenhower, and the findings of the Party-to-People program which had conducted hearings in various parts of the nation. Despite the fact that the Goldwaterites dominated the platform committee, their product reflected the views of Scranton on issues other than civil rights and extremism. The *Nation* did comment, "It is . . . a container for bits of pure ignorance that are Goldwater's hallmark,"[7] but *Time* observed that although Barry Goldwater could run on it, "so for that matter, could most any other Republican."[8] Significantly, the right-wing *National Review* found the foreign policy and military sections "the clearest and best."[9] This may have been the most conservative platform that the GOP had adopted since 1936, but it still was conservative rather than reactionary, despite the claim of Nelson Rockefeller that it was "wholly inadequate."[10]

Examining this document in more detail, John Kessel has pointed out that "In general, the domestic portions of the platform approved by the committee were not very different than they had been in 1960."[11] The Republicans expressed faith in the individual, faith in the competitive system, and faith in limited government, picturing Democratic leaders as "Federal extremists." Calling for a prayer amendment to the US Constitution, they also came out against obscenity and political corruption in high places. Perhaps the most controversial plank was that dealing with civil rights; while the 1960 platform had devoted fifteen hundred words to this issue, its 1964 counterpart limited itself to less than a hundred. Nevertheless, the latter document did pledge the party to "full implementation and faithful execution" of the Civil Rights Act of 1964, which Barry Goldwater had voted against on Constitutional grounds, although it also opposed "inverse discrimination" against whites in both schools and jobs. With respect to its more conservative features, the pledge to balance the budget and cut federal spending by $5 billion was in line with the economy-in-government theme; whereas the 1960 platform had endorsed federal aid for the building of public schools, its 1964 counterpart opposed it, except with respect to higher education. Nor was there any mention of the 1960 promises to expand unemployment insurance, inaugurate a system of federal grants for the needy, or implement a federal health

insurance system with a private option. Thus, instead of dismantling the monument that the Democratic New Deal-Fair Deal-
New Frontier-Great Society administrations had erected, the
Goldwaterites merely contented themselves with chipping pieces
off it.

Turning to foreign policy, James Reston commented at the time
that "The Republicans who traditionally were against foreign
entanglements now insist on being much more involved in the
world than the Democrats."[12] There was considerable emphasis
on NATO—"The Great Shield"—as well as on SEATO and
CENTO. Rather than abandon the United Nations, as many
right-wing extremists have advocated, this document instead
called for a revitalization of its original purpose, and for changing
the voting procedures in the General Assembly so as to reflect
population disparities. Less flexible was its attitude towards
"atheistic imperialism-Communism," which it pictured as a
monolithic evil: "We reject the notion that Communism has
abandoned its goal of world domination, or that fat and well-fed
Communists are less dangerous than lean and hungry ones. We
also reject the notion that the United States should take sides in the
Sino-Soviet rift." Returning to the spirit of the 1952 platform, this
document talked in terms of eventually liberating fifteen Communist-dominated nations; its 1960 counterpart had merely hoped for
freedom in the case of ten. On the other hand, while the 1960
platform had proposed that the rate of immigration be at least
doubled, its 1964 counterpart merely advocated as much as would
"re-unite families."

With respect to Democratic shortcomings, this document complained that the Kennedy-Johnson administration had "increased
Soviet influence in southeast Asia . . . stood by as a wire blockade in
Berlin became a wall of shame . . . turned its back on the captive
peoples of eastern Europe . . . forever blackened our nation's honor
at the Bay of Pigs." In the latter connection the Republicans
promised recognition of a Cuban government-in-exile and assistance for Cuban freedom fighters. There also was an attack on the
so-called "hot line" on the grounds that it had been employed first
with a "sworn enemy" rather than a "proven friend," and a blast at
the international prestige polls that the Democrats had used
against the Republicans four years earlier in condemning the
latter's foreign policy.

For the first time since 1932, a floor fight over a Republican platform took place. Five minority planks were offered, two on extremism (one naming the Communist party, the Ku Klux Klan, and the John Birchers), two on civil rights, and one on Presidential control of nuclear weapons. While the galleries, which were even more right-wing oriented than the delegates, booed Governor Nelson Rockefeller, they were kinder to Michigan Governor George Romney, who offered minority planks on extremism and civil rights that Barry Goldwater actually could have swallowed without too much difficulty. During the course of the debate conservative Senator Peter Dominick of Colorado observed that back in 1765 an imaginary *New York Times* editorialist might have described Patrick Henry as an extremist, while liberal Senator Jacob Javits of New York pictured the platform fight as "a historic confrontation between the moderate and conservative wings of our Party."[13] There was a roll call on only one of the five minority planks, one of the two dealing with civil rights, and the delegates rejected it 409 to 897; later 883 delegates were to cast their votes for Barry Goldwater on the first ballot, in what was apparently a significant correlation of voting strength.

Far more cut-and-dried was the Democratic convention at Atlantic City in August, in many respects more of a coronation than a convention. Lyndon Johnson was renominated for President by acclamation. LBJ did keep the delegates in suspense up to the last minute as to his choice of a running-mate, but he finally settled on Senator Hubert Humphrey of Minnesota. Passed over was Attorney General Robert Kennedy, who nevertheless received a twenty-minute ovation when he appeared in person to make a speech praising his late brother, which closed with a quotation from Shakespeare's *Romeo and Juliet*. The only real excitement of the convention was generated by the credentials fight involving the delegations from Mississippi and Alabama, both strongly anti-Johnson; they were eventually seated after they had agreed to sign pledges of support for the party's ticket.

The lengthy platform, which technically was drawn up by the Resolutions Committee chaired by Representative Carl Albert of Oklahoma, but actually was written almost in its entirety at the White House, stressed the theme "One Nation, One People." To the *New Republic* it bore an "eerie resemblance" in certain parts to the Republican one four years before.[14] While there was an endorsement of the principles enumerated in the Democratic platform of 1948, "The Record" section of this document also took the unprecedented step of quoting planks from the 1960 platform, demonstrating how JFK and LBJ had faithfully executed them. Rather than dealing in generalities, it unleashed an attack on extremist groups, citing specific organizations: "We condemn extremism, whether from the Right or Left, including the extreme tactics of such organizations as the Communist Party, the Ku Klux Klan, and the John Birch Society." In the case of civil rights, the Democrats, like the Republicans, endorsed the Civil Rights Act of 1964; they also proclaimed their opposition to racial quotas and "inverse discrimination," while coming out strongly for law and order.

Admittedly this document did contain liberal planks on labor, urban affairs, education, Congressional procedures, and immigration, but as one commentator has observed, the 1964 platform was far more moderate, far less militantly liberal, than its 1960 counterpart.[15] On a more materialistic note, there also was the expected reference to "42 months of uninterrupted expansion under Presidents Kennedy and Johnson . . . the longest and strongest peace-time prosperity in modern times." Significant omissions included an endorsement of the Supreme Court's one-man, one-vote ruling on legislative reapportionment, and a reaffirmation of the attack on natural gas and oil depletion allowances found in the 1960 platform.

With respect to foreign policy, the Democrats supported the nuclear test ban treaty, unlike the Republicans, and adopted a statement resembling the Republican minority plank on the Presidential control of nuclear weapons. Stressing heavy outlays for national defense as its counterpart had done in 1960, this platform still clung to the theory that it was possible to have both guns and butter. John Kennedy was praised for his handling of the Cuban missile crisis and Lyndon Johnson for his of the Gulf of Tonkin incident; Castro was to be isolated further, while our commitments to South Vietnam were to be honored with "unflagging devotion." To the Democrats the Peace Corps was "the most powerful idea in recent times," while the Alliance for Progress was "the greatest undertaking of social reform and international cooperation in the history of the Western Hemisphere."

During this same month the Prohibition party assembled in St.

Louis to nominate Professor Earle Harold Munn for President
and Mark Shaw for Vice President. Its platform largely consisted
of the same planks that had appeared in 1960, some of them
verbatim, and in the same basic order. One new plank consisted of
a brief statement on national sovereignty: "We declare our belief
in national sovereignty and oppose surrender of this sovereignty
to any international group." Of greater importance was the longer
statement on civil rights. This recognized the Constitutional
guarantee of equal treatment for all American citizens, regardless
of race, religion, or national origins, deplored the use of violence
and/or arbitrary pressure tactics, and opposed those proposals
which would destroy the system of neighborhood schools through
a program of artificial integration. That this would be the one
important new plank in this minor party's platform demonstrates
the significance of this issue.

While Goldwater and Miller monopolized the right-hand side
of the road during the campaign, Johnson and Humphrey cut a
broad path down the middle. Little, in fact, went right for the
Republican nominee, who developed a penchant for saying the
wrong thing at the wrong time and the wrong place. Not only did
traditionally Republican newspapers embrace LBJ, but so did
many businessmen who never had backed a Democrat before; in
fact, even such a prominent Republican party leader as George
Romney disassociated himself from the Arizona Senator. With
respect to the voters in general, a large number were turned off by
Goldwater's sword-rattling relative to Vietnam and his proposed
cutbacks in social programs. Even the so-called "white backlash"
failed to materialize on a large scale for the Republican candidate,
who took the position that what the voters wanted was "a choice
not an echo."

Amassing the largest plurality of popular votes and the largest
percentage of popular votes in American history, Lyndon Johnson crushed Goldwater, 43 million to 27 million, also annihilat-
ing him in the Electoral College, 486 to 52. The Arizona Senator
carried only five southern states—Louisiana, Mississippi, Alabama, Georgia, and South Carolina—and his native Arizona.
Even worse for the Republicans, the Democrats increased their
majorities in both houses of Congress. Thus, it might indeed be
said that LBJ was standing on top of the mountain. But
unfortunately for Johnson, the dropoff on the other side proved

sharp and precipitous; within four years his political reputation
was to lie more or less in ruins, and it was not even safe for him to
ride through the streets of America's cities. *Sic transit gloria
mundi.*

XXXIV. 1968

The Resurrection of Nixon

The eighty-ninth Congress elected with Lyndon Johnson
contained heavy Democratic majorities, and during its early days
it passed a body of legislation comparable in bulk to that enacted
during the first three months of Franklin Roosevelt's Presidency, a
generation before. Examining the measures written into law
during LBJ's second term, one discovers such key items as the
Elementary and Secondary Education Act of 1965, the Higher
Education Act of 1965, medicare legislation (1966), the Voting
Rights Act of 1965, the Civil Rights Act of 1968, the establishment
of the Department of Housing and Urban Development (1965) and
the Department of Transportation (1966), model cities legislation
(1966), and the Housing and Development Act of 1968. Despite the
enactment of this and other Great Society measures, however,
there was simultaneously occurring an unprecedented number of
demonstrations, marches, riots, and bombings, both in the cities
and on the campuses. Blacks in the Watts area of Los Angeles
revolted in August 1965; an assassin shot and killed Negro leader
Martin Luther King, Jr., in April 1968; the Kerner Report of the
same year blamed white racism for the polarization of the country.
The Johnson administration was thus faced with a highly ironic
situation: as more social legislation was passed, there was more
and more social discontent. In the words of Henry Wallich,
"Despite mounting fulfillment, the expectations gap has risen
because of unreasonable promises."[1]
Foreign affairs were intensified in June 1967, when Israel warred

and won—in six days—against the combined forces of Egypt, Jordan, and Syria. The outcome was a severe blow to Russian prestige, but the United States managed to remain on the sidelines. Nor did the American government intervene when the Russians invaded Czechoslovakia in August 1968, just before the Democratic convention. On a more positive note, the United States and the Soviet Union reached an agreement in 1967, on a treaty to prevent the use of nuclear weapons in outer space, and another in 1968, to obligate non-nuclear powers not to produce or receive nuclear weapons. But the most critical problems in the foreign relations area that confronted the Johnson administration was that of the Vietnam War; by the time LBJ left office, the number of American troops serving there had passed the half-million mark, and the war was costing American taxpayers approximately $30 billion a year (fifty-five thousand Americans also had given their lives in the process.) In March 1968 a weary and frustrated LBJ informed his television audience that he would not seek another term as the President of a nation now split between "hawks" and "doves" on the conduct of the war.

In nominating Fred Halstead for President and Paul Boutelle for Vice President, the Socialist Workers placed a heavy emphasis on the linkage between the Vietnam War and the racial situation in this nation. "While US troops are in Vietnam attempting to crush a popular revolution," it observed, "police, national guard and army units are used to viciously smash the uprisings of black people in our own cities." Correctly perceiving that many young people in America were forging a new way of life for themselves, this document advocated that eighteen-year-olds be given the right to vote, and that free public education be furnished through the university level.

On the other hand, the Socialist Labor party, in designating Henning Blomen as its standard-bearer, with George Taylor as his running-mate, largely ignored the Vietnam War and the racial situation as specific issues, instead focusing its attack on the failures of the Great Society and the war on poverty. Like in 1964 the platform quoted both William O. Douglas and Thomas Carlyle, but this time it also included quotes from the National Committee for an Effective Congress, and from Thomas Jefferson: "There is in the land a certain restlessness of questioning." New Leftists and liberals were repudiated, along with the Republicans

and the Democrats. Confronted with the growing material prosperity of America under the capitalist system, the Socialist
Laborites took comfort in the thesis that "experience shows that
revolutions occur when expectations of a better, more secure and
more happy life are rising."

A somewhat different approach was offered by the Socialist
party, which instead of offering a Presidential candidate allied
itself with the liberal elements in the Democratic party. On the
other hand, the Communists nominated a black woman, Mrs.
Charlene Mitchell, for President, thus selecting its first candidate
for the highest office in the land since 1940. The New York City
convention of that party, in July, also picked the twenty-three-
year-old Michael Zagarell as her running-mate. Other parties in
the field included the New party, the Best party, the Peace and
Freedom party, the Universal party, the Constitution party, and
the Freedom and Peace party. (Complex as this narrative is at
times, it would be even more so if splinter-group platforms were
included.)

That July, the Republicans met at Miami Beach, with a
resurrected Richard Nixon again seeking the Presidency. Despite
the fact that he failed to receive a majority of the votes of any of the
major, northern industrial states, other than Illinois, Nixon
received 692 votes on the first ballot, to 277 for liberal New York
Governor Nelson Rockefeller, and 182 for conservative California
Governor Ronald Reagan. His surprise choice for Vice President
was Governor Spiro Theodore Agnew of Maryland, who had
defected from the Rockefeller camp after the latter had announced
that he would not actively seek the Presidency. Although the
delegates approved Agnew by a lopsided majority, 178 of them also
voted for Governor George Romney, who had once been the front-
runner for his party's Presidential nomination, until he made the
unfortunate statement that he had been brainwashed about
Vietnam.

The platform, which was drafted under the direction of Senator
Everett Dirksen of Illinois, has been described by English observers Chester, Hodgson, and Page as "a program of supreme
meaninglessness,"[2] but a number of important planks were
nevertheless included. Based heavily on the policy papers issued
during the previous four years by the Republican Coordinating
Committee, the platform was acceptable to all factions, avoiding a

fight on the floor like the one that had marred the previous convention. The florid oratorical style of Dirksen was most apparent in the "Preamble, Purposes and Pledges." Three of the more innovative aspects of the section on domestic policy were its advocacy of the right of eighteen-year-olds to vote, the creation of a volunteer army, and a program of massive tax credits to lure private enterprise into the ghettos. Of equal interest was the section on human development, containing an endorsement of a Human Investment Act, which would provide tax credits to employers to train disadvantaged citizens, and a national Job Opportunity Data Bank. Among the various minority groups, the plight of the American Indians and Eskimos was singled out as a national disgrace.

Turning to the government itself, this document advocated the reforming of the Presidential election process, the reorganizing and modernizing of Congress, and improved postal service. With respect to the distribution of expenditures, the Republicans pledged that "Such funds as become available with the termination of the Vietnam War and upon recovery from its impact on our national defense will be applied in a balanced way to critical domestic needs and to reduce the heavy tax burden." Unlike the Democrats in 1964, the Republicans were hesitant to promise both guns and butter; unlike the GOP four years previously, there was no talk of a balanced budget.

Vietnam quite naturally was the focal point of the section dealing with foreign policy, and the Republicans renounced bipartisanship to proclaim that "The Administration's Vietnam policy has failed—militarily, politically, diplomatically, and with relation to our own people." The result of this failure was a prolonged war of attrition. Accusing LBJ of paying inadequate attention to the political framework, the Republicans favored a progressive de-Americanization of the war effort, rather than an American-led military victory; there was no mention either of a bombing pause or negotiations with the NLF A synthesis of the thinking of Nixon, Rockefeller, Romney, and the "hawks," this section has been described by Theodore H. White as "a masterpiece of political carpentry."[3]

Elsewhere in the platform, the Democrats were attacked for having "frittered away superior military capabilities," despite the fact that the defense budget doubled during the Kennedy and

Johnson administration. In this connection there were references to the Fll-B (TFX) airplane as "second-best weaponry," and to the USS *Pueblo* seizure as a "shameful, humiliating episode." Foreign aid should only be extended to those nations which urgently require it, and manifested a desire to help themselves; East-West trade should be explored only when the Communists begin acting in a more peaceful manner. Although the Republicans blasted the Democrats relative to Cuba for abandoning the Monroe Doctrine, they adopted a less militant stance towards the Soviet presence in eastern Europe than they had in their previous platform. On the other hand, they clearly aligned themselves with the Jews in the aftermath of the Arab-Israeli War. Despite various and sundry American involvements abroad, this document nevertheless proclaimed, "We do not intend to conduct foreign policy in such [a] manner as to make the United States a world policeman."

There was relatively little strife both inside and outside the convention hall during the Republican gathering at Miami Beach, but when the Democrats assembled at Chicago later in August, it became necessary to employ the tightest security regulations in the history of national conventions. Both the Chicago police and the national guard were called in to subdue rioting dissidents outside, while the people of America watched these developments at home on their television screens. (For various reasons, LBJ did not attend.) The candidate of the doves was Senator Eugene McCarthy of Minnesota, an enigmatic intellectual who had made a strong showing in New Hampshire against the President; McCarthy later defeated Senator Robert Kennedy in Oregon just prior to the latter's victory in California— the day before his assassination. In contrast, the candidate most acceptable to Johnson was Vice President Hubert Humphrey, who entered the race too late to file for any of the Presidential preference primaries, and who had to withhold his criticism of the administration's handling of the Vietnam situation lest he incur the wrath of LBJ. College students and intellectuals backed McCarthy, but enough labor leaders and urban bosses threw their support to Humphrey to enable him to win on the first ballot.

The Vice President picked as his running-mate Senator Edmund Muskie of Maine, a Catholic who had spoken for the majority plank on Vietnam; in his acceptance speech Humphrrey declared that "Our most urgent challenge is in urban America."[4]

In another significant development, the convention voted by the relatively narrow margin of 1,350 to 1,206 to throw out the unit rule. Despite the tension, the only party leader of note to take a walk was segregationist Governor Lester Maddox of Georgia, a recently declared Presidential candidate, who left town complaining about "socialists, beatniks, and misfits" after Julian Bond had challenged the credentials of the Georgia delegation.[5]

Although Representative Hale Boggs of Louisiana was the chairman of the Resolutions Committee, the stamp of the White House was on the platform, especially that portion of it dealing with the Vietnam War. Unlike its 1964 counterpart, there was no quoting from the previous document, showing how earlier pledges had been implemented; instead, the 1968 platform began with a reference to Thomas Jefferson and James Madison, and then progressed with a catalogue of Democratic achievements during the past eight years. At various points there was praise for the war on poverty, Head Start, the Model Cities program, JOBS, and the Neighborhood Youth Corps. There likewise was a call for federal financing of the welfare program and governmental support for the "family incomes of the working poor." One of the more controversial aspects of this document was its endorsement of the work of the Kerner Commission; liberals on the drafting committee inserted this plank while Boggs was in Washington, despite the fact that LBJ had been rather cool to its work. On the other hand, Boggs did manage to water down an indictment of television to a complaint about the "all too frequent exploitation of violence as entertainment," the only change in any plank between the drafting of the platform and its later adoption by the full convention.

With respect to future reforms, the Democrats followed the example of the Republicans by advocating a Constitutional amendment granting eighteen-year-olds the right to vote, and favoring the increased participation by youthful delegates at future Democratic conventions. Like the Republicans, the Democrats endorsed law and order in the guise of justice and law, but with the qualification that "We will further this campaign by an attack on the root causes of crime and disorder"; the latter did progress beyond their own 1964 platform by recognizing the principle of one man, one vote, in all elections. Turning to less momentous concerns, there also was a plank lauding "Lady Bird"

Johnson for her work in beautifying the highways of the nation. But aside from this cornucopia of assorted reforms, perhaps the best argument set forth in this document for keeping the party in office was the reference to the ninety-month period of sustained economic growth—the longest such period in American history. The profits arising from this, however, were to be subjected to a revised tax structure that closed loopholes, and imposed a minimum income tax on persons of high income.

Unfortunately, the Democrats under LBJ had fewer achievements to point relative to foreign policy than they had in the domestic field. Like the Republicans, they called for restraint in the formulation and implementation of American diplomacy, declaring that we must "Resist the temptation to try and mold the world, or any part of it, in our own image, or to become the self-appointed policeman of the world." In the case of the Near East, the platform also followed the Republican example by adopting a pro-Israel stance. The recent Russian takeover of Czechoslovakia merely provoked a plank expressing moral outrage, rather than calling for military or other action on the part of the United States.

Yet these planks faded into insignificance when compared with those on Vietnam. The first of these asserted that the United States should "Stop all bombing of North Vietnam when this action would not endanger the lives of our troops in the field; this action should take into account the response from Hanoi," while the second declared that the American government should "Negotiate with Hanoi in an immediate end or limitation of hostilities and the withdrawal from South Vietnam of all foreign forces—both United States and allied forces, and forces infiltrated from North Vietnam." Neither in this or in the other two planks was there any specific mention of the Viet Cong. Endorsing the concept of Vietnamization, this document called for an honorable and lasting settlement to what it described elsewhere as the "tragic" Vietnam War.

On the afternoon of August 28 there was a three-hour debate on the Vietnam plank, which the Resolutions Committee had approved by approximately a two-to-one majority. Such Presidential possibilities as Senators Eugene McCarthy, George McGovern, and Edward Kennedy all favored an unconditional halt to the bombing of North Vietnam, while Hubert Humphrey continued to uphold LBJ; after the campaign was over, however, the latter confirmed reports that he had been opposed to the initial decision for bombing North Vietnam. Speaking on behalf of the majority report, Senator Gale McGee of Wyoming invoked the "domino" theory, while Governor Warren Hearns of Missouri warned against jeopardizing the lives of American servicemen in Vietnam. Resolutions Committee Chairman Boggs made the most effective plea, with his claim that a bombing halt would cause a five-fold increase in North Vietnamese capabilities in the demilitarized zone. Despite the fact that the New York delegation voted 148 to 42 to uphold the minority plank, the delegates defeated the substitute measure by 1,041-¼ to 1,567-¾.

In terms of ideology, the candidates and platform of the American Independent party proved as interesting, if not more so, than those of the two major parties. Dispensing with a national convention, the AIP presented a ticket of Governor George Wallace of Alabama for President and General Curtis Le May for Vice President. Among other things, Wallace attacked the movement in this country away from states' rights, the desegregation rulings of the Supreme Court, "pointy-headed" intellectuals, and our nation's failure to achieve victory in Vietnam. To some of his critics, Wallace was simply a racist posing as a law-and-order man, but subsequent developments proved that his appeal was far more broad and complex. His running-mate was a hawk of hawks, an individual of whom it might be said that he was even more committed to a military victory in Vietnam than Barry Goldwater.

While more than one individual (perhaps without actually reading it)accused the AIP platform of being outside the political mainstream, on closer perspective it appears somewhat less extremist than one might expect after such accusations. After complaining about the Federal government's encroachment upon state and local powers, it charged that civil rights legislation (in particular that passed in 1964) had "set race against race and class against class." In this connection the Supreme Court, which had handed down its school desegregation ruling in 1954, was attacked for having enacted judicial legislation; as a partial solution, it was proposed that members of the Federal judiciary at the district level be required to face the voters regularly, and those at the appellate and Supreme Court levels to confront the US Senate periodically.

Taking the side of free enterprise against socialism, this document nevertheless pledged, "We will eliminate the favorable treatment now accorded the giant, non-tax-paying foundations and institutions." The rebuilding of the cities should be a joint enterprise for Federal, state, and local authorities involving the relocation of expanding industry away from metropolitan centers, while jobs for the poor and health care should be the concern of private enterprise as much as the government. The AIP also devoted no less than seventeen planks to agriculture, a subject the Republicans and Democrats had tended to neglect in their growing preoccupation with urban affairs; one of these advocated price supports at 90/100 percent of parity, with the last endorsing a campaign against the imported fire ants. Despite the charge that the Wallace movement was racist in nature, there was a plank calling for Federal assistance to two "ancient and noble races," the American Indians and the Eskimos.

Approximately one-third of this document was devoted to foreign affairs. It pledged aid to those countries "who need, deserve, and have earned the right to our help", and endorsed a protective tariff when necessary to safeguard American industry. The plank on the Middle East walked the tightrope between the Jews and Arabs rather than take an anti-Semitic line, while that on eastern Europe showed restraint by merely expressing concern rather than promising liberation. With respect to Castro, the solution offered was economic sanctions; with respect to De Gaulle, patient and firm dealing. Although the platform did give qualified support to the emerging nations of Africa and Asia, it also announced, "We disagree with present economic sanctions and pressures applied to Rhodesia and the Union of South Africa," a position which brought the AIP under fire from civil rights groups. The plank on Vietnam did call for a military victory over the enemy and the abandonment of a no-win policy, but only in the event that peaceful negotiations did not work. Far more extreme was the sword-rattling nuclear weapons plank, which declared that parity rather than superiority was not enough, and the statement that the armed services should be responsible for the exercise of military force provided that it was in line with national policy. The ghost of the Barry Goldwater of 1964 hovers over this part of the platform, which although occasionally employing the first person, seems more representative of Le May than of Wallace.

Quite different in orientation was the platform of the Prohibition party, which had held its convention at Detroit in June 1967, and selected a ticket of Earle Harold Munn and the Reverend Rolland E. Fisher. As usual, the planks were rehashes of what had been proposed four years before, or even earlier, with two prominent exceptions. That on the income tax gave the Prohibitionists credit for first proposing the idea as early as 1896, but complained about the "graduated tax and confiscatory rates" which had not been originally contemplated. More original, perhaps, was the new plank dealing with tax sharing. This suggested that "appropriate amounts of the tax collected in each state [be] distributed to each of the state governments before becoming the property of the federal government." Of the Vietnam War and disturbances in cities and on campuses, there was nothing said.

The fall campaign began with Richard Nixon enjoying a comfortable lead, and George Wallace looming large in the polls. It appeared at first as if Hubert Humphrey faced a seemingly impossible task in attempting to put the shattered Democratic party back together again, but with the help of organized labor and other groups, he began picking up support, largely at the expense of the AIP Even Eugene McCarthy, who had withdrawn to his tent after the convention for a long sulk, belatedly jumped on the Humphrey bandwagon, while LBJ picked up votes for the Democratic nominee by ending the air raids over North Vietnam several days before the election. Fortunately for Richard Nixon, however, his support held relatively constant during the campaign. Edging out Humphrey by a margin of 500,000 popular votes out of a total of 72 million, the Republican nominee obtained a more clear-cut victory in the Electoral College, 302 to 191, carrying 32 states to 13 for the Democratic nominee. Still, the triumphant Nixon received 3 million popular votes less than he had in 1960, and failed to carry a single large city. Wallace made the strongest showing by a third-party nominee since Robert La Follette in 1924, winning five southern states with 45 electoral votes and amassing nearly 10 million popular notes.

The combined Nixon/Wallace popular vote was approximately 58 percent, apparently a decisive antiadministration mandate. But even though the largest number of voters in American history turned out, the percentage of eligible voters who participated was not remarkably high. Richard Nixon, moreover, was confronted with another dilemma: the voters had returned a

Democratic Congress for him to work with and had given him
only 43 percent of the popular vote. Perhaps Nixon, in retrospect,
could find solace in the fact that such Presidential greats as
Abraham Lincoln and Woodrow Wilson won their first terms
with popular vote percentages falling far short of a majority.

XXXV. 1972

Democratic Doldrums

During the course of the 1972 Presidential campaign, a break-in
occurred at the national headquarters of the Democratic party,
located at the Watergate complex in Washington. Although the
total implications of this burglary were not immediately obvious,
by the midway point of his second term as chief executive, the
mushrooming scandal that followed had forced Richard Nixon
out of office. Since he was the first President in history to resign,
the circumstances leading up to this unprecedented action have
tended to overshadow his record as chief executive in all of its
aspects. Especially during Nixon's first term, before he was
inundated by the Watergate flood, a number of key developments
took place that are worthy of mention.

Like Harry Truman, the majority of Nixon's greatest achievements were in the foreign relations field. With the brilliant Henry
Kissinger advising him on foreign affairs, he brought American
participation in the war in Vietnam to a halt early in 1973, after
having instituted such bold actions as the Cambodian invasion
and the mining of North Vietnamese ports. The most travelled
President in history, Nixon journeyed to both Russia and China,
in an attempt to inaugurate a new era of relations with these two
giant Communist powers; although failing to recognize the
mainland China regime diplomatically, he did negotiate a nuclear
arms limitation pact with the Soviet Union. The winding down of
the war in Vietnam not only led to a cooling off of discontent on

the campuses of America, but also allowed Nixon to move towards the termination of the draft and the creation of an all-volunteer army.

Less amenable to solution were the economic problems facing America, successively a recession, unemployment, and inflation; once Nixon dealt with one of these, another reared its ugly head. In the international sphere, in 1971 imports exceeded exports for the first time since 1893, with the result that he floated the dollar on the international exchange after having devalued it by 11 percent. Nixon also saw fit in August of that year to establish wage and price controls, thus inaugurating a series of economic programs known as phases. His attempts to deal with pressing domestic problems were complicated by Democratic control of both the House and the Senate; to cite only two examples, Congress dragged its feet on both revenue sharing and welfare reform. Turning to his other innovations, Nixon's concept of the New Federalism visualized a return of some of the powers now exercised by the Federal government to the states, while he also de-emphasized the Cabinet and the various departments by con-centrating more and more executive power in the White House. The latter reform, which was designed to by-pass the top-heavy Federal bureaucracy, instead set the stage for Watergate.

During the first Nixon administration, former Governor Spiro Agnew of Maryland served as Vice President. Acting as "Nixon's Nixon," Agnew's slashing but articulate indictments of various individuals and groups won him the undying enmity of liberals and Democrats, as well as the fervent admiration of frustrated conservatives and partisan Republicans. In the year before the 1972 Republican convention, there was some talk of Nixon replacing Agnew with another running-mate, but prior to the Republican meeting at Miami Beach in August, the President announced that he was not going to break up a winning team. With this uncertainty removed, the GOP gathering proved to be the least exciting one since 1956, when the Republicans renominated the ticket of Eisenhower and Nixon, a near landslide winner in 1952.

Unlike 1964, when Democratic incumbent Lyndon Johnson ran as the candidate of the American mainstream against the Re-publican right-winger Barry Goldwater, in 1972 a GOP President established himself as the spokesman for Middle America against George McGovern and the forces of the far left. To quote the

Republican platform, "No Americans before have had a clearer option." Not surprisingly, the domestic planks endorsed the record of the Nixon administration, although a statement favoring right-to-work laws was excluded as a sop to labor, and a commitment to federally assisted day care centers was included only after a fight in the platform committee. A conservative delegate from Utah also sponsored a plank favoring a strictly balanced Federal budget, but he was then stopped by another delegate, who stated that this would embarrass Nixon. More successful was the move to include a plank delineating more clearly the problems of the American Indian, along with some proposed GOP remedies.

Looking at some of the key domestic planks, the GOP took a step away from the welfare state by opposing a governmentally guaranteed income and soak-the-rich tax which would affect the middle class as well. Perhaps more original was the request that individuals be allowed to buy, hold, or sell gold. The Republicans also warned against an excessive dependence on foreign oil, and stressed the importance of domestic development to fill the gap until nuclear energy would become plentiful; in this connection they called for the creation of a Department of Natural Resources, "to develop a national, integrated energy policy and implement that policy." The influence of Ralph Nader was present in that plank calling for a clean-burning automobile engine, and in that advocating an independent consumer advocate agency and a product safety agency, but the GOP nevertheless affirmed its opposition to "punitive" proposals that were more antibusiness than anticonsumer. There should be, it declared, "a workable balance between a growing economy and environmental protection."

Among the other reforms supported by the Republicans were the lowering of the legal age to eighteen, equal rights for women, and an emphasis on the family farm rather than giant agrobusinesses. The right of responsible citizens to own firearms for legitimate purposes was also upheld. Taking the position that "The Nation's welfare system is a mess," the GOP came out for reforms in this area; favoring the bolstering of Social Security, medicare, and private pension planks, it attacked compulsory national health insurance, and endorsed a joint program involving the government, employers, and employees. Generally speaking, this document was probably less conservative than the politics of most of the delegates who renominated Nixon, although the chairman of the Resolutions Committee was right-of-center Representative John Rhodes of Arizona, who followed many of the procedures established in 1968 by Everett Dirksen.

With respect to foreign affairs, the Republicans proudly stated that "historians may well regard these years as a golden age of American diplomacy." Amnesty for draft evaders acting in the name of a "higher morality" was rejected, along with the "meat-ax slashes" in defense spending proposed by Senator McGovern. In the opinion of the GOP, the United States should expand contacts with eastern Europe and China, show concern for the Soviet Jews, keep Cuba isolated, and reconcile Israel and the Arabs. "The Nixon Doctrine," observed the platform, "recognizes that continuing defense and development are impossible unless the concerned nations should bear the principal burden." Turning to foreign economic policy, it attacked the practice of locating plants in foreign countries solely to take advantage of low wage rates, noted that multinationals pose problems as well as offer opportunities, and promised that workers and industries harmed by changing trade patterns would get more help. With the Vietnam War now nearing its end relative to American participation, the Republicans proudly boasted that US forces in Vietnam had been reduced by 93 percent, and total American forces abroad had been trimmed by more than 1 million men and women. Elsewhere, in a blast at the war prosperity of the Kennedy and Johnson years, this document declared that "We stand for full employment . . . in an economy . . . not dependent upon war or massive military spending."

Quite different in orientation was the platform approved at the Democratic convention at Miami Beach the proceeding month, in July. This was the gathering that many commentators a year earlier had expected to nominate Senator Edmund Muskie of Maine for President; Muskie, however, faltered in the primaries, while 1968 candidate Hubert Humphrey proved unable to put together a majority coalition of delegates four years later. Alabama Governor George Wallace did pose a serious threat for a while, in the North and in the Border States as well as in the South, but an attempted assassin's bullet in Maryland removed him from the scene as a serious Presidential contender. A political vacuum thus existed, and into this vacuum moved the "Prairie Populist," Senator George McGovern of South Dakota. In a brilliant political maneuver, liberal McGovern capitalized on the support of the "New Left," to win the Democratic Presidential nomination on the first ballot; unlike the 1968 convention at Chicago, the war protesters, reformers, and minority groups were present inside the hall at Miami Beach, not outside. Although the parallels are not complete, one invariably thinks of the metamorphosis that took place in the Democratic party between 1892 and 1896, with the "free silver" Bryanites seizing control of the party from the Cleveland "gold bugs."

Under the reform rules adopted in the wake of the 1968 fiasco, it was stipulated that the platform must be completed and available to the delegates ten days before the convention. Preliminary platform hearings were held in a number of cities, with the most important ones taking place in Washington, with black Newark mayor Kenneth Gibson presiding; the chairman of the platform committee was not a politician, but a professor, noted Presidential scholar Richard Neustadt. Three days before the first session, however, a drafting committee of fifteen, chaired by Gibson, had roughed out the main sections of the platform; of the committee members, six were committed to McGovern, two each to Humphrey and Wallace, one to Muskie, and four were uncommitted. Among those groups having the greatest "input" were the liberal Democratic Policy Council, Common Cause, the United Farm Workers and the "new leftist" New Democratic Coalition. In contrast, spokesmen at the regional hearings had only a limited impact on this document.

Both in the platform hearings and on the convention floor, the politically realistic McGovernites were forced to rely on support from the issue-oriented Wallacites and delegates supporting other candidates to keep some of the more extreme planks out of the platform. On the convention floor the Alabama Governor did attempt to present a minority report, which criticized judges who ignored Congress to make laws, Presidents who ignored Congress to wage war, and bureaucrats who ignored Congress to "pursue abstract and artificial social theories,"[1] but the convention defeated his package on a voice vote without taking a roll call on a single issue. According to one survey, Wallace delegates apparently were most concerned about the busing of students. Unfortunately for the "New Left," the platform debate was so arranged that extremist planks were offered in the middle of the night, when only a handful of viewers were watching their television sets.

To Tom Geoghegan writing in the *New Republic*, " . . . the platform—this year, for once, an important document—was a showpiece of populist zip"[2] whose true ancestor was the Students for a Democratic Society charter drafted by Tom Hayden a decade earlier at Port Huron. Nevertheless, Geoghegan did admit that "In brief, the Democrats promise more old-left new deals in the language of the New Left,"[3] and an examination of the domestic section of this document does reveal that in many ways it merely extended the programs inaugurated under the Great Society, while waffling on some of the more controversial reforms proposed by the New Left. To Benjamin I. Page, it "blended continuity and change."[4] There was, for example, no call for more liberal abortion laws and for the legalization of the use of marijuana; in fact, one plank stated that there should be a national effort against the use of drugs and drug addiction! This sometimes cautious approach on specific issues is to be found in a document which nevertheless loudly proclaims that "It is time now to rethink and reorder the institutions of the country."

Although the platform bypassed the demand of the National Welfare Rights' Organization for a guaranteed income of $6,500 a year for a poor family of four, there was a plea for top-to-bottom welfare reform, an "income security program," and a pledge to make the government the employer of last resort. It was also recommended that welfare rights organizations be recognized as representative of welfare recipients. The Democrats parted company with the Republicans, too, in their endorsement of a system of universal national health insurance; they advocated the use of general revenues as necessary to supplement payroll tax receipts in the financing of Social Security. McGovern's tax reform proposals were abandoned in favor of support for Wilbur Mills's plan for the Congressional review of all tax deductions, but the removal of "all unfair corporate and individual tax preferences" were urged along with the reduction of local property taxes. A redistributive tax reform plank favored by Senator Fred Harris of Oklahoma, which was offered from the floor of the convention, narrowly lost on a voice vote.

In what was perhaps the strongest antimonopoly plank adopted by a major party since 1912, the Democrats came out for the curbing and breaking up of conglomerates, and the deconcentration of shared monopolies such as the auto, steel, and tire industries. As a result, on June 28 the *Wall Street Journal* described the proposed document as "Unfriendly to Big Business."[5] The platform committee did reject a proposal to ban offshore oil drilling outright, but it still included a pledge strictly to enforce offshore safety regulations; one plank called for the abolition of oil import quotas. The Democrats also endorsed the termination of the "unfair, bureaucratic Nixon wage and price controls," which a Democratic Congress had originally authorized, and which the Republicans promised to end as soon as possible.

Turning to the consumer, there was a plank advocating an independent consumer protection agency (but with erroneous wording), liberalized provisions for class action suits, and more comprehensive product labelling. An unsuccessful attempt to court labor featured an increase in the minimum wage to $2.50 an hour; the call for the boycott of nonunion lettuce was designed to appeal to Cesar Chavez's United Farm Workers and the Mexican-Americans (Chicanos). With respect to education, that plank came out for the equalization of school spending, increased Federal aid to education, and even the use of busing ("another goal [sic] to accomplish desegregation"). There was no special section on blacks, but one on "rehabilitation" offered prisoners a variety of rights, while a plank adopted from the floor favored preferential treatment for the Indians relative to surplus public lands. Despite the call for the ratification of the equal rights amendment for women and other antidiscrimination measures, spokesmen for some of the more esoteric minority groups had to find solace in a statement to the effect that "Americans should be free to make their own choice of lifestyles and private habits without being subject to discrimination or persecution." Everyone, however, was conceded the right of privacy against wire-tapping, electronic surveillance, and computer data banks.

Although a Great Society liberal might have been able to consent to the domestic sections of this platform, but with qualifications, Democrats committed to a strong posture on defense (such as Senator Henry Jackson) could hardly regard these planks with much sincere enthusiasm at all. While it is true that this document did not specifically endorse the defense cuts proposed by Senator McGovern, and did pledge "to maintain adequate military forces for deterrence and effective support of our international position," it also advocated that the United States reduce both military spending and overseas bases and forces. One area where the Democrats were in agreement with the Republicans was the mutual call for the abolition of the draft; this was not the case relative to amnesty, where the Democrats adopted a much softer line.

To the delight of the "doves," the Vietnam plank advocated the "immediate total withdrawal" of all American forces, adding that "after the end of US direct combat participation, military aid to the Saigon government, and elsewhere in Indochina, will be terminated." Outside the convention hall Senator McGovern caused a stir by promising to keep some residual US forces in Thailand until the POW's were returned. On the other hand in what probably was the most hawkish Israel plank in memory, there was a call for the removal of the US embassy from Tel Aviv to Jerusalem, and the stationing of a major naval force in the Mediterranean "to deter the Soviet Union from putting unbearable pressure on Israel." (This was added from the floor of the convention.) As for Europe, the Democrats recommended a termination of support for the Greek military dictatorship, expressed concern for the oppressed minorities of the Soviet Union and eastern Europe, urged that the voice of the United States be heard in Northern Ireland, called for an end to military aid to Portugal, and favored cancellation of the Azores base deal. Elsewhere in the world, they called for sanctions against Southern Rhodesia, opposition to South Africa, reduced military assistance to Latin America, regular diplomatic relations with China, and US support for Bangladesh. Although from the standpoint of military withdrawal, one might label this as an isolationist document, in the nonmilitary realm it by no means advocated a position of noninvolvement.

While Nixon was pre-empting the middle of the road and McGovern was off in left field, the forces of the far right coalesced behind a ticket consisting of conservative Republican Congressman John Schmitz of California and conservative farm magazine publisher Thomas Jefferson Anderson of Pigeon Forge, Tennessee. The national convention at Louisville, Kentucky, attracted almost two thousand delegates from forty states, but not George Wallace, who had chosen this year to operate within the confines of the Democratic party. Significantly, the preamble to the platform approved at this August gathering stressed problem-solving rather than ideology; its two main targets were welfare recipients and multimillionaires who paid no taxes, while the average man bore the brunt of the tax burden. Unlike the rather "hawkish" platform that was adopted in 1968 when General Curtis Le May was George Wallace's running-mate, this somewhat isolationistic document makes reference in the preamble to the never-ending use of American troops "for gunfodder in futile international involvements."

Domestically, the American party advocated quality education, the neighborhood and private schools, and voluntary prayer, while indicting business, sex education, sensitivity training, and drug experimentation. Among the more conservative planks were those affirming the right of every citizen to keep and bear arms, and opposing the legalization of marijuana, pornography, the liberalization of abortion laws, and women's liberation. There also was an endorsement of local government, as well as an attack on the "unrepresentative, unresponsive, dictatorial, federal judiciary," which should be subject either to popular election or to periodic reconfirmation. With respect to economic matters, the American party recommended that the government stop competing with private enterprise, that deficit spending be ended, that individual ownership of gold be allowed, and that the Federal Reserve System be liquidated. It balanced off a call for withdrawal of governmental subsidies to agriculture with a blast against foreign imports from "slave" nations, and sought to win labor with a plank opposing compulsory arbitration and an "acceptable" level of unemployment. While attacking welfare chiselers and federal funding for public assistance programs, the American party came out for various reforms in Social Security and for the expansion of privately financed health care. Nevertheless, despite the rather conservative flavor of the platform, one might cite planks dealing with consumer protection, the environment, and governmental secrecy that at least pay lip service to liberalism.

Relative to foreign policy, the American party placed great emphasis on the unconstitutional nature of American involvement in the Vietnam conflict, and indicted both postwar aid to

North Vietnam and amnesty for military deserters and draft dodgers. Adopting a friendly stance towards South Africa and Rhodesia, it called for neutrality in the Middle East and a hands-off policy towards the Cuban exiles, while blasting increased US contacts with mainland China. In its espousal of a generally isolationistic position relative to diplomacy, the American party pronounced an anathema against those post-World War II treaties entangling the United States in other nations' affairs, along with American membership in the United Nations, the World Bank, the International Monetary Fund, and the General Agreement on Tariffs and Trade. Other objects of attack included foreign aid, a liberalized immigration policy, disarmament, the Peace Corps, and the United States Information Agency. To the American party, future American defense policy should emphasize a strong navy, withdrawal to the Western Hemisphere, and the Monroe Doctrine, but not universal military training. All foreign debts stemming from previous wars should be collected, if necessary by the confiscation of foreign property. One passage in this decidedly nonliberal document, however, did parallel a complaint frequently voiced in recent years by liberals: "Through our involvements abroad, our country is being changed from a republic to a world empire in which our freedoms are being sacrificed on an altar of international involvement."

Of the other "third" parties which selected Presidential candidates and adopted political platforms in 1968, perhaps the one that attracted the most attention was the People's party, which nominated antiwar pediatrician Dr. Benjamin Spock for President at its St. Louis convention in July. Its platform asked the immediate withdrawal of all US troops abroad, free medical care, a family allowance of $6,500, the legalization of abortion and marijuana, and an end to discrimination against women. Less publicized but more unorthodox was the Libertarian party, whose ideological stance might be described as a mixture of laissez-faire economics, avant garde morality, and a Jeffersonian suspicion of "big government, big spending and government bureaucracy."[6] Its Presidential candidate, University of Southern California philosophy professor Dr. John Hospers, observed that the key principle of his party's platform was that "a person should not be interfered with by the government unless he interferes with the freedom of another individual."[7]

Also playing an active role in this campaign was the Communist party, whose Presidential candidate was its long-time general secretary, Gus Hall. Meeting at Brooklyn in February, the Communists adopted a platform advocating an end to the war in Indochina and the payment of reparations to the Vietnamese, diplomatic recognition of China, North Korea, Albania, and Cuba, and the nationalization of the arms, space, and nuclear power industries. Its rival on the left, the Socialist Workers party, had chosen its Presidential nominee, Atlanta secretary Linda Jenness, at a convention held the previous August. The Trotskyites came out for an immediate end to the Vietnam War, while supporting black and Chicano political movements, women's liberation, and prison reform. More economically oriented was the Socialist Labor party, which nominated Chicago dry-cleaning plant worker Louis Fisher for President at its Detroit convention in April. According to its platform, inflation, high unemployment, and the need for wage and price controls indicated that the capitalist system was approaching a crisis even greater than that of 1929.

Finally, one might point to that political perennial, the Prohibition party, which assembled at Wichita the previous June to select Earle Harold Munn for President. Its rather long platform came out against inflation and governmental spending, while voicing environmental concern; although striking Federal employees and civil disobedience were censured, year-round Daylight Savings Time was endorsed. Other objects of attack included the nation's welfare system, the guaranteed annual income, and the change of dates for national holidays. The Prohibitionists did admit that the drug problem had become worse, but they still denounced alcoholism as a more deadly social evil. In their opinion the news media, which quite naturally paid considerable attention to the forces of the "New Left" that had taken over the Democratic party, were guilty of "sensationalizing a growing moral permissiveness."[8]

Throughout the campaign that followed the conventions nothing seemed to go right for George McGovern, aside from the fact that, thanks to small contributors he was able to raise in the neighborhood of $35 million—approximately four times the amount available to Hubert Humphrey in 1968. But McGovern never was able to shake the radical image that had descended upon him by the time of the Democratic convention; his numerous far-out stands and ideological flip-flops on key issues alienated the New Left and regular Democrats, the youth vote and organized labor, and George Wallace, who made no Presidential endorsement. To make matters worse, McGovern's dumping of Senator Thomas Eagleton of Missouri, after it had become known that the latter had a psychiatric record, quite seriously crippled his campaign from the start. More fortunate were the Republicans, who enjoyed a $50 million war chest, favorable economic conditions aside from an overly high unemployment rate, and good prospects for a settlement of the Vietnam War in the not-too-distant future. Equally important was the fact that they proved able to keep the lid on the Watergate break-in until after the election was over.

Bolstered by public opinion polls that showed him far ahead, Richard Nixon did little actual campaigning, although he did deliver some political addresses over television and radio. In one of the greatest landslides in history, the incumbent President annihilated the "Prairie Populist," 45,000,000 popular votes to 28,000,-000, in an election which saw only 55 percent of the eligible voters go to the polls; McGovern carried only Massachusetts (the home of Eagleton's replacement as running-mate, R. Sargent Shriver, Senator Edward Kennedy's brother-in-law) and the District of Columbia, with its overwhelming black population. Deprived of George Wallace as its Presidential candidate, the American party popular vote total dropped from 10 million in 1968 to 1 million in 1972. But despite his near-record triumph, Richard Nixon was unable to carry in a Republican Congress with him, as the GOP actually lost two seats in the Senate while picking up a dozen in the House. With a divided government to preside over, the stage was set for the President's great confrontation with Congress over the Watergate investigation.

XXXVI.   1976

A Tentative Appraisal

Writing at the end of the 1976 Presidential campaign, it is no easy task to place the nominees, events, and platforms in perspective. Nevertheless, some sort of tentative evaluation may prove a valuable addition to the narrative, since the major party platforms for 1976 are of considerable interest. So, too, are the Presidential candidacies of former Minnesota Senator Eugene McCarthy and former Georgia Governor Lester Maddox, and the meteoric rise of Jimmy Carter as a national political figure. Not since Wendell Willkie, perhaps, has an individual so far removed from the party leadership seized his party's Presidential nomination; during the 1950s Dwight Eisenhower was the candidate of the Republican "Eastern Establishment," even if he was not really a member of this group.

But then never in history has a President resigned; such was the fate of Richard Nixon, who surrendered office on August 9, 1974, when the controversy over the cover-up of the Watergate break-in had reached the point where it appeared certain Congress would impeach him and remove him from the chief executiveship. Less than a year earlier his Vice President, Spiro Agnew, resigned in disgrace after pleading no contest to a charge of tax evasion. Under a newly approved Constitutional amendment Representative Gerald Ford of Michigan, the Republican minority leader in the House of Representatives, was approved by Congress to replace Agnew after Nixon had nominated him as Vice President.

As was the case during his first term as President, Richard Nixon's record in the foreign affairs field continued to outshine that in the domestic area, one case in point being the conclusion of the Vietnamese peace negotiations in January 1973. When still another war broke out in the Middle East between the Israelis and the Arabs in October, Secretary of State Henry Kissinger obtained both a cease-fire and a disengagement accord by means of "shuttle" diplomacy; in the aftermath of this conflict the United States resumed diplomatic relations with Egypt for the first time since 1967. President Nixon also continued his much publicized trips abroad, visiting Moscow in mid-1974 to sign three nuclear pacts, and the Middle East itself (Israel, Egypt, Syria, Jordan, and Saudi Arabia) in June of that year. On the other hand, at home growing inflation spearheaded a large number of economic problems which chronically plagued the nation during 1973 and 1974, and which the Nixon Administration failed to solve.

Upon becoming President, Gerald Ford caused a sensation by issuing a "full, complete, and absolute" pardon to Richard Nixon for any possible misdeeds which he may have committed while in the White House. Ford also aroused controversy by setting forth a program of earned clemency for those individuals who refused military service in Vietnam. The new President did defer to Congress by making an unprecedented appearance before a House Judiciary Subcommittee on October 17 to defend the Nixon pardon, but during the two years that followed he was to be unusually active in vetoing legislation passed by the predominantly Democratic Congress. Early in his administration that body approved former Governor Nelson A. Rockefeller as Ford's replacement as Vice President after the chief executive had selected him for that position.

Although inflation and unemployment both had declined by the time of the 1976 Presidential election, both still remained high, and the President and the Congress were unable to reach an understanding as to how they should be reduced. Equally explosive was the energy controversy, which had erupted in the wake of the Arab oil embargo at the time of the 1973 war with Israel; here the President was in disagreement as to policy with a Congress which was contemplating the divestiture of the oil companies. Nor were they in accord with respect to what to do about debt-plagued New York City, then on the verge of default. Ford originally took a hard line, but by December was willing to approve a $2.3 billion federal loan by Congress after New York State had agreed to raise taxes and reduce future expenses.

In the foreign affairs field South Vietnam fell following a rather abrupt military collapse during March and April of 1975. Cambodia also surrendered during the latter month, but in May President Ford took the controversial step of sending in U. S. troops to recapture the American merchant ship *Mayaguez* after the Communists had seized it in the Gulf of Thailand. Then on December 7, 1975, when visiting Honolulu, Ford proclaimed a six point "Pacific Doctrine" which reaffirmed that the United States was not withdrawing from Asia.

During 1975 the President also attended meetings in Brussels, Helsinki, and France on such topics as NATO, post-World War II territorial boundaries, and mutual economic cooperation, and at home attacked Congressional policy towards Turkey and Angola. Burned by the unpleasant American experience in Vietnam, Congress was hesitant to extend aid and assistance to that war-torn state, and during 1976 the Marxist led forces gained a victory there. Fearful of Communist regimes emerging elsewhere in Africa, Secretary of State Henry Kissinger called for the white dominated government of Rhodesia to give way to black majority rule; the Ian Smith regime did agree to the holding of talks to effect this end, although with considerable reluctance.

Thanks largely to the furor over Watergate, the Democrats picked up 43 seats in the House (but only three in the Senate) and four governorships in the 1974 off-year election. They looked ahead with confidence to victory in the 1976 Presidential contest, forgetting the fact that earlier in American history the Republicans had retained the White House in the next Presidential election, despite the scandals of the Grant and the Harding administrations. In any event, Democrat after Democrat announced his candidacy, including a number of well-known national figures. Quite a few experts, though, predicted an inconclusive string of primaries, following which the delegates assembled at New York City would select some one who had not formally entered the race, most likely Senator Hubert Humphrey of Minnesota.

But as is so often the case in politics, the unexpected took place instead. Capitalizing on a growing anti-Washington sentiment in this country and a desire to return to earlier religious, moral, and ethical values, former naval officer and Georgia governor Jimmy Carter took the New Hampshire Democratic Presidential primary. The wealthy peanut farmer then went on to capture a majority of the other state primaries, winning enough delegates to secure his party's Presidential nomination by the time that the Democrats convened at New York City in July. A last minute string of defeats did not keep Carter from becoming the first Democratic (and major party) Presidential nominee from the South in the present century; Virginia-born Woodrow Wilson later became identified with New Jersey, while Lyndon Johnson's Texas is a south-western state.

At the convention itself Carter easily won nomination on the first ballot, with Morris Udall and Edmund Brown trailing with approximately 300 votes apiece. Carter then selected as his running mate Senator Walter "Fritz" Mondale of Minnesota, a protege of Hubert Humphrey, whose voting record in the Senate was the most liberal of any of the serious Vice Presidential possibilities whom Carter considered. Some observers detected a swing to the left here by the Georgian following a more middle of the road stance in the primaries, but there remained a widespread public uncertainty as to whether the former Georgia governor was a conservative, a moderate, a liberal, or a mere opportunist. Having no voting record in Congress, he forced political analysts to turn to his one term in the state house at Atlanta for clues; there his big achievement was the reorganization of the state government into fewer departments and agencies, but without reducing the cost of operating it.

The Democratic platform in its final version appeared to be more a Great Society document than a McGovernite one; it was written under the direction of platform committee chairman Governor Wendell Anderson of Minnesota. Its call for more spending by the federal government did not square with the anti-Washington approach which Carter had frequently employed during the primaries. But even before Carter had clinched his party's Presidential nomination, a Democratic Advisory Council of Elected Officials had been working on a report for over three years which was to form the basis of the 1976 Democratic platform. Not surprisingly, this document drawn up in an era of recession emphasized economic issues, especially the creation of more jobs and the establishment of safeguards against inflation. (Earlier in the year President Ford had vetoed a major jobs bill.) As for foreign affairs, the task force chairman was party elder statesman W. Averell Harriman; this part of the report took the position that the United States needed to implement a new internationalism blending realism and idealism, with less emphasis on Russia and China and more on our allies. While it largely sidestepped the touchy Middle Eastern situation, this report heavily indicted the Ford Administration's policy towards black Africa.

Likewise, the platform itself—which Jimmy Carter described as "a binding contract with the American people"[1]—took a liberal stand on the racial question by supporting the use of busing as a judicial tool of last resort to achieve racially integrated schools. Two of the more controversial domestic planks were those endorsing a ban on cheap handguns ("Saturday night specials") and opposing an anti-abortion Constitutional amendment. Conspicuously absent was an attack on capital punishment. There was a call for a minimum income guarantee for both the working and non-working poor, as well as for a complete overhaul of the tax structure; supporters of the future Presidential candidate, however, blocked the inclusion of a plank advocating the public financing of a comprehensive national health insurance system. (Carter favored some employer-employee contributions and a phased-in approach.) Turning to economics, the Democrats called for an adult unemployment rate of only three per cent within four years, in the process endorsing governmental action via the Humphrey-Hawkins bill, and accused the Republicans of bringing about "stagflation" by their economic policy. Stand-by wage and price controls also were advocated.

While it did not endorse the break-up of the major oil companies, this document did oppose both the deregulation of natural gas prices and oil company ownership of other energy sources. Significantly, a reliance on nuclear power was downgraded. Planks favorable to labor included a call for the repeal of Section 14B of the Taft-Hartley Act, and the granting to public and agricultural workers of the right to organize and bargain collectively, as well as the right of construction workers peacefully to picket a job site. The platform also came out for federal financing of Congressional elections. However, it did not advocate the restoration of the postal service as a governmental agency, thanks to the urging of Carter supporters, despite its backing of the so-called sunset law concept and zero-based budgeting. In general the forces of the Georgia governor succeeded in moderating a document which otherwise might have been much closer in philosophy to its predecessor of 1972.

In the area of foreign affairs the Democrats endorsed both detente and a strong American military deterrent, including a bigger Navy. Yet there was a call for a five to seven billion dollar cut in defense spending, and a delay in the decision to produce the B1 bomber. With the acrimony over the Vietnam war having subsided, the platform came out in favor of pardons for draft dodgers. Elsewhere in the Far East, the Democrats attacked the admittedly dictatorial regime in South Korea, but they sidestepped a European "hot spot" by rejecting a proposed plank favoring the creation of a united Ireland. More comprehensive was the declaration that "the United States should not provide aid to any government—anywhere in the world—which uses secret police, detention without charges, and torture to reinforce its powers." In view of the tremendous amount of unfavorable publicity surrounding certain activities of the C.I.A. over the years, it is not surprising that this document also favored a prohibition on covert or illegal operations by governmental bodies, except where national security considerations mandated it. In this connection the Democrats proclaimed that "governmental decision-making behind closed doors is the natural enemy of the people."

While Jimmy Carter was sewing up the Democratic Presidential nomination, the Republicans were being torn apart by a bitter struggle between the incumbent chief executive, Gerald Ford, and former California governor (1967-75) Ronald Reagan. Although many commentators failed to see much difference between their political philosophies other than to label Ford a pragmatic conservative and Reagan an ideological one, Reagan and Ford in fact did differ on at least several foreign policy issues, specifically the Panama Canal and detente, and more generally the conduct of Henry Kissinger as Secretary of State. Although he had shown little inclination to run for a second term early in his administration, Ford nevertheless became more eager for the Presidency as time went on, despite two assassination attempts on him during September 1975 in California. In November of that year Vice President Nelson Rockefeller, under pressure from the right wing of his party, which had never forgiven him and still distrusted him, announced that he would not be a candidate for another term.

That same month Reagan announced his Presidential candidacy. The one-time actor, television personality, and liberal Democrat seized an early lead over Ford in the Gallup Poll which he shortly was to lose and never regain. When Ford faced Reagan in the February New Hampshire primary, Ford won a narrow victory, following which Reagan faltered somewhat in his campaign, even losing such "Sun Belt" states as Florida to Ford. But just as it appeared that his Presidential hopes had been damaged beyond repair, Reagan made a comeback in North Carolina and then Texas and Indiana, climaxing his drive with a triumph in California.

At Kansas City, though, the Ford forces managed to win over most of the uncommitted delegates, and beat down Reagan's attempt to force Ford to announce his Vice Presidential candidate in advance of the Presidential balloting. (Reagan's previously revealed choice, Senator Richard Schweiker of Pennsylvania, was not only from the Northeast, but also was a liberal as well.) Ford then narrowly won his party's Presidential nomination on the first ballot, 1187 to 1070, staving off the most serious challenge to an incumbent President since William Howard Taft defeated Theodore Roosevelt in 1912. After Reagan had announced in advance that he would not accept his party's Vice Presidential nomination under any circumstances, Ford turned somewhat unexpectedly to Senator Robert Dole of Kansas. Dole, a former Republican national chairman and at times a sharp partisan infighter, balanced the ticket neither ideologically nor geographically. Fortunately for Ford, the bitterness of the Reagan forces in defeat was not as great as many had anticipated, and the President significantly narrowed Jimmy Carter's lead over him in the Gallup Poll following the convention.

Even before the Democrats had assembled in convention the chairman of the 1976 Republican platform committee, Governor Robert Ray of Kansas, had begun holding public hearings. Correctly foreseeing that disagreement was most likely to occur in the field of foreign affairs, Ray declared that the main thrust of the platform would be to "reassert this nation's commitment to the freedom of the individual," to "develop a sense of internationalism," to endorse "productivity and efficiency," and to "commit the Republican Party to responsibility."[2] The first clash over a controversial issue at the hearings, though, was about abortion, which was to prove a more serious problem for the Democrats.

At the convention itself the actual drafting of the platform was done in closed session, following the example of the Democrats. The resulting document was perhaps the most conservative one offered by the G.O.P. since the Goldwater debacle of 1964; neither here nor in the balloting for President did the once powerful Eastern liberal wing of the party manifest much clout. Unlike the Democrats, the Republicans came out for a Constitutional amendment prohibiting abortion, a development most pleasing to the supporters of Ronald Reagan. The latter, however, were thwarted at the last moment in their attempt to include a plank favoring laws to ensure equal treatment for women without specifically endorsing the Equal Rights Amendment. The Reagan forces, moreover, absorbed several defeats in the area of foreign policy. Here the platform committee rejected a plank opposing negotiations with Panama which would relinquish American sovereignty over the Canal Zone, along with another recommending that the United States avoid policies "which undercut the stability of African nations through unrealistic or impractical demands."[3] This was an obvious slap at Ford and Kissinger's support of black majority rule there. Also defeated were Reaganite proposals critical of detente and inviting Soviet author Alexander Solzhenitsyn to address Congress.

With respect to those parts of the platform which the Reagan forces did not challenge, in the domestic field the Republicans opposed a guaranteed annual income program [unlike the Democrats], and made a plea both to remove ineligible recipients from welfare rolls and to tighten food stamp eligibility requirements. The energy plank called for the lifting of price controls from oil and newly discovered natural gas, while attacking the Democrats for attempting to break up the major oil companies. In rejecting a broad federal gun control program—which it felt should be left to the states—the GOP also took a different stand from its opponents. Other planks attacked national health insurance and grain reserves, while advocating less governmental regulation and revenue sharing for the cities. Mandatory busing for racial balance in the schools was censured as expected, as was the Humphrey-Hawkins bill. "No nation can spend its way into prosperity," observed the platform; "a nation can only spend its way into bankruptcy."

Turning to foreign policy, this document basically endorsed the Ford Administration's policies towards Panama, Africa, and Russia. Yet it also rejected the concept of nuclear sufficiency relative to the Soviets, instead favoring a stance of superiority, which obviously would undercut future strategic arms limitations talks with Russia. In addition, in its commitment to "fulfill and keep its commitments, such as the mutual defense treaty with the Republic of China (Taiwan)," the platform apparently backed away from the attempt to normalize relations with the mainland

regime begun during the Nixon Administration. To James
Weighart the foreign policy section as a whole "is couched largely
in cold war rhetoric of the 1950's."[4]

Although the Republican platform was not completely satisfactory to such right-wing organs as William F. Buckley's *National
Review, Newsweek* found it "a model of present-day conservatism," and "almost a reverse image of the Democrats' emphasis."[5]
This assessment was typical of most overtly non-ideological
publications. Less enthusiastic was the left-leaning *Nation*, which
concluded that it was the most reactionary platform which the
Republicans had adopted in years.[6]

Yet liberal news and opinion magazines were not overly
enthused by the Democratic document, either. Thus the *Nation*,
while proclaiming that it "gleams in comparison with the
Republicans',"[7] nevertheless complained that "Its style is Common
Denominator Bland."[8] The more moderate *Time*, which found
the Vietnamese issue the most sensitive one which the Democrats
faced, proclaimed their platform to be "a monument to sweet
unity;"[9] to *Newsweek*, it was "solidly middle-of-the-road in
tone."[10] Considering its attitude towards the GOP platform, it is
not surprising that the *National Review* would complain of
Democratic "economic witchcraft."[11] Equally critical was *Business Week*, which offered the assessment: "when in doubt,
mumble."[12]

For those dissatisfied with both the Republican and Democratic
nominees and platforms, there remained the option of either not
voting or backing one of the minor parties. Of these perhaps the
most publicized was the American Independent Party; this organization, which met at Chicago in late August, had polled a
million votes in 1972 with former Republican Congressman John
Schmitz of California, a John Bircher, as its Presidential candidate. This time the delegates rejected the candidate of the
intellectual faction, former judge and university president Robert
Morris, and instead chose former Georgia Governor Lester
Maddox. Maddox, who had once chased Negroes out of his
restaurant, in recent years had become a bitter enemy of Carter.
Although there was a disagreement on foreign policy between
hardline Reaganite anti-Communists and isolationist Wallacite
Populists, the convention settled on a platform which, in the
words of *Time*, "opposed drugs, gun control, busing, welfare,

ERA, Washington, the United Nations and Communism, and endorsed police enforcement, America First and the family."[13]

Also in the field as usual were the candidates of the parties of the far left: Gus Hall (Communist); Frank P. Zeidler (Socialist); Julius Levin (Socialist Labor); and Peter Camejo (Socialist Workers). The Communists in particular took a strong stand in favor of detente. Prohibitionist nominee Ben C. Buber, Jr.'s party favored a return to morality and a ban on alcohol, while National Libertarian candidate Roger L. MacBride's party advocated a sharp reduction in governmental activities and a corresponding increase in personal freedom. Former Minnesota Senator Eugene McCarthy, who unsuccessfully challenged Lyndon Johnson for the Democratic Presidential nomination in 1968, ran as an independent without even bothering to form an official political party to support his highly innovative candidacy.

The fall Presidential campaign saw President Ford erase Jimmy Carter's huge lead in the polls at the time of the Republican convention, and engage in a series of debates with his Democratic challenger. These three debates, the first to be held at the Presidential level since the Kennedy-Nixon ones of 1960, stressed in order domestic policy, foreign policy, and general subjects; Ford may have been the narrow winner in the first and Carter in the second, with the third possibly a draw. Although the President made a serious error in describing eastern Europe as being independent of Russian domination during the second debate, it would appear that style was just as important to the viewers as substance in these encounters, which apparently did not effect the outcome of the election as much as they had in 1960. (The 1976 debates, however, probably did stimulate a greater interest in the Presidential race among potential voters.) Vice Presidential candidates Dole and Mondale also debated, but here, too, there was no great victory for either side.

On the eve of the election pollster George Gallup observed that "For the first presidential election year since 1936, the American electorate is concerned chiefly about domestic problems and not questions related to war and peace."[14] These included such economic issues as inflation, governmental spending, and unemployment, as well as such non-economic ones as crime. Religion, moreover, was a key concern for the first time since 1960, not just because of Jimmy Carter's evangelical religious beliefs and his controversial interview in *Playboy* magazine,[15] but also due to Catholic distaste for abortion. Political ethics likewise were an issue, from Watergate and the Nixon pardon to alleged and actual examples of Congressional impropriety. This is not to say that foreign policy did not arise aside from eastern Europe, since Carter criticized Secretary of State Henry Kissinger's handling of his office, while President Ford in praising him pointed to an America at peace. In fact, Kissinger's domination of US diplomacy contributed to the widespread belief among voters that Ford lacked certain leadership qualities; on the other hand, critics of the former Georgia governor viewed him as less politically experienced than the President and more inconsistent and unpredictable on the issues.

Although many commentators predicted a voters' turnout of less than 50 per cent—which probably would have worked to President Ford's advantage in a close election—approximately 53 per cent actually showed up at the polls. Heavy southern and black and labor support enabled Jimmy Carter to defeat the incumbent President in the popular vote, 40.3 to 38.6 million, but Carter's victory in the Electoral College (297 to 241) was the narrowest since 1916. Despite his loss, Ford did carry every state from the Great Plains westwards aside from Texas and Hawaii. Independent candidate Eugene McCarthy only received one per cent of the popular vote, but he may have been a decisive factor in at least several close states; in fact, a switch of less than 10,000 votes in both Ohio and Hawaii would have given Ford another term as President. As for Congress, there was no change in the Senate, while the Democrats picked up several seats in the House of Representatives, bolstering their existing two-to-one majority. With the focal point of national power now shifting to Plains, Georgia, President-elect Jimmy Carter announced his intention to follow through on his campaign promises, a pledge which, as we have seen, different chief executives have honored to varying degrees.

Notes

Throughout the manuscript the author has attempted to note systematically two main types of material: (1) direct quotations; and (2) assessments of entire platforms or single planks made by individuals, newspapers, magazines, etc. Because of the availability of the Porter and Johnson volume, direct quotations from the platform have not been noted.

Introduction

1. Marvin R. Weisbord, "Again the Platform Builders Hammer Away," *New York Times Magazine,* July 5, 1964, p. 10.

2. Gerald M Pomper, " 'If Elected, I Promise': American Party Platforms," *Midwest Journal of Political Science,* August 1967, p. 319.

3. Milton C., Cummings, *The National Election of 1964* (Washington: The Brookings Institution, 1966), p. 25.

4. "The Republican Platform," *Nation,* July 3, 1948, p. 3.

5. William S. White, "For Virtue, Valor and Votes," *New York Times Magazine,* July 27, 1952, p. 12.

6. Seymour Harris, *The Economics of the Political Process* (New York: The Macmillan Company, 1962), p. 68.

7. Henry Hazlitt, "Republican Platform Economics," *Newsweek,* July 5, 1948, p. 21.

8. Raymond Moley, "Make It Short," *Newsweek,* November 18, 1963, p. 116.

9. "Slippery Political Platforms," *Catholic World,* August 1948, p. 390.

10. Pomper, p. 318.

11. Weisbord, p. 10.

12. Paul T. David, "Party Platforms as National Plans," *Public Administration Review,* May-June 1971, pp. 303 and 305.

13. Austin Ranney, "The Platforms, the Parties, and the Voter," *Yale Review,* September 1952, pp. 10-11.

14. Cummings, p. 25.

15. David Hinshaw and Bruno Shaw, "Platform Promises are the Bunk," *Saturday Evening Post*, May 1, 1948, p. 142.

16. David, p. 309

17. Ibid, p. 308.

18. Hinshaw and Shaw, p. 141.

19. Weisbord, p. 28.

20. David, p. 307.

21. Ibid, p. 309.

22. David Hinshaw, "We Point with Pride, We View with Alarm," *New York Times Magazine*, July 2, 1944, p. 40.

23. "Politics and Platforms," *Commonweal*, August 24, 1956, p. 505.

24. John P. Hendrickson, "Legislative Record of Republicans in the Seventy-Third Congress in Relation to the Republican Platform of 1932 and the Campaign Speeches of Mr. Hoover" [Ph.D. diss., Iowa State University, 1952]. See *Dissertation Abstracts*, XII (1952), pp. 744-45.

25. "Political Pledges," *North American Review*, August 1916, pp. 161-71.

26. Hinshaw and Shaw, p. 25.

27. Hendrickson, Ph.D. diss.[see abstract].

28. John K. Galbraith, "The Days of Boom and Bust,"*American History: Recent Interpretations*, ed. Abraham Eisenstadt, 2 vol. (New York: Thomas Y. Crowell, 1962), II:319.

29. David, p. 312.

30. Weisbord, p. 28.

31. David, p. 314.

32. Weisbord, p. 28.

33. David, p. 310.

34. Ibid, p. 311.

35. Ibid, p. 314.

36. Harris, p. 69.

37. Victor L. Profughi, "Party Platforms and Performances: 1900-1964" [Ph.D. diss., University of Pittsburgh, 1967]. See *Dissertation Abstracts*, XXVIII (1967), p. 1110-A.

38. John P. Bradley, "Party Platforms and Party Performance: Social Security 1920-1960" [Ph.D. diss. University of Washington, 1962]. See *Dissertation Abstracts*, XXIII (1963), pp. 4405-6.

39. David, p. 311.

40. Ibid, p. 304.

The 1830's

1. Samuel Rhea Gammon, *The Presidential Campaign of 1832* (Baltimore: Johns Hopkins Press, 1922), p. 140. Johns Hopkins University Studies in Historical and Political Science XL:1.

2. Richard C. Bain, *Convention Decisions and Voting Records* (Washington:The Brookings Institution, 1960), pp. 18-19.

3. Richard B. Morris, *Encyclopedia of American History* (New York: Harper and Row, 1970), p. 178.

1840

1. Robert Gray Gunderson, *The Log-Cabin Campaign* (Lexington: University of Kentucky Press, 1957), p. 65

2. Ibid.

3. Henry Minor, *The Story of the Democratic Party* (New York: The Macmillan Company, 1928), p. 194.

4. Morris, p. 714.

5. Ibid, p. 183.

1848

1. Arthur M. Schlesinger, Jr. ed. *History of American Presidential Elections 1789-1968*, 4 vol. (New York: Chelsea House Publishers, 1971), II:884.

1852

1. Bain, p. 48.

2. Schlesinger, II:944.

1856

1. Hinshaw and Shaw, p. 141.

2. Eric Foner, *Free Soil, Free Labor, Free Men: The Ideology of the Republican Party Before the Civil War* (New York: Oxford University Press, 1970), p. 130.

1860

1. Morris, p. 225.
2. Reinhard H. Luthin, *The First Lincoln Campaign* (Gloucester: Peter Smith, 1964), p. 150.
3. Melvin L. Hayes, *Mr. Lincoln Runs for President* (New York: The Citadel Press, 1960), p. 57.

1864

1. Morris, p. 228.
2. William F. Zornow, *Lincoln and the Party Divided* (Norman: University of Oklahoma Press, 1954), p. 79.
3. William Starr Myers, *The Republican Party: A History* (New York: The Century Company, 1928), p. 142.
4. Zornow, p. 151.
5. Jules Abels, *The Degeneration of Our Presidential Election: An Institution in Trouble* (New York: The Macmillan Company, 1968), p. 101.
6. Schlesinger, II:1170.
7. Ibid, II:1168.

1868

1. Morris, p. 245.
2. George H. Mayer, *The Republican Party 1854-1966* (New York: Oxford University Press, 1967), p. 167.
3. Charles H. Coleman, *The Election of 1868: The Democratic Effort to Regain Control* (New York: Octagon Books, 1971), p. 204.
4. Minor, p. 301.

1872

1. Bain, p. 94.
2. Schlesinger, II:1319.
3. Minor, p. 306.

4. Howard P. Nash, *Third Parties in American Politics* (Washington: Public Affairs Press, 1959), p. 110.

5. Fred E. Haynes, *Third Party Movements since the Civil War with Special Reference to Iowa* (New York: Russell and Russell, 1966), p. 19.

6. Schlesinger, II:1318.

7. Ibid.

8. Ibid, II:1320.

1876

1. Lloyd Robinson, *The Stolen Election: Hayes versus Tilden—1876* (Garden City: Doubleday and Company, 1968), p. 61.

2. Republican National Convention, *Proceedings* (Concord: Republican Press Association, 1876), p. 59.

3. Ibid, p. 61.

4. Minor, p. 314.

1880

1. Bain, p. 114.

2. Republican National Convention, *Proceedings* (Chicago: Jno. B. Jeffrey Printing House, 1881), p. 165.

3. Ibid, p. 166.

4. Herbert J. Clancy, *The Presidential Election of 1880* (Chicago: Loyola University Press, 1958), pp. 159-60.

5. Schlesinger, II:1505.

1884

1. H. Wayne Morgan, *From Hayes to McKinley: National Party Politics, 1877-1896* (Syracuse: Syracuse University Press, 1969), p. 202.

2. "Politics and Platforms," p. 505.

3. Frank R. Kent, *The Democratic Party: A History* (New York: The Century Company, 1928), p. 285.

4. Ibid.

5. National Democratic Convention, *Official Proceedings* (New York: Douglas Taylor's Democratic Printing House, 1884), p. 206.

6. Mayer, p. 210.

1888

1. Democratic National Convention, *Official Proceedings* (St. Louis: Woodward and Tiernan Printing Company, 1888), pp. 101-2.

2. Minor, p. 358.

1892

1. Richard Hofstadter, *The Age of Reform* (New York: Alfred A. Knopf, 1955), p. 132.

2. Solon J. Buck, *The Agrarian Crusade: A Chronicle of the Farmer in Politics* (New Haven: Yale University Press, 1920), p. 142.

3. Malcolm Moos, *The Republicans: A History of Their Party* (New York: Random House, 1956), p. 189.

4. George Harmon Knoles, *The Presidential Campaign and Election of 1892* (Stanford: Stanford University Press, 1942), p. 113. Stanford University Publications Series: History, Economics, and Political Science vol.V, no. 1.

1896

1. Morris, p. 286.

2. "The Republican National Nominee," *Nation*, June 25, 1896, p. 484.

3. Republican National Convention, *Official Proceedings* (Minneapolis, 1896), p. 90.

4. Leland D. Baldwin, *The Stream of American History*, 2 vols. (New York: American Book Company, 1957), II:301.

5. Democratic National Convention, *Official Proceedings* (Logansport: Wilson, Humphreys and Company, 1896), p. 199.

6. Ibid, p. 234.

7. Schlesinger, II:1811.

8. Paul W. Glad, *McKinley, Bryan and the People* (Philadelphia: J.B. Lippincott Company, 1964), pp. 136-37.

9. James McGregor Burns, *The Deadlock of Democracy* (Englewood Cliffs: Prentice Hall, 1963), p. 79.
10. Ibid.

1900

1. Myers, p. 352.
2. "The Two Platforms," *Gunton*, August 1900, p. 129.
3. "The Menace of Mr. Bryan's Platform," *Harper's Weekly*, July 21, 1900, p. 667.
4. Schlesinger, III:1896-97.

1904

1. Moos, p. 246.
2. Bain, p. 166.
3. "The Platform," *Nation*, June 30, 1904, p. 507.
4. "A Bad Blunder," *Outlook*, July 23, 1904, p. 677.
5. Schlesinger, III:1969.
6. Kent, p. 365.
7. Moos, p. 247.
8. Morris, p. 268.

1908

1. Moos, p. 259.
2. W.B. Fleming, "The Republican Platform Unmasked," *Arena*, September 1908, pp. 204-9.
3. "The Republican Platform," *Outlook*, June 27, 1908, p. 413.
4. "The Independence Party: Its Platform and Nominees, Its Strengths and Its Weakness," *Arena*, September 1908, pp. 229 and 232.

1912

1. "The Ravishing of the Socialist Party," *Independent*, August 29, 1912, p. 506.

2. Ibid, p. 507.
3. Baldwin, II:401.
4. "Mr. Bryan's Views of Governor Wilson and the Democratic Platform," *Outlook*, September 7, 1912, p. 27.
5. Mayer, p. 328.
6. Hinshaw and Shaw, p. 141.
7. George E. Mowry, *Theodore Roosevelt and the Progressive Movement* (Madison: University of Wisconsin Press, 1947), p. 273.
8. Amos R.E. Pinchot, *History of the Progressive Party 1912-1916* (New York: New York University Press, 1958), p. 172.

1916

1. "A Comparison of the Chicago Platforms," *Literary Digest*, June 17, 1916, p. 1762.
2. "The Party Platforms," *Review of Reviews*, July 1916, p. 19.
3. Paul U. Kellogg, "Three Platforms," *Survey*, June 24, 1916, p. 336.
4. Democratic National Convention, *Official Report of the Proceedings* (Chicago, 1916), p. 142.
5. "The St. Louis Platform," *Nation*, June 22, 1916, p. 662.
6. "The Political Campaign: The Platforms," *Independent*, July 10, 1916, p. 44.
7. "The Minor Parties: Their Candidates and Platforms," *Review of Reviews*, September 1916, p. 320.
8. Ibid.

1920

1. Minor, pp. 457-8.
2. David J. Hill, "The Issues at Stake," *North American Review*, August 1920, p. 153.
3. Schlesinger, III:2357.
4. Norman Hapgood and Talcott Williams, "The Republican Platform: A Debate," *Independent*, July 24, 1920, p. 107.
5. Edward T. Devine, "The Republicans at Chicago," *Survey*, July 17, 1920, p. 401.
6. Republican National Convention, *Official Report of the Proceedings* (New York : Tenny Press, 1920), p. 110.
7. David Burner, *The Politics of Provincialism: The Democratic Party in Transition, 1918-1932* (New York: Alfred A. Knopf, 1968), p. 64.

8. "The League of Nations as the Dominant Issue," *Current Opinion*, August 1920, p. 151; "The Two Platforms," *Outlook*, July 21, 1920, p. 526.
9. "The Fighting Creed of the Democrats," *Literary Digest*, July 17, 1920, p. 15.
10. Hapgood and Williams, p. 112.

1924

1. "The Democracy States Its Case," *Literary Digest*, July 12, 1924, p. 7.
2. "Democratic Economics, 1924," *New Republic*, July 9, 1924, p. 174.
3. Democratic National Convention, *Official Report of the Proceedings* (Indianapolis: Bookwalter-Ball-Greathouse Printing Company, 1924), p. 307.
4. Ibid, p. 289.
5. Ibid, p. 274.
6. Ibid, p. 263.
7. "The La Follette Platform," *New Republic*, June 18, 1924, p. 89.
8. "La Follette and His Platform," *Forum*, November 1924, p. 688.
9. Kenneth C. MacKay, *The Progressive Movement of 1924* (New York: Octagon Books, 1966), p. 144.
10. See the bibliography covering the year 1924 for a complete listing of these articles.

1928

1. Baldwin, II:552.
2. Roy V. Peel and Thomas C. Donnelly, *The 1928 Campaign: An Analysis* (New York: Richard R. Smith, Inc., 1931), p. 32.
3. Schlesinger, III:2595.
4. Nellie Tayloe Ross, "Two Platforms," *Woman's Journal*, August 1928, p. 15.
5. "The Platforms," *World's Work*, August 1928, p. 346.
6. Burner, p. 196.

1932

1. "The Republican Convention," *World Tomorrow*, July 1932, p. 196.

2. "The Two Platforms," *Nation*, July 13, 1932, p. 23.
3. "The Platform Plank on Prohibition," *Review of Reviews*, July 1932, p. 14.
4. "The Republican Convention," p. 196.
5. Republican National Convention, *Official Report of the Proceedings* (New York: The Tenny Press, 1932), p. 129.
6. Morris, p. 340.
7. Karl Schriftgiesser, *This Was Normalcy: An Account of Party Politics During Twelve Republican Years 1920-1932* (Boston: Little , Brown and Company, 1948), p. 292.
8. Hinshaw and Shaw, p. 25.
9. "The Democratic Repeal Smash," *Literary Digest*, July 9, 1932, p. 4.
10. Democratic National Convention, *Official Report of the Proceedings* (Washington, 1932), p. 206.
11. Schriftgiesser, p. 292.
12. Morris, p. 340.

1936

1. "All Dressed Up . . .," *Nation*, June 24, 1936, p. 793.
2. "The Democrats' Call to Arms," *New Republic*, July 8, 1936, p. 255.
3. "Towards the Left," *Business Week*, July 4, 1936, p. 44.
4. Schlesinger, III:2823.
5. David H. Bennett, *Demogogues in the Depression: American Radicals and the Union Party, 1932-1936* (New Brunswick: Rutgers University Press, 1969), p. 193.

1940

1. Moos, p. 415.
2. Herbert S. Parmet and Marie B. Hecht, *Never Again: A President Runs for a Third Term* (New York: The Macmillan Company, 1968), p. 139.
3. Moos, p. 414.

1944

1. Morris, p. 366.

2. Keith Hutchison, "Mr. Willkie's Challenge," *Nation*, June 24, 1944, p. 726.

3. Donald Bruce Johnson, *The Republican Party and Wendell Willkie* (Urbana: University of Illinois Press, 1960), p. 290.

4. "Advice from Mr. Willkie," *Time*, June 26, 1944, p. 22.

5. Schlesinger, IV:3032.

6. Baldwin, II:692.

1948

1. Jess Conway, "The Socialists See Daylight," *New Republic*, September 13, 1948, p. 12.

2. "The Republican Platform," p. 3.

3. Henry Cabot Lodge, *The Storm Has Many Eyes: A Personal Narrative* (New York: W. W. Norton and Company, 1973), p. 71.

4. Abels, p. 91

5. Murray S. Stedman and Susan W. Stedman, *Discontent at the Polls: A Study of Farmer and Labor Parties 1827-1948* (New York: Russell and Russell, 1950), p. 28.

6. David J. Saposs, *Communism in American Politics* (Washington: Public Affairs Press, 1960), p. 174.

7. Karl M. Schmidt, *Henry A. Wallace: Quixotic Crusade 1948* (Syracuse: Syracuse University Press, 1960), p. 189.

8. Curtis D. MacDougall, *Gideon's Army* (New York: Marzani and Munsell, 1965), p. 568.

9. Ibid, p. 561

10. Ibid, p. 571

11. Ibid, p. 572

1952

1. "The Platform Was the Payoff," *Nation*, July 19, 1952, p. 42.

2. "The Dilemma of Candidate Eisenhower," *New Republic*, July 21, 1952, p. 5.

3. Schlesinger, IV:3233.

4. Wayne Morse, "The GOP Platform," *New Republic*, August 4, 1952, pp. 12-13.

5. Schlesinger, IV:3234.

6. Henry Hazlitt, "You Never Had It So Good," *Newsweek*, August 4, 1952, p. 74.

7. Baldwin, II:766.

1956

1. "Harry's New-Old Platform," *Life*, August 27, 1956, p. 36.
2. "Straddle on Civil Rights," *New Republic*, August 27, 1956, p. 5.

1960

1. Henry Hazlitt, "The Total Welfare State," *Newsweek*, August 1, 1960, p. 70.
2. "Befuddled Donkey: The Democrats Ignore the Lessons of the Postwar Era," *Barron's*, July 18, 1960, p. 1.
3. "Rights of Man—1960 Style, " *Time*, July 25, 1960, p. 18.
4. "The G. O. P. Appeal Is Not to Members of Pressure Groups," *Saturday Evening Post*, October 1, 1960, p. 10.
5. Theodore H. White, *The Making of the President 1960* (New York: Atheneum Publishers, 1961), p. 218.
6. "GOP's New Guard Takes Over," *Business Week*, July 30, 1960, p. 28.
7. Schlesinger, IV:3464.

1964

1. *Inaugural Addresses of the Presidents of the United States* (Washington: U.S. Government Printing Office, 1974), p. 269.
2. Schlesinger, IV:3585.
3. Ibid.
4. Ibid.
5. New York Times, *The Road to the White House: The Story of the 1964 Election* (New York: McGraw Hill Book Company, 1965), p. 64.
6. Cummings, p. 25.
7. "GOP Platform," *Nation*, July 25, 1964, p. 5.
8. F. Clifton White, *Suite 3505: The Story of the Draft Goldwater Movement* (New Rochelle: Arlington House, 1967), p. 388.
9. "The Platform," *National Review*, July 28, 1964, p. 633.
10. "Republicans Hit Kennedy-Johnson Record," *Engineering News-Record.* July 16, 1964, p. 21.
11. John H. Kessel, *The Goldwater Coalition: Republican Strategies in 1964* (Indianapolis: The Bobbs-Merrill Company, 1968), p. 110.
12. New York Times, p. 61.

13. Republican National Convention, *Official Report of the Proceedings* (Washington: Republican National Committee, 1964), p. 254.
14. "Johnson vs. Goldwater," *New Republic*, September 5, 1964, p. 3.
15. Schlesinger, IV:3587.

1968

1. Henry C. Wallich, "Platform Paradox," *Newsweek*, September 9, 1968, p. 85.
2. Lewis Chester, Godfrey Hodgson, and Bruce Page, *An American Melodrama* (New York: The Viking Press, 1969), p. 452.
3. Theodore H White, *The Making of the President 1968* (New York: Atheneum Publishers, 1969), p. 286.
4. "Platforms Draw the Battle Lines," *Engineering News-Record*, September 5, 1968, p. 11.
5. Chester, Hodgson, and Page, p. 378.

1972

1. Tom Geoghegan, "Miami and the Seeds of Port Huron," *New Republic*, September 2, 1972, p. 17.
2. Ibid, p. 16.
3. Ibid, p. 17.
4. Denis G. Sullivan, Jeffrey J. Pressman, Benjamin I. Page, and John J. Lyons, *The Politics of Representation: The Democratic Convention 1972* (New York: St. Martin's Press, 1974), p. 78.
5. Ibid, p. 84.
6. Alfonso A. Narvaez, "A Party is Formed by 'Libertarians,' " *The New York Times*, July 5, 1972, p. 24.
7. Ibid.
8. Roger C. Storms, *Partisan Prophets: A History of the Prohibition Party* (Denver: National Prohibition Foundation, 1972), p. 69.

1976

1. Democratic Planners Told to Remain Loyal to Busing," in Fort Worth *Star-Telegram*, June 14, 1976.

2. "No plank fight seen for G.O.P.," in Dallas *Morning News*, June 22, 1976.

3. "Platform hews to Ford line," in Fort Worth *Star-Telegram*, August 14, 1976.

4. James Weighart, "GOP Platform Dead Weight," in *Charleston Daily Mail*, August 20, 1976.

5. "Battleground," in *Newsweek*, August 30, 1976, pp. 24-25. The quote appears on p. 24.

6. "The Right Wing's Triumph," in *Nation*, August 28, 1976, pp. 130-1. See p. 130.

7. Ibid, p. 131.

8. "Jimmy Built," in *Nation*, July 3, 1976, pp. 2-3. The quote appears on p. 2.

9. "The Joyous Risk of Unity," in *Time*, June 28, 1976, pp. 18-19. Consult p. 18 for the quote. The *New Republic* attacked the Democratic position on desertion in "Fudging Amnesty," June 26, 1976, pp. 4-5.

10. "The Democrats' Magna Carter," in *Newsweek*, June 28, 1976, p. 21.

11. William F. Buckley, Jr. "The Democratic Platform, 1976," in *National Review*, July 23, 1976, pp. 802-3. The quote appears on p. 803.

12. "Democrats Carterize their economic stand," in *Business Week*, June 28, 1976, pp. 25-6. See p. 25 for the quote.

13. "Conclave in Chicago," in *Time*, September 6, 1976, pp. 10-11. The quote appears on p. 11.

14. George Gallup, "Unusual aspects mark '76 presidential race," in Dallas *Morning News*, October 31, 1976.

15. This rather lengthy interview appears between p. 63 and p. 86 of the November issue, which went on sale on the newstands early in October, although highlights from the interview did appear in the press earlier. Carter's comments on sexual morality aroused more of a furor, but the most politically shocking assertion occurs in the very last paragraph: "I don't think I would *ever* take on the same frame of mind that Nixon or Johnson did—lying, cheating and distorting the truth." Aside from the fact this was perhaps not the most appropriate place of publication for an interview with a Presidential candidate, Carter later expressed regrets about undergoing it.

Annotated Bibliography

Several items appearing in the notes which deal only obliquely with political platforms have not been included here.

PART I: THEORETICAL AND MULTIELECTIONAL

Books

ABELS, Jules, *The Degeneration of Our Presidential Election: An Institution in Trouble* (New York: The Macmillan Company, 1968). Touches on the following platforms: 1856, 1864, 1904, 1912, 1916, 1920, 1924, 1928, 1932, 1944, 1948, 1960, and 1964.

BAIN, Richard C., *Convention Decisions and Voting Records* (Washington: The Brookings Institution, 1960). The standard work on political conventions, but sketchy at times on the platforms.

BRADLEY, John P., "Party Platforms and Party Performance: Social Security 1920-1960," Ph.D. dissertation, University of Washington, 1962. Deals only with the Republicans and the Democrats.

BUCK, Solon J., *The Agrarian Crusade: A Chronicle of the Farmer in Politics* (New Haven: Yale University Press, 1920). Analyzes the elections of 1872, 1876, 1880, 1884, 1888, and 1892.

BURNER, David, *The Politics of Provincialism: The Democratic Party in Transition, 1918-1932* (New York: Alfred A. Knopf, 1968). Discusses the Democratic planks in 1920, 1924, 1928, and 1932.

DAVID, Paul T., Ralph M. Goldman, and Richard C. Bain, *The Politics of National Party Conventions* (Washington: The Brookings Institution, 1960). Surveys American political history with occasional references to platforms.

HARRIS, Seymour, *The Economics of the Political Parties* (New York: The Macmillan Company, 1962). Looks at the Eisenhower administration relative to the platform planks of both the Republicans and the Democrats in 1956 and 1960.

HAYNES, Fred E., *Third Party Movements since the Civil War with Special Reference to Iowa* (New York: Russell and Russell, 1966). Examines the third-party platforms of 1872, 1876, 1880, 1884, 1888, 1892, 1896, and 1912.

HICKS, John D., *The Populist Revolt* (Minneapolis: University of Minnesota Press, 1931). Contains material on the platforms of 1892 and 1896.

HOLLINGSWORTH, J. Rogers, *The Whirligig of Politics: The Democracy of Cleveland and Bryan* (Chicago: University of Chicago Press, 1963). Deals with the Democratic platforms of 1896, 1900, and 1904.

JOHNSON, Donald Bruce, *The Republican Party and Wendell Willkie* (Urbana: University of Illinois Press, 1960). Surveys the Republican platforms of 1936, 1940, and 1944 and dissects Willkie's ideas.

JONES, Charles O., *The Republican Party in Politics* (New York: The Macmillan Company, 1965). Touches on the Republican platforms of 1960 and 1964.

KENT, Frank R., *The Democratic Party: A History* (New York: The Century Company, 1928). A standard work covering the platforms from 1840 to 1924.

KIPNIS, Ira, *The American Socialist Movement 1897-1912* (New York: Columbia University Press, 1952). Looks at the Socialist platforms for 1904, 1908, and 1912.

MORTON, Ralph G., *Ballots and Bandwagons* (Chicago: Rand McNally and Company, 1964). Surveys the Republican platforms of 1912 and 1920 and the Democratic one of 1932.

MAYER, George H., *The Republican Party 1854-1966* (New York: Oxford University Press, 1967). A standard work on the Republicans which examines the platforms from Fremont to Goldwater.

MINOR, Henry, *The Story of the Democratic Party* (New York: The Macmillan Company, 1928). A standard work that looks at the Democratic platforms between 1840 and 1924.

MOOS, Malcolm, *The Republicans: A History of Their Party* (New York: Random House, 1956). A standard work on the Republican party which covers the platforms from Fremont to Eisenhower.

MORGAN, H. Wayne, *From Hayes to McKinley: National Party Politics, 1877-1896* (Syracuse: Syracuse University Press, 1969). Treats major party platforms in 1880, 1884, 1888, 1892, and 1896.

MOWRY, George E., *Theodore Roosevelt and the Progressive Movement* (Madison: University of Wisconsin Press, 1947). Analyzes the Republican platforms of 1908 and 1916 and the Progressive platform of 1912.

MYERS, William Starr, *The Republican Party: A History* (New York: The Century Company, 1928). A standard work on the Republican party which examines the platforms through 1924.

NASH, Howard P., *Third Parties in American Politics* (Washington: Public Affairs Press, 1959). A far-ranging treatment of platforms with more emphasis on the nineteenth century than on the twentieth.

OGDEN, Daniel M., and Arthur L. Peterson, *Electing the President: 1964* (San Francisco: Chandler Publishing Company, 1964). Looks at major party platforms in 1960 and 1964.

POLSBY, Nelson W., and Aaron B. Wildavsky, *Presidential Elections: Strategies of American Electoral Politics* (New York: Charles Scribners Sons, 1968). Examines the evolution of the Republican and Democratic platforms between 1932 and 1952.

POMPER, Gerald M., *Elections in America* (New York: Dodd, Mead and Company, 1968). Chapter 7 features a content analysis of the platforms, chapter 8 an examination of their fulfillment.

————.,*Nominating the President: The Politics of Convention Choice* (Evanston: Northwestern University Press, 1963). Discusses the implementation by the Truman and Eisenhower administrations of party platform planks, and attempts to categorize major party planks over the years by means of a table.

PORTER, Kirk H., and Donald Bruce Johnson, compilers, *National Party Platforms 1840-1968* (Urbana: University of Illinois Press, 1970). The standard, up-to-date compilation of the platforms of American political parties, both major and minor.

PROFUGHI, Victor L., "Party Platforms and Performances: 1900-1964," Ph.D. dissertation, University of Pittsburgh, 1967. Examines both major party platforms with respect to agriculture, labor, the tariff, and taxation.

SCHLESINGER, Arthur M., Jr., ed. *History of American Presidential Elections 1789-1968*, 4 vol. (New York: Chelsea House Publishers, 1971). A monumental collaborative work that contains a great deal of material on the platforms over the years. Scope of coverage: volume 1, 1789-1844; volume 2, 1848-1896; volume 3, 1900-1936; volume 4, 1940-1968.

SCRIFTGIESSER, Karl, *This Was Normalcy: An Account of Party Politics During Twelve Republican Years 1920-1932* (Boston: Little, Brown and Company, 1948). Looks at the major party platforms in 1920, 1924, 1928, and 1932.

STEDMAN, Murray S., and Susan W. Stedman, *Discontent at the Polls: A Study of Farmer and Labor Parties 1827-1948*. (New York: Russell and Russell, 1950). Chapter 2 focuses exclusively on the platforms.

STORMS, Roger C., *Partisan Prophets: A History of the Prohibition Party* (Denver: National Prohibition Foundation, 1972). The product of twelve years of study on the part of the author, much of this work is biographical; its most original contribution is its treatment of the period since 1926.

Articles

"Anti-trust Planks in the Democratic Platforms 1892-1932," *Congressional Digest*, June 1933, pp. 178-80. Quotes the pertinent material in chronological order.

BLACK, Anna M., "Teaching the Presidential Campaign in Junior High School," *Historical Outlook*, October 1924, pp. 302-3. Features a most useful list of general issues in the Presidential campaigns as reflected in the party platforms.

BRATTER, Herbert M., "What Do We Know about the Candidates' Monetary Policies," *Commercial and Financial Chronicle*, October 27, 1960, pp. 1, 24-25. Surveys political platform planks dealing with the money question between 1856 and 1960.

DAVID, Paul T., "Party Platforms as National Plans," *Public*

Administration Review, May-June 1971, pp. 303-15. Analyzes various aspects of major party platforms between 1944 and 1968.

HINSHAW, David, "We Point with Pride, We View with Alarm," *The New York Times Magazine*, July 2, 1944, pp. 13, 40-41. A brief and rather critical account of political platforms that stresses the innovative role of minor parties.

HINSHAW, David, and Bruno Shaw, "Platform Promises are the Bunk," *Saturday Evening Post*, May 1, 1948, pp. 25, 141-42. Touches on a number of platforms in a generally hostile treatment.

MOLEY, Raymond, "Make it Short," *Newsweek*, November 18, 1963, p. 116. Favors short platforms in a generally negative assessment of those documents.

MERRILL, Justin S., "Erratic Platforms of the Democracy," *North American Review*, September 1892, pp. 268-79. Examines platform planks on the tariff between 1840 and 1892.

NELSON, Frederic, "Do Platforms Need All Those Planks?" *National Review*, June 30, 1964, pp. 533-34. A look at platform utterances from 1924, 1944, 1948, 1952, 1956, and 1960.

"Platforms," *Nation*, May 28, 1896, p. 410. Surveys money planks in party platforms between 1872 and 1896.

"Political Platforms," *American Journal of Politics*, 1892, pp. 206-18. A panoramic view of key nineteenth century platform planks, 1800-1872.

POMPER, Gerald M., "'If Elected, I Promise': American Party Platforms," *Midwest Journal of Political Science*, August 1967, pp. 318-23. Discusses concept of voter-rationality and party-rationality.

WEISBORD, Marvin R., "Again the Platform Builders Hammer Away," *The New York Times Magazine*, July 5, 1964, pp. 10, 27-29. A general treatment covering many aspects of this subject.

WHITE, William S., "For Virtue, Valor and Votes," *The New York Times Magazine*, July 27, 1952, p. 12. A generally critical assessment of political platforms.

PART II: INDIVIDUAL ELECTIONS

The 1830s

GAMMON, Samuel Rhea, *The Presidential Campaign of 1832* (Baltimore: Johns Hopkins Press, 1922). Johns Hopkins University Studies in Historical and Political Science XL:1. Looks at the National Republican Young Men's addresses and resolutions in 1832.

1840

GUNDERSON, Robert Gray, *The Log-Cabin Campaign* (Lexington: University of Kentucky Press, 1957). Goes into Democratic commitments and Whig evasions in 1840.

1848

RAYBACK, Joseph G., *Free Soil: The Election of 1848* (Lexington: University of Kentucky Press, 1970). See for both the Free Soil and Democratic platforms of 1848.

1856-1860-1864

Proceedings of the First Three Republican National Conventions (Minneapolis: Harrison and Smith, 1893). Especially valuable for 1856 and 1860, when there was significant floor debate.

1856

CRANDALL, Andrew Wallace, *The Early History of the Republican Party 1854-1856* (Gloucester: Peter Smith, 1960). Focuses on the Republican platform.

DEMOCRATIC NATIONAL CONVENTION, *Official Proceedings* (Cincinnati: Enquirer Company, 1856). Consult for platform debate.

FONER, Eric, *Free Soil, Free Labor, Free Men: The Ideology of the Republican Party Before the Civil War* (New York: Oxford University Press, 1970). Discusses the Republican platform of 1856, as well as that of 1860.

1860

FITE, Emerson D., *The Presidential Campaign of 1860* (Port

Washington: Kennikat Press, 1967). See for both the Republican and Democratic platforms of 1860.

HAYES, Melvin L., *Mr. Lincoln Runs for President* (New York: The Citadel Press, 1960). Concentrates on the Republican platform of 1860.

HESSELTINE, William B., ed. *Three Against Lincoln: Murat Halstead Reports the Caucuses of 1860* (Baton Rouge: Louisiana State University Press, 1960). First-hand accounts of the Republican and Democratic conventions of 1860.

KNOLES, George Harmon, ed. *The Crisis of the Union 1860-1861* (Baton Rouge: Louisiana State University Press, 1965). Emphasizes the Republican platform of 1860.

LUTHIN, Reinhard H., *The First Lincoln Campaign* (Gloucester: Peter Smith, 1964). Traces the shaping of the Republican platform in 1860.

NICHOLS, Roy Franklin, *The Disruption of American Democracy* (New York: The Macmillan Company, 1948). Focuses on the Democratic platform of 1860.

POTTER, David M., *Lincoln and His Party in the Secession Crisis* (New Haven: Yale University Press, 1942). A look at the Republican platform of 1860.

1864

DEMOCRATIC NATIONAL CONVENTION, *Official Proceedings* (Chicago: The Times Steam Book and Job Printing House, 1864). Consult for platform debate.

ZORNOW, William F., *Lincoln and the Party Divided* (Norman: University of Oklahoma Press, 1954). Looks at the Radical, Union (Republican), and Democratic platforms of 1864.

1868

COLEMAN, Charles H., *The Election of 1868: The Democratic Effort to Regain Control* (New York: Octagon Books, 1971). Concentrates on the major party platforms of 1868.

NATIONAL UNION REPUBLICAN CONVENTION, *Proceedings* (Chicago: Evening Journal Print, 1868). Consult for platform debate.

1872

DEMOCRATIC NATIONAL CONVENTION, *Official Proceedings* (Boston: Rockwell and Churchill, 1872). Consult for platform debate.

1876

DEMOCRATIC NATIONAL CONVENTION, *Official Proceedings* (St. Louis: Woodward, Tiernan, and Hale, Printers, 1876). Consult for platform debate.

HAYWORTH, Paul Leland, *The Hayes-Tilden Disputed Presidential Election of 1876* (New York: Russell and Russell, 1966). Analyzes both the Republican and Democratic platforms of 1876.

REPUBLICAN NATIONAL CONVENTION, *Proceedings* (Concord: Republican Press Association, 1876). Consult for platform debate.

ROBINSON, Lloyd, *The Stolen Election: Hayes versus Tilden—1876* (Garden City: Doubleday and Company, 1968). Examines the major party platforms of 1876.

UNGER, Irwin, *The Greenback Era: A Social and Political History of American Finance* (Princeton: Princeton University Press, 1964). Looks at the Greenback platform of 1876, as well as the Democratic and Republican ones.

1880

CLANCY, Herbert J., *The Presidential Election of 1880* (Chicago: Loyola University Press, 1958). Inspects both major party platforms in 1880, as well as the minor party ones.

REPUBLICAN NATIONAL CONVENTION, *Proceedings* (Chicago: Jno. B. Jeffrey Printing House, 1881). Consult for platform debate.

1884

NATIONAL DEMOCRATIC CONVENTION, *Official Proceedings* (New York: Douglas Taylor's Democratic Printing House, 1884). Consult for platform debate.

THOMAS, Harrison Cook, *The Return of the Democratic Party to Power in 1884* (New York: Columbia University Press, 1919). Studies in History, Economics and Public Law, vol. 89, no. 2.

Discusses state platforms 1874-1884, but most valuable for its comparisons and contrasts of the Democratic and Republican platforms of the latter year.

1888

DEMOCRATIC NATIONAL CONVENTION, *Official Proceedings* (St. Louis: Woodward and Tiernan Printing Company, 1888). Consult for platform debate.

BLACKBURN, J. C. S., "The Republican Platform," *Forum*, September 1888, pp. 10-18. A hostile treatment that one should also see for 1884.

1892

DEMOCRATIC NATIONAL CONVENTION, *Official Proceedings* (Chicago: Cameron, Amberg, and Company, 1892). Consult for platform debate.

KNOLES, George Harmon, *The Presidential Campaign and Election of 1892* (Stanford: Stanford University Press, 1942). Stanford University Publications University Series: History, Economics, and Political Science, vol. V, no. 1. Looks at both major and minor party platforms in 1892.

"The Democratic Platform," *Nation*, June 30, 1892, pp. 480-81. Praises the tariff and silver planks.

"Platforms and Principles," *Nation*, December 1, 1892, p. 297. Discusses the evolution of the Republican party from the Liberty party.

1896

DEMOCRATIC NATIONAL CONVENTION, *Official Proceedings* (Logansport: Wilson, Humphreys, and Company, 1896). Consult for platform debate.

GLAD, Paul W., *McKinley, Bryan, and the People* (Philadelphia: J. B. Lippincott Company, 1964). Covers both the Democratic and Republican platforms, with more on the former.

JONES, Stanley L., *The Presidential Election of 1896* (Madison: University of Wisconsin Press, 1964). Treats both the major and minor party platforms for 1896.

REPUBLICAN NATIONAL CONVENTION, *Official Proceedings* (Minneapolis, 1896). Consult for platform debate.

LOUPP, F. E., "The Republican Convention," *Harper's Weekly*, June 27, 1896, p. 642. Analytical but not one-sided.

"The St. Louis Platform," *Nation*, June 25, 1896, pp. 484-85. A
vicious attack on the Republican platform.

1900

"The Menace of Mr. Bryan's Platform," *Harper's Weekly*, July 21,
1900, p. 667. Critical of Bryan and the Democratic platform in
general.
"The Platform That Failed," *Nation*, July 5, 1900, p. 291.
Examines the behind-the-scenes maneuvering in the formulation of the Republican platform.
"The Silver Coinage Platform," *Independent*, July 12, 1900, pp.
1687-88. Discusses the Democratic silver plank and criticizes
Bryan.
"The Two Platforms," *Gunton*, August 1900, pp. 126-34. A
comparative study that is pro-Republican.
WEST, Henry Litchfield, "The Republican and Democratic Platforms Compared," *Forum*, October 1900. Prefers the Democratic stand on the Philippines and on a number of other
issues.

1904

"A Bad Blunder," *Outlook*, July 23, 1904, pp. 677-79. Critical of
the Republican platform for attacking the South relative to
disenfranchising the Negro.
"Discussion of the Democratic Platform," *Current Literature*,
September 1904, pp. 205-6. A sampling of newspaper senti-
ment.
"The Platform," *Nation*, June 30, 1904, pp. 506-7. Blasts the
Republican stand on the tariff.

1908

REPUBLICAN NATIONAL CONVENTION, *Official Report of the Pro-
ceedings* (Columbus: Press of F. J. Heer, 1908). Consult for the
platform debate.
"The Democratic Platform," *Outlook*, July 18, 1908, pp. 597-99.
Compares and contrasts the Republican and Democratic
platforms.
"The Denver Platform," *Independent*, July 16, 1908, pp. 159-61.
Examines the Democratic document analytically.

FLEMING, W. B., "The Republican Platform Unmasked," *Arena*, September 1908, pp. 204-9. A satire.

"The Independence Party: Its Platform and Nominees, Its Strength and Its Weakness," *Arena*, September 1908, pp. 229-34. Praises the Independence party but criticizes Hearst.

Low, Seth, "The Writ of Injunction as a Party Issue," *Century Magazine*, October 1908, pp. 911-16. Prefers Republican to Democratic plank.

"Making the Party Platform," *American Review of Reviews*, July 1908, pp. 8-16. Emphasizes the injunction plank in the Republican platform.

"The Republican Convention: Its Platform and Ticket," *Arena*, September 1908, pp. 224-28. Critical of the Republicans.

"The Republican Platform," *Independent*, June 25, 1908, pp. 1419-20. Examines document analytically.

"The Republican Platform," *Outlook*, June 27, 1908, pp. 412-13. A highly laudatory evaluation.

"The Socialist Platform," *Outlook*, August 29, 1908, pp. 974-76. A gentlemanly attack on the Socialists.

1912

KELLY, Frank K., *The Fight for the White House: The Story of 1912* (New York: Thomas Y. Crowell, 1961). Analyzes the Republican, Democratic, and Progressive platforms.

PINCHOT, Amos R. E., *History of the Progressive Party 1912-1916* (New York: New York University Press, 1958). Focuses on the Progressive platform of 1912.

REPUBLICAN NATIONAL CONVENTION, *Official Report of the Proceedings* (New York: The Tenny Press, 1912). Consult for platform debate.

"The Democratic Platform," *Independent*, July 11, 1912, pp. 102-3. A somewhat hostile treatment.

"The Democratic Platform," *Outlook*, July 13, 1912, pp. 560-61. Describes this document as better than average.

"Following the Campaign: Shaky Platform Planks," *Outlook*, August 10, 1912, pp. 812-13. Discusses only the Democratic and Progressive platforms.

KELLOGG, Paul D., "The Industrial Platform of New Party," *Survey*, August 24, 1912, pp. 668-70. Analyzes the labor provisions of the Progressive party platform and the appeal of the party to social workers.

MacFarlane, Peter Clark, "Measures—Not Men: What the Five National Platforms Really Mean," *Everybody's Magazine*, October 1912, pp. 484-92. A detailed comparative study of these documents plank by plank.

"Mr. Bryan's Views of Governor Wilson and the Democratic Platform," *Outlook*, September 7, 1912, pp. 27-28. Disagrees with the Democratic platform on the tariff, the bosses, taxing power, and states' rights.

"New Progressive Party," *Independent*, August 15, 1912, pp. 260-61. Generally favorable to the Progressive party platform.

"A New Way of Building a Political Platform," *Review of Reviews*, October 1912, pp. 482-84. Describes the writing of the Progressive party platform.

"The Platform: Its Character," *Outlook*, June 29, 1912, pp. 454-55. Notes the differences between Taft's record and the Republican platform planks.

"Platform Solemnities," *Nation*, May 28, 1914, p. 621. An examination of the Democratic abandonment of the Panama tolls plank—which the writer does not regard as a bad thing.

"The Ravishing of the Socialist Party," *Independent*, August 29, 1912, pp. 506-7. Deals with the unfair charge that Theodore Roosevelt and the Progressives stole from the Socialist party.

Roosevelt, Theodore, "Platform Insincerity," *Outlook*, July 27, 1912, pp. 659-63. Attacks both the Republican and Democratic platforms.

"The Socialist Platform and Candidates," *Outlook*, June 1, 1912, p. 235. Shows the trend towards moderation.

1916

Democratic National Convention, *Official Report of the Proceedings* (Chicago, 1916). Consult for platform debate.

Republican National Convention, *Official Report of the Proceedings* (New York: The Tenny Press, 1916). Consult for platform debate.

"A Comparison of the Chicago Platforms," *Literary Digest*, June 17, 1916, pp. 1762-63. An outstanding treatment of the Republican and Progressive platforms.

Kellogg, Paul U., "Three Platforms," *Survey*, June 24, 1916, pp. 336-40. A detailed examination of the Democratic, Progressive, and Republican platforms.

"The Minor Parties: Their Candidates and Platforms," *Review of Reviews*, September 1916, pp. 318-20. Discusses the American party, a splinter of the Prohibition party, as well as the other third parties.

"The Party Platforms," *Review of Reviews*, July 1916, pp. 19-21. Finds the Republican and Democratic platforms similar, with the Progressive platform briefer and better phrased.

"Platforms and Common-Sense," *Nation*, June 15, 1916, pp. 635-36. Looks at the three major party platforms, and downgrades the importance of these documents in general.

"The Political Campaign: The Platforms," *Independent*, July 10, 1916, pp. 44-45. Prefers the Republican to the Democratic platform where there are differences.

"Political Platforms and Candidates," *Bankers Magazine*, July 1916, pp. 1-4. Emphasizes the pro-Federal Reserve plank of the Democrats, quoting speeches, etc.

"Political Pledges," *North American Review*, August 1916, pp. 161-71. Critical of the Democratic failure to execute its pledges of 1912.

"The St. Louis Platform," *Nation*, June 22, 1916, pp. 661-62. Generally favorable to this document.

1920

BAGBY, Wesley M., *The Road to Normalcy: The Presidential Campaign and Election of 1920* (Baltimore: Johns Hopkins Press, 1962). Johns Hopkins University Studies in Historical and Political Science, LXXX(1962):1. Treats major party platforms.

DEMOCRATIC NATIONAL CONVENTION, *Official Report of the Proceedings* (Indianapolis: Bookwalter-Ball Printing Company, 1920. Consult for platform debate.

REPUBLICAN NATIONAL CONVENTION, *Official Report of the Proceedings* (New York: Tenny Press, 1920). Consult for platform debate.

W. L. C., "The Democratic Platform," *Survey*, July 17, 1920, pp. 511-12. An in-depth analysis that neither blames nor praises.

DEVINE, Edward T., "The Republicans at Chicago," *Survey*, June 19, 1920, pp. 401-2. A complex evaluation that also is somewhat critical of the Wilson administration.

"The Fighting Creed of the Democrats," *Literary Digest*, July 17,

1920, pp. 15-16. Newspaper comments, with emphasis on the League of Nations.

GOMPERS, Samuel, and Matthew Woll, "Read! Think! Choose! The Democratic and Republican Platforms," *American Federationist*, August 1920, pp. 729-43. Prefers Democratic platform on labor and other issues.

HAPGOOD, Norman, and Talcott Williams, "The Republican Platform: A Debate," *Independent*, July 24, 1920, pp. 107-12. Takes the form of an opening statement by pro-Democrat Hapgood, a rebuttal by pro-Republican Williams, and a counter-rebuttal by Hapgood, plus some remarks by John Spargo.

HILL, David J., "The Issues at Stake," *North American Review*, August 1920, pp. 145-55. Claims that the Republicans have kept their promises more faithfully than the Democrats.

"Labor in the Party Platforms," *Nation*, July 17, 1920, p. 61. Critical of both major party platforms.

"Labor's Disappointment at the Republican Platform," *Literary Digest*, June 26, 1920, pp. 16-17. Quotes from labor publications.

"The League of Nations as the Dominant Issue," *Current Opinion*, August 1920, pp. 149-52. Stresses the similarities between the Republican and Democratic platforms.

"Planks—San Francisco Style," *Independent*, July 10, 1920, p. 41. Compares the Republican and Democratic platforms issue by issue.

"The Republican Call to Battle," *Literary Digest*, June 19, 1920, pp. 18-19. Newspaper comments, with emphasis on the League of Nations.

"The Republican Platform," *New Republic*, June 23, 1920, pp. 100-2. A critical treatment hedged with a few words of praise.

"The Two Platforms," *Outlook*, July 21, 1920, pp. 526-27. Stresses the similarities rather than the differences in analyzing four key issues.

WILLIAMS, Talcott, and Norman Hapgood, "The Democratic Platform: The Main Issues," *Independent*, August 21, 1920, pp. 207-9. Takes the form of an opening statement by Williams, a rebuttal by Hapgood, and a counter-rebuttal by Williams.

————.,"The Democratic Platform: Nullifying the Constitution," *Independent*, August 7, 1920, pp. 142-45. Takes the form of an opening statement by Williams, a rebuttal by Hapgood, and a counter-rebuttal by Williams.

1924

DEMOCRATIC NATIONAL CONVENTION, *Official Report of the Proceedings* (Indianapolis: Bookwalter-Ball-Greathouse Printing Company, 1924). Consult for platform debate.

MacKAY, Kenneth C., *The Progressive Movement of 1924* (New York: Octagon Books, 1966). Focuses on the Progressive platform of 1924.

REPUBLICAN NATIONAL CONVENTION, *Official Report of the Proceedings* (New York: The Tenny Press, 1924). Consult for platform debate.

WHITE, William Allen, *Politics: The Citizen's Business* (New York: The Macmillan Company, 1924). A contemporary account of the Democratic (and Republican) platforms of 1924.

CATT, Carrie Chapman, "Thirteen Planks—in Two Platforms," *Woman Citizen*, July 12, 1924, p. 10. Compares and contrasts the Republican and Democratic documents.

————., "Watch Your Planks," *Woman Citizen*, August 9, 1924, p. 12. Features specific criticisms of the three major party platforms—especially the planks of special interest to women.

"The Democracy States Its Case," *Literary Digest*, July 12, 1924, pp. 6-8. Offers a wide sampling of editorial opinion.

"Democratic Economics, 1924," *New Republic*, July 9, 1924, pp. 173-74. A skeptical assessment of the Democratic platform.

"The Democratic Platform and the Popular Will," *Outlook*, July 9, 1924, p. 373. Regards the Democratic platform as closer to public opinion than the Republican one.

"La Follette and His Platform," *Forum*, November 1924, pp. 673-89. Includes an article by Zona Gale examining the implementation of Republican minority platform planks over the years, and another by Washington Pezet critical of La Follette's judicial reforms, plea for a Presidential primary, and attacks on monopoly.

"The La Follette Platform," *New Republic*, June 18, 1924, pp. 88-90. Stresses the agrarian emphasis of this document.

LINDSAY, Samuel M., "Political Platforms of 1924," *Review of*

Reviews, August 1924, pp. 193-96. Downgrades the 1924 platforms in general.

————., "Underpinning the Platforms," *Survey*, March 15, 1924, pp. 671-72. Examines the growing role of pre-convention research in the writing of party platforms.

"Pink Ballots for the Ku Klux Klan," *Outlook*, June 25, 1924, pp. 306-8. Analyzes Ku Klux Klan responses to a public opinion poll on political platforms.

"Platforms of the People," *Outlook*, May 7, 1924, pp. 24-29. Points out that popular opinion towards platform demands does not vary widely from section to section.

"Platforms of the People," *Outlook*, May 14, 1924, pp. 60-63. Reveals that sectional attitudes towards platform demands are most apparent in the South.

"Platforms of the People," *Outlook*, May 28, 1924, pp. 133-36. Finds that men and women do not differ in their views, although this generalization is not always true of Democratic women.

"Platforms of the People," *Outlook*, June 4, 1924, pp. 185-87. Constructs a hypothetical Republican platform based on public opinion.

"Platforms of the People," *Outlook*, June 18, 1924, pp. 263-65. Constructs a hypothetical Democratic platform based on public opinion.

1928

DEMOCRATIC NATIONAL CONVENTION, *Official Report of the Proceedings* (Indianapolis: Bookwalter-Ball-Greathouse Printing Company, 1929). Consult for platform debate.

PEEL, Roy V., and Thomas C. Donnelly, *The 1928 Campaign: An Analysis* (New York: Richard R. Smith, Inc., 1931). Analyzes the Republican and Democratic platforms of 1928.

REPUBLICAN NATIONAL CONVENTION, *Official Report of the Proceedings* (New York: The Tenny Press, 1928). Consult for platform debate.

ALLEN, Devere, "A Survey of the Parties," *World Tomorrow*, October 1928, section two/sheet (fold). Presents content analysis of the major and minor party platforms.

"The Democratic Platform," *New Republic*, July 11, 1928, pp. 188-89. Lambasts the Democratic platform for criticizing the

Republicans without offering a comprehensive alternative program.

FOSTER, William T. and Waddill Catchings, "Planks Without Platforms," *Atlantic Monthly*, November 1928, pp. 700-9. Stresses the similarity between the Democratic and Republican platforms, and favors the Keynesian approach to government and the economy.

"The Pasteboard Platform," *New Republic*, June 27, 1928, pp. 136-37. Attacks the Republican platform for being too general.

"The Platforms," *World's Work*, August 1928, pp. 346-47. Prefers the Republican platform to the Democratic one.

"Platforms and Realities," *Outlook*, June 20, 1928, p. 293. Views the 1928 platforms in the light of those of 1856 and 1860.

ROSS, Nellie Tayloe, "Two Platforms," *Woman's Journal*, August 1928, p. 15. A defense of the Democratic platform.

1932

DEMOCRATIC NATIONAL CONVENTION, *Official Report of the Proceedings* (Washington, 1932). Consult for platform debate.

HENDRICKSON, John P., "Legislative Record of Republicans in the Seventy-Third Congress in Relation to the Republican Platform of 1932 and the Campaign Speeches of Mr. Hoover," Ph.D. dissertation, Iowa State University, 1952. Finds that the following Republican Congress did honor the Republican platform promises and Hoover's campaign pledges.

OULAHAN, Richard, *The Man Who: The Story of the 1932 Democratic National Convention* (New York: The Dial Press, 1971). Looks at the major party platforms in 1932, with emphasis on the prohibition issue.

PEEL, Roy V., and Thomas C. Donnelly, *The 1932 Campaign: An Analysis* (New York: Farrar and Rinehart, 1935). Analyzes the Republican and Democratic platforms of 1932.

REPUBLICAN NATIONAL CONVENTION, *Official Report of the Proceedings* (New York: The Tenny Press, 1932). Consult for platform debate.

TUGWELL, Rexford G., *The Brains Trust* (New York: The Viking Press, 1968). Focuses on the Democratic platform in 1932.

ALLEN, Devere, "A Program for Revolt," *Nation*, July 27, 1932, pp.

80-82. A discussion of the League for Independent Political
Action and its support of the Socialist ticket and platform.

————., "A Survey of the Parties—1932," *World Tomorrow*,
September 28, 1932, section two/sheet (fold). Presents content
analysis of the major and minor party platforms.

"Asks Economy in War Expenditures," *Christian Century*, July
20, 1932, p. 916. Discusses the model platform of the Young
Democratic Club of America drawn up by Robert M.
Hutchins.

"Democratic Platform Demands," *Review of Reviews*, August
1932, pp. 16-17. A plank-by-plank summary of the Democratic
platform, with some analysis.

"The Democratic Repeal Splash," *Literary Digest*, July 9, 1932,
pp. 4-5. Examines newspaper sentiment towards major party
prohibition planks.

"A Four Year Plan," *World Tomorrow*, March 1932, pp. 67-68. A
critical assessment of the pre-convention platform of the
League of Political Action.

LEWIS, Grace H., "The Democrats," *Delineator*, October 1932, pp.
23, 71. Evaluates the Democratic platform as the best one
written in twenty years.

"Mr. Hoover and His Dry Constituency," *Christian Century*, July
13, 1932, pp. 878-79. Sees little difference between FDR and
Hoover and criticizes the Democratic prohibition plank.

"Party Platforms Mark Peace Progress," *Christian Century*, July
13, 1932, pp. 877-78. Notes the similarity of peace planks in the
two major party platforms.

"Planks in Democratic Platform That Bear on Business Problems," *Business Week*, July 13, 1932, p. 22. Describes the
Democratic planks in this area and compares and contrasts
them with the Republican ones.

"Planks in Republican Platform That Bear on Business Problems," *Business Week*, June 29, 1932, pp. 12-13. Summarizes
the business planks in the Republican platform.

"The Platform Plank on Prohibition," *Review of Reviews*, July
1932, pp. 14-15. A favorable assessment of the Republican
platform.

"The Republican Convention," *World Tomorrow*, July 1932, p.
196. A bitter attack on the Republican platform.

"Take Your Choice," *New Republic*, July 27, 1932, pp. 286-87.
Places its main emphasis on the Republican, Democratic, and

Socialist platforms in a comparative analysis of some key planks.
"A Third Party Platform," *New Republic*, February 10, 1932, pp. 335-36. A discussion of the League for Independent Political Action platform.
"The Two Platforms," *Nation*, July 13, 1932, p. 23. Lukewarm to the Democratic platform, hostile to the Republican one.
"What the Party Platforms Promise," *Literary Digest*, July 16, 1932, p. 5. Newspaper comment on the two major party platforms and an analysis of their similarities and differences.

1936

BENNETT, David H., *Demagogues in the Depression: American Radicals and the Union Party, 1932-1936* (New Brunswick: Rutgers University Press, 1969). Relates Union party platform of 1936 to the program of the National Union for Social Justice.
"All Dressed Up. . . ," *Nation*, June 24, 1936, pp. 791-93. A general condemnation of the Republican platform.
"Business and the Conventions," *Business Week*, July 4, 1936, pp. 12-13. Emphasizes the failure of both parties to endorse the World Court and the St. Lawrence Seaway.
"Chickens Come Home to Roost," *Saturday Evening Post*, June 27, 1936, p. 22. A pre-convention attack on the Democratic platform.
"Compare the Platforms," *Nation*, July 18, 1936, p. 60. Divides party platforms into three categories.
"Comparison of Platforms," *New Republic*, September 23, 1936, pp. 205-6. A typical comparative analysis.
"Controversial Issues in the Party Platforms of 1936," *Congressional Digest*, August 1936, pp. 203-4. Summarizes the key planks in the various platforms, both major party and minor party, on a half-dozen issues.
"The Democrats' Call to Arms," *New Republic*, July 8, 1936, pp. 254-55. Generally laudatory towards the Democratic platform, but with some reservations.
"G.O.P. Platform: Borah Demands Three Planks, Gets Two; Committee Besieged by Scores," *Literary Digest*, June 20, 1936, pp. 6-7. Discusses Borah's role and press opinion.
HOOVER, Herbert, "Constructive American Alternatives," *Vital*

Speeches, June 1, 1936, pp. 555-59. Former President Hoover's proposal for a platform.

"Mr. Facing-All-Ways," *New Republic,* June 24, 1936, pp. 189-91. Pictures Governor Landon and the Republican platform as ideologically contradictory.

"Mr. Roosevelt Holds Fast," *Nation,* July 4, 1936, pp. 3-5. Points out where the generally superior Democratic platform might be improved.

"Planks and Implications," *Time,* June 22, 1936, p. 19. An analysis of the shaping of the Republican platform and its provisions.

"Platforms," *Literary Digest,* July 4, 1936, p. 5. Compares and contrasts the Republican and Democratic platforms on a dozen key issues.

SAYRE, Wallace S., "Major Party Platforms of 1936," *Current History,* August 1936, pp. 51-55. Stresses the similarities as well as the differences between the Republican and Democratic platforms.

"Towards the Left," *Business Week,* July 4, 1936, p. 44. Criticizes Democratic platform for its leftward drift.

"What Will the Parties Do?" *New Republic,* September 23, 1936, pp. 195-97. Discusses six platforms one-by-one.

1940

DEMOCRATIC NATIONAL CONVENTION, *Official Report of the Proceedings* (Washington, 1940). Consult for platform debate.

DONAHOE, BERNARD F., *Private Plans and Public Dangers: The Story of F.D.R.'s Third Nomination* (Notre Dame: University of Notre Dame Press, 1965). Emphasizes the Democratic platform of 1940.

MOSCOW, WARREN, *Roosevelt and Willkie* (Englewood Cliffs: Prentice-Hall, 1968). Treats both the Republican and Democratic platforms of 1940.

PARMET, Herbert S., and Marie B. Hecht, *Never Again: A President Runs for a Third Term* (New York: The Macmillan Company, 1968). Looks at both the Democratic and Republican platforms for 1940.

"Heads I Win, Tails You Lose," *Independent Woman,* August 1940, p. 228. Discusses women's rights planks in major party platforms.

"What They Promise," *New Republic,* October 7, 1940, p. 487.

Compares Republican and Democratic planks on major issues.

1944

BERNARD, Ellsworth, *Wendell Willkie: Fighter for Freedom* (Marquette: Northern Michigan University Press, 1966). Discusses Willkie's platform ideas in 1944.

DEMOCRATIC NATIONAL CONVENTION, *Official Report of the Proceedings* (Chicago, 1944). Consult for platform debate.

"Advice from Mr. Willkie," *Time*, June 26, 1944, pp. 21-22. A point-by-point analysis of Willkie's platform ideas.

"The Convention Proposes, Dewey Disposes," *Business Week*, July 1, 1944, p. 19. Stresses flexibility of the Republican platform.

"The Democratic Platform," *Nation*, July 29, 1944, p. 114. Regards this document as superior to its Republican counterpart.

HUTCHISON, Keith, "Mr. Willkie's Challenge," *Nation*, June 24, 1944, pp. 726-27. Emphasizes Willkie's liberal ideas.

"The Republican Platform," *Nation*, July 8, 1944, pp. 32-33. Portrays this document as contradictory and inconsistent.

ROBEY, Ralph, "The Democratic Platform," *Newsweek*, July 31, 1944, p. 56. Finds the platform to be well-written, but platitudinous, and evasive towards the money question and the public debt.

————, "The Republican Platform," *Newsweek*, July 3, 1944, p. 56. Examines the fight over the tariff.

"What They Want," *Business Week*, April 15, 1944, pp. 16-17. Farmers' testimony before the Republican platform committee.

WILLKIE, Wendell, "Cowardice at Chicago," *Colliers*, September 16, 1944, pp. 11, 77-79.

1948

ABELS, Jules, *Out of the Jaws of Victory* (New York: Henry Holt and Company, 1959). Discusses the Democratic, Dixiecrat, and Progressive platforms in 1948.

DEMOCRATIC NATIONAL CONVENTION, *Democracy at Work: The Official Report* (Philadelphia: Local Democratic Political Committee of Pennsylvania, 1949). Consult for platform debate.

LODGE, Henry Cabot, *The Storm Has Many Eyes: A Personal Narrative* (New York: W.W. Norton and Company, 1973). As much on President Harry Truman's reaction to the Republican platform as on that document itself.

MACDOUGALL, Curtis D., *Gideon's Army* (New York: Marzani and Munsell, 1965). An exhaustive treatment of the events surrounding the Progressive platform of 1948.

REDDING, Jack, *Inside the Democratic Party* (Indianapolis: Bobbs-Merrill Company, 1958). Touches on the Democratic platform of 1948.

ROSS, Irwin, *The Loneliest Campaign: The Truman Victory of 1948* (New York: New American Library, 1968). Examines the Democratic, Republican, and Progressive platforms of 1948.

SAPOSS, David, J., *Communism in American Politics* (Washington: Public Affairs Press, 1960). Focuses on the Progressive platform of 1948.

SCHMIDT, Karl M., *Henry A. Wallace: Quixotic Crusade 1948* (Syracuse: Syracuse University Press, 1960). Looks at the Progressive platform of 1948.

"A. F. of L.'s Proposals," *American Federationist*, July 1948, pp. 5-7, 31. Emphasizes opposition to the Taft-Hartley Act.,

"The Cantilevered Roof," *Time*, July 19, 1948, p. 24. Stresses the civil rights issue before the platform committee.

"Comparing the 1948 Platforms," *U.S. News and World Report*, July 23, 1948, pp. 22-23. Analyzes Republican and Democratic stands on key issues.

CONWAY, Jess, "The Socialists See Daylight," *New Republic*, September 13, 1948, pp. 11-13. A detailed analysis of the Socialist platform.

HAZLITT, Henry, "Democratic Platform Economics," *Newsweek*, July 26, 1948, p. 24. A general and specific indictment of this document.

———, "Republican Platform Economics," *Newsweek*, July 5, 1948, p. 21. Points out the contradictions in this document.

"The Party Platforms," *Senior Scholastic*, October 6, 1948, pp. 11A-13A. Summarizes Republican, Democratic, and Progressive stands on key issues.

"Platforms vs. Performance in Congress," *Congressional Quarterly Almanac*, vol. V (1949), (Washington: Congressional Quarterly News Features, 1950). Examines the record of the eighty-first Congress.

"The Republican Platform," *Nation*, July 3, 1948, pp. 3-4. Emphasizes the hypocrisy of this document relative to the record of the eightieth Congress.

"Shaping the G.O.P. Platform," *Business Week*, June 19, 1948, p. 23. Describes Henry Cabot Lodge as favoring brevity and broadness.

"Slippery Political Platforms," *Catholic World*, August 1948, pp. 385-92. Highly critical of the Republican foreign policy plank.

1952

CARIDI, Ronald J., *The Korean War and American Politics: The Republican Party as a Case Study* (Philadelphia: University of Pennsylvania Press, 1968). Traces the shaping of the Republican platform of 1952.

COOKE, Edward, "The Platform and Resolutions Committees of the 1952 National Political Conventions," Ph.D. dissertation, Northwestern University, 1953. Contrasts Republican and Democratic procedures.

DAVID, Paul T., *Presidential Nominating Politics in 1952: The National Story* (Baltimore: Johns Hopkins Press, 1954). Treats both the Republican and Democratic platforms of 1952.

LURIE, Leonard, *The King Makers* (New York: Coward, McCann, and Geoghegan, 1971). Discusses the watered-down civil rights plank and the abortive attempt to formulate a minority substitute at the Republican convention of 1952.

"Bridging Dissension," *Newsweek*, July 21, 1952, p. 30. A general discussion of the shaping of the Republican platform, quoting some key planks.

"Civil-Rights Again," *Newsweek*, July 28, 1952, pp. 20-21. Points out the liberal pressures on the Democratic platform committee.

"A Civil-Rights Plank," *New Republic*, May 12, 1952, p. 6. Analyzes the evolution of the Democratic position between 1944 and 1952.

COOKE, Edward F., "Drafting the 1952 Platforms," *Western Political Quarterly*, September 1956, pp. 699-712. Discusses the formulation of both major party documents and compares these with their 1948 counterparts.

"The Dilemma of Candidate Eisenhower," *New Republic*, July 21, 1952, pp. 5-6. A negative evaluation of the Republican platform.

"The Harmony Boys," *Time*, July 28, 1952, p. 9. Examines the backstage maneuverings relative to the civil rights plank in the Democratic platform.

HAZLITT, Henry, "GOP Platform Economics," *Newsweek*, July 21, 1952, p. 76. Points out the ambiguities of this document.

_____"'You Never Had It So Good,'" *Newsweek*, August 4, 1952, p. 74. Pictures the Democratic platform as spendthrift.

"How the Platforms Differ," *Business Week*, August 16, 1952, p. 172. Contrasts Republican and Democratic documents.

McWILLIAMS, Carey, "The Price of Unity," *Nation*, August 2, 1952, pp. 83-84. Laments that the Democratic platform is not liberal enough.

MORSE, Wayne, "The GOP Platform," *New Republic*, August 4, 1952, pp. 12-13. Blasts the civil rights, labor and foreign policy planks.

"1952 Promises Matched Against Action," *Congressional Quarterly Weekly Report*, vol. 13, December 30, 1955, pp. 1317-40. An examination of the Republican and Democratic execution of their 1952 platform pledges.

"Platform Gives Comfort to All Pros and All Antis," *U.S. News and World Report*, July 18, 1952, p. 42. An investigation of the ambiguities in the Republican platform.

"The Platform Was the Payoff," *Nation*, July 19, 1952, pp. 42-43. Paints the Republican document as reactionary in character.

"The Politic Generalities," *Time*, July 21, 1952, pp. 14-15. An examination of the Republican platform emphasizing foreign policy and civil rights.

"Promises and Portents: How the Platforms Compare," *Newsweek*, August 4, 1952, p. 27. A comparison of the key planks of the Republican and Democratic platforms.

RANNEY, Austin, "The Platforms, the Parties, and the Voter," *Yale Review*, September 1952, pp. 10-20. Generally critical in its attitude towards the major party platforms.

WINNER, Percy, "Europe Views the Convention," *New Republic*, August 11, 1952, p. 9. Finds the Democratic platform preferable on foreign policy.

1956

DEMOCRATIC NATIONAL CONVENTION, *Official Report of the Proceedings* (Richmond: Beacon Press, 1956). Consult for platform debate.

MARTIN, Ralph G., and Ed Plant, *Front Runner, Dark Horse* (Garden City: Doubleday and Company, 1960). Focuses on the Democratic platform of 1956.

THOMSON, Charles A. H., and Frances M. Shattuck, *The 1956 Presidential Campaign* (Washington: The Brookings Institution, 1960). Looks at the platform hearings as well as the platforms of both major parties in 1956.

BENDINER, Robert, "The Compromise on Civil Rights—I," *Reporter*, September 6, 1956, pp. 11-14. Analyzes the Republican and Democratic civil rights planks.

"Business Issues in the Campaign," *Business Week*, August 25, 1956, pp. 23-26. Contrasts the Democratic and Republican platforms on such issues as taxes and the budget, defense, credit policy, etc.

"Civil Rights: Stronger or Weaker?" *Newsweek*, August 27, 1956, p. 32. Examines the civil rights plank fight at the Democratic convention.

"Did Parties Keep Their 1956 Platform Promises?" *Congressional Quarterly Weekly Report*, vol. 17, December 25, 1959, pp. 1573-85. An examination of the Republican and Democratic execution of their 1956 platform pledges.

"Drive Opens for Farm Vote," *Farm Journal*, October 1956, pp. 8-10. Contrasts Republican and Democratic stands on agriculture.

"Harry's New-Old Platform," *Life*, August 27, 1956, p. 36. Blasts Democratic economic planks.

HAZLITT, Henry, "Democratic Claptrap," *Newsweek*, September 3, 1956, p. 69. An attack on the platform.

————,"GOP Double-Think," *Newsweek*, September 10, 1956, p. 89. Damns Republican platform with faint praise.

"The Issues," *Time*, September 3, 1956, pp. 12-13. A comparison of the Democratic and Republican platforms.

LAWRENCE, David, "The People Want to Know," *U.S. News and World Report*, September 7, 1956, p. 144. Questions various Democratic planks.

"The Platform: Civil-Rights 'Peace,'" *Newsweek*, August 20,

1956, p. 23. Traces the preconvention maneuverings relative to the Democratic civil rights plank.

"Platform Committees Hear From the Churches," *Christian Century*, August 22, 1956, pp. 963-64. Sets forth the National Council of Churches recommendations to the Republican and Democratic committees.

"Politics and Platforms," *Commonweal*, August 24, 1956, p. 505. Examines the attitudes of leading Democrats towards their civil rights plank.

RABINOWITCH, Eugene, "Walking the Plank to Nowhere," *Bulletin of the Atomic Scientists*, October 1956, pp. 282-83, 320. Critical of both the Democratic and Republican foreign policy planks for not grappling with the basic issues.

"Republicans Better on Civil Rights," *Christian Century*, August 29, 1956, p. 987. Finds the Republican civil rights plank preferable to the Democratic one.

"Something to Live With," *Time*, August 27, 1956, pp. 18-19. A discussion of the Democratic platform, with emphasis on civil rights.

STANFORD, Neal, "Middle East in Party Platforms," *Foreign Policy Bulletin*, September 15, 1956, p. 3. Contrasts Republican and Democratic Middle Eastern planks.

"Straddle on Civil Rights," *New Republic*, August 27, 1956, pp. 5-6. Pictures Democratic civil rights plank as a politically expedient compromise.

"Three Small Changes," *Newsweek*, September 3, 1956, p. 24. Describes minor alterations proposed by Southerners in the Republican civil rights plank.

"The Two Party Platforms . . .," *Newsweek*, August 27, 1956, pp. 20-21. Contrasts Republican and Democratic platforms on some key issues.

"What the Democrats Promise," *U.S. News and World Report*, August 24, 1956, pp. 104-105. A summary of the Democrats platform.

"What the Republicans Promise," *U.S. News and World Report*, August 31, 1956, pp. 84-85. A summary of the Republican platform.

"What the Two Parties Stand for in 1956," *U.S. News and World Report*, August 17, 1956, pp. 37-38. An overall examination of the 1956 major party platforms in connection with some 1952 planks.

1960

DAVID, Paul T., *The Presidential Election and Transition 1960-1961* (Washington: The Brookings Institution, 1961). Treats both the Democratic and Republican platforms of 1960 extensively.

DEMOCRATIC NATIONAL CONVENTION, *Official Report of the Proceedings* (Washington: National Document Publishers, Inc. 1964). Consult for platform debate.

TILLETT, Paul, ed., *Inside Politics: The National Conventions, 1960* (Dobbs Ferry: Oceana Publications, 1962). Published for the Eagleton Institute of Politics at Rutgers—The State University. Looks at the platform hearings as well as the platforms of both major parties in 1960.

WHITE, Theodore H., *The Making of the President 1960* (New York: Atheneum Publishers, 1961). Most valuable for its treatment of the Republican platform in 1960.

"Befuddled Donkey: The Democrats Ignore the Lessons of the Postwar Era," *Barron's*, July 18, 1960, p. 1. Criticizes Santa Claus philosphy underlying the platform.

BENDINER, Robert, "The Scent of Victory," *New Statesman*, August 6, 1960, p. 170. An English view of Nixon's platform maneuverings.

"The Bold Stroke," *Time*, August 1, 1960, pp. 9-12. A discussion of the Nixon-Rockefeller meeting.

"The Defense Issue," *New Republic*, August 8, 1960, pp. 5-7. Examines "Ike's" dislike of the Nixon-Rockefeller manifesto.

"Democrats Plan Pricing Pressure," *Iron Age*, August 25, 1960, p. 51. Analyzes Democratic attitude towards the iron and steel industries.

"Demos Pledge Better P.O., Consumer Aid," *Advertising Age*, July 18, 1960, pp. 2, 85. Focuses on the provisions of the Democratic platform relating to consumers.

G. DuS., "A Plank for Science," *Science*, August 12, 1960, pp. 385. Points out similarities and differences in the Republican and Democratic stands.

EASTMAN, Ford, "Democrats Pledge Reorganization of Military and Space Programs," *Aviation Week*, July 18, 1960, p. 32. A detailed look.

———, "Republicans Pledge New Defense Efforts," *Aviation*

Week, August 1, 1960. Examines Rockefeller-Nixon revision of platform.

GARDNER, Richard N., "Aid and Trade—Party Views," *Foreign Policy Bulletin*, September 15, 1960, pp. 1-2, 8. Compares and contrasts Democratic and Republican positions.

"The G.O.P. Appeal Is Not to Members of Pressure Groups," *Saturday Evening Post*, October 1, 1960, p. 10. Laments that the Democratic platform is oriented to minority groups.

"GOP's New Guard Takes Over," *Business Week*, July 30, 1960, pp. 25-29. Analyzes shift of the Republican platform towards the left.

GORDON, William E., "Presidential Platforms, 1960," *Contemporary Review*, October 1960, pp. 530-39. Discusses the philosophical aspects of the Republican and Democratic platforms.

HAZLITT, Henry, "The Total Welfare State," *Newsweek*, August 1, 1960, p. 70. A bitter onslaught on the Democratic document.

"How Bowles Did It," *New Republic*, July 25, 1960, pp. 6-7. Describes Chester Bowles's role in the shaping of the Democratic platform.

"It's Kennedy for the Democrats," *Business Week*, July 16, 1960, pp. 25-27. Discusses unique features of the Democratic platform.

LAWRENCE, David, "The Rights of What Man?" *U.S. News and World Report*, August 1, 1960, p. 92. A critical view of the Democratic document.

MILES, Thomas W., "The Platforms' Economic Labels: Some Ideas Behind Them," *Banking*, September 1960, pp. 82-84. Contrasts Republican and Democratic economic philosophies.

"One Man's Platform," *Time*, July 18, 1960, p. 14. An examination of Nelson Rockefeller's ideas for the Republican platform.

"The Other Big Issue: A Sound Dollar Is Essential for the Republican and National Growth Program," *Life*, August 28, 1960, p. 28. Prefers Republican to Democratic fiscal policy.

"Parties, Platforms, Candidates: The Why of the Endorsement," *American Federationist*, September 1960, pp. 3-9. Supports Kennedy and the Democrats.

"Party Platforms Consider Cities," *National Civic Review*, September 1960, pp. 426-27. Contrasts Republican and Democratic stands.

"Party Platforms on Labor," *U.S. News and World Report*, August 8, 1960, pp. 85-86. Compares Republican and Democratic positions.

"Republicans Adopt 1960 Platform after Conflicts . . .," in *Congressional Quarterly Weekly Report*, vol. 18, July 29, 1960, pp. 1334-35. Examines the changes in this document as a result of the Nixon-Rockefeller Manifesto.

"Rights of Man—1960 Style," *Time*, July 25, 1960, pp. 18-19. An incisive analysis of the Democratic platform.

RODGERS, Raymond, "Money Rates, Politics and International Realities," *Bankers Monthly*, September 15, 1960, p. 13. Contrasts the Republican and Democratic positions.

"Science Planks Important," *Science News Letter*, August 13, 1960, p. 98. Compares major party stands on science and technology.

SMITH, McLellan, "The Two Great Differences in Conception Between the Republicans and Democrats," *Magazine of Wall Street*, August 13, 1960, p. 564. Highly critical of the Democratic platform.

"Something for Most Everybody from Republicans, Too," *U.S. News and World Report*, August 8, 1960, pp. 64-65. A capsule summary of the Republican platform.

"The Urban Planks in the Party Platforms," *American City*, September 1960, p. 7. Finds that the Democrats place more emphasis on federal action.

"What Democrats Offer Country: Something for Most Everybody," *U.S. News and World Report*, July 25, 1960, pp. 66-67. A capsule summary of the Democratic platform.

"What the Platforms Say about Education," *Saturday Review*, October 15, 1960, pp. 86-87. Contrasts Republican and Democratic views.

WHITE, William S., "Public and Personal," *Harper's*, October 1960, pp. 96-101. Critical of both major party platforms.

1964

CUMMINGS, Milton C., *The National Election of 1964* (Washington: The Brookings Institution, 1966). Includes more on the Republican platform than on the Democratic one.

GILDER, George F., and Bruce K. Chapman, *The Party That Lost*

Its Head (New York:Alfred A. Knopf, 1966). Shows the conflicting forces that shaped the 1964 Republican platform.

KESSEL, John H., *The Goldwater Coalition: Republican Strategies in 1964* (Indianapolis: The Bobbs-Merrill Company, 1968). Traces the forming of the Republican platform in 1964.

LAMB, Karl A., and Paul A. Smith, *Campaign Decision-Making: The Presidential Election of 1964* (Belmont: Wadsworth Publishing Company, 1968). Surveys the evolution of the Republican platform in 1964.

McDOWELL, Charles, *Campaign Fever* (New York: William Morrow and Company, 1965). Discusses at length the Republican platform of 1964 and also touches on the Democratic one.

NEW YORK TIMES, *The Road to the White House: The Story of the 1964 Election* (New York: McGraw Hill Book Company, 1965). Looks at both the Republican and Democratic platforms of 1964.

NOVAK, Robert D., *The Agony of the GOP 1964* (New York: The Macmillan Company, 1965). Discusses the strife over the Republican platform in 1964.

REPUBLICAN NATIONAL CONVENTION, *Official Report of the Proceedings* (Washington: Republican National Committee, 1964). Consult for platform debate.

WHITE, F. Clifton, *Suite 3505: The Story of the Draft Goldwater Movement* (New Rochelle: Arlington House, 1967). Written with the assistance of William J. Gill, this work traces the shaping of the 1964 Republican platform.

WHITE, Theodore H., *The Making of the President 1964* (New York: Atheneum Publishers, 1965). Treats both the Republican and Democratic platforms of 1964.

BAILEY, Fred, "Johnson Versus Goldwater: A Surprise Package for Farmers?" *Banking*, October 1964, pp. 88-90. Accuses both the Republicans and Democrats of avoiding the farm issue.

"Both Parties Woo Business; But Courting Tactics Vary," *Iron Age*, September 3, 1964, pp. 25-26. A comparison of Republican and Democratic planks.

CRAWFORD, Kenneth, "Where They Stand," *Newsweek*, September 7, 1964, p. 31. A discussion of the Republican and Democratic platforms.

"Democratic Platform: Will It Lead to the Great Society," *Time*, September 4, 1964, p. 30. Contrasts specific planks in the major party platforms.

"Goldwater-Scranton Conflict Dominates GOP Platform Hearings," *Congressional Quarterly Weekly Report*, vol. 22, July 10, 1964, pp. 1417-20. Includes day-by-day analysis plus a copy of the letter from William Scranton to the Republican platform committee.

"GOP Platform," *Nation*, July 25, 1964, pp. 5-7. Compares and contrasts the 1960 and 1964 platforms.

GREENBERG, D.S., "Democratic Platform," *Science*, September 11, 1964, p. 1161. Examines the background of this document as well as the specifics re: space, oceanography, and atomic energy.

HECHT, George J., "Where the Democrats and the Republicans Stand on School Aid," *Parents Magazine*, October 1964, pp. 42, 106, 121. Contrasts the major party platform stands on education.

HUMPHREY, Hubert H. "The G.O.P. 'Jihad,'" *Christian Century*, September 23, 1964, p. 1172. A critical view of the Republican platform by the Democratic Vice Presidential nominee.

"Johnson vs. Goldwater," *New Republic*, September 5, 1964, pp. 3-4. Prefers Democratic platform to the Republican one.

LAMBERT, Don E., "Petroleum and the Party Platforms," *World Oil*, October 1964, pp. 11-12. Contrasts the Republican and Democtratic stands on oil and other issues.

MAYNARD, Paul J., "The Candidates and The Platforms," *Magazine of Wall Street*, September 19, 1964, pp. 8-10, 46-48. Compares and contrasts 1960 and 1964 platforms of the major parties.

"Michigan's Romney Fights for Moderate GOP Platform," *Congressional Quarterly Weekly Report*, vol. 22, July 10, 1964, pp. 1449-50. Examines George Romney's stand on various issues.

"New Voice of the GOP," *Newsweek*, July 27, 1964, pp. 30-31. Compares and contrasts the 1960 and 1964 Republican platforms.

O'HANLON, Thomas, "Business—and the Party Platforms, *Dun's Review and Modern Industry*, October 1964, pp. 55-57, 132. An examination of the philosophical differences between the Republicans and the Democrats.

"One Platform for All," *Time*, July 10, 1964, pp. 22-23. Focuses on the role of Melvin Laird in shaping the Republican platform.

"One Team, One Theme," *Time*, August 28, 1964, p. 18. Discusses the testimony of cabinet officials at Democratic platform hearings.

"The Platform," *National Review,* July 28, 1964, p. 633-34. Evaluates the strong and weak points of the Republican document.

"A Platform Built for Barry," *Newsweek,* July 20, 1964, pp. 22-27. An examination of the Republican platform committee hearings.

"Platforms Differ on Defense and Space." *Aviation Week and Space Technology,* August 31, 1964, pp. 20-21. Contrasts the Republican and Democratic stands on various issues.

"A Prosperity Theme—and Problems," *U.S. News and World Report,* August 31, 1964, p. 28. Surveys the testimony before the Democratic platform committee.

"Republicans Hit Kennedy-Johnson Record," *Engineering News-Record,* July 16, 1964, p. 21. A deatiled summary of the key features of the 1964 Republican platform.

P.W., "Education in the Party Platforms," *Saturday Review,* October 17, 1964, pp. 51-52. Contrasts Republican and Democratic positions.

"Washington and the Utilities," *Public Utilities Fortnightly,* September 24, 1964, pp. 43-44. Examines the Democratic stand on rural electrification.

"What the Democratic Platform Promises," *U.S. News and World Report,* September 7, 1964, pp. 34-35. A capsule summary of the major planks.

"What the Platform Says," *Time,* July 24, 1964, pp. 21-22. Discusses the Republican platform fight and the contents of that document.

"What the Republican Platform Promises," *U.S. News and World Report,* July 27, 1964, pp. 34-35. A capsule summary of the major planks.

"When Republicans Tackled Their Platform," *U.S. News and World Report,* July 20, 1964, p. 35. Surveys testimony before the platform committee.

1968

CHESTER, Lewis, Godfrey Hodgson, and Bruce Page, *An American Melodrama,* (New York: The Viking Press, 1969). An elaborate examination of the Democratic platform of 1968, with some attention to its Republican counterpart.

HERZOG, Arthur, *McCarthy for President* (New York: The Viking Press, 1969). Focuses on the Democratic platform fight in 1968.

LARNER, Jeremy, *Nobody Knows: Reflections on the McCarthy Campaign* (New York: The Macmillan Company, 1970). Looks at the struggle in 1968 over the Democratic platform.

MAILER, Norman, *Miami and the Siege of Chicago: An Informal History of the Republican and Democratic Conventions of 1968* (New York: World Publishing Company, 1968). The major party platforms of 1968 as viewed through the eyes of a self-proclaimed literary genius.

The Presidential Nominating Conventions 1968 (Washington: Congressional Quarterly Service, 1968). Contains a running chronological summary of the Democratic platform debate.

WHITE, Theodore H., *The Making of the President 1968* (New York: Atheneum Publishers, 1969). Treats both the Republican and Democratic platforms of 1968.

"A Close Call in Chicago," *Broadcasting*, September 2, 1968, pp. 26-27. Examines the Democratic planks on the telecommunications industry.

"Democrats Agree on Economic Planks," *Business Week*, August 31, 1968, pp. 13-14. Describes the push by the Democrats beyond the New Economics to greater equity.

"Democrats Nail Down a Platform," *Engineering News-Record*, August 29, 1968, pp. 29-30. Concentrates on urban problems.

"GOP Platform Writers Back Depletion," *Oil and Gas Journal*, August 12, 1968, p. 32. Emphasizes the Republican stands on oil and gas and East-West trade.

"GOP Quietly Planks Its Platform," *Engineering News-Record*, August 8, 1968, pp. 9-11. Shows how Republicans succeeded in appealing to all factions of the party.

"How Platform-Makers See the Issues," *Nation's Business*, June 1968, pp. 90-91. Cites the opinions of Republican leaders in various states.

"How The Parties Stand on Trade," *Business Abroad*, October 1968, pp. 9, 14. Compares and contrasts the Democratic and Republican positions.

KINNEY, Gene T., "Platforms and Candidates Differ Markedly on

Depletion," *Oil and Gas Journal,* September 9, 1968, pp. 84-86. A look at both major party documents.

"Meanwhile, in Miami Beach," *Chemical Week,* August 10, 1968, pp. 17-18. Finds that the Republicans have abandoned free trade for protection.

"Platform Shows New Party Look," *Business Week,* August 10, 1968, pp. 23-24. Emphasizes taxes and trade.

"Platforms Draw the Battle Lines," *Engineering News-Record,* September 5, 1968, pp. 11-12. Compares and contrasts the Republican and Democratic documents.

"Promises the Democrats Make: Platform for 1968," *U. S. News and World Report,* September 9, 1968, pp. 50-52. Examines the highlights of this document.

"The Republican Promises—A Look at the Platform," *U. S. News and World Report,* August 19, 1968, pp. 78-79. Surveys the key planks in this platform.

"The Vietnam Plank," *Newsweek,* September 2, 1968, pp. 24-25. Describes the struggle between the doves and the hawks at the Democratic platform committee hearings.

"Vietnam Planks," *New Republic,* September 21, 1968, pp. 10-11. Breaks down the votes at the Democratic convention.

"Vietnam: The Dissidents Walk the Plank," *Newsweek,* September 9, 1968, pp. 32-33.

WALLICH, Henry C., "Platform Paradox," *Newsweek,* September 9, 1968, p. 85. Accuses the Democrats of over-promising.

"What Republicans Offer on Labor," *U. S. News and World Report,* August 19, 1968, pp. 63-64. A detailed analysis of this plank.

1972

SULLIVAN, Denis G., Jeffrey J. Pressman, Benjamin I. Page, and John J. Lyons, *The Politics of Representation: The Democratic Convention 1972* (New York: St. Martin's Press, 1974). An excellent description of the background, writing, and reception of the platform, picturing McGovern as a political pragmatist gradually moving towards the center. See chapter 4 by Benjamin I. Page, "Innovation and Compromise: The Making of a Party Platform."

"Democratic Platform—What's Being Proposed," *U. S. News and*

World Report, July 10, 1972, pp. 78-79. Summarizes the key passages from this document.

"Empty Platform," *Economist,* August 26, 1972, pp. 45-46. Discusses the right-to-work and day-care center issues.

GEOGHEGAN, Tom, "Miami and the Seeds of Port Huron," *New Republic,* September 2, 1972, pp. 16-18. A brilliant critique of the Democratic platform.

"Hearing," *New Yorker,* July 8, 1972, pp. 19-20. Looks at the regional hearing on the Democratic platform in New York City.

"Hightlights of the 1972 Republican and Democratic Platforms," *Congressional Digest,* October 1972, pp. 234-55. The most complete set of direct quotations currently available.

"Just Trust George," *Economist,* July 15, 1972, pp. 46-48. Examines abortion and subsidization of the poor, relative to the Democratic platform.

KINNEY, Gene T., "Voters Given Clear Choice on Most Key Energy Issues," *Oil and Gas Journal,* September 4, 1972, pp. 41-44. Compares and contrasts the Republican and Democratic stands on energy.

"The Latest Edition of McGovern's Economics," *Business Week,* September 2, 1972, pp. 14-15. Analyzes how the South Dakota Senator's ideas changed during the course of 1972.

"Lions and Lambs," *Newsweek,* July 10, 1972, p. 18. Examines the drafting of the Democratic platform.

"McGovern I: The Platform," *National Review,* July 21, 1972, pp. 782-83. A conservative attack on various Democratic planks.

"Open Platform," *Newsweek,* June 12, 1972, p. 30. Discusses the regional hearing on the Democratic platform in Boston.

"A Platform Appeal to Democrats," *Business Week,* August 26, 1972, pp. 20-21. Describes the Republican document and contrasts it with its Democratic counterpart.

"The Platform: 'The American Party Is Committed to . . . ,'" *Texas Eagle,* vol. 4, no. 10A, 1972, p. 6.

"Promises Republicans Make," *U. S. News and World Report,* September 4, 1972, pp. 28-29. Cites key passages from the Republican platform.

"Promises the Democrats Make," *U. S. News and World Report,* July 24, 1972, pp. 32-33. Quotes the main planks from the Democratic document.

"What McGovern Would Do As President," *U. S. News and World Report*, July 24, 1972, pp. 22-24. A summary of the South Dakota Senator's positions as of mid-1972.

Since the minor party platforms had not been collected and published at the time of completion of this manuscript, the author turned to *The New York Times* for highlights of these documents. The October 29 article is by far the most comprehensive; the others treat only a single party. In no case did this newspaper print the actual platform of any of these minor parties.

"Communists Here Dropping the Use of Term American," *The New York Times*, February 22, 1972, p. 43.

MALCOLM, Andrew H., "Spock Nominated by People's Party," *The New York Times* July 30, 1972, p. 27.

NARVAEZ, Alfonso A., "A Party is Formed by 'Libertarians," *The New York Times*, July 5, 1972, p. 24.

"Other Presidential Aspirants Offer Wide Choice," *The New York Times*, October 29, 1972, p. 46.

SALPUKAS, Agis, "Socialist Labor Party Plans Presidential Campaign," *The New York Times*, April 11, 1972, p. 24.

WALDRON, Martin, "A Female Trotskyite Nominee Stumping in Texas," *The New York Times*, January 2, 1972, p. 57.

1976

The author wrote the chapter on the 1976 platforms as the campaign progressed, so that quite naturally there were no retrospective accounts available. He did add to his narrative a sampling of contemporary assessments of these documents by leading news and opinion magazines, but did not attempt to assemble a comprehensive, annotated list of every article mentioning the platforms. Those selected items which he did employ are cited in the footnotes to the chapter on 1976; anyone wishing to investigate other articles might turn to the standard periodical guides.

Index

Socialist Party, 27, 30, 32, 35, 106, 142, 146, 149, 150, 153, 155, 162, 164, 169, 170, 177, 181, 182, 184, 185, 190, 192, 201, 207, 208, 209, 214, 215, 221, 232, 233, 241, 242, 248, 257, 266, 295

Socialist Workers Party, 30, 221, 222, 223, 233, 242, 249, 257, 265, 284, 295

Soldiers Bonus Act, 177

Solzhenitsyn, Alexander, 293

South, 20, 22, 23, 24, 54, 61, 62, 63, 65, 66, 67, 69, 72, 73, 74, 76, 78, 80, 81, 83, 84, 86, 87, 88, 89, 90, 91, 93, 96, 103, 104, 105, 115, 120, 121, 124, 134, 146, 166, 168, 175, 179, 183, 190, 195, 226, 237, 239, 250, 254, 255, 277, 288

South Africa, 281, 283

South Carolina, 50, 54, 69, 73, 74, 80, 103, 131, 143, 226, 231, 236, 247, 263

South Dakota, 119, 122, 184, 278

South Korea, 291

Southeast Asia Treaty Organization, 260

Southern Rhodesia, 281

Southgate, J. H., 128

Southwest, 112, 288

Southwestern Social Science Association, 13

Spain, 222, 229

Spanish-American War, 29, 135, 136, 137

Spargo, John, 175

Sparkman, John, 236

Specie Resumption Act, 97, 98, 101, 102

Spock, Benjamin, 283

Springfield (Ill.), 144, 180

Springfield *Republican*, 173

"Sputnik", 247, 248

Square Deal, 142

Stagflation, 290

Stalin, Joseph, 208, 223, 233, 242, 249

"Stalwarts", 98, 104, 105, 108, 109, 110

Standard Oil, 154

Stanton, Edwin, 87

Stassen, Harold, 215, 223, 233, 234, 244

States' rights, 22, 24, 42, 53, 63, 64, 67, 70, 78, 85, 105, 160, 195, 204, 216, 225, 226, 271

States Rights Party, 226, 230

Stedman, Seymour, 170

Stephens, Alexander, 80, 94

Stevens, Thaddeus, 47, 69, 88

Stevenson, Adlai I, 124, 138

Stevenson, Adlai II, 236, 239, 243, 246, 249

Stewart, Gideon, 102

Stimson Doctrine, 194

Stimson, Henry, 191, 210

Stone, William J., 166

Straight Out Democratic Party, 94

Streeter, Alson, 116, 121

Student sit-in campaign, 248

Students for a Democratic Society, 279

Suez Canal, 221, 241

Suez crisis, 25, 244, 245, 246

Sulzer, William, 168

Sumner, Charles, 60, 72, 91

Sun Belt States, 291

Sunset laws, 290

Supreme Court, U. S., 32, 33, 48, 73, 75, 103, 110, 131, 133, 150, 154, 162, 163, 199, 204, 207, 232, 240, 241, 243, 244, 251, 262, 271

Survey, 165

Sutton, Mike, 18

Swallow, Silas, 145, 146

Syria, 265, 287

Taft, Charles, 202

Taft-Ellender-Wagner Act, 221

Taft-Hartley Act, 24, 25, 42, 43, 220, 221, 222, 223, 225, 230, 231, 232, 233, 234, 236, 238, 250, 290

Taft, Robert, 209, 213, 215, 216, 223, 233, 234, 239

Taft, William Howard, 145, 146, 148, 151, 153, 154, 155, 156, 157, 160, 161, 162, 163, 164, 170, 292